CHILD EDUCATION AND SOCIAL DEVELOPMENT

CHILD EDUCATION AND SOCIAL DEVELOPMENT

JANARDAN PRASAD
VIJAY KUMARI KAUSHIK

KANISHKHA PUBLISHERS, DISTRIBUTORS
NEW DELHI - 110 002

KANISHKA PUBLISHERS, DISTRIBUTORS
4697/5-21 A, Ansari Road, Daryaganj
New Delhi-110 002
Phones : 2327 0497, 2328 8285
Fax : 011-2328 8285
E-mail: kanishka_publishing@yahoo.co.in

Child Education and Social Development

First Published-1996
Edition-2018

ISBN: 978-81-7391-149-5

PRINTED IN INDIA

Published by Madan Sachdeva for Kanishka Publishers, Distributors, 4697/5-21A, Ansari Road, Daryaganj, New Delhi-110 002, Typeset by Sunshine Graphics, Delhi, and Printed at Rajdhani Printers, Delhi.

Preface

The subject of child development has attracted the attention of biologists, psychologists, anthropologists and educationists alike. The concept of child development has many dimensions; they are biological, psychological and educational. It has now been realized that the primary focus in the educational process is the child and not the subject and the teacher. The child study approach to curriculum creation involves an effort to create curriculum in such a way that the child's organic nature, "the child own needs" and "his immediate interests are to furnish the starting point of education. The main concern is with the children rather than theories about children, with sensitivity and responsiveness to children rather than with scholarly exercise in the study of children, and with the facilitation of these learnings of immediate concern to the child rather than with teaching the child what be "needs" to know. The child study developer begins not with the needs of society or the academic disciplines but with the needs and concerns of the individual child as seen by the developer himself. This involves an effort, while developing curriculum to apply to the education of children the lessons learnt from children themselves.

For example it is important to note that with in the organic school "play is not distinguished from work as the predominant mode of learning. In fact with in the organic school the distinction between work and play is an in appropriate one. It is more appropriate to distinguish between "involvement in an activity" and lack of involvement in an activity, since it is believed that if a child is fully involved in and having fun with an activity, learning is taking place. As a result, the atmosphere of the organic school is viewed by the child study developer to be one in which children are actively involved in experiences. In contrast, the atmosphere of the traditional school is viewed as one in which children are forced to partake in tedious work.

The organic school is also different from the traditional school because it is believed that individual children learn and grow in a free atmosphere.

The very aim and end of the child study developers endeavours is to meet the needs of the growing child.

In focussing directly upon the child, child study developers focus upon all round growth of the whole child, his intellectual growth, his affective growth, his psycho social growth, his physical growth, his moral growth.

In this way, it will be seen that efforts have been made to analyse and discuss all the aspects of child development in the light of the recent theoretical and practical experiences by the educators, administrators psychologists and the general public.

Efforts to bring out a book on a subject like psychology and child development are comparatively new in the Indian publishing. It is true that the concepts and most of the data used are western. Every effort has been made to make the book easy, readable and useful.

Editors

Contents

1

Nature of Man

Biology is related to psychology in the sense that the two subjects represent different ways of looking at the same life process. Whereas a biologist primarily is interested in the organic, physiological, or somatic aspects of living creatures, a psychologist is, or should be, chiefly interested in their psychological, mental, or motivational dimension. However, because of the interrelationships of the two sciences—biology and psychology—students in each field need to know the major findings of the other. Furthermore, a student interested in the psychological nature of man should in some way incorporate biological man into his total scheme of thought.

In this chapter, we view biological man in his most generalized aspects. In so doing, we describe certain facets of human beings, and of life in general, as a biologist might. We also undertake the exploration of certain questions relating to man's biological or "original" nature.

It should be realized that, although a substantial amount is known about human biology, there are still many unanswered questions. So far, biologists have asked more questions than they have been able to answer, yet there is no assurance even that the best questions have been formulated.

Some of the material covered in this chapter reviews the work of freshman or sophomore biology and physiology courses. However, the chapter delves into matters, such as the nature of mind, which students rarely encounter in lower-division college courses.

Furthermore, it focuses primarily on a particular school of thought in biology—that commonly labeled *organismic.* Just as there are different positions concerning the psychological nature of man[1], there also are different views about his biological nature. We herein describe some of these views and show how they contrast. Our treatment of biological man grapples with fundamental questions which often have philosophical implications. Hence, to a student of biology, there is no question more fundamental than the one posed in the following heading.

WHAT IS LIFE?

Living creatures, including man, seem in much of their functioning to act like complicated, exquisitely constructed mechanisms which obey many of the common law of chemistry and physics. At the same time, such life processes as assimilation, metabolism, and muscular contraction appear to be under some sort of central control. Life is coordinated. Also, life seems to display a coordination of effort directed toward certain ends, such as preservation and propagation of a species and the maintenance of as much physical comfort as possible. In lower forms of life such as plants, sea anemones, and amoebas, a control center is not visible. However in higher forms, control appears to be centered in the neuroendocrine system, *i.e.*, brain, nerves, and the regulatory glands. The higher an animal on the phylogenetic scale, the more important is the brain, and particularly the cerebrum, as a control center.

But to explain this is not to explain much. How does the control center work? What makes it go? Perhaps there is as yet no scientifically defensible answer. We know that in the higher life forms there is continuous electrical activity in the central nervous system and that the waves, or pulsations, which can be measured, vary greatly depending on the state of the animal—whether it is at rest, asleep, thinking, or engaged in physical activity. But to the question of the significance of the apparent autonomous electrical activity of the central nervous system a well-known psychologist, D. O. Hebb, tells us, "Not even a tentative answer is available."[2] One of the pioneers and present ranking experts in the measurement of electrical activity of living creatures of E. D. Adrian. He states, "Perhaps the chief impression which will be left by this account [Adrian's discussion of the significance of brain waves] is the complete inability of contemporary science to give a satisfactory picture of any kind of mental activity."[3]

In very recent years, research on brain functions has been greatly accelerated and many interesting data have emerged, such as the strong correlation between brain chemistry and speed of learning.[4] However, "... the nature of the physiological change that occurs during learning ... is far from being understood."[5]

Although little can be demonstrated scientifically in this regard, one of the favorite subjects of human speculation through the ages has been the basic nature of life, and particularly that aspect of life which we call mind. Out of this speculation several hypotheses have arisen. We discuss three of them on the pages to follow. The first two—vitalism and mechanism—have ancient origins; the third—organismic biology —is largely a product of twentieth-century thought.

Vitalism

According to a majority of vitalists, a living organism may be compared to a living piece of machinery which *in itself* is incapable of experiencing consciousness. It is unable in itself to will, purpose, reflect, imagine, or have aesthetic experience. Like an electronic computer, it requires something of an entirely different and unique order to direct it. A person who defines a physiological organism in this manner must assume the presence of some kind of "life force" which "makes the body go." McDougall's "hormic psychology" is an example of a vitalistic position. The life force, or *élan vital* as it is often called, is nonmaterial, nonmechanical, and nonchemical. To use a simple analogy, the body is an automobile, the life force its driver; or the body is a piano, the life force its player.

To a vitalist, the *élan vital* is mind, or at least one aspect of mind. One theory has been that mind is a substance, or entity, but obviously a substance utterly unlike the material objects of experience.[6] Mind substance is as real as anything can be, yet it has no length, no breadth, no thickness, and no mass. Mind has been regarded as a substance because of its assumed unchanging qualities (compare oxygen, a material substance, which, so long as it remains oxygen, continues to have the same properties). What are the properties of mind substance according to those who think it exists. It is nonmaterial, invisible, indestructible, the same among all men, and possessed of certain powers, all of which come under the general head of thinking. Examples of the powers of mind substance are willing, purposing, reflecting, imagining, and remembering.

Plato usually is regarded as one of the first persons to systematize and popularize the idea that mind is a substance. Later, Rene Descartes (1596-1650) centered his thinking on the concept *mind* and its relation to an organic body. Descartes asserted that mind is sharply separated from nature. Thus, in essence, it is a substance completely different from matter. Accordingly, whereas the essence of mind is *pure thought*, the essence of matter is extension; it has length, breadth, thickness, and mass.

Descartes felt that mind resides in the body. Moreover, he specifically pinpointed its location in the pineal gland, a tiny organ imbedded in the base of the brain. Here, a human mind uses the body as its instrument, but mind also can act independently of brain and other parts of the body.

Descartes' outlook commonly is referred to as mind-body dualism. Cartesian, *i.e.*, deriving from Descartes, dualism has been a subject of much dispute and criticism. Its critics argue that no dualist has ever provided an adequate explanation of how a nonmaterial substance can act upon a material substance. Furthermore, the evidence of common-sense suggests that mental functioning is profoundly affected by physical states; for example, people who are ill, or who have suffered brain damage, think less well than those in a normal physical condition. Dualists have never explained how, if mind is a nonmaterial substance independent of matter, it can be so affected.

Many philosophers, and psychologists with a philosophical turn of mind, have tried to retain the idea that mind is a nonmaterial substance, equivalent to soul or spirit, and at the same time eliminate the difficulties arising from trying to explain how a nonmaterial substance can act upon a material one. In short, they have avoided a mind-body dualism by simply eliminating one side of the mind-body pair—they retain mind but assume that physical matter is such in superficial appearance only. Adherents of this position assume that in actuality the physical body, and indeed all material substance, is a *projection* either of the finite minds of individuals or of the infinite mind of God.

A leading exponent of the idea that perception of a thing is what gives it existence was an Irish philosopher and bishop, George

Berkeley (1685-1753). His position is known as *subjective idealism*. The more extreme notion that Mind is the only reality existent in the universe, and that material substance is an illusion, is associated with a philosophical school of thought known as *absolute idealism* and identified with G. W. F. Hegel.

Another point of view regards mind as a nonmaterial entity but not as a substance in the sense that its properties are fixed. According to this view the properties of mind evolve, and there is no telling what the outcome may be. We see here the influence of the concept of evolution. Although there have been a great many exponents of the idea that mind is an emergent spiritual force, two persons who stated the position sharply were the Frenchman Henri Bergson (1859-1941) and the Italian Giovanni Gentile (1875-1944). Bergson went a long way toward eliminating mind-body dualism by declaring the supremacy of mind. In this respect, we can see in him a Berkeleian influence. But, Bergson talked of the mind's using the body as an instrument and of the separability of mind from body. He also talked of mind as having unity, in contrast to matter, which is divisible. Such ideas are obviously dualistic.

Gentile did not refer to mind as an existent but rather as pure activity from which all that we know as existence springs. Since, according to Gentile, mind is activity or process in an everlasting state of change, and since all material substance is a product of mind-acts, it follows that all material substance is likewise in a state of constant flux. To Gentile, the universe consists basically of acts of thought, that is, acts of mind. Mind has no existence apart from its acts and its actions have no limitations in space and time. Thus, Gentile went about as far as one can go in making mind or spirit the basis of everything man is aware of and at the same time eliminating any kind of eternal law or governing principle.

To students, all of this may seem abstruse and even irrelevant. Nevertheless, we have been dealing with one of the bedrock issues in connection with the question, What is life? Our attitudes toward children, and the way we go about working with them, are likely to be coloured by whether we take a vitalistic or some alternative position.

Most contemporary biologists is the United States reject vitalism in favour of one or the other of the two outlooks described next. However, we cannot ignore the fact that a number of brilliant scientists have, in despair, given up trying to explain the full range of behaviour among animals and men without introducing a mental force separate from, but interacting with, the physical body. The well-known physicist, A. S. Eddington, has expressed what is essentially a dualistic position. (*The Philosophy of Physical Science,* 1939). C. S. Sherrington, a pioneer in neurophysiology, adopted a dualistic outlook (see his *Man on His Nature,* 1951). E. D. Adrian, one of the world's leading authorities on neural electrical phenomena, talks in terms of a mind-brain dualism and says "the addition of mental events... seems to rule out a purely physical description of all that happens..." and "...if it is found that physical mechanisms cannot even explain all that happens in the brain, we shall have to decide when and where *the mind* intervenes."[7] Another neurophysiologist, John C. Eccles, frankly espouses a Cartesian dualism, *i.e.*, the theory of mind-body dualism proposed by Rene Descartes, and attempts to develop a scientifically respectable theory of how a brain could interact with a life force which is not detectable by any instruments we now have.[8]

Mechanism

Mechanists (also sometimes called materialists) try to explain the whole of life in terms of operation of the laws of physics and chemistry. They assume that living protoplasm is nothing more than a highly complex organization of chemical and electrical phenomena. They staunchly refuse to accept, as necessary in explaining life, any sort of nonmaterial mental or spiritual force. Behaviour, they maintain, is best explained as responses to stimuli from either outside or inside an organism. H. G. Wells, J. S. Huxley, and G. P. Wells compare the mammalian body to a gasoline motor and go on to say, "Now is this analysis sound? Is a living man fundamentally a machine? That is a question capable of experimental decision. We can measure the amount of food that a man or an animal consumes over a given period of time, and we can measure the energy yielded during the same period. If we burn an equal weight of similar food in a suitable apparatus and find out how much energy its combustion yields, and if this value is equal to the energy yielded by the experimental subject, then evidently the living organism, so far as its energy-output is concerned, is really and precisely a combustion engine."[9] After citing experiments designed to test this proposition, these authors conclude that "man and the animals generally are fundamentally mechanisms, driven by the energy liberated in the oxidation of food."[10] They concede, however, that the machinelike properties of the body do not explain everything. For example, they do not explain growth, reproduction, and consciousness. But the latter phenomena are explainable, they reason, without resorting to a belief in soul, spirit, or mysterious "life force."[11] However, Huxley in his later writings, such as *Evolution in Action* and certain essays in *Man in the Modern World*, seems to move toward an outlook more like what we describe under our third—organismic— category.

Mechanists have given much attention to the task of explaining mental phenomena in physical terms. The development of electronic computers ("electronic brains") has stimulated attempts to describe what we call mind as a product of a complex system of computation, making use of electrochemical processes. In a provocative paper delivered before the Hixon Symposium in 1948 the late John von Neumann, a brilliant mathematician associated with the Princeton Institute for Advanced Study, explored the question of whether it would be possible to build a computer having the essential attributes of a living organism. Von Neumann states, "...some regularities which we observe in the organization of ... [natural organisms] may be quite instructive in our thinking and planning of... [automata, or computers]; and conversely, a good deal of our experience and difficulties with our artificial automata can be to some extent projected on our interpretations of natural organisms."[12] Von Neumann compares an individual neuron with a vacuum tube of a computer. A vacuum tube in a digital computer is a yes-or-no organ; similarly, individual neurons discharge on a yes-or-no basis. Computing machines are capable, he says, of logical calculations and of memory. Von Neumann also elaborates on the idea that it is theoretically possible to build an artificial automation which can reproduce itself.[13]

Mechanists historically have favoured some sort of reflex arc theory for explaining behaviour. A reflex arc is defined as a circuit which consists of a sense organ, such as an eye, a nerve leading from the sense organ to a central "switching area" (the spinal cord or brain), and a nerve leading outward from the switching area to a muscle or gland. When the sense organ is stimulated, a "message" tours the circuit and produces a response of muscle or gland.

The reflex arc concept in biology has a long history. Descartes came to conceive of all the lower animals as simple machines. He noted that muscular reactions seemed to follow predictably from stimulation of sense organs and reasoned that there were incoming and outgoing pathways which provided fixed channels for an animal's whole repertory of acts. (As we have seen, Descartes placed man in a different category—man had a soul, or mind.) Pierre Cabanis (1757-1808), a French philosopher and physician, argued that human beings exhibit a level of behaviour as mechanical as that of the lower animals. He asserted that stimulus response connections in man which do not reach the brain but are channeled through the spinal cord show the same reflex quality which Descartes thought he had observed in the behaviour of lower animals.[14] The term *reflected movement* (or reflex) was coined in 1736. Boring attributes the first detailed treatment of the subject to the German physiologist, Muller, who published his work on the subject between 1833 and 1840.[15]

It remained for psychologists of the late nineteenth and early twentieth centuries to extend the reflex arc concept to include all, or virtually all, of human behaviour. Reflexes were thought to be either inborn—a part of a person's original biological equipment—or learned. In the latter case, they involved the fixing, or "stamping in," of some new connection between specific afferent (incoming) and efferent (outgoing) nerves. The afferent "messages," it was thought, may be channeled through the spinal cord only, or through both cord and brain. Stimulation of the receptor (sense organ) was held to cause an automatic, predictable, and almost instantaneous response in the effector (reacting muscle or gland). Reflex arcs presumably are illustrated by such phenomena as knee jerk, blinking (when an eye is threatened), withdrawal from a painful object, and the like. We associate such a development in biological and in psychological thought with the names of I. P. Pavlov (1849-1936), a Russian biologist, Vladimir Bekhterev (1857-1927), a Russian neuropathologist, and, in this country, Edward L. Thorndike (1874-1949), and John B. Watson (1878-1958).

The reflex arc concept, particularly in the simple form in which it was held early in the twentieth century, now has fallen into disrepute. However, since the intent of this section of the chapter is to present positions and to keep pros and cons to a minimum, we shall not describe here specific criticisms which have been leveled against it.

Most modern mechanists take for granted the inadequacy of the original reflex arc theory and describe behaviour in different, but still essentially mechanistic, terms. For example, D. O. Hebb has constructed a rather elaborate theory which takes into account the criticisms of the reflex arc concept. Hebb is a mechanist who believes that persons wishing to stay in his camp must be able to account for higher thought processes (such as purposing, valuing, and reflecting) as a product of the electrochemical activity of the body.[16] G. L. Freeman, also a mechanist, likewise develops a highly sophisticated conception of the life process in which he meets many of the traditional objections to a biology based on mechanistic premises. However in so doing, Freeman's mechanistic view borrows from the organismic in the sense that he prefers to define a life form as a "system" which operates purposively.[17] In fact, it would not be far wrong to say that a majority of biologists and experimental psychologists today place themselves within the mechanistic frame of reference but that they also are moving toward the organismic position which is described in the next section.

So far we have said nothing about how mechanists define mind. If a person is a pure mechanist, *i.e.*, if he has eliminated every trace of dualism, obviously he must reject the notion that mind is a nonmaterial vital force. If he is true to his materialist principles, he must deny that any kind of nonmaterial force exists; or if he concedes its existence, he must at least hold that such a force is inconsequential.

In what way, then, can a mechanist use the term *mind?* He can use it only if he regards mind as a function—as a manner of behaving and not as a thing in itself. To a mechanist mind is learning, i.e., the building and storing of new reflex arcs. Most mechanists, however, avoid any use of the term *mind,* since from their point of view the term connotes a nonmaterial spiritual force. To them, an electronic computer is analogous to a mammalian brain; and a computer, even though it can solve many problems if the data are fed in correctly, cannot be said to *have* a mind.

We have asserted that mind to a mechanist can be nothing more than a function—a pattern of behaviour resulting from the environmental forces acting upon a living organism. Adherents of the position we are to describe next also regard mind as a function. However, they define the nature and role of functional mind in a fundamentally different manner.

Organismic Biology

The organismic view is rather popular among biologists of the twentieth century. Those who accept this general frame of reference tend to reject both vitalism and mechanism on the ground that neither provides an adequate explanation of the life process. Organismic biologists object particularly to mechanists' tendency to explain the behaviour of living creatures in terms of a collection of reflex arcs. They also oppose vitalism, but because of its postulation of an unproved life force. A central feature of the organismic outlook is an emphasis on study of life forms by *wholes,* rather than in terms of a collection of response connections. Accordingly, organismic biologists are interested in how a total creature, or organism, behaves as it interacts with its environment.

It is true that some who call themselves organismic biologists regard life forms as machines. These biologists are likely to adopt a behaviouristic psychology. But others, and probably the great majority, avoid entirely the machine analogy. One of the originators and most prominent figures of organismic biology was Ludwig von Bertalanffy. He describes three points on which the organismic position diverges from traditional mechanism. These are as follows.

1. *Life is a "system" rather than a collection of cooperating parts.* To state the idea differently, life is characterized by organization—an interdependence of parts and some kind of coordinating agency. Further, a living organism is a "system of systems." That is, a single cell is a system in itself, although it is under the general control of the organ of which it is a part; likewise, a single organ, such as the stomach, is a system but under the general control of the entire organism; and a total organism is a system whose behaviour is influenced by a still larger system—the "organism-in-its-environment." An analogy of systems within systems might be our solar system. The sun with all its planets behaves as a unit. Nevertheless, each planet has its own system of interacting forces, as does each moon or manmade satellite of each planet.

2. *Life is dynamic rather than static.* That is, life is purposive in the sense that it tries to maintain and better itself in its environment. Its fundamental pose is "activity, exploration, movement." Life does not wait for environmental stimuli to impinge upon it and thus excite it to action; action is its normal state. Purposiveness of higher life forms is likely to involve conscious design, growing from unpredictable wants, and not at all times being related to physiological drives.

3. *Life is interactive rather than reactive.* Since the fundamental orientation of an organism is toward exploration and manipulation of its environment, it is unlike a slot machine, which is passive until someone pulls the lever. On the other hand, life forms are modified

by environment: living is a two-way process in which a life form and its environment exert simultaneous influence upon each other. This viewpoint contrasts with the traditional mechanists' view that life is reactive, that its fundamental pose is waiting, that it acts only after stimulation.[18]

In addition to what Bertalanffy states, it should be noted that organismic biologists have devoted much study to that side of life which we call "psychological"—in contrast to a mechanist's almost exclusive interest in the physical side of life. Although organismic biologists do not presuppose substantive minds, in one sense the organismic and vitalistic views are alike. They both have no objection to studying the physical aspects of life—in fact, they would insist that much which is valuable may be learned only in this way. However, they insist that we can achieve useful definitions of the life process only if we include theories of "central control," *i.e.*, purposiveness, which we can do only through study of the mental as well as the physical characteristics of life forms.

An eminent American biologist, H. S. Jennings, asserts that, with reference to human beings, biologists have two kinds of data to work from: one kind results from observation of how living beings act (outer, or behavioural, data), the other from observation of mental lives (inner, or cognitive, data). It is proper, Jennings says, to label what we can discover through the use of outer data *physical,* and what we can discover through inner data *mental.* Jennings then points out that many biologists and some psychologists have largely ignored the mental aspect of life. He obviously thinks those scientists who have dismissed mind as unimportant, or non-existent, are misguided. "The universe," says Jennings, "is a system that brings forth life, sensation, emotion, thought." With the development of life, the universe "... begins to become conscious of itself, it begins to feel, to think, to have ideas and purposes and ideals."[19]

How do organismic biologists conceive of mind? They regard it as a function, but in a way very different from that of mechanists. To an organismic biologist, mind is a function that arises in interactive situations—that is, situations in which experience is incurred. The role of this function is to further an organism's purposes which consist of the shaping and fulfilling of organic need and the creating and fulfilling of nonorganic need.

To be more explicit, mind is the capacity of an organism, in an interactive situation, to see and be guided by meanings. Meaning is the "sign-quality" or "pointing-quality" which objects come to have as a result of an organism's having experienced them. For example, the "sign-quality", of a hot stove soon becomes apparent to a small child; a stove means. "Touch me and you will get burned." To extend the illustrations: growling dogs *mean* bite, thunderheads *mean* rain, paddles *mean* spank, the smell of cooking food *means* dinner. A human being probably begins acquiring his first meanings during his prenatal period, long before he can verbalize them. But mind becomes of major effectiveness in the life of a human person only after he is old enough to verbalize meanings and only after he has learned to socialize with others. The foregoing reference to human beings should not be construed to mean that mind, as defined above, is confined to humans. It is evident that all the higher animals may acquire meanings as they interact with their environments. Furthermore, although the "mental" experiences of an amoeba must be very different from those of a Harvard professor, all forms of life may do likewise.

In a single paragraph C. W. Morris, drawing mainly from the thinking of John Dewey, sums up a definition of mind which probably would be satisfactory to most organismic biologists:

> When the ongoing activity of the organism is blocked there arises a situation with the character which Dewey calls "doubtful" or "tensional." It is in such situations that mind and consciousness make their appearance, serving the purpose of resolving this ambiguity so that the situation can be controlled in the service of the frustrated organic demands or interests. It should be noted that this view does not make thought instrumental to sheer activity but to specific interests. Nor does it specify the limits of such interests—they may range from the need of food to a solution of the problem of mind. The insistence is simply that thought is inseparably linked with the demands of interested behaviour, and is instrumental to the satisfaction of such demands.[20]

Although the organismic approach may present enormous complexities, it is also probably a fairly good safeguard against some of the oversimplification of the atomistic, piecemeal approach. If we understand the organismic principle, and apply it, we never cease looking for relevant factors in a web which we recognize at the outset as being very complex.

The remainder of the chapter treats certain aspects of human biology from a basically organismic point of view; however, certain of the facts which we recount would be equally acceptable to a vitalist, a mechanist, or an organismic biologist.

WHAT IS THE FIELD CONCEPT IN BIOLOGY?

At one time biologists tended to regard living organisms as "collections of parts" capable of being understood only through careful analysis of the structure and functioning of each part. When one looks at life in this way, he conceives of an organism as a mosaic or perhaps as an assembled jigsaw puzzle. Although this atomistic analysis of living creatures still has its uses, it now is supplemented with a concept of the "organism-as-a-whole" in which the organism is seen as a unit or organic entity. Many biologists go even further than this by assuming that an organism cannot be fully understood except when it is studied in the context of its environment. Hence, the unit of study is an "organism-in-an-environment."

In biology, the organismic point of view makes use of what many scientists call the *field concept*. The idea of the field first appeared in physics. It has since come to be used in biology, psychology, and the social sciences. However, the field concept in biology is not identical with the field concept is psychology; the differences will become apparent in later chapters. A simple definition of a field is "a totality of coexisting facts which are conceived of as mutually interdependent....."[21] A characteristic feature of a field is that, because of the interdependence of its elements, it tends to maintain some degree of balance or stability. If the equilibrium of a field of forces is disturbed, counterbalancing forces tend to arise which reinstate equilibrium. However, since the new equilibrium may incorporate factors not previously present, it will not necessarily consist of the same state of affairs as existed prior to the disturbance.

If a living organism is regarded as a field of forces, an example of disturbance and restoration of a different but useful state of balance would be as follows: A four-legged animal loses a leg. It "compensates" by learning a new gait which permits walking with three legs; further, the muscles of the three remaining legs grow stronger. To take an example incorporating both animal and environment: a certain species of squirrel, let us say, subsists on a certain kind of pine seed. But a disease kills the pines in the area. The squirrels learn to substitute a different kind of nut and, although less well nourished, continue to exist in depleted numbers. A new equilibrium has appeared.

There is nothing in nature guaranteeing that new equilibria necessarily will be better for a particular form of life; sometimes a change in a field destroys a life form (as happened to the dinosaurs). But when a field of forces includes one or more life forms, reorganization of the field usually is influenced by the attempts of the life forms to preserve and better their conditions of living.

The field concept also includes the notion that a total field has qualities unlike those of any single element of the field. In physics, the nature of elements in chemical combination illustrates this. A compound is, on its own level, one kind of field. Water is an example of a chemical compound. Consider how different are the qualities of water from either of its components—hydrogen and oxygen—taken singly. Conversely, all the components of a field, while a part of the field, take their qualities from their location and role in the field. If a field changes, the properties of its constituent parts change.

Biologists for some time have been aware that animals have "electrical systems." These are characterized by differences in potential and by resulting flow of electrical current. The flow of electrical current produces electromagnetic fields. There is good reason to believe that there is a continuous reciprocal relationship between these electrical phenomena and metabolic processes. That is, changes in metabolism are associated with changes in electrical phenomena; but it is impossible to say that one is the "cause" of the other. They are both aspects of the same underlying life process.

Thus, the term *electrometabolic field* has come into use in biology. A total organism can be regarded as a field of forces but it consists also of a number of subfields, each overlapping and continuously interacting with the others. The nature of the small fields is not well understood; undoubtedly each organ, and each cell in an organ, exhibits field characteristics. (We are saying here what Bertalanffy says when he asserts that a living creature consists of "systems within systems.")

Of what significance is all this for teachers? In studying a child or youth, it seems wise to take into consideration as much of the "field" as one can encompass. Insofar as possible, that part of environment which affects a person's biological functioning must be seen in its entirety. How well is he nourished? What pattern of rest and activity does he follow? What kind of medical attention does he receive? In what ways have his more pressing organic drives been satisfied, redirected, or frustrated? Along with consideration of the environment of an organism, it seems wise to interpret specific physiological traits in their relationship to a total organism. For example, Johnny's tooth cavities may be partially a result of genetic inheritance, partially a result of his mother's illness while he was a fetus, and partially a result of a general bodily malaise produced by emotional upset or other factors.

IN WHAT WAY IS LIFE PURPOSIVE?

Central to the organismic view is the idea that life is purposive. This is an easy statement to make, but knotty problems appear when we try to become more specific.

One level of purpose appears to be simply the maintenance of normalcy. As John F. Dashiell puts it, "Through all animal life an outstanding characteristic runs—the tendency of the organism to maintain its normalcy against internal or external disrupting agencies."[22] This characteristic often is referred to as *homeostasis,* a term popularized by Walter Cannon earlier in the century.[23] A good example is the way a person fights disease often successfully without aid of medicine. Other examples are the ways in which wounds heal, broken bones knit, or a kidney increases its functioning to compensate for loss of its twin. Some animals seem to have developed homeostasis more fully than man: they can "regenerate" lost tails or legs. Homeostasis produces kinds of behaviour which appear purposive; it makes a creature appear to be trying to regulate itself in terms of a goal—survival.

As defined by Cannon, homeostasis is the process by which a disturbed organism eliminates the disturbance and returns to its former state. Defined in this way, the concept is too static to explain much that we now know. C. A. Mace has developed some extensions of the original theory which seem helpful. He has suggested that what is maintained or restored in homeostasis is not so much an internal state of an organism—although to a degree this happens—but also a satisfactory relation of the organism and its environment. Also, a specific equilibrium is rarely maintained; it is better to refer to the attainment of "a new equilibrium" than to "restoration of equilibrium."[24]

Students will note at this point that homeostatic theory ties in very closely with the general statement of field theory (pp. 40-41).

Organic Drives and Needs

An organic drive is a tendency to act in fulfilment of an organic need. That is, when a physiological need appears it produces a state of tension which is uncomfortable; to relieve discomfort and thus restore a state of normalcy an organism engages in appropriate behaviour—the manifestation of drive. Since organic needs are never completely satisfied (unless an organism is dead) *some level of tension is normal to life.* In short, a field is never completely relaxed but only at times relatively so.

A moment's thought is all that is required for us to identify several organic needs common not only to man but to most other members of the animal kingdom. These needs have become embedded in the biological organism through long evolutionary processes; they are indispensable, in the sense that their satisfaction contributes to well-being and survival.

1. The need for food and drink. The role of this need in permitting continued metabolism and maintenance of chemical balances is obvious.
2. The need for regular elimination of waste products from the organism.
3. The need for satisfactory rest-activity rhythms. A certain amount of rest is needed to permit repair of fatigued tissue. Apparently activity, varying in amount and kind according to the organism, also plays an important role in promoting physical well-being.
4. The need for protection of the physical organism from threats of the physical environment—from poisons, extremes of noise, and various physical dangers.
5. The need for a modicum of physical comfort. Generally speaking, animals avoid discomfort and seek comfort. Discomfort may come from a variety of causes—extremes of hot and cold, extremes of light, disease, insect-pests, and the like.
6. The need for sexual release, which is not always so specific as to require for its satisfaction the mating act.

Levels of Purposiveness

Although organic needs are relatively specific in that we can describe the processes involved and understand fairly well the drive-reducing behaviour which leads most directly to satisfaction, the kinds of behaviour human beings have devised in the satisfaction of organic need are immense in number and highly complex. Man, because of his capacity to think, symbolize, and transmit his ideas from one generation to another, is the culture-building animal par excellence. Consequently human culture may in many ways become far removed from the task of organic-need satisfaction. In fact, man among all the earth's creatures seems to have been the only one to invent the notion that some organic needs are evil and ought to be denied. Accordingly, in a study of man, we must make a sharp distinction between what organic need demands and what human desire wills. For example, a person may *feel* as his strongest need a fast of thirty days or a whiplashing. Lest modern Americans scorn too much the religious ascetics who have deliberately practiced "mortifying the flesh," they should remember that in numerous ways they punish their physical organisms, perhaps not so painfully but in ways even more damaging. (The smog of some of our larger cities is perhaps more damaging to the physical organism than any forms of penitence yet devised.)

Life then is purposive on different levels. It is purposive on a level where what happens seems fairly automatic, as in the case of the internal homeostatic processes of digestion, assimilation, and respiration. It is purposive on the level of the organic drives of which human beings are consciously aware. Furthermore, it is purposive on a level which we might call psychological need, wish, or desire. The latter may be unrelated to organic need and does not necessarily contribute to either physical health or survival.[25]

In the final section of Chapter 3, we point out that our most pressing psychological need is maintenance and enhancement of the perceived self. This means, approximately, keeping one's psychological person in a state which permits self-respect, security, self-expression, etc. Students should note that this is a psychological and not an organic need. As a matter of fact, it is often necessary for persons to deny organic needs in order to achieve satisfaction of psychological needs. And in many persons psychological needs become far more pressing than the organic; in an extreme case one might even get in a position where he can serve his psychological needs best only by committing suicide.

How many teachers use the understandings which we have sought to communicate in this section? Young persons basically have the same organic needs as adults. Thus, if teachers understand the nature of organic drives, they will understand children better. Any school programme which takes advantage of the impulses of young people resulting from organic needs stands a better chance of success, in the sense that motivation of students to do hard and original work will be higher. However, psychological needs, which are highly individualistic and often have to be revealed and stimulated through skilled teaching, can provide even stronger motivation than that arising from organic drives.

WHAT SHOULD TEACHERS KNOW ABOUT GENETICS?

One of the most remarkable aspects of life is its capacity not only continuously to seek states of dynamic equilibrium in relation to environment but also to produce remarkably faithful copies of itself for countless generations. Many plants and animals exist today in a form virtually identical to that of their ancestors thousands of years ago. Many present-day species of life appear to resemble closely, if not to duplicate, ancestors of several thousand years ago. Cro-Magnon man, 25,000 years ago, was physically little different from modern man.

The Carriers of Heredity

Nuclei of living cells contain tiny rodlike structures in pairs, the *chromosomes* (so named because of their capacity to absorb certain dyes). The two sets appear upon examination to be identical or nearly so. Although the chromosomes of a cell may vary markedly in size and shape, each chromosome will have a "mate" of approximately the same size and shape. Where reproduction is sexual, one set represents the inheritance from the father, the other set the inheritance from the mother. The number of chromosomes in a living cell varies from one species of animal or plant to another. In human beings there are twenty-three pairs.

Chromosomes carry what Schrödinger has called a "code script."[26] This code script directs the development of the organism from the time the egg is fertilized to the adult state and in major ways governs the biological functioning of the organism throughout life.

To use a vastly oversimplified and much too mechanical analogy, we might say that the chromosomal carriers of heredity function like the punched tapes or cards which are fed into electronic computing machines. They cause a machine to run through a series of predictable steps. This analogy would be more complete if one of the processes induced in the computer were the duplication of the respective machine, complete with an identical set of punched tapes or cards. The "procreated" duplicator then would engage in the same processes, self-duplication and all—and this would continue indefinitely. For the analogy to be perfect, the reproduction of a computer would require the functions of two parent computers, "male" and "female," each of which would contribute to the offspring a set of its own punched tapes or cards which would work jointly in directing the offspring's functioning.

Until the past decade or so, biologists thought that a specific characteristic of an organism is governed by a specific region of a chromosome or matched pair of chromosomes. This region was referred to as a *gene.* Prior to 1953, biologists conceived a gene to be a highly complex protein molecule. However, gene theory has in late years undergone a revolution. First, it was discovered that the chemical carrier of hereditary traits is not protein but a chemical, deoxyribonucleic acid—DNA for short—which is centered in the nuclei of cells. Ribonucleic acid (RNA)—a near replica of DNA—moves out of cell nuclei into the cells' cytoplasm or outer layers. Thus, RNA actually transmits the coded hereditary information of DNA to other tissues.

Chromosomes consist mainly of molecules of DNA. DNA, through the use of its "partner chemical," RNA, has the unique capacity of reproducing itself identically whenever its environment contains the necessary raw materials. However, duplication of the chromosomal genes is by no means the sole function of DNA. Through the pioneering work of Andre Lwoff, Jacques Monod, and Francois Jacob of the Pasteur Institute in Paris, it appears established that, when a foreign substance is introduced into a cell, it triggers the cell's DNA to produce precisely to enzyme needed to convert the substance to a chemical form which cells can use to develop and multiply.

Thus, in a sense, the basic function of genes can be turned on or off—they can perform tasks other than merely transmitting hereditary characteristics. Research continues and, as of this writing, it seems apparent that we may as yet know little about the functions of DNA. It is evident, however, that it serves as a kind of "brain within the cell" (to use a crude analogy), the full implications of which forces us to revise fundamentally our concept of the cell and perhaps the nature of life itself.[27]

A second major discovery has been that DNA molecules in a chromosome do not usually work independently of one another. They tend to work in teams, in the sense that the functioning of one affects the functioning of others. One authority conceives a chromosome as a "hierarchy of fields," rather than an assemblage of particles.[28] The gene concept is still useful but it now seems best to think of a gene as a function of a region of a chromosome rather than as a specific particle.

As we have seen, chromosomes occur in body cells in matched pairs. Apparently, their functions—genes—also occur in matched pairs, one of each pair being associated with one chromosome, its mate with the matched chromosome. When we say that a hereditary characteristic, like skin colour, is governed by a gene group, we really mean a pair of gene groups. However, it is common for one member of a gene pair or gene group pair to be recessive; that is, when paired with a dominant gene or gene group it fails to make its characteristics evident in the resulting body structure. Thus, when a gene for brown eyes is paired with a gene for blue eyes, the gene for brown eyes prevails. For a person to have blue eyes he must carry two recessive genes for blue.

Eye colour is one of a few characteristics in human beings apparently governed by a single gene pair. Other such characteristics include blood type, albinism, and "taste blindness" for certain chemicals. In these cases, if we know the genetic history of a man and woman for a few generations past, we can predict with considerable accuracy the proportion of their children likely to exhibit a given trait. This type of inheritance follows Mendelian principles, *i.e.*, the principles of heredity formulated by Gregor, Mendel (1822-1884). Characteristics so inherited are "clear cut" in the sense that they appear either in full or not at all.

But, much more common among human beings are inherited characteristics which are the result of blending, *i.e.*, the interplay of gene teams. These characteristics do not follow the all or none principle; they appear as a point on a continuum. Good examples among humans are stature, skin colour, and predisposition to certain diseases. It is very hard to predict the outcome of blending; for example, even if we knew the skin colours of a baby's ancestors, for several generations, it would still not be safe to predict the baby's colour before his birth.

Of course, because of the ways in which environmental factors seemingly can influence physical traits, one is never safe in predicting that any particular kind of hereditary trait will appear in an adult offspring. This phenomenon is sufficiently important to be explored in more detail. The pattern of genes of an organism is referred to as the organism's *genotype,* its internal chromosomal structure. The genotype governs what an organism can become in a given environment and also determines the hereditary characteristics which an organism can transmit to its offspring (though, if reproduction is heterosexual, the genotype of the offspring is of course a product of the genotype of both father and mother).

The external appearance of an organism is called its *phenotype.* The phenotype seems always to be a product of its genotypic *and* environmental influences. Phenotypes may vary considerably even when genotypes remain the same. For example, when persons of Asiatic extraction move to the United States, their children (if reared in this country) tend to be larger than the parents, and their grandchildren larger still. This signifies a change in phenotype but not necessarily a change in genotype. Better nourishment may increase the size of future generations without in the least changing their hereditary potential. Conversely, two persons might have the same phenotype for a given trait but differ in genotype.

Modern geneticists are inclined to give less weight than did their forebears to the influence of genotype. Certainly, genetic inheritance counts for a good deal in determining the kind of adult a person will become, but the fact is, we do not know the exact role genotype plays in determining phenotype. Scientists used to debate what they called the nature-nurture issue. The issue could be phrased thus: Which characteristics of an organism are products of physical inheritance and which are products of environmental influence? But, modern scientists have virtually abandoned debate on this issue; many say that, since we have no adequate means of ascertaining the facts, continuing such a debate is futile.

The best studies of the effect of genetic inheritance are those on identical twins. Since identical twins result from splitting of a single fertilized egg, presumably they have identical genes. What is determined by heredity should therefore appear in exactly the same form in the two twins—subject, of course, to such environmental modification as may have occurred. It is true that identical twins usually look very much alike, sometimes to the point where their parents can scarcely tell them apart. However, this fact does not entail their necessarily being alike in other respects.

According to one study, the IQ difference of identical twins who have been reared together is 3.1 points; that of fraternal twins reared together, 8.5 points. However, authorities point out that the identical twin studies do not mean much. Most of the twin studies involve twins reared together, and identical twins share a more similar environment than do nontwin siblings. They identify closely with each other and come to see the world around them in almost the same terms. Furthermore, they normally share the same diet and medical care.

The most valid type of study with respect to the nature-nurture controversy is that of identical twins who were separated in infancy and reared out of contact with each other and in dissimilar environments. Under these conditions, twins tend to be less alike; for example, the average difference in IQ scores in double that of identical twins reared together. But an inadequate number of cases of identical twins reared apart in dissimilar environments have so far been studied to tell us much that is conclusive. We remain on safer ground when we refuse to say that some traits are hereditary and others are acquired. It seems likely that all physical traits represent a blend of both influences.[29]

Are Personality Traits Inherited?

This question has an easy answer: No evidence! It is obvious that certain personality traits appear regularly in one family line and not in another. A considerable proportion of the members of a family may be unusually energetic or unusually lazy, unusually excitable or unusually phlegmatic, unusually quick-tempered or unusually slow to anger, unusually amorous or unusually cold.

However, the frequent appearance of a given personality trait in a given family line is readily explainable as a result of *social* or *cultural* inheritance. John Jr. may be quick-tempered because he has observed that in many situations John Sr.'s equally quick temper gets desired results. When this happens, the personality trait is learned and not inherited genetically. So far as we know, *all* personality traits are learned. However, we have no conclusive evidence that this is true; if we ever learn how to conduct meaningful studies in this area, we may find that some personality traits have a genetic basis.

Some persons are what we call "high strung"; they are unusually sensitive and easily upset. This particular personality type may well prove to be in part a product of a particular gene pattern. But we do not know this is the case.

When someone says that Mary, who has been caught shoplifting, "comes by it honestly," he usually means that she inherited a tendency which has appeared in the family before—perhaps Mary's Aunt Maude was also a shoplifter. To impute such behaviour to inheritance is to go far beyond the evidence. This way of thinking is a part of our "folklore biology" just as some of the notions about psychology described in Chapter 3 are "folklore psychology."

The wisest stand for a teacher to take is that physical inheritance in itself is rarely of any crucial importance. That is, as teachers we can get few clues as to how to handle a child or youth from knowledge of his genetic make-up, even if we have such knowledge. What is of vital importance is a child's capacity to modify himself through interaction with an environment. All but the hopelessly defective have this capacity.

Race and Genetics

Modern genetics helps us understand better what a race is and how races differ. Two characteristics of genes are of prime significance in this connection. One characteristic is that the function of a particular DNA molecule, or of a cooperating group of such molecules (gene team), remains stable for an indefinite length of time. Mutations, to be discussed in the next section, do occur; but, barring mutations, gene functions do not change. Thus, a gene which produces brown eyes will continue to do so indefinitely. Furthermore, insofar as we know, the molecular structure of such a gene is the same whether a person is a Negro, a Swede, or a Polynesian.

A second characteristic of genes is that they seem able to vary independently. At first thought, this statement may seem to contradict the earlier assertion that most physical traits are products of gene teams and that a chromosome may be better understood as a "field of forces" with highly complex lines of interaction. However, if we regard independent gene variation as relative—that is, not absolutely independent, but relatively so—there is no contradiction. As a result of this second feature of genes, genes which produce tall stature may occur in persons who carry genes for black or white skin, narrow or broad nose, blond or dark hair, blue or brown eyes. Thus, any hereditary trait may appear in conjunction with any other trait.

These two genetic principles give meaning to the following definition of race: "Races are populations which differ in the relative commonness of some of their genes."[30] Thus, in a particular race a given trait, such as tallness, may occur more often than in another race. A particular shade of skin may be more common in one race than in another. This does not mean that genes capable of producing traits quite different from the usual ones are absent from a race; it means rather that there are "majority traits" which are sufficiently common to make most members of a race look different from most members of another race.

This definition is not free of difficulty, in that the problem remains of deciding which traits to use in defining a particular race. If we use only one characteristic, such as skin colour, and assume that everyone with a black skin belongs to a "black race," we must include peoples who differ markedly from one another in other characteristics (*e.g.*, Asian Indians, Melanesians, and Africans). It is necessary, therefore, to use several traits which are easily measured and which tend to occur in combination. Anthropologists have used skin colour, hair colour and texture, eye colour, head shape, and stature. Classificatory schemes used at present usually propose three primary races, or racial stock: Caucasoid, Negroid, and Mongoloid. Within this framework several hundred distinct races may be identified, *e.g.*, Nordic, Alpine, Mediterranean, Armenoid, Hindi, and so on. Since the base now commonly used for classifying people racially are arbitrary, and since racial mixing apparently has occurred since the first development of distinctive races, we can only conclude that the concept of race is not very meaningful. In Dunn and Dobzhansky's words. "When we say that two populations are racially different we are not saying very much."[31]

There may be vast differences *culturally* between the races, but this is a matter of learning and not a product of biological difference. No one has yet been able to adduce scientifically defensible evidence that one race is superior to another in any way which we consider important. Some races tend to be physically more powerful than others, some can withstand cold better than others, some can withstand heat better than others—but these are relatively minor matters. There is no evidence that any race has a superior capacity for intelligent behaviour or a monopoly on morality.

Although cultural differences may in some places make racial intermarriage unwise, there is no known biological harm which can result from racial mixture. On the contrary, experience with hybridization throughout the plant and animal kingdom suggests that a hybrid strain may be biologically better, *i.e.*, stronger and more vigorous, than the parent varieties. Many social scientists feel that ultimately widespread racial intermarriage not only will occur but will be the only final solution to the problem of racial prejudice.

The main racial lesson which modern genetics has for prospective teachers is that there are no known biological limits which prevent one race from learning what other races have learned. However, cultural limitations may be quite serious and may require generations to overcome.

Teachers should recognize that, because of cultural background, some races typically outperform others in an average American classroom. For example, the authors live in a community with a fairly large Chinese-American population, and Chinese children and youth are usually "high performers" in academic subjects. A cultural tradition of prizing scholarship, which extends backward thousands of years, undoubtedly explains the Chinese performance.

HOW DO SPECIES EVOLVE?

In the previous section we stressed the permanence of species. But it is obvious that species change. Plant and animal breeders, in seeking new varieties, deliberately induce or take advantage of genetic change. Permanent change in an organism from the characteristics of its forebears results only from genetic change, *i.e.*, a change in the functioning of the genes. Insofar as is known, there are only two ways in which this can occur: (1) sexual recombination of hereditary units, as when we crossbreed two different strains or varieties and get a new type of organism; and (2) mutation, or internal change, of the chromosomal DNA.

Just how mutations occur is still a matter of speculation. Beadle suggests that when a DNA molecule creates a copy of itself it sometimes makes a mistake. As a result, the new molecule has a different atomic arrangement from that of its parent. As a simple but hypothetical analogy, Beadle compares mutations to typographical errors, of which there are four basic types; (1) extra letters inserted

(2) letters omitted; (3) letters substituted; and (4) letters transposed. The new faulty molecule, with its added, missing, or rearranged atoms, goes on duplicating itself in its new form with its normal precision. What causes a DNA molecule to make a mistake? We know of at least two causes: one is high energy radiation, the other the action of various chemicals which an organism ingests from its environment.[32]

Errors in replication, *i.e.*, DNA reproduction, would accumulate steadily in a species and thus make species-stability impossible, except that they tend to be self-destructive. Present species are already highly selected, *i.e.*, relatively perfect in relation to environment. Since present species represent a high order of development, in terms of potential for survival, almost all new mutations are harmful. New mutant strains of a species usually have a poor survival potential and die out—unless human beings intervene to provide a type of environment which will permit survival.

It would be in exceptionally rare instances that both sets of a gene pair would mutate at the same time in exactly the same way. Hence, in almost all cases, mutations affect only one gene of a gene pair. The mutation may produce either a recessive or a dominant character; however, the former is much more common. Since mutations are so often recessive, a new characteristic may not appear immediately in the offspring of a mutated parent. Until enough descendants have been produced so that they can inbreed, a new trait is unlikely to appear as a detectable change in bodily characteristics. Undoubtedly, because of taboos on incest and on the marriage of cousins, many damaging mutations in human beings never have become apparent in phenotypes.

The Mechanism of Evolution

The changes induced by mutation are usually small. However, occasionally they are quite large, as when, apparently as a result of a single mutation, a strain of mice known as the "varitint waddler" appeared.[33] Evolution operates when changes appear giving a species, or a strain, some advantage or disadvantage which is significant in the struggle for survival. The crucial period in the life of a member of a species, with respect to the survival of the species, is the period through the age of reproduction. For example, if individuals of a particular species tend to remain fertile through the age of, say, seven years, then any mutation which enhances their chances of survival, or increases their fertility, during the first seven years will have survival value for the species. Some types of insects exist in their adult, reproductive form for only a few hours before they die. However, because of their ability to survive in large numbers just long enough to breed, they represent highly viable species. In human beings, any mutation which increases survival or enhances fertility through about the first forty or forty-five years of life would tend to have survival value for the species.

Natural selection is the name given to the process by which, through the failure of their carriers to survive, some mutated genes are lost; and by which, because of their relatively higher survival value, other mutated genes form the basis of a new and flourishing strain or species. In nature, it is often the case that several species compete for scarce food or scarce habitat. Successful species tend to multiply until their numbers create a food or space shortage or create other problems. Evidently, therefore, a life form often may exist in a rather delicate state of balance with hostile environmental influences. If a mutation gives its bearers only a slight advantage over the rest, then over the long run the new strain will prevail; just as, conversely, an adverse mutation which confers only a slight disadvantage will in time make its bearers extinct.

Natural selection may operate in a highly competitive situation; there may be so many of a species in relation to food supply that only the strongest or craftiest survive. But, it is easy to draw unwarranted conclusions from this fact. And wrong conclusions have indeed been drawn. Many persons have assumed that competition is the natural state of animals in nature. This is the so-called "law of the jungle"—the stronger devour the weaker; the weaker devour those weaker still; and so on.

Biological studies of the twentieth century have led to a rather drastic modification of this point of view. It is now common opinion among biologists that ability of the members of a species, or of different species, to cooperate may have much more "survival value" than competition of one individual against another. Wolves hunting in packs find this to be a successful means of procuring food. Crows and ravens find that more food can be had if sentinels are placed to warn of impending danger. Prairie dogs survive better in cooperative colonies.[34] Human beings likewise furnish an excellent example of the survival value of cooperation. Except in occasional isolated instances, human life outside societies governed by a large measure of internal cooperation is unknown.

Evolution and Man

It is now generally accepted by biologists that human beings are a product of natural selection and also that they represent the "pinnacle" of the evolutionary process because of their superior adaptability. Beadle, in the reference cited, hypothesizes that all physical substance started as hydrogen and is still evolving. From hydrogen the more complex elements developed. The next step was the combination of elements into molecules. From simple molecules evolved more complex ones until finally the first life appeared. Beadle suggests that life began as single DNA molecules. At this point we approach the virus level of existence: a virus is a bundle of DNA molecules with a protective protein coating. From viruses the next step was to cells; then to multicellular organisms and finally man.

Has man ceased changing biologically? There is no reason to believe so. However, biological evolution has ceased to be very important, at least for the time being. With the appearance of a culture-creating organism, evolution can operate in another realm—that of ideas. Julian Huxley calls this stage in the evolutionary process the *psychosocial*. In this stage changes in ideas take the place of genetic change. New ideas enable man to adapt to a changing environment. Ideas themselves undergo a process comparable to natural selection: those with survival value tend to persist and those which reduce the potential for survival are lost.

This does not mean that ideas, because they survive, are necessarily good; we undoubtedly harbour many very ancient ideas which have the effect of reducing human well-being. Such ideas can survive if they do not markedly reduce the birth rate or increase thew death rate.

Even though human life flourishes without need for further biological change, nevertheless man cannot escape biological change. Dobzhansky states that human sperm and ova contain mutations at the rate of one in every 10,000 to 250,000 cells produced. This does not seem like a very high rate of mutation. However, Dobzhansky suggests that the mutation rate has probably increased in recent years and may increase still more in the future. Industrialization not only increases the level of radiation to which everyone is subjected but also necessitates human contact with mutation-producing chemicals.

Since natural selection no longer operates in man, there is a risk that the human race will accumulate a large stock of harmful mutations.

As a specific example, Dobzhansky points out that as we eliminate infectious diseases we protect genes for susceptibility. If natural selection were operating, many persons carrying the genes for susceptibility would die young and thus the genes would be destroyed. Conceivably, through preserving mutants for susceptibility, the level of susceptibility could become so high that if our artificial means of controlling the disease were to break down we would be disastrously vulnerable.[35]

Of what significance for teachers is our treatment of genetic change? Its significance is certainly not so obvious as is the case with some other aspects of human biology. Our hope is that prospective teachers will be impressed with the idea that man is a piece of "unfinished business," biologically, psychologically, and culturally. Such an idea should be of significance in helping teachers find a sense of direction.

Another idea of possible significance is simple that man does not have all of his biological problems solved. In spite of the tremendous strides he has made in conquering disease, he dare not forget that evolution works inexorably but not necessarily in his favour. Although we know enough about the nature of genetic change to be able to control the spread of harmful mutations, it is most unlikely that this will happen. Rather, the mutant will survive through increased medical attention and contribute to the pollution of the genetic pool.[36]

REFERENCES

1. D. O. Hebb, *The Organization of Behaviour*, Wiley, 1949, p. xvi.
2. *Ibid.*
3. E. D. Adrian, *The Physical Background of Perception*, Oxford University Press, 1947, p. 1.
4. See Ernest R. Hilgard and Gordon H. Bower, "Neurophysiology of Learning," *Theories of Learning*, 3rd ed., Appleton-Century-Crofts, 1966, esp. p. 462.
5. *Ibid.*, p. 454.
6. Most of the discussion in this chapter on the nature of mind is influenced by Charles W. Morris, *Six Theories of Mind*, University of

Chicago Press, 1932. Also highly pertinent is Boyd H. Bode, *How We Learn,* Health, 1940.

7. Adrian, *op. cit.,* p. 4.
8. John C. Eccles, *The Neurophysiological Basis of Mind,* Clarendon, 1953, especially Chapter 6.
9. H. G. Wells, Julian S. Huxley, and G. P. Wells, *The Science of Life,* Literary Guild, 1934, pp. 29-30.
10. *Ibid.,* p. 30.
11. *Ibid.,* pp. 1270-77.
12. John von Neumann, "The General and Logical Theory of Automata," in Lloyd A. Jeffrss, ed., *Cerebral Mechanisms in Behaviour,* Wiley, 1951, p. 2.
13. Advanced students who wish further to study modern attempts to explain life in physicalist terms may find of interest Norbert Wiener's *Cybernetics,* Wiley, 1948, or W. Ross Ashy's *An Introduction to Cybernetics,* Chapman & Hall, 1956. Also by the same author, *Design for a Brain,* Wiley, 1952. John von Neumann's posthumously published *Computer and the Brain,* Yale University Press, 1958, is also pertinent.
14. Gardner Murphy, *Historical Introduction to Modern Psychology,* Harcourt, Brace 1949, pp. 18, 38.
15. Edwin G. Boring. *A History of Experimental Psychology,* Appleton-Century, 1929. p. 39.
16. Donald O. Hebb, *A Textbook of Psychology,* W. B. Saunders, 1958, Chapters 2-5.
17. G. L. Freeman, *The Energetics of Human Behaviour,* Cornell University Press, 1948.
18. See Ludwig von Bertalanffy, *Problems of Life; an Evaluation of Modern Biological Thought,* Wiley, 1952, Ch. 1.
19. H. S. Jennings, *The Universe and Life,* Yale University Press, 1933, p. 16.
20. Morris, *op. cit.,* pp. 294-95.
21. Kurt Lewin, "Behaviour and Development as a Function of the Total Situation," in Leonard Carmichael, ed., *Manual of Child Psychology,* 2nd ed., Wiley, 1954. Lewin's formulation is derived from a statement by Albert Einstein. See p. 919.
22. Quoted in Arthur W. Combs and Donald Snygg, *Individual Behaviour,* rev. ed., Harper & Row, 1959, p. 41.
23. See Walter Cannon, *The Wisdom of the Body,* Norton, 1932, for many excellent examples of homeostasis at work.
24. C. A. Mace, "Homeostasis, Needs and Values," *British Journal of Psychology,* August, 1953, p. 3.

25. A discussion of psychological purposiveness.
26. For one of the most provocative treatments of this subject, see Erwin Schrödinger, *What Is Life?* Cambridge University Press, 1955. See especially Chapters 2-5. Schrödinger's discussion of the nature of genes is now obsolete, but most of his thesis remains valid.
27. See Gunther S. Stent, "1965 Nobel Laureates in Medicine or Physiology, *Science,* October 22, 1965. Less technical but helpful is Philip E. Hartman and Sigmund R. Suskind, *Gene Action,* Prentice Hall, 1965.
28. See Edmund W. Sinnott, L. C. Dunn, and Theodosius Dobzhansky, *Principles of Genetics,* McGraw-Hill, 1958, p. 387.
29. *Ibid,* p. 30.
30. L. C. Dunn and Theodosius Dobzhansky, *Heredity, Race, and Society,* New American Library, 1952, p. 114.
31. *Ibid.,* p. 125.
32. George Beadle, "The Chemical Basis of Modern Genetics," *Proceedings,* Plant Science Seminar, Camden, N. J., 1960.
33. John L. Fuller and W. Robert Thompson, *Behaviour Genetics,* Wiley, 1960, pp. 19-20.
34. See the provocative discussion of animal cooperation in Ashley Montagu, *The Direction of Human Development,* Harper, 1955, pp. 17-58. For a fuller treatment of the same subject, see. W. C. Allee, *The Social Life of Animals,* Beacon, 1958.
35. Theodosius Dobzhansky, "The Present Evolution of Man," *Scientific American,* September, 1960.
36. See Norman J. Berrill, *Biology in Action,* Dodd Mead, 1966, p. 831.

2

Physical Growth and Development

The most important, most helpful, most deceiving, most confusing, most neglected fact in education is growth. Most important, because the first consideration throughout the school years should be that healthy growth be achieved; most helpful, because the plasticity and vigor of the growth period offer multiple opportunities for education; deceiving, because education is constantly mistaking for its own accomplishment what has really come about through maturing; confusing, because growth involves constant change; neglected, because it is so obvious and yet so subtle.

Growth in intellect, personality, and character can be adequately understood only in relation to physical growth. To appreciate the fundamental biological character of growth in intelligence, the similarity between the curves for growth in intelligence and in physique should be noted. Only after consideration of the physiological changes going forward in childhood and adolescence can one come to full appreciation of the profound changes in interests and attitudes occurring in this same period. Anomalies of physical development are the explanation of many a "problem child."

For a child, the fact that he is constantly growing and changing is not simply a fact; it is an experience, presenting to him very difficult problems. Moreover, since in his world physical size and prowess play a large part, the growth which he has achieved determines in large degree the group of children with which he will associate, and his position and prestige in that group. In the adolescent period physical growth may, and usually does, present manifold embarrassments to the youngster of either sex. It is not easy for the grown and relatively stabilized person to realize how bewildering it is to be growing, especially since these problems of childhood and youth probably once caused him so much unhappiness that he now does not wish to remember them.

The concrete significance of differences and changes in physical size will be clearer if the reader will recall their bearings on his or her own childhood and adolescence. He may remember how very big adults seemed—how big even children in the fifth grade appeared—when he was in the second grade, or how awkward and immature he felt as a high school freshman in comparison with the seniors. It is also well to recall cases one has known in which growth factors have played a large part in a child's life. One school had the bright boy whose ambitious parents pushed him ahead in school until he was with others against whom he was so helpless in play that he became a diffident recluse; the exceedingly tall boy who withdrew completely from games with his fellows because he literally could not compete on a level with them; the stupid sixth-grade bully who tyrannized because he had been held back in the grades among boys too small to fight back successfully; and the slight youngster who worked himself into physical and emotional exhaustion trying futilely to make good in some form of athletics. Then there was the girl, small for her age, who became the pampered pet of both the teacher and the other girls in her class, and the big raw-boned girl who was acutely unhappy because she was so tall and large that most of the boys did not want to dance with her. If the reader will look back critically at his or her own adolescence there will probably emerge unpleasant recollections of bewilderment and anxiety over the changes of puberty. Very likely there was embarrassment over sleeves and trouser legs that had become too short, accentuating wrists and ankles proportionately too thin, with hands and feet too big. Perhaps there was awkwardness that caused accidents at dinner table or in classroom, a voice that broke at inopportune times, teeth and nose too prominent in a childish face, a downy beard that was not enough to shave but too much to escape comment. All too likely the maturing of the sex organs was an event about which the surprised youngster had not been adequately informed, and which was regarded with fear and shame as something abnormal. Anyone who has forgotten these manifold difficulties involved in merely growing should carefully review his or her childhood and youth by glancing at such books as Tarkington's *Seventeen*, Sherwood Anderson's *Tar: A Mid-West Childhood*, or Leonard's *The Locomotive God*, noting the importance of physical changes as a background against which the story unfolds.

To begin the study of educational psychology by a consideration of physical growth is, then, of twofold value. Some understanding of the background physiological factors involved in psychological development is thus obtained. And the peculiar and difficult psychological problems presented to a child because he is physically a growing and changing organism can thus be systematically studied.

GROWTH IN SIZE

Most elementary of all data regarding growth are measurements of height and weight. In a given child size is only a rough indication of his stage of growth. But massed data on height and weight tell much about the course of growth and the relation of various factors to growth.

Curves of Growth in Height and Weight—The total sweep of the growth process is well shown by Chart 2.1, which gives curves of growth in height and weight. The curves indicate a rapid growth in infancy, a slower rate in middle childhood, an upsurge at adolescence—more noticeable on the curves for weight—and an adult leveling off toward 20 for the boys, earlier for the girls.[1]

The magnitude of the total growth process through the years, and especially in adolescence, must be emphasized. Thus over the twelve years from 6 to 18 boys increase over one-half in height and over three times in weight. The powerful nature of the forces of growth and the insistency of the demands of the organism as regards food, exercise, sleep, and other factors involved in physical well-being can hardly be overemphasized. Little wonder that there are times in the lives of many children when—very likely to the distress of their teachers—the youngsters seem to be

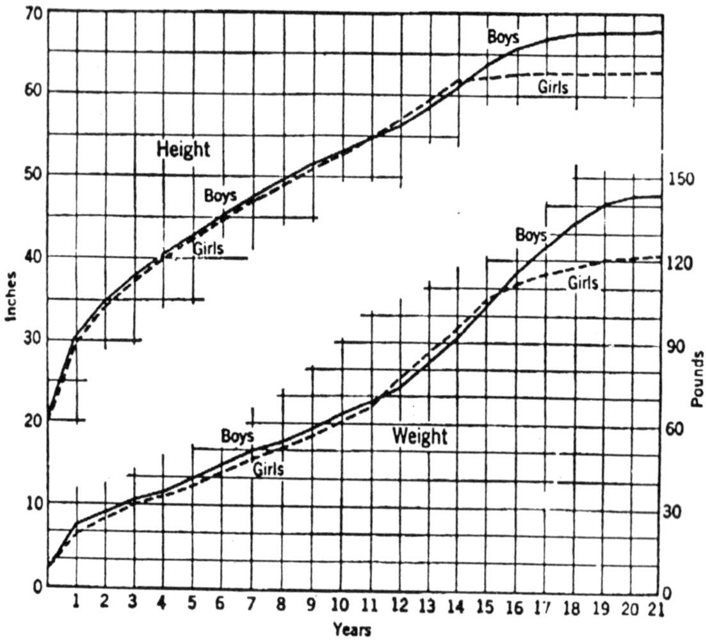

Chart 2.1—Growth in height and weight from birth to 21 years. (Adapted from Baldwin [2], Davenport [12], and Burgess [7].)

preoccupied with merely growing. Variations in rate of growth at different ages and the size of the adolescent acceleration are well brought out in Chart 2.2, which shows not the height and weight at each age but the gain in each year.

Physical Size and "Child Society"—The great significance, for who may be called "child society," of these marked differences from age to age in physical size must be clearly understood. Childhood and yours are rough-and-tumble periods, and a youngster's position among be fellows is determined in large part by his physical size, strength, and vigor. In proportion as a child can associate and compete physically he will achieve confidence and ability to get along with others and will have a happy or a miserable childhood. These differences of height and weight from one age to the next thus give chronological age a special significance in the associations of childhood.[2]

The pervasive effects of differences in physical size may be illustrated by the story of two brothers, one unusually large

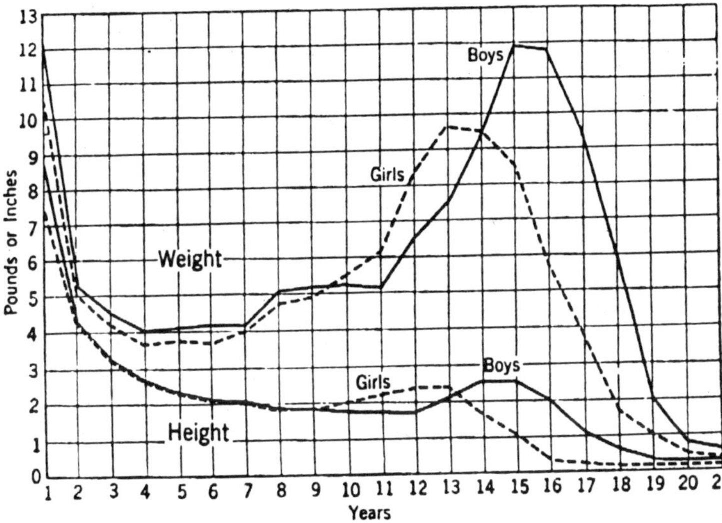

Chart 2.2—Average gains each year in height and weight for boys and girls . One division on the chart equals 1 pound, 1 inch, or 1 year. The chart shows that from birth through the first year boys average 12.2 pounds gain in weight and 8.7 inches in height. They gain 5.2 pounds and grow 4.4 inches during the second year, etc. (Birth to age 3, adapted from Baldwin [2]; ages 4-18, from Davenport [12]; 18-21, from Stuart [44]; height, 2-21, from Burgess [7].)

for his age, and the other not only a year younger but small for his age. As far back as the younger one, James, could remember, his brother had imposed on him, teased him, made him do the unpleasant chores—backing up his impositions by actual physical combat whenever James rebelled. By the time the two boys had reached adolescence James had been so thoroughly cowed that he did not dare drive the family car, have a date, or wear the kind of clothes he liked. He did somewhat poorer work in school than his brother, largely because his feelings of inadequacy became acute whenever he was faced with an examination. To compensate for his inabilities, James withdrew more and more from the social life of his fellows and developed a dream world in which he was the successful person he might have become in real life had he only been as large as his brother. It was not until his senior year in college that James began to study subjects that gradually showed him the source of his difficulties; he still remains shy and unsure of himself, and is frequently harassed by his earlier feelings of inferiority—the basis of which was a few inches less than his brother in height and a few pounds in weight, during his childhood years (4).[3]

Adult-Child Relationships and Size—Almost wholly neglected in discussions of the psychology of childhood is the pervasive importance of the child's physical inferiority to adults. Even in their relations with one another, shrewd adults recognize differences of physical size and vigor as of subtle but very great significance. Thus the small man feels inferior and becomes either submissive or defensively aggressive; the man of powerful physique may be either domineering or patronizing. But physical differences between children and adults are even more marked (and are accentuated by multiple other differences of intellectual and emotional maturity and of prestige).

Adult-child differences in physique are strikingly illustrated in the remarkable series of photographs in Chart 2.3. The pictures show at regular four-year intervals the growth of a girl from one year of age to 17—taken each time with her father who thus serves as an adult standard of comparison. The smallness of the young child compared to an adult is obvious, as is the growth in size over these years. Notably well shown are the changes in proportion and total physical personality which also occur—a matter so important that the next section will be devoted to it. The little girl is plump and short-limbed; the 9-year-old is slim and boyish; adolescence has been entered by 13, and the 17-year-old girl is beginning to show the rounded fullness of young womanhood.

The young child is a pygmy among adult giants. Childhood attitudes of dependence, submissiveness, fear, or resentment, and adult protectiveness or domineering could hardly develop as they do if it were not for the crude animal fact of the child's physical inferiority. And it may be a very important factor in a child's attitudes in school. Whatever the relations between a 100-pound boy and a 200-pound principal, the mere difference in physical size is for both a fundamental factor in the situation. Some of the most obstinate cases of discipline in high school seem to have their root in the feeling of the youngster that he has at last grown to the point where he can fight back. A splendid feature of the modern school is this: that adult physical superiority is playing a smaller part [4] and is being supplanted by a felling of mutual cooperation, friendship, and respect.

Chart 2.3—"Mr.Chadwick's little girl grows up." Growth of a girl, as shown by pictures at four-year intervals, the father serving in each one as a standard of comparison. (Pictures reproduced by; permission of Mr. F. H. Chadwick and *Life*. For the above plate certain of the pictures were rephotographed so that the father was the same size in each picture, and the figures were aligned so that comparisons could be made easily.)

Sex Differences in Growth Rate—It is also evident that growth proceeds at different rates for the two sexes. The maximum adolescent rate is reached by girls about two years earlier—around 12 to 14, as compared with around 14 to 16 for boys, as shown in Chart 2.2. From about 12 to 14, girls average both taller and heavier than boys. Shrewd observers of children know that there are interesting consequences as regards the social relations between the two sexes. The vigor and physical superiority of many girls during this period frequently bring participation (as never before or later) in boy's sports and amusements, and the development of a splendid physical confidence and poise. As a result, the boys either admit the girls to comradeship or else draw away from them and assume a scorn which seems in no small part a defense reaction—to which the girls respond by a great show of independence.

It should also be noted that throughout childhood girls appear to be on an average more mature physiologically than boys; even at 6 they are already about a year in advance, as shown by such evidence as the replacing of certain cartilages by bone. Although the point is in dispute, there is also evidence to indicate that puberty is reached by girls on the average about a year earlier than by boys. Adult leveling off in growth appears at about 17 for the girls as compared with 19 for the boys (the outcome being that by 20 men average over 4½ inches taller and 22 pounds heavier than women). Further, most intelligence tests show girls through the elementary school period to average slightly above boys of the same age. And in the secondary school the girls seem to show a greater sex-social maturity, as compared with the boys of the same chronological age. All these facts have a manifold significance for the schools; they present social, moral, and educational problems, the full import of which the average high school teacher seems not to realize. The average 16-year-old girl is physically and emotionally almost a woman, whereas the average 16-year-old male is often yet little more than a boy.

Relation of Growth Rate to Intelligence—One other group comparison requires brief mention. It is a common belief that intellectually superior children are physically delicate or retarded in growth. However, investigations are almost unanimous in finding brilliant children to average somewhat superior in height and weight. Thus, Terman (45) reports a superiority of brilliant over average children in height of 1 to 3 inches at all ages (with a final height of at least 2 inches above the normal group), and in weight of 5 to 12 pounds (with an average final weight of at least 10 pounds more than the normal group). Intellectually superior children also tend to reach puberty at an earlier age. To move a bright child through school at a somewhat more rapid rate than the average child thus need not take him "out of his class" physically; rather it may put him more where he belongs as regards physique and physiological as well as social and intellectual maturity.

The assumption of physical delicacy on the part of the intellectually superior may be due in part to generalizing from the occasional extreme case, and in part to confusing real intellectual superiority with the studiousness and the verbal facility sometimes developed by the weak or sickly child as a compensation for his inadequacies in play and as a result of greater association with adults and more reading. In part it is due to the fact that educationally advanced children are in schoolrooms with children chronologically and physically older and thus bigger. And in part this assumption is perhaps a defense mechanism of the average and inferior person.

On the other hand, intellectually inferior children average inferior physically. Thus Wheeler (48) has found that dull children average 2 or 3 inches shorter and 5 to 8 pounds lighter per age than children of average ability. For both brilliant and dull groups the differences from the average are small in early childhood but tend to increase as the children grow older, resulting in final averages of significance for the three groups.[5]

Individual Differences—So far the consideration has been of averages. But in physical growth—as in connection with every other topic discussed in this volume—even more important than general trends is the fact that individuals may differ greatly from the average. Thus a group of 2276 boys 15 years of age were found to vary in height from 4 feet 8 inches, to 6 feet 2 inches; and in weight from 80 pounds to 161 pounds (2). Chart 2.4 shows distributions of height of children from 6 through 18. A few boys at 7 are as tall as the shortest boys of 16.

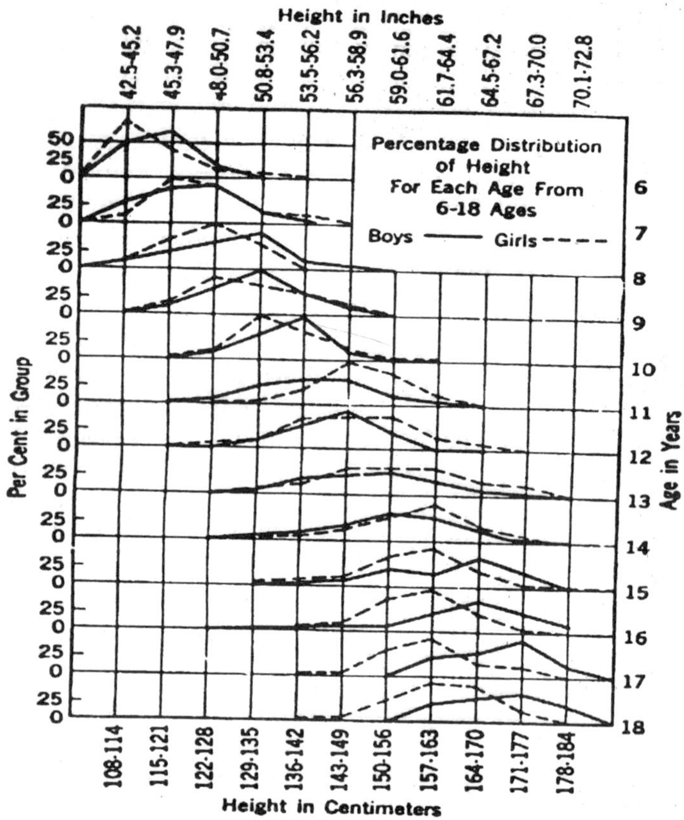

Chart 2.4— Individual differences in the height of boys and girls at each age from 6 to 18. The chart shows that, for example, about 75 per cent of the 6-year-old girls are in the 108-114 cm. group in height, and that girls of this age range in height from 101 to 142 cm. (From Baldwin [2], p. 149)

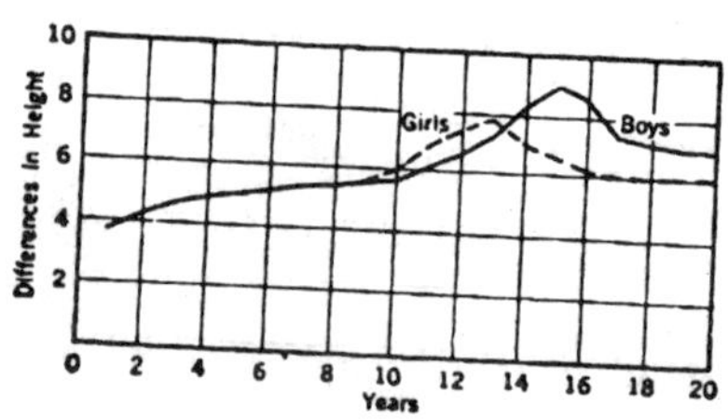

Chart 2.5— Range (from 10th to 90th percentile) in height, ages 1—20. (From date of Burgess [7].)

Through the adolescent years (roughly from 12 through 16) the range is especially great, for reasons which will be returned to shortly. This fact is shown clearly in Chart 2.5. The difference in height between girls at the 10th and at the 90th percentiles[6] broadens from 6 inches at 10 years to 8 inches at 13 years, then narrows to 6 inches at 17. Boys show a similar spread two years later.

It may justifiably be inferred that such differences are in large part normal. Decided differences in height, weight, and other physical characteristics may be expected between youngsters of the same age; in consequence, care must be exercised before deciding, for instance, that a given boy is underweight, overweight, or otherwise abnormal in any unhealthy sense. Marked individual differences are also found in the total growth curves. The pubertal acceleration in growth may (as will be seen shortly) come at different ages, and a given child may show special times of growth, pause, or acceleration. However, individual curves for growth, especially in weight, may show certain fluctuations suggesting the operation of special factors such as ill health.

The fundamental question regarding each child is this: What is normal *for him?* Thus the mother of a rather short, slight child was much worried and stuffed him with food. Inquiry showed that both parents were short and slight—but in excellent health—and had in childhood been short and slight like their child. They were told to cease worry, that the youngster was entirely normal and healthy for his total build and constitution, that in fact statistics on health and longevity showed it was best to be a little under average in height and weight.

GROWTH AND CHANGE

It is certainly of importance that the average child triples his weight and adds 50 per cent to his stature during the years from 6 to 18, but the mere increase in size is by no means the most important feature of the growth process. Such striking changes occur that he becomes a different being. Every proportion of his body alters; there are also changes in the internal organs, in the processes of digestion and metabolism. The sex organs mature, the lymphatic system grows and them decreases, and there are subtle alterations in the composition of all the tissues. The organism not only enlarges; it is transformed. When this fact is taken into consideration in connection with the changes already shown in size, it is small wonder that the adult teacher and the child or adolescent frequently misunderstand each other. Nor is it surprising that many educational mistakes are made in providing for the child's learning.

Changes in Proportions of the Body—Differences in the gross facts of total proportion were shown in Chart 2.3 above and are made more evident in Chart 2.6. It is evident that in the proportion of head to body, length of body in relation to legs—in fact, in all such respects—the child is different. Nevertheless, this chart does not show adequately these differences in appearance. The shape and proportions of the head may continue to change until the end of adolescence. During adolescence the features alter in ways that are often embarrassing; for instance, the shape and size of the jaws change and the nose becomes prominent. Pictures of a person in childhood, then in the teens, and finally in young manhood often show differences so great that one might often well doubt it was the same individual. As the child moves into adolescence there is a

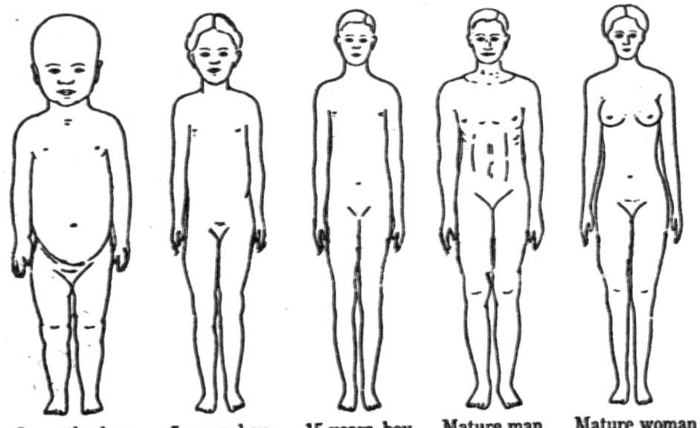

Chart 2.6—Change in body proportions with age, and sex differences. (From Bardeen [3], pp. 490, 493.)

lengthening of the long bones of the arms and legs. Another skeletal change that is a repeated source of irritation is the development, then the discarding, of one set of teeth, the final dentition being completed only during adolescence, or even later.

Changes in the Internal Organs—During the school years there are not only outward changes in size and proportion but internal changes in every system of the body—muscular, digestive, circulatory, genital, nervous. The nature of some of these changes is exhibited in Chart 2.7. As shown there, the nervous system has almost reached the final gross size by the age of 12, the lymphatic system grows with great rapidity at first and then becomes actually smaller, the genital organs grow hardly at all until after thee 12th year, and each of the various tissues of the body has a typical curve

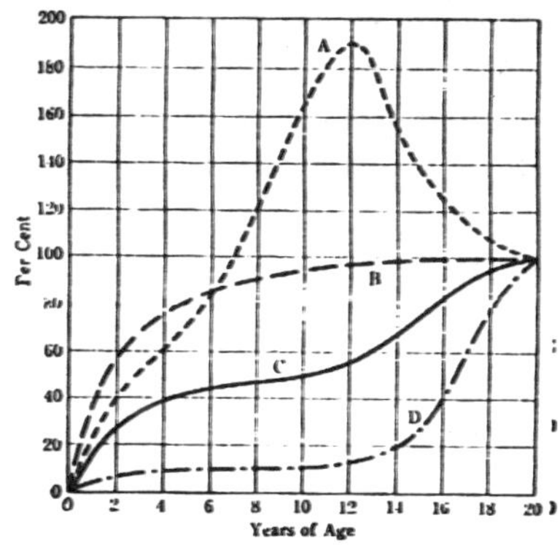

Chart 2.7— The major types of postnatal growth of the various parts and organs of the body. The several curves are drawn to common scale by computing their values at successive ages in terms of their total postnatal increments (to 20 years). (From Harris, *et atl.* [24], p. 193.)

A. Lymphoid type: Thymus, lymph nodes, intestinal lymphoid masses.

B. Neural type: Brain and its parts, dura, spinal cord, optic apparatus, many head dimensions.

C. General type: Body as a whole, external dimensions (with exception of head and neck), respiratory and digestive organs, kidneys, aorta and pulmonary trunks, spleen, musculature as a whole, skeleton as a whole, blood volume.

D. Genital type: Testis, ovary, epididymis, uterine tube, prostate, prostatic urethra, seminal vesicles.

Whereas in the newborn child the muscular system constitutes about 23 per cent of the weight of the entire body, in the adult it is 43 per cent (42). The nature of the muscular tissue is somewhat different in child and adult. Moreover, muscular growth is not uniform; the muscles of the legs, arms, and back have growth curves of their own. Nor is muscular growth always perfectly coordinated with growth of the skeleton so that there may be, especially at the adolescent age, embarrassing awkwardness of movement.[7]

The striking growth and then decline of the lymphatic system is well exhibited by the chart; and since lymphatic circulation is largely dependent upon muscular activity, the need for a vigorous childhood is emphasized. Metabolism is more rapid in children than in adults. Accordingly, appetite is great. And especially is adolescent appetite marked, and often peculiar. Because of changes in internal chemistry involved in the physiological transformations of adolescence, plus the injudicious diet usually resulting from the adolescent's own selection of foods, the boy or girl may have periods of indigestion, an unhealthy skin, and headaches.

Central and most important of all in this total process of change are the growth and maturing of the sex organs. The most significant date in the total period is the age of onset of puberty. Table 2.1 shows age of first menstruation of a group of mothers and daughters, and age of appearance of pigmented hair in the pubic region for two groups of boys, in 1908 and 1937. The great individual differences must especially be emphasized. Thus first menstruation may not uncommonly come as early as 11 or late as 15.

Of distinct interest is the evidence in this table to suggest that both boys and girls are now reaching puberty a little earlier than

TABLE 2.1

Age of First Menstruation of 357 Mothers and 680 Daughters, and of the Pubescence of 1406 Boys in 1937 and 3835 Boys in 1908[8]

	Percentage at Each Age			
Age	*Mothers*	*Daughters*	*Boys,1908*	*Boys, 1937*
9	1	—	—	—
10	1	2	—	1
11	6	8	7	14
12	17	20	21	25
13	27	35	27	29
14	25	22	26	22
15	15	9	15	8
16	5	3	4	—
17	2	1	—	—
18	1	—	—	—
	100	100	100	99
Mean	13.99	13.61	13.4	13.08

a generation ago. Such earlier maturing might be due to better nutrition and health in the present generation. Conceivably also the sex repression and lack of knowledge of sex a generation ago may have tended to retard healthy sex development: present-day movies and adolescent social life might tend to stimulate sex maturing.

Of great interest is the further finding that in general the taller and heavier children, and those who are healthy and from good neighbourhoods, tend to reach puberty earliest. To these youngsters already bigger than their later-maturing fellows is then added the rapid growth just preceding and at pubescence; growth in weight at this period is usually double the growth during later childhood. Individual differences are thus greater at this time than ever before or in the ages immediately following, as shown in Charts 2.4 and 2.5 and include adolescent changes in proportion and tissue so that in total these differences are striking, as indicated by the boys of the same chronological age but at different stages of maturing shown in Chart 2.8.

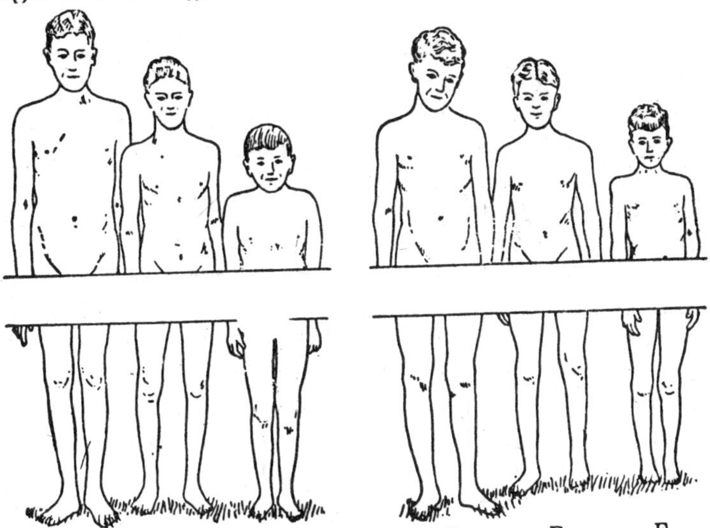

Chart 2.8 — A concrete illustration of individual differences in physical development. The three boys at the left (A, B, C) are 15 years of age. A is post-pubescent; B is pubescent, and C is pre-pubescent. The three to the right (D, E, F) have chronological ages in reverse order to their physical size. D is 13 years 1 month of age, and pubescent; E is 13 years 5 months of age, and pubescent; F is 14 years 6 months of age, and pre-pubescent. (From Dimock [17], p. 229.)

Consequent Educational Problems—Clearly a high school teacher or a director of athletics has here a very difficult problem, all too often inadequately recognized. In the same lass may be some small youngsters who are physiologically yet children, and others, usually much taller and heavier, who are physiologically well on the way to maturity. The biggest may be not only twice as heavy and strong as the smallest of the same age but also sexually adult, with the build and voice and the sex-social interests of early adulthood; the smallest has the build, voice, and interests of a child. In sports, in reading and movie interests, and above all in social trends and problems of social adjustment these two are in different worlds. The relatively unimportant fact of chronological age may throw them together in school. Nowhere else in the educational system is such a difficult diversity to be found. Yet many high school teachers seem not to recognize these facts. And rare is the secondary school which has any consistent programme for dealing with them. A school which rejects with indignation, on the ground that it would "get him out of his natural group," the suggestion that a bright child be moved ahead academically a little faster, usually has no scruples about keeping such adult and child pupils together.

DEVELOPMENT OF STRENGTH AND SKILL

Growth in physical size, in proportion, and in tissue has been briefly outlined above. The next question is concerned with development in strength and skill. Are increases in strength as remarkable as those in weight? Does strength as well as weight increase especially rapidly at adolescence? Is there a real motor incoordination at that time? Are individual differences in strength and skill as marked as in poundage? All these questions are of great importance. They are obviously so for programmes of physical education and athletics. But evidence on these matters should also be of significance in many phases of the regular school programme. For instance, too much may often be expected of young children in handwriting, art, and crafts, However, findings regarding growth in strength and skill should have still larger implications. They indicate development in functioning which might well be of some help in understanding the growth of more intellectual abilities and have some bearing on the growth of "intelligence." It therefore seems strange that educational psychology has not given more attention to this topic.

Chart 2.9 indicates growth, over the school years, in a simple skill (rate of tapping with a pencil stylus on a metal plate), and a simple act of strength (grip of the right hand). The chart shows the average boy as doubling his rate of tapping from 6 to 18, and in the ten years from 7 to 17 he more than triples in strength of grip. Here are two elementary findings emphasizing the extent of development over the school years, findings which should constantly be kept in mind in planning school programmes.

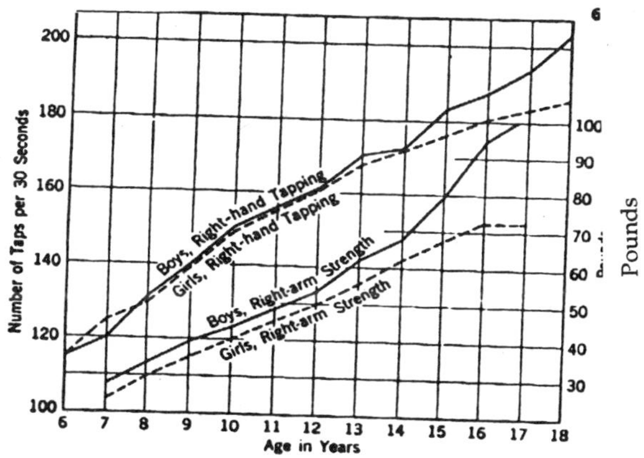

Chart 2.9— Growth in strength of arm and rate of tapping, boys and girls. (Adapted from Baldwin [2], and Brooks [6].)

Rate of tapping and strength of grip are simple elements in the total of physical efficiency. May not some measure be obtained which involves more varied acts of strength and evidence of physical ability? Chart 2.10 summarizes findings from an effort to obtain a general measure of "muscular power."

> Indices of physical strength were obtained by combining the results of seven physical tests such as lung capacity, strength of back, legs, arms. The combined result of such a series of tasks might be considered to show general physical ability in somewhat the same fashion as the total score on many different questions in tests of intelligence gives an indication of an individual's general mental ability. Such tests of strength and skill have been given to many thousands of young people of various ages. Chart 2.10 shows growth of physical efficiency as determined by these tests.

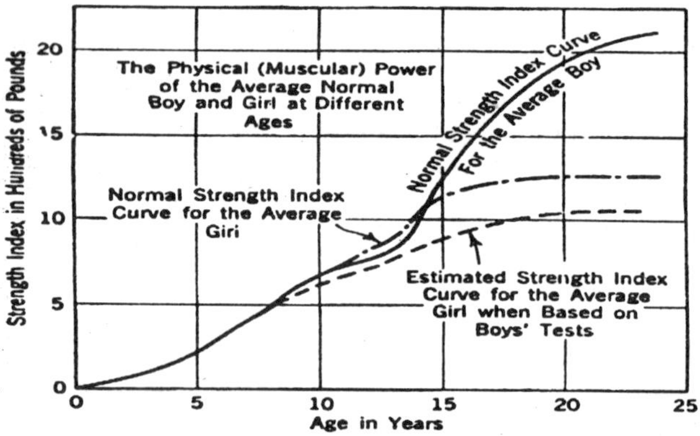

Chart 2.10—Growth in general muscular power as shown by rise in average strength index through childhood and adolescence. The strength index was based on seven tests: lung capacity in cubic inches, strength of right. and left-hand grip, strength of back, strength of legs, strength of arms in extension and in flexion (38).

The course of growth in strength and skill is similar to the curves for growth in physical measurements such as weight. Again the total growth over the school years and particularly at adolescence is great; the boys' strength index doubles in the four years from 13 through 17. As adulthood is reached, male muscular superiority becomes greater. Presumably much of this greater strength of the male is a constitutional difference between the sexes. However, there are some results to suggest that feminine inferiority is becoming less, as a result of increase in physical sports for girls and other opportunities for healthy development.

That individual differences in physical strength and skill are great need hardly be mentioned. Table 2.2 shows the percentages of a group of 13-year-old boys with different strengths of grip and, in the line below, similar results for a group of boys 18 years old. At each age, the strongest is about three times as strong as the weakest. At 18 the weakest in no stronger than the average at 13; one 13-year-old boy is distinctly stronger than the average 18-year-old.

Clearly, athletic abilities among children of a given age will be exceedingly various. At any given age, strength and skill and size will differ so much that different sports seem obviously needed for persons of various physical abilities. Play involving children of different ages, as in a one-room country school, must obviously be of a sort in which boys and girls who differ greatly in strength and skill can participate. Also to be expected are great differences in

TABLE 2.2

Percentages of Groups of Boys 13 and 18 Years Old showing Different Strengths of Grip of the Right Hand[9]

Age	*Pounds of Pull*																	
	20	25	30	35	40	45	50	55	60	65	70	75	80	85	90	95	100	105	M
13	3	8	19	40	12	9	5	3					1						37
18				1	2	5	5	14	21	16	14	9	5	3	2	1	1	1	65

ability in handwriting, typing, sewing, shopwork. The young child will on the average be much inferior to the older child. But the teacher of young children who is distressed by their crude and clumsy work can find comfort in the fact that the processes of growth and maturation will in their own good time bring improvement. As will be seen in a later chapter, she can usually do little, as by intensive training, to hurry that development, somewhat as she can do little to hasten the child's growth in height. She can only help him to attain such strength and skill as is natural for him at his age, and (the most important point) keep optimal the conditions for his growing. As will also be seen later, "intelligence" appears to grow and reach an adult level in somewhat the same fashion; at each age there are great individual differences in mental "strength."

FACTORS INVOLVED IN PHYSICAL GROWTH

The school years are thus a period of extraordinary growth and change in size, biochemical constitution, strength, and skill. What are the factors influencing this development? In particular, what conditions may retard healthy development, and what may be done to remove such handicaps and further desirable growth?

Biological Constitution—Indubitably the most important factor is the marvelous biological constitution which brings it about that individuals do develop in an ordered, coordinated, and basically similar fashion. Certain conditions, as of nutrition, may hamper or further this development; yet under ordinary conditions growth goes forward in its own way and in its own good time, surprisingly independent of circumstances. Weight increases, proportions change, strength and skill grow, in accord with these fundamental facts of growth; educational programmes must also keep step. It is not possible, for instance, to train babies to walk before their neuromuscular systems have developed to the point where they are ready for this activity. Somewhat as extra food cannot make a baby grow faster than a "normal" rate, so extra practice will not bring progress in such skills beyond what the organism's own processes of maturation permit. Talking comes only with the proper maturation. Perhaps a certain stage of maturation has to be reached before a child can learn to read. This problem of maturation will be returned to later.

In gross, human beings are thus alike and develop in similar fashion. Nevertheless, as already emphasized, individual differences are relatively great. The first factor to be mentioned as causing them is individual differences in constitution. Some people are "naturally" tall and others short; some fortunate men and fewer women can eat all they wish and never grow stout, whereas others take on fat with even a relatively moderate diet.

As racial characteristics are inherited by the race, so individual differences in constitution are inherited in the family. Tall parents tend to have tall children; the individual who never has to worry about taking on excess weight probably has a father who was similarly blessed. Colour of hair and eyes, shape and size of chin and nose and head, physical strength and energy (also temperament and mental abilities) are all more or less clearly recognized as tending to run in families. Thus the heights of fathers and sons have been found to correlate .51, of brothers. .51 of fraternal twins .64, of identical twins .93 (31).

However, it is also commonly recognized that sons may differ markedly from their fathers, and usually do differ considerably; a correlation of .51 shows that the father-son relationship averages as only rough; occasional extreme differences are possible. In part these differences, as well as the similarities between father and son or between two brothers, are to be accounted for genetically; each son inherits traits not only from the mother as well as the father but also from the grandparents and other more remote ancestors. These elements of inheritance will be different for two brothers (unless they are identical twins). Exceptional combinations may occur, producing exceptional individuals.

Physical Environment and Nutrition— However, growth is not completely determined by inherited organic constitution, nor is individuality. The environment in which the growth takes place is also of major importance. Before the child is born the environment of the mother's body may be so affected by injury or gross disease as to affect the child's development. A birth injury may affect both physique and intellect. Later injury or such diseases as syphilis, tuberculosis of the spine, or poliomyelitis may very evidently affect development.

More important in the number of persons involved and the effects on the well-being of the general population are diet and conditions of living. Thus in certain groups in France during the First World War, the growth of young children was retarded one or two years and of older children as much as four or five years, with marked delay in pubescence. An investigation involving a total of about 20,000 German children in Leipzig showed an increase of 4 inches in height and 24 pounds in weight from 1918 to 1935, with an acceleration of over a year and a half in rate of growth (10). (The question at once arises as to what is now happening to the children in these countries!) Adolescent boys and girls in school average taller and heavier than youngsters of the same age who are working, and they reach maturity in size at least a year earlier that the working children. Elementary school children in slums have been found to average 3 to 5 inches shorter and 8 to 12 pounds lighter than children from good neighbourhoods. Boys from one-room tenements of an American city averaged 2 inches shorter and 6 pounds lighter than boys from apartments of three or more rooms. The skeptic may argue that working-class and tenement groups are constitutionally below more privileged groups in the total population. This may be one factor in the above data, But Chart 2.11 shows that when the depression reduced certain families from comfort to poverty, the weights of the children in these families fell off relatively, while in families who remained either comfortable or poor the weights of the children did not shift. Table 2.3 shows how the simple procedure of giving milk to undernourished children at recess brought about gains in height and weight over a similar group not so helped.

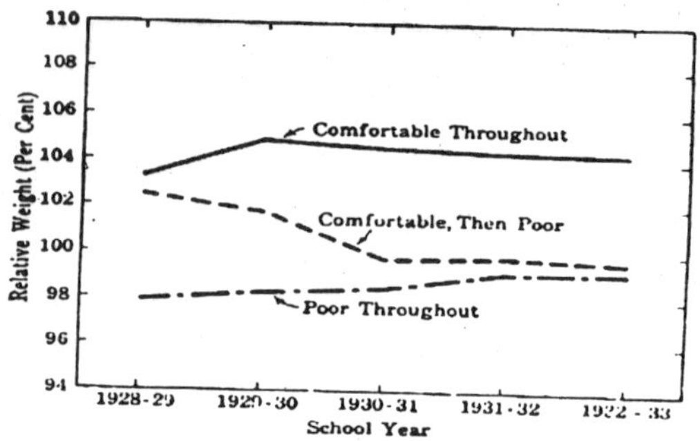

Chart 2.11— Relative weight of children, aged 6 to 9, according to economic status of family: *(a)* family in comfortable circumstances throughout period; *(b)* family in comfortable circumstances in 1929, becoming poor by 1932; and *(c)* family in poor circumstances throughout period. ("Comfortable" means income of $ 250 or more per year per capita; "poor," less than this amount.) (From Palmer and Collins [33].)

TABLE 2.3

Average Increase in Height and Weight of Boys (a) Given Milk and (b) Not Given Milk [10]

	Height (in.)	*Weight (lb.)*
Milk group	1.47	3.62
Non-milk group	1.21	2.97
Difference	.26	.65

Since diet, living conditions, and medical care are now in general better than fifty or a hundred years ago, a somewhat more rapid physical growth and greater height and weight at a given age might be expected now than previously. Considerable scattered evidence supports this expectation. Measurements of the skeletons of medieval Englishmen have led to the conclusion that they are about 4 cm. shorter than Englishmen of the present (10). Of more immediate interest to the student reader will be this finding, that at Harvard sons of alumni are about $1^3/_4$ inches taller and 10 pounds heavier than their fathers; and in four eastern women's colleges the superiority of daughters over mothers was 1.1 inches in height and 3.9 pounds in weight—nevertheless, the daughters were more slender! (5.)

From the above findings it might be expected that immigrant groups which have come from very unfavourable conditions would herein later generations show improved physique, and this does seem to be the case. Thus Japanese children born and reared in America are larger than children of the same racial type in Japan; similar findings have been reported for immigrants from Europe.

There is thus much scattered evidence to show that unfavourable diet and living conditions retard growth, delay adolescence, reduce height and weight for each age, and produce adults who are below what they might have been in physique. Undoubtedly such unfavourable environmental conditions cause not only smaller physique but less physical strength, energy, resistance to disease. And there is evidence that with improvements in living conditions and diet—improvements in which the schools have had a part and which they may do much to foster—accelerations of growth and improved physique have come about. To the modern teacher such findings should be of multiple significance. She is concerned with the physical as well as the mental growth of her pupils, and here is evidence that such growth may be furthered. But there are many very important psychological ramifications. As already emphasized, adequate physique is desirable if a child is to compete with and obtain status and confidence in his relations with other children. Energy and good nature are less likely in the stunted than in the well-developed child. The same is true as regards readiness in learning.

Psychological Factors Affecting Growth— In a later chapter evidence will be presented that emotional distress, worry, or excitement interferes with digestion and elimination, disturbs sleep, affects circulation. Surely the inference is not unreasonable that emotional strain which was continued over a long period of childhood might affect growth. The marked retardations in growth in French and German children during and immediately after the First World War might well be in part a product of such factors (and the continuing air raids and destruction of the Second World War may well have such effects). The repressive school and home discipline and punishments of the past may perhaps have played a part in the small physique of past generations.

The lack of constraint, and the sympathetic furthering of child life which is characteristic of the best modern schools and homes—surely it is not altogether fanciful to suppose that such influences, operating cumulatively throughout a child's life, might further his physical growth. As explanation for the data showing puberty to be reached earlier now than a generation ago it was suggested that perhaps the less repressed and more informed present-day attitude toward sex (and perhaps the more frequent stimuli to sex feeling as in the movies and in teen-age social life) had played a part. Presumably psychological factors may operate not only negatively but positively to affect growth and maturing. The change in psychological atmosphere from cold repression to fostered freedoms of activity and understanding, and the great psychological stimulation from movies, radio, reading, social life—surely it is not too much to suppose that in total such changes might have not only psychological but even physiological effects.

And if there are such effects, clearly a teacher should consider them in her attempts to understand individual children. A repressive, drab home might stunt the development not only of a child's personality but even of his physique. If his teacher can help this child, she may hope for improvement not only in his emotional and intellectual but in his physical well-being.

PHYSICAL GROWTH AND CHANGE AS THE FOUNDATION FACT FOR EDUCATIONAL PSYCHOLOGY AND EDUCATION

Physical growth is thus the great underlying biological phenomenon which must ever be held in mind if the facts of educational psychology are to be understood or its theories kept sound. The crude fact of the child's physical inferiority and immaturity is dominant in determining his status in his family and community and his concept of himself. His growth in size as well as in strength and skill calls for continuing readjustments in programmes of recreation, handicraft, music, and art. The striking changes not only in size but also in constitution which accompany sexual maturing bring changes in interests and emotions which are a continuing problem to the youngster and those who have to deal with him. As will be seen later, the major and comparatively neglected fact regarding learning is the great increase in capacity to learn, with growth. The fact that conditions of living affect physical growth means that they, as a product of that fact, pervasively affect the growth of the total personality as well.

Clearly, then, educational programmes must be congruent with growth. Lack of such congruence in school is the cause of major problems of educational ineffectiveness and discipline. Surely it is no dream to suppose that if the processes of growth and education can be brought harmoniously to work together, healthy growth will be furthered, and nature may thus support and further the efforts of education.

One further point must be stressed for perspective regarding physical growth through the school years, and as partial explanation for the school's difficulties in understanding and dealing with growing children. The growth years are a special phase of the total life span. Physical growth curves through 20's show that phase as ended; the curves fall over to a level. As a matter of fact, they soon do more than that; in the 20's they almost imperceptibly dip over into the slow decline which continues throughout the rest of life. As undergraduate reader of 20 is at the height of his growth curves. Around these years he is more healthy than he has been before or ever will be again. Death comes least often to this age and the ages just preceding than any others. In the 20's he reaches his greatest strength and skill. The 20-year-old reader may well feel that, physiologically he is at the high point of his life.

From about 20 on, the nature of the physiological trends is very different from what it has been during the previous years of surging growth. This fact (and the larger fact that adult life is far different from life during the school years) makes it difficult for adults really to understand young people. Adequate perspective calls for consideration of development and change throughout the life span. The adult teacher should understand herself, and the differences between herself and her pupils;[11] she should see herself as well as her pupils in a total developmental perspective. The psychology of the teacher is a much-neglected but very important topic. "My most difficult problem," remarked a high school principal, "is due not to the pubescence of our pupils but to the menopause of a teacher."

SUMMARY

Basic for any sound and adequate understanding of the development of interests, abilities, social adjustments, attitudes, character, and personality through the school years is an understanding of physical development. The major facts regarding physical development which are thus significant are as follows:

1. The extent of increase in size is indicated by the fact that in the twelve years from 6 to 18 the average boy increases over 50 per cent in height and over three times in weight. Evidently the young child is a pygmy among giants; attitudes of dependence or fear on the part of the child, and of protectiveness or domination on the part of parent or teacher, can in such a situation readily develop. Sex differences in growth rate have their correlate in attitudes between the sexes. Bright children tend to be somewhat heavier and taller than average children, dull and feeble-minded children smaller than average. Individual differences are marked; one 10-year-old child may be twice as heavy as another; a few 7-year-old boys are as tall as the shortest 16-years-olds. In play and physical competition such individual differences, and differences between younger and older children, are of great importance. And the total growth process is of such magnitude that important psychological correlates and consequences would be expected.

2. Different parts and organs of the body grow at different rates, and the total proportion and constitution of the body changes markedly over the growth years. The 20-year-old is not simply a larger person than the 6-year-old child; in proportion and internal constitution he is physiologically a different being. That he is a different being psychologically is obviously to be expected. Individual differences in amount, rate, and age of change may be marked; in the same high school class there may be a pre-adolescent boy and a youngster of the same age who is sexually mature—and probably also much heavier and taller. Evidently such situations create many psychological problems.

3. The average boy triples in strength of grip in the ten years from 7 to 17 and doubles his quickness as shown by tapping. His "strength index" doubles in the four years from 13 to 17. At a given age, the strongest boy may be as much as three times as strong as the weakest. Clearly such development and such individual differences in physical effectiveness are of great importance in athletics or any activity involving strength or skill, and are significant regarding the individual's total psychological development.

4. Growth goes forward under the impulsion and control of biological determiners which remain mysterious in essence. And

individual differences are in part the product of individual differences in constitution which are also largely unknown. But research has shown growth to be clearly affected also by housing and other conditions of living, and by nutrition and disease. Hence the community and the school have a responsibility for healthy growth.

5. Physical growth is thus the foundation for and influences the nature of intellectual and emotional growth and the development of the personality. To be effective, education must be based on these facts. But education (and psychology also) should have a yet longer perspective—should see growth as one phase of the total life span. The special character of the growth experience, as compared with adulthood, will then be sensed. And the physiological backgrounds of adult mental life will be seen as playing their part in the total educational situation.

REFERENCES

1. Most books dealing with child development or adolescence treat of growth only through 16 or 18. Wherever possible, this volume presents data showing growth through 20 or 21. This is done partly because now for a large portion of American young people the school years extend through 20, partly because it is desired that the data should extend to include the average undergraduate reader. But the most important reason is this: only by such extension is the reaching of the adult level shown—with the sex differences clearly apparent—and the growth phase of the total life span really covered. It is important that this phase be thus fully described, and that the change in direction of the life processes be thus clearly indicated. This point is so important that it will be returned to at the end of this chapter.
2. It is interesting to note here that the boxing world considers the increase of weight made by the average boy between 14 and 15—about 15 pounds—as more than sufficient to move a man from one boxing group into another, as from featherweight to lightweight. The average boy, between the ages of 14 and 17, puts on enough pounds to change a man all the way from a lightweight to a heavyweight. It must be remembered that 15 pounds is proportionately more in the youth than in the man.
3. Figures in parentheses refer to the readings at the end of the chapter.
4. It is interesting here to contrast the descriptions of childhood misery in the stories of Dickens and the Brontes with modern novelists' descriptions of childhood.

5. As further indication of the relation between lack of physical vitality and mental defect, the following facts may be presented concerning the life span of defective and normal persons: The normal male child of 2 has an average expectation of 56.8 more years of life; the male moron of the same age has an average expectation of 52.2 years; the average male imbecile, 29.6 years; and the idiot, 20.1 years. Two-year-old male defectives as a group have an average expectation of only 30.1 more years of life, or 26.7 years less than for normal babies (14).
6. A 10th percentile means that 10 per cent of the group (in this instance the children of a given age) score at or below that level. And the score found at the 90th percentile would be equal to or greater than that of 90 per cent of the group. Chart 2.5 presents the differences between the scores representing these two percentile ranks at each age.
7. Even if there is no actual decline in neuromuscular coordinations some clumsiness might be expected merely from the rapid increase in size and change in proportion. Bigger feet and longer limbs take more room , and until this fact is learned, some knocking against things may be expected.
8. Adapted from (21) and (17). The criterion of pubescence for the boys is "the appearance of pigmented hairs in the pubic region" (17, p. 208). This criterion presumable marks an earlier stage in the total process of pubertal change than the very different criterion (first menstruation) for the girls, and thus accounts for the anomalous implication in the above table of earlier puberty for boys than girls. As already indicated, most other evidence shows girls to mature earlier than boys. Girls have more erupted teeth at each age, skeletal development as shown by ossification is more advanced, adolescent acceleration in growth in height and weight comes earlier. As will be seen later, interests seem to mature earlier. It thus seems reasonable to conclude that puberty is reached between one and two years earlier by girls than by boys.
9. Data modified from (39). The careful reader may catch the fact that medians in the above table (given to the right and their position in the distributions indicated by italics) are much lower than those indicated for the same ages in Chart 2.10. The discrepancy is probably due to different types of apparatus and method. Table 2.2 is derived from English findings obtained some time ago.
10. The data are from (49), Part III, p. 431. They represent a total of about 1200 boys 5 to 14 years old in seven communities in Great Britain, and show effects of about one pint of milk five days a week over approximately seven months.
11. In *Life: A Psychological Survey* (35), such a treatment of the pubescence has been attempted, with emphasis on the adult years.

3

Health and Psychology

Health is a major neglected topic in psychology, of pervasive importance. It should be obvious that a child who has defective and uncorrected vision or is deaf, malnourished, or ill cannot carry on his school work effectively. But other and less recognized results of handicap or ill health are often far more serious. Physical defect of illness is likely to affect energy and temperament; the child thus burdened may be apathetic or irritable and emotionally unstable. Many disciplinary problems are really health problems. Long-time effects upon personality, often determining the entire course of the individual's life, may result from childhood sickness or handicap. A crippled or underdeveloped or half-sick or blur-visioned youngster cannot participate in play on equal terms with normal children. Social isolation and feelings of inferiority may thus begin, and grow. At home a handicapped or sickly child may be indulged and become habitually dependent, or he may be resented as a burden and develop feelings of inferiority or bitterness. At school this same child may suffer from too much sympathy, from neglect, or even from unmistakable hostility (the handicapped youngster is often unattractive in both person and personality). And the teacher has the problem not only of her relations with the child but also of other children's relations with him, which may be similarly various. At adolescence all such problems may be intensified. The handicapped or sickly youngster may not be attractive to the other sex. Even minor defects or blemishes may become a matter of acute distress to a shy teen-age boy or girl trying to find his or her place in "heterosexual" society. It may well be claimed that the most serious consequences and the most difficult problems presented by physical defect or disease are usually not medical but psychological! Moreover, a later chapter will point out that sundry physical indispositions and illnesses are largely psychological in origin—the products of emotional strain and frustration.

Further, problems of physical defect and illness cannot be put to one side as involving only a few unfortunates. Careful estimates indicate that less than one-third of school children are free from physical defect (aside from one or two decayed teeth); one-third have minor physical difficulties, and the remaining third are seriously handicapped by ill health or defect of some sort (45). Each year about half the children in the average school have at least a minor illness (7). These problems occur in every classroom. They are in the background of many of the most persistent and puzzling difficulties of disinterest, discipline, and personality development faced by every teacher. A brief survey of the health problems of childhood and adolescence, with special reference to psychological relationships, is thus called for, if educational psychology is adequately to cover the problems of learning and development of ability and personality with which modern education is concerned.

PHYSICAL DEFECTS AND CHRONIC CONDITIONS

It was stated above that considerable majority of children suffer from some physical defect. Chart 3.1 shows the frequency of various types of physical defect and chronic disease condition among school children. It is obvious that these defects vary in seriousness and may vary in degree. It must not be forgotten that often a child may suffer from several handicaps and that in fact defects often go together. Thus a child whose nasal passages are largely blocked by adenoids will be a mouth breather, may have defective tonsils and chronic nasal catarrh, is likely to have impacted teeth, and may develop middle-ear infection.

Sensory Defects— Most obvious of the difficulties which affect schoolwork are sensory handicaps, and of these most frequent are the visual defects. Chart 3.1 indicates that about one-third of all children have some defect of vision. Many of these defects are slight, and a large proportion can be corrected with properly fitted glasses. But even in present-day schools regular testing of pupils' eyes may be lacking or inadequate, or glasses may not be provided or not worn.

Some years ago, while giving a group test to a fourth-grade class, one of the writers noticed a boy who went through each test at breakneck speed and then put his head down in his arms on his desk. The teacher remarked that she had tried in vain to stop this procedure, and added that the lad's work was slipshod and slapdash. He also would hold anything he was reading at arm's length—she had tried to make him stop that! He was occasionally truant. Inquiry of the child revealed that he had frequent headaches and occasional nausea (from

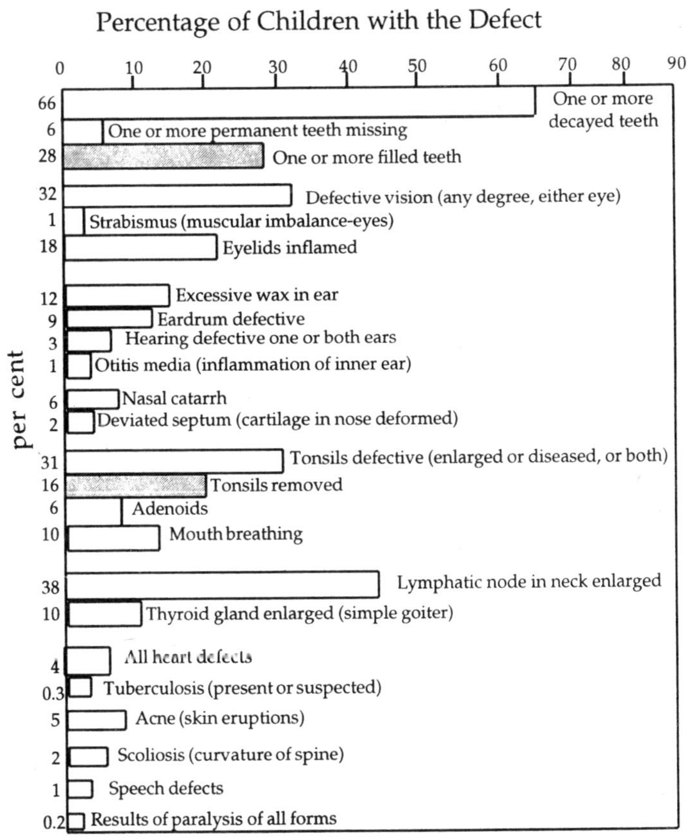

Chart 3.1— Average prevalence of certain physical defects and diseases among several groups of white school children. In the case of two defects, frequency of treatment (teeth filled, tonsils removed) is shown by shaded bars.

eyestrain, though of course he did not know that this was the cause). The book at arm's length and the frequent brief rest periods were devices he had hit upon for minimizing his discomfort. And his teacher had stupidly tried to prevent him from thus getting what little relief he could. Small wonder that, what with the discomfort and the perverse nagging, he occasionally stayed away from school!

This boy was suffering from farsightedness (hyperopia or hypermetropia), the defect most common among children, and often missed in routine testing of the eyes with the ordinary visual testing chart because most cases can by special effort briefly force the lens of the eye into sufficient accommodation so that even near objects can be seen clearly. The boy described above had thus "passed" the perfunctory test of vision given in that school. But such cases cannot long maintain the extra effort; the eyes become uncomfortable from fatigue, and whenever the muscles relax, vision blurs.

Evidently glasses which will do the extra focusing necessary because of the defect (because the eyeball is too short) are needed. Teachers should be alert for evidences of farsightedness in classroom behaviour, such as were shown by the boy described above—holding things at a distance, efforts to rest the eyes, complaint of visual discomfort or headache. When visual defect is suggested, a careful examination of the eyes should be arranged for.

The opposite condition of nearsightedness (myopia) is less often overlooked. The tendency to hold a book extra close is readily noted and its significance understood. And in routine tests of vision (as with the Snellen chart) the child cannot force his eyes into even brief adjustment for far vision; thus his inability to read smaller type at 20 feet is readily detected and the extent of the defect roughly measured. Further, since there is no extra effort of accommodation there is no extra visual fatigue or discomfort, headache, nausea, or other distress such as plagues the farsighted youngster. The farsighted child is thus more likely than the nearsighted child to be irritable, recalcitrant to school tasks, or truant. But the nearsighted individual has his own difficulties, and glasses (concave, to allow for the act that the eyeball is too long) may make more difference in a youngster's life than might at first be realized.

For instance, one teacher, early in the school year, reproved a boy for leaving his seat and coming up front to read something on the blackboard. Instead of recognizing this symptom of nearsightedness for what it was, she resented the act as disturbing the attention of the other children. The boy was embarrassed and resentful. Thereafter when he could not read what was on the board he either made a whispered inquiry of a classmate, or guessed and made mistakes which were sometimes ludicrous and further irritated the teacher.

Fortunately about this time the parents took the boy to an oculist, his trouble was diagnosed, and glasses were obtained. The classroom difficulty cleared up at once; the boy could see adequately, and the teacher now knew what the trouble had been and was anxious to make amends for her former harshness. But the benefits reached much further. Upsets with his bicycle became less frequent now that he could see clearly where he was going.

Now when he was downtown he could see at a distance what street car was coming and need not ask some impatient stranger—one had retorted disdainfully, "Can't you read?" Before he had seemed socially stupid; he did not recognize people or he missed the innumerable little cues of expression, gesture, or almost suppressed movement which often tell more than words. Now he began to catch on to such cues. Most encouraging to him was his improvement in sports. Now he could see a baseball when it came toward him; his batting and his catching became much improved. He had almost come to the conclusion that he was "just no good" in sports and tended to pull off by himself. He grew much more alert and very much happier. As his father remarked six months later, he seemed almost like a new boy.

Astigmatism is due to some irregularity in the curvature of the eyeball or the lens; this irregularity may of course appear with nearsightedness but it is more frequent with farsightedness. There is some astigmatism in the majority of cases of defective vision. Because of inability to get clear focus on anything the astigmatic person is likely to be restless and greatly handicapped. Glasses correcting this irregularity put clarity into a hitherto blurred and distorted world.

A fifth-grade girl had peculiar difficulty in reading. She would

> read ten or twêlves words correctly, her head turned to one side and with and effortful frown, then suddenly produce a jumble of words partly from the page and partly from imagination. A careful examination showed that she had astigmatism which made it impossible for her to keep the total adjustment of position and focus that gave best vision for more than a few seconds. The whole reading process then broke down, and she continued what she had read with whatever words next occurred to her.

The eyeball may, then, be too long or too short, or its surface irregular, thus causing errors of refraction. These are the common difficulties. But there may also be difficulty with the muscles which control the eyes so that the two eyes do not coordinate perfectly; especially when the individual is not well or is fatigued there is visual discomfort, perhaps blurring, dizziness, or nausea. Muscular imbalance may cause loss of sight of the squinting eye. Cross-eyedness is both handicapping and disfiguring. As shown by Chart 3.1, inflammation of the eyelids (acute of chronic conjunctivitis and blepharitis) is common. In short, the eyes are a major health problem. An uncorrected visual defect may be a major handicap both in and out of school.

Diagnosis and treatment of such defects is a matter for experts. But here, as in other problems of health, teachers should be a first line of defense. In the first place, they should be alert to symptoms which suggest that reference to the doctor is needed. Some of these symptoms—holding a book closer or farther away than average, having difficulty with blackboard or map work, complaining of visual discomfort or headache after reading, making frequent attempts to rest the eyes, holding the head in an odd position—have been mentioned. Other evidences of probable trouble of some sort with the eyes are blinking, attempting to brush away blur, rubbing the eyes, shutting one eye when reading, and inflamed eyes. A pupil showing any such symptoms should be referred to someone competent to diagnose and deal with visual difficulties.

> Both teachers and parents often do not realize that symptoms of visual defect may be not apparently related to vision (headache and nausea, for example) and that a child who sees poorly may not recognize that fact. He does not know how things look through good eyes, and so does not sense his own

> trouble. How should he know that his failure in both reading and sports is due to poor vision rather than ineptitude! Unfortunately the teacher may not see any connection between a lad's restlessness and astigmatism, or his dislike for school and a muscular disbalance so slight that only an oculist can discover it. Little wonder that children are often totally unaware of even marked defects.

Teachers should also do what they can to relieve eyestrain in the classroom. Lighting should be adequate, though all too often even in study halls and libraries it is not. The light should come over the left shoulder (except for left-handed children) and be softly reflected from walls and ceilings; it should never shine directly into a child's eyes or on the desk or books. The teacher cannot redesign the school lighting system, but she can do much by the way she adjusts the shades and arranges the seating, uses artificial light, and minimizes eye work on dark days. Short recesses of work not imposing a strain on the eyes give visual rest. Children should be taught to stop occasionally when reading, to rest the eyes. They should not be forced to do close work or copying which involves much eyestrain. Special sight-saving classes for children with serious visual defect are now common; adequate lighting is provided, and material with extra large print. Children needing such a class should of course be sent to it, if available. When glasses have been prescribed, the teacher should see to it that they are obtained and worn. In short, she should first be a lookout who spots possible visual troubles and refers them to a specialist, and second she should be the friendly supervisor who sees that the specialist's recommendations are carried out and that conditions for the use of eyes are as good as they can be.

Chart 3.1 shows about 3 per cent of children having defective hearing in one or both ears. It also shows defective eardrums in 9 per cent of the cases, and excessive wax in ears, which may cause trouble, in still more.

> Deafness in children is often not recognized for what it is. Perhaps the most common sign of inadequate hearing is an appearance of stupidity. Not hearing much that goes on about him, the child seems not alert, and without understanding of what is happening. If he has been partially deaf since early childhood, he may have imperfections or blurrings of speech

due to his never having heard quite accurately. A slightly deaf child may be very irritating to a teacher who does not recognize the situation. She speaks to him and he pays no attention. To check whether he may be deaf she repeats the question in the same tone of voice and this time he replies, thus convincing her that he is not deaf but merely inattentive. What she does not realize is that a nudge from another boy following her first remark had made the deaf youngster look up and that by turning directly toward her and watching her lips he was then able to understand. A deaf child is also handicapped in relations with other children. Their chatter goes on about him unnoticed. He misses the calling back and forth in games. Soon he pulls off by himself. Increasingly in adolescent and adult life the deaf person is shut off from social intercourse and is either depressed, oversensitive, or suspicious, wondering if people may be talking about him.

Periodic examinations by the school physician or nurse should find cases of deafness or other conditions which may affect hearing. The first location of such cases may nevertheless devolve upon the teacher. If she notes inattentiveness, a flat voice, perhaps a turning of one ear toward the speaker, perhaps a discharging ear, medical attention should be obtained.

The markedly deaf child will need special care in an institution or class where lip reading is taught. The mild case who may stay in the regular class will need tactful help. The teacher should place the child in front and to her right so that he can see as well as possible to read her lips and expression. (Somewhat deaf children thus secure some help, even though they have never been taught lip reading.) She should try to speak slowly and clearly, to bring the child into things rather than let him be left out, and to have the other children try also to do these things. Special help may be needed on such subjects as reading and spelling where failure to hear a word accurately may bring misconception. And if the child is helped not only with his schoolwork but also with his social adjustments, he may learn to take his handicap in his stride.

The teacher should also do what she can to prevent deafness. Congenital deafness is almost always hereditary. Acquired deafness may follow such diseases as measles, scarlet fever, or diphtheria, or result from chronic conditions of the nose and throat which may spread throughout the Eustachian tubes (connecting the middle ear and pharynx). Damage to the ear may also come from carelessness in diving or swimming. The majority of cases of deafness begin in early childhood. The teacher should do everything possible to see that children convalescing from serious contagious disease do not have neglected infections in the ear, that infected tonsils or adenoids are removed, and that chronic catarrh is treated.

Miscellaneous Chronic Conditions of the Mouth, Nose, and Throat—As well exhibited by Chart 3.1, these physical handicaps are in total most frequent of all. Partly because so common, their medical and even more their psychological seriousness tends to be neglected. Enlarged adenoids cut off the passage from the back of the mouth into the nose, thus causing mouth breathing. And since discharges from the nose cannot freely escape into the mouth, infection may be spread into the sinuses or the Eustachian tubes, with possible effects on hearing as above mentioned. The nose tends to become thin, the upper lip short, the chin dropped, and the teeth irregular in position with the upper teeth protruding; the expression is stupid. At night there is likely to be snoring, and when eating some bother in swallowing, because of the blocking of the passage at the back of the mouth. The youngster may not play as much as other children because of discomfort in breathing. In short, enlarged adenoids are not merely an interference with normal physiological functionings. They are a serious burden upon normal child existence, and may cause such deforming of facial appearance as to be a handicap throughout life. Tonsils, if enlarged, may also interfere with breathing or swallowing; if infected they are a constant health hazard. Any such focal infection, discharging its poisons back into the body, is likely to make the child irritable and restless or listless, and easily fatigued. Rheumatism and heart disease may be an outcome of the spread of the infection.

Some dental decay is almost universal. But serious decay may be again a source of infection and possibly cause serious infectious disease. Imperfect teeth may prevent adequate mastication of food, and dental deformity may seriously affect appearance. The writers know a girl whose social life during her first year in high school was dominated by her sensitiveness about her protruding teeth and the band on them which was to bring them into somewhat better position but which in the meantime constantly reminded her of her peculiarity. Enlargement of a lymph node or gland in the neck may come from infection of tonsils or adenoids or teeth or gums. Serious malfunctioning of such ductless glands as the thyroid may cause manifold physical and psychological effects which will be touched on later.

Deformities, Paralyses, and "Crippling" Diseases— Chart 3.1 shows frequency of paralyses and of lateral curvature of the spine. If to these two types of cases are added all individuals with other deformity of the back, a clubfoot, a deformed hand, or a limb lost in an accident, the total is much larger. And if to these are also added those with any physical deformity or blemish which presents a psychological problem (such as a misshapen jaw or nose, a birthmark, a disfiguring scar, or acne or pimples on the face), the entire sum of all persons having some sort of physical handicap or blemish is evidently very great. The psychological problems these individuals present are various but almost always difficult. The seriously crippled must learn to do what may be possible by way of getting about and taking part in the routines of life. If possible, a vocation must be found and preparation made for it. But it is the less extreme cases which are not only far more numerous but often seem to present more difficult psychological problems and indeed to suffer more from their handicaps. That is, these last cases are out with other youngsters but handicapped in their relations with them. And their handicap is often not so extreme as to arouse sympathy; it may even cause dislike or ridicule. Some sample cases will make clearer certain of these problems.

> Kurt suffered from an attack of infantile paralysis when he was ten. His parents did everything they could for his happiness—had a private tutor for him, were always with him, the father never crossing him in anything. His sister and he were inseparable. This extreme dependence on the family became a problem for all concerned. Another case was normal in childhood—active in all childhood games, average in appearance, and confident. Then paralysis followed an attack of diphtheria at twelve. Vigorous play was stopped. As a result of efforts on the part of the family to teach him again to swim and play with others of his own age some adjustment was brought about, but feelings of inferiority persisted.
>
> Mary was a hunchback. Childhood play and adolescent social life were largely impossible for her. But from early childhood

her parents had wisely taken an "objective" attitude toward her deformities. There were, to be sure, certain things she could not do, but then everyone has limitations and difficulties which must be accepted. The thing to do was to find out what one could and could not do, locate a few things one could learn to do well, and for the rest take things in one's stride. Her companions admired Mary for her good nature and matter-of-fact acceptance of her handicap. Some things (making little humorous sketches, for instance) she could do extra well and for these she was admired and sought after. Though it is often not considered desirable that a cripple should teach, Mary obtained a position teaching the first grade. She was friendly, patient, and somehow her short stature seemed to get her down on a level with her children, so that she was in a desirable way with them, rather than over them. The children both liked her and were sorry for her, and as a result behaved themselves extra well. As the superintendent remarked, he thought it was a good thing for the children to have some experience in contacts with a handicapped person. He considered her one of the ablest teachers in his school system.

Charles had a crippled right arm, as a result of birth injuries, about which he was exceedingly sensitive. In childhood his parents had limited him to quiet games he could easily play—it seemed never to have occurred to them that he might learn to throw with his left hand, or otherwise participate in boyhood games. In adolescence, whenever possible, he avoided shaking hands, so that people would not have his deformity called to their attention. He went to no dances or other social affairs. In interesting contrast was Henry, who had somewhat the same defect. But somehow, from his mother, he had got the idea that his handicap was a challenge; there were sundry things which he could and would do anyhow and he would find a few things in which he could excel. Thus he could throw a baseball with his left hand better than the average boy could with his right. And he wrote with his left hand exceptionally well.

Hortense was short, squat, thick-lipped, very near-sighted, and clumsy. In childhood she "got along fairly well," but in adolescence she apparently decided she was socially hopeless, was careless and sloppy in appearance, thought of herself as an intellectual and a free thinker, liked to attract attention by her radical ideas (she did not have many ways in which she could attract attention). Her peculiarities of physique were quite clearly background determining factors in her personality. They probably were products of some obscure glandular imbalance.

The handling of cases of tuberculosis or heart disease is so dominated by medical necessities that little need be said about them here. But it should be pointed out that psychologically they present somewhat the same problems as a cripple; their lives are restricted and they must learn to adapt to that fact.

Can any generalization be drawn from this diversity of cases, from almost complete paralysis to little more than pimples on the face? The following conclusions seem warranted. In the first place, over and above any consideration of physical effectiveness or health, it is highly important psychologically that physical handicaps or blemishes be lessened so far as possible. Acne may not be a health hazard, but it may prevent a sensitive adolescent from making important social adjustments. In the second place, even more than with the normal person, it is important that the handicapped youngster make good in some way. The prestige of the second boy with the crippled right hand as a left-handed pitcher, and of the hunchbacked girl as a clever artist, was vital for their psychological health. But it is foolish to try to make good along lines where the handicap especially operates and failure is particularly likely. A boy with a crippled arm who was bound he could play the violin, and a cross-eyed girl with dramatic ambitions wore themselves out to no good purpose. Finally, the handicapped person should associate with normal people, learning all the time to accept his handicap and be accepted as he is.

Speech Defects— Speech defects may be of various types and come from various causes. Children with blurring or peculiarity of speech due to some anatomical peculiarity like cleft palate are relatively rare. Most common are stammering and stuttering, which are best thought of as having their origins in emotional strain of some sort. Undoubtedly every reader of this paragraph has at some time unexpectedly been called upon to speak to a group or meet some important person, and found that his mouth was dry, voice weak, and enunciation indistinct and somewhat incoherent.

In general it will be convenient to think of speech difficulties as possibly due to any one of five causes and check these off in considering a particular case, (1) Defective speech may be one feature of a general mental inferiority or delay of development. Idiots cannot speak at all, and imbeciles relatively little. Speech defects are more common among children below average in ability. (2) Some difficulty in speech may be one feature of a total picture of malnutrition, infection, or nervous disease. (3) Poor speech may be due to some structural defect in the speech organs such as cleft palate, a tongue misshapen or tied, a dental deformity, an obstruction in nose or throat like enlarged tonsils or adenoids. (4) Infantile habits of speech (such as lisping) may be continued from babyhood usually because doting parents thought them cute. Not infrequently an adult has a slight lisp or other peculiarity of speech which seems like an affection but of which he is largely unaware and which is simply a bad habit carried over from childhood. (5) The difficultly may be essentially of the "embarrassment" type. The individual feels insecure and thus much more readily than the average person stutters or repeats a syllable, or stammers and is unable to articulate freely. Clearly each case must be dealt with according to its cause. The second and third types call for medical or surgical attention. The last involves problems of emotional strain which will be discussed later. The important point here is this: Whether in a given instance a speech defect is psychological in origin or not, almost always such defects have important psychological consequences. Doubtless every reader knows of some such instances.

> A college student reported that until he was about six years old he lisped. This lisp his brothers delighted to imitate and he would then become angry and cry, thus gaining a reputation of crybaby. He would then protest to his mother and thus obtained the additional reputation of tattletale. As a result he early developed solitary habits which persisted into adult life. Another young man wrote of stammering at an early age, being laughed at by other children, and getting into frequent fights as a consequence. College students often tell of complete unwillingness to recite having its origin in such speech defects.

Malnutrition— A word remains to be said, in addition to what has already been indicated at the close of the preceding chapter, about the complex condition of inadequate nourishment which is usually complicated by one or more physical defects, frequent illness, and bad health habits. Vitamins and a balanced diet are now enough a matter of common talk so that no discussion is needed here. But teachers may forget that dullness may be largely malnourishment, and also that malnourishment may occur in prosperous homes, the food being sufficient but not such as a growing child needs. Many cases are pitiful indeed.

> Eleven-year-old Marie was failing her school work. She was twenty pounds underweight, round-shouldered, pallid, and much of the time sat motionless and expressionless, seeming often in a daze. Colds were frequent. Her voice was flat and indistinct. Inquiry showed that this girl never had any breakfast before coming to school, that her mother worked and lunch was thus whatever the child could find in the icebox, and that the evening meal consisted chiefly of bread, potatoes, and gravy. A little later an active tuberculosis developed.

ILLNESS AND ITS PSYCHOLOGICAL REPERCUSSIONS

Table 3.1 summarizes an extensive study of illness and shows well that sickness is part of the total life experience of almost everyone. About half of all school children in a given year are ill, many of them several times in the course of a year. Most common are respiratory illnesses such as colds or influenza. Next come communicable diseases such as measles. And next in order come accidents. Out of a thousand school children, about two die every year. Here are sundry intrusions upon life, and sundry special circumstances which affect living.

Psychological Symptoms of Physical Ailments— It should be mentioned first of all that a physical disease is practically never without its psychological symptoms in mood (such as irritability or depression) and conduct (like restlessness or lethargy). Typical of contagious diseases in the first period is fever. This may show in classroom conduct disorder.

> An elementary school teacher once told one of the writers of her experience with two very will-behaved twin boys. They ordinarily worked together and were most likable youngsters. But one winter day she noticed that they were frequently cross

and were having trouble with each other. She decided that they should be separated and put one on either side of the room. A day or so later they were absent with measles. Soon other children near where she had put each boy came down with measles. In short, she had taken the almost perfect step to spread the infection from these boys around her room as widely as possible.

Another teacher during an epidemic made a special point of watching each child closely every day and sending anyone who showed any possible symptoms at once to the school nurse. Not only was the room without such conduct problems, but the epidemic made less headway among the children under her charge.

A college student was doing failing work and was also something of a classroom and dormitory problem. She was very restless, chattered almost constantly, was irritable, would lose her temper and then weep. Medical examination showed chronic appendicitis and infected tonsils. She was twenty pounds underweight, had a temperature, and looked feverish and half-sick, Her academic and conduct problems quite clearly had their cause in her ill health.

TABLE 3.1

Illness [a] and Death Rates per 1000 Population from Birth Through 19 years of Age[1]

Age Group	*Number of Illnesses*	*Number of Persons Sick*	*Sickness Group[b]*						*Annual Death Rate*
			Respiratory	*Communicable*	*Digestive*	*Accidents*	*Skin*	*Ear*	*All Others*	
Under 5	1212	676	537	235	156	71	42	41	130	17.11
5-9	978	585	424	241	69	86	41	28	89	1.92
10-14	679	459	303	97	51	86	43	—	99	1.46
15-19	599	411	253	40	55	81	48	—	122	2.41

[a] Illness is defined as any symptom, disorder, or affection which persists for one or more days or for which medical service was received or medicine purchased. Illnesses include the results of both injury and disease. Illness rates are based on sole or primary causes; a continuous period of sickness is never counted as two sicknesses.

[b] Only groups with rates of more than 20 per 1000 are listed.

[c] Puerperal and female disorders in the years 15-19 total 24.7.

Psychological Recovery After Physical Illness— When a child has been out of school because of illness, there are problems not simply of making up missed schoolwork but also of his return to the play group and more generally of social adjustment. Probably the child is still not very strong. He finds himself bewildered by work the other children are doing which he does not understand. When he tries to enter into their active play during recess, he finds himself feeling weak and unable to keep up. Some children never get back into easy association with other youngsters.

> When Leroy was ten, influenza kept him out of school most of the winter. Other pupils and the teacher herself had also been ill, and she felt unable to give each one special help to make up missed work. Leroy had been a good student and did not like to show it when something came up he did not understand. He had difficulty particularly in arithmetic and was greatly disturbed by almost failing. Not until two years later did he regain his academic self-confidence.

> Harold was in a hospital and then a nursing home for eight months as a result of a near-fatal automobile accident. Upon his return home he was shy with his family, seemed afraid to go out into the neighbourhood, hung back near the door when his class went out to recess, and was timid about speaking in class. He made a good physical recovery but seemed unable to romp again with other boys of his own age. When he entered high school, however, the new group and the variety of sports seemed to give him courage to try again, and he gradually began to participate in recreational and social affairs.

Nervous Diseases—Certain conditions remain to be mentioned which are not highly frequent but which have such psychological involvements that they should be known. Epidemic encephalitis is sometimes incorrectly known as sleeping sickness—incorrectly because it is not the same as African sleeping sickness and because there are not always unusual amounts of sleep. In mild cases diagnosis may be very difficult (the patient should always, of course, have expert medical attention). The child may seem simply to have a mild influenza, be just sleepy, or have a head cold. Usually there is some fever, drowsiness, and ocular disturbances such as double vision. Important here, however, are conditions following the acute illness. The child may wander around the house at night unable to sleep, be overtalkative, his face may show a mask-like immobile appearance, his movements be slow, or there may be overactivity. Emotional disturbances such as extreme irritability, violent temper, and occasional delinquency are a frequent accompaniment. In young children there may be some arrest of intellectual development.

> One writer tells of a girl who came to the investigator's attention when she was eight. She frequently ran away from home, and did queer things like mixing salt and pepper and refilling the shakers with the mixture. Investigation showed that when three months of age she had been "sick with a high fever," but the diagnosis of encephalitis had not been made at that time. The case was lost track of, but later, when the girl was almost 20, she was found spending the night in railroad stations and wandering about the city. Such cases are obviously very difficult conduct problems. Consistent intractability in the classroom may have such origins. Many of these cases need special class or institutional care (45).

Chorea is a disease most obviously characterized by jerking movements; it is often called St. Vitus's dance. But these movements are not the only symptoms. Often the first symptoms are emotional; the youngster is irritable, restless, and fidgety, drops things, stumbles, and makes faces. The condition is most common from about five to the middle teens, and is about three times as frequent among girls as boys. It is believed to be the result of infection frequently beginning with diseased tonsils; the infection may spread to the heart muscles. There is here a group of serious medical problems. But all too often at the beginning of chorea or in very mild cases the teacher treats the irritability and clumsiness from a disciplinary point of view, thus only aggravating the situation.

Encephalitis and chorea may serve as illustrations of the fact that nervous disease may show important psychological symptoms. Malfunctionings of a ductless gland may so manifest themselves. The individual may be irritable, erratic, excitable, or contrariwise, he may be lethargic and slow. And usually subtle differences in physical development may be noticed. In any case where such factors are suspected, medical attention is obviously called for.

A teacher may have an epileptic pupil. A convulsive seizure may occur, or a petit mal attack— an episode of confusion or "fainting." Odd irresponsible behaviour may be an epileptic equivalent. Mood may be gloomy or suspicious. But it must be at once added that most instances of fainting are not epilepsy but simply mild episodes of a digestive or circulatory origin. Odd behaviour and gloominess may have many other causes; some epileptics show no peculiarities of personality. Seizures may be hysteroid rather than epileptoid, emotional rather than organic in origin. These last types of seizure will be discussed later.

HEALTH HABITS

It remains to be pointed out that there are involved, in health, sundry physiological routines and habits with which the teacher may be concerned. Food habits are clearly important. The nursery school tries to provide its children with proper food and then teaches them how to behave when eating. Most elementary schools have children chronically torpid because of inadequate or ill-chosen and ill-cooked food at home, and sallow-faced restless boys whose troubles appear to have their origin in innumerable confections at all hours and no appetite at mealtime. The high school encourages its students to eat a sensible lunch in the school cafeteria, not to eat foolishly at the corner drugstore, and not to develop dietary oddities.

> A quick survey of a college group will discover plenty of illustrations of bad dietary habits and attitudes still persisting. A home economics major did not until her senior year course in dietetics finally teach herself to drink milk regularly. Another girl visiting at a friend's home "just didn't like tongue" and "never ate beans" and "wouldn't touch asparagus" and "eggs just didn't agree with her." Dietary broad-mindedness and a willingness to try new foods *should* be developed in pre-school days. A thrifty freshman makes a lunch out of ten cents' worth of sugar buns which he gulps while playing chess at the Y. M. C. A., and then wonders why he is constipated.

In high school the teachers of home economics and physical education often do much to improve dietary habits. Not only do they inform the students. The training diet for the school teams is used as an object lesson. A good choice of food in the cafeteria is rewarded by a special ticket placed on the tray. In a small high school greatly addicted to Coca-Cola the teacher fed one group of white rats with that drink instead of mild. Both students and their parents at a parent-teacher meeting were much impressed by the undersized nervousness of the Coca-Cola rodents. In elementary school, problems may be both less evident and harder to deal with.

> Rosalia's widowed mother leaves for her work early and comes back late; the children have a grown-up breakfast, a picked-up lunch, and a late, heavy, ill-cooked dinner. The mother is grateful for the milk and crackers the school gives Rosalia at recess. But Gwendolyn presents a more ticklish problem. Her socially overactive mother is rarely up in time to get breakfast for her daughter, and gives her money for her lunch which she buys at a confectioner's.

Sleep habits are dealt with wisely by the nursery school; although largely out of the school's control in later years, they are often a factor in its problems. In every one of a number of groups of children (aged 10 through 17) investigated as to their sleep habits, some youngsters reported having been up until one o'clock or later during the preceding week. Only about a third had a room to themselves and about half shared a bed with some other member of the family. All too often the radio or adult activities keep children up. Multifarious goings-on may affect the sleep of high school students. That this may occur is suggested by the finding that 20 per cent of a large group of high school boys were away from home at least part of every evening in the week (27). Money-earning may intrude upon sleep habits; thus a high school boy may rise at five in the morning to take care of a morning paper route and be out till after eleven in the evening with a late edition. Lack of sleep causes difficulty in maintaining attention on a task, and drowsiness or irritability. An inattentive, cross, mistake-making pupil may be primarily a child without enough sleep.

Other health habits need only be mentioned. Habits of elimination are learned in the pre-school years. But occasionally enuresis (bedwetting) may persist; a teacher may discover that nervous youngster who was greatly disturbed at a plan for an overnight class trip was fearful lest he shame himself. Routines of elimination may be disturbed by the earlier start and changed hours of high school. Elementary habits of cleanliness may be lacking.

The teacher seeking to understand the problem pupil must, then, consider whether faulty habits as regards diet, sleep, or elimination may be a factor. They will be, in a majority of these cases. She should see the establishment of such basic habits for physical well-being as an important educational responsibility for both healthy development and comfortable social living together.

To be sure that pupils are informed is the obvious first step. Prerequisites for the desired habit are sometimes strangely lacking. Thus a school recently visited had no soap in the washroom. To save trouble the cafeteria tables had been piled in a corner and the students ate hurriedly and disgustedly from trays in their laps. Habits of cleanliness and of unhurried eating could hardly be fostered under these circumstances. Recognition of desirable habits, as by a health score card, will foster them.

THE INTERRELATIONS OF HEALTH AND PSYCHOLOGICAL DEVELOPMENT

This chapter has touched upon a great variety of problems—from dentistry to delinquency and enuresis to epilepsy! Are any helpful generalizations possible?

1. In dealing with any psychological or educational problem it is well, first of all, to consider whether some physical defect or disease may be in the background. What seems to be stupidity may be deafness. Intractability may be really encephalitis. To deal with such cases as if they were simply stupid or delinquents is cruel—and stupid. It is a cheering thought that a teacher may hope to have certain of her most persistent problems solved for her by medical treatment. The erratic, irritable, and truant boy may become a star pupil when glasses take care of his farsightedness. The listless and inattentive failure may markedly improve, once diet and sleeping habits have been changed. The chronic troublemaker may quiet down, once infection in teeth and tonsils has been removed. It is a mercy for teacher, class, and herself that the choreic girl is now resting at home in bed under the care of her family physician; her recent grimacing, dropping of books and pencils, and talkativeness had become a problem for all concerned.

2. Problems of physical health involve educational and psychological responsibilities. Glasses are no help in school if they are not worn. The task is not simply to cajole Johnny into wearing them, but to bring about a desirable attitude in the matter on the part of both John *and* his friends. Does he resent the glasses as a confession of weakness or does he take pride in them? Do the other boys yell

"four eyes," or do-they either take the glasses for granted or show friendly interest? The former victims of malnourishment or of focal infection may now be much healthier. But they may need special help to bring them up from their former poor work, and the teacher must not continue her former attitude of discouragement or exasperation regarding them. The victim of encephalitis does not like the teacher, nor she him. It is her responsibility to change the attitude of both parties, and also to help this child, not popular with his fellows, to find a better relationship with them. After choreic Mary, having been in bed for two months, and John, out of school half a year following a near-fatal accident, are back in school once more, neither feels physically strong. Both feel a little shy and strange after their absence. It is easy for them, weak as they still are, to become discouraged about the schoolwork they have missed. The other children are doing long division which the returning youngsters don't understand at all. On the playground they try to run with the others but soon feel tired and can't seem to keep up. These problems of psychological recovery are often far more difficult than is physical recovery.

Health thus presents sundry psychological and educational as well as medical problems. Many psychological problems are partly or even entirely medical problems. In consequence, improvement of physical health may solve many baffling problems of conduct or ineducability.

3. However, the relation of health to psychology must not be thought of simply with reference to certain special cases or problems. The pervasive importance of health as a factor in personality must be emphasized. It is fairly obvious—at least once attention is called to it—that a child with cross-eyes or a clubfoot or tuberculosis is bound to have a markedly different personality from a completely healthy child. A child slightly deaf, undernourished, or chronically heavy from lack of sleep is not the person he might have been in interests, abilities, or mood. But effects of ill health may be more subtle, and they may operate over long periods of time. As has been mentioned, encephalitis so mild as to be unrecognized may cause marked aberrations of personality which persist for years after. Lack of some vitamin or other special element in the diet may affect temperament and capacity for work. Thus special mid-morning feedings of milk and food concentrate to build up calcium metabolism were found to reduce nervousness in the

classroom (excitability, worry, jumpiness) by 13 per cent (26). College students who have at any time had a serious illness appear to be more subject to fear and anger than persons who have not thus suffered (42).

Even more general and pervasive effects of health may be possible. The next chapter will take the attitude that mental ability is not something in the central nervous system aloof from the rest of the organism. Hardy in certain respects though it is, the nervous system may be affected in various ways by the body's total condition. Glandular disfunction may grossly derange it. But functioning ability involves still more. Energy and liveliness are important. If one child does twice as many things as another child, he is likely to develop more intellectually—and to know more and be able to do more things. Succeeding chapters will point out that the healthy child is livelier in interests; he also is liked better and is at a social advantage. The organism's health and vigor are indeed of pervasive importance as regards the total personality.[2]

SUMMARY

About two-thirds of all school children have some more or less serious physical defect (not counting one or two decayed teeth). About one-third of all children have some visual defect, which if uncorrected may handicap both schoolwork and play and cause headache or other distress. Three per cent have defective hearing which handicaps the child in all his contacts with other people. Defects involving the nose and throat, such as infected tonsils and enlarged adenoids, are also common. They may interfere with normal breathing, they usually lower vitality, and (in the case of adenoids) they may adversely affect the growth and shape of the face. Deformities, paralyses, and blemishes may handicap the individual physically and in any case put a burden of adjustment upon him.

In a given year, over half of any group of children are likely to be ill. And about two in a thousand children will die. The teacher must often be the person who first notices evidence of illness. She is often the one most responsible for bringing about educational and psychological recovery after the illness is over.

Reasonable habits of diet, sleep, elimination, and recreation are important for health, both physical and mental.

In all these problems of health, the teacher must often be the one who notes the first symptoms and sees that remedial steps are taken. Almost always there are problems of bringing the child back into his place in both his schoolwork and his associations with other children after the health problem has been dealt with. The larger effects of health upon intellectual as well as physical vigor, activity, and tone are of great importance and should also be recognized by her.

REFERENCES

1. Adapted from (7), pp. 244, 248, 249.
2. As a later chapter will emphasize, what happens to a person psychologically affects his health.

4

The Nature and Nurture of Abilities

It is common in everyday speech to say that so-and-so is an able fellow, that this other person is for about average ability, and that a third individual is not very bright. And what is meant is so generally recognized that no elaborate definitions or explanations are necessary. The reference is to the general level of effectiveness and understanding which the person in question has shown in dealing with the variety of issues which come up in everyday life. It is evident to everyone that people differ greatly in their competence in meeting the problems which come to them. It is also obvious that a twenty-year-old man has much more such ability than a six-year-old boy. Ability is something that increases, during the years with which this volume deals, and something the increase of which may possibly be furthered or hindered by various agencies including the school.

This practical and obviously important topic must now be considered. What are the factors involved in a person's general level of effectiveness? How does such ability develop over the years of childhood and youth? Is it possible to increase an individual's effectiveness—one's own, for instance? Can a school increase the abilities of its pupils? If so, how? Here is a central problem of every ambitious person, and a major issue of educational theory and practice.

A FIRST OVERALL ANALYSIS

Evidently the everyday concept of ability is a very broad one. The question concerns the individual's effectiveness in various real life situations. Many factors are involved. Which are most important and significant for understanding educational problems?

Factors Involved in Realized Ability as Manifested in Everyday Life—A first factor in the adequacy with which an individual meets a situation is the information and skill helpful in dealing with it which he possesses. Where the task, and the information or skill needed to deal with it, are very specific (as in repairing a piece of electrical equipment), this factor is well recognized. But it is hardly less important in other situations where it is less evident. Thus the average traveler feels much at a loss during his first days in a foreign country. Not only the language but a hundred and one different manners and customs and attitudes confuse him. This experience in incompetence can be had without foreign travel, however. The back-country boy in the city for the first time probably feels himself quite as much without ability to deal with the hurrying confusion about him. A city man trying for the first time to manage farm animals feels terribly stupid. It will be well to keep all this in mind when, a little later, data are reviewed which seem to imply that country children and immigrants average below native American youngsters in "intelligence."

A second factor is less immediately evident, but very important and usually inadequately dealt with. A person is able, in dealing with a problem, in proportion as his methods of work and attack upon problems are effective. Some people go right at a task, whereas others fiddle around. Some give up quickly if a solution is not soon found, but others stay with it. Some try this and then that at random and before long do over again what has already been found not to work, whereas others go at the matter systematically, checking off possibilities in order. Some housewives are chronically distraught and their homes in confusion, but others move with easy methodicalness through housekeeping crises. In school some students settle down quickly to study, but others fuss and glance about and are distracted by every passing coed. One student has his notebook always with him and his notes are systematic; another makes rambling jottings on the back of an envelope which is soon lost. In office, factory, home, and school a large element in effectiveness is method of work and attack upon a problem. This factor is so important that it will be returned to in a later chapter.

A third factor in an individual's competence is the extent to which emotional interference or facilitation affects his thinking and doing. Many persons who appear to have excellent intellectual capacity are ineffective because emotional distractions or blockings interfere with a free and consistent dealing with a situation. Others, apparently of less intellectual potentialities, react with easy confidence in a crisis and "excel themselves."

In everyday life individuals thus show themselves able in dealing with situations in proportion as (1) they have needful information and skill for dealing with the problem in hand, (2) their ways of going about their work or attacking the problem are efficient, (3) they are not emotionally distracted or distraught, but rather emotionally stimulated by the situation. A basic factor still remains: (4) a general capacity or potentiality. It was pointed out in Chapter 2 that although conditions of nutrition and living affect an individual's height, still some people are constitutionally tall and others short. Somewhat analogously, individuals differ in their constitutional potentialities for intellectual tallness or shortness. Some people's nervous systems are much more effective than others. And it is to be expected that this factor, popularly called general intelligence, will put a limit or ceiling upon the extent to which the other factors mentioned above can operate. It should also be clear, however, that most people actually do not develop their potentialities up to their limits. Because they do not have all the needed information or skill, or the best of work habits, or adequate emotional adjustment, their actual abilities are distinctly below their potentialities. Feeble-minded children may be close to their limits. But many capable individuals may be far below. And within the great group of more or less average people differences as regards these four factors may be very important in determining comparative effectiveness in everyday living.

The reader may find it interesting and instructive to consider his acquaintances with respect to these various factors. The importance of being adequately informed with reference to a topic was well shown by the contrast between students in a course on medieval history who had read many good historical novels dealing with this period and other students who had had no such previous information. To many in the latter group medieval ways were hardly more understandable than a report of happenings on another planet. For contrast as to methods of work, the reader may well keep a little record of several students during a study hour in the library, as to the number of minutes it takes each one to settle down to work and the number of times each one glances up or moves around. Sample notebooks may also be examined to see how students differ in the orderliness of their memoranda. Great differences in all these respects will almost certainly be found. The very diffident, hesitant, anxious person who recites stumblingly because of embarrassment and seems chronically interrupted in his work by emotional distresses may be compared with the expansive, ready-spoken, enthusiastic youngster who displays all his wares with great fluency and intrigues everyone with his enthusiasm. As for the last factor—constitutional capacity or potentiality—everyone knows some people who seem to have a gift for seeing the crucial issue in a discussion, grasping the essential point in a situation, and seeing significant relations which escape the average person. Other people who may be referred to as just naturally "not very bright" are inferior in these respects. Such differences in original capacity are clearly fundamental.

The basic factor limiting an individual's actually realized abilities is thus his constitutional capacity or potentiality. But the extent to which his potentialities are realized depends on various factors, of which the four above-mentioned are most important. In interpreting any effort at measurement of ability, any experiment aiming at the improvement of ability, or any educational programme directed toward either improvement of ability or adjustment to differences therein, all these factors should be kept in mind. Since their interrelation is somewhat more evident in connection with special abilities and disabilities than with ability in general, such special traits may well be next examined.

Special Abilities—Certain children show decided differences in ability along a particular line. Thus a teacher notices that one child has a knack in dealing with mechanical gadgets; another shows musical talent, a third has artistic gifts. Clearly marked special abilities may be of great vocational importance. If they are based on constitutional special potentialities or capacities, they must be definitive in any programme of vocational planning. On the other hand, if they are more the product of the four factors mentioned in the preceding section, they may be the product of special circumstances which may change. They may even be undersirable (as when a boy turns to a mechanical hobby because he is not getting along well with other youngsters). An understanding of such matters may be helped by considering a particular individual and the way in which special abilities may develop as a result of circumstances.

Ellen was the only child of a woman whose husband had been killed in a tragic accident shortly before Ellen's birth. The mother had done a good deal of oil painting, designing of Christmas cards, photography, and so on, for her own amusement. She had an income sufficient for herself and Ellen, and so could continue her dabbling in art. Her two consuming passions became her daughter and the child's artistic productions. As soon as Ellen could hold a pencil in her hand she was shown how to draw simple objects. The drawing lessons were short, but there were several of them in the course of a day. Frequently the mother would point out how some old house would make a lovely picture, how a tree was beautiful against the sky, how the colour of a cream pitches contrasted charmingly with the wallpaper behind it, and so on. By the time Ellen was seven years old she had visited more museums than most people do in a lifetime. And always her mother was with her, commenting, explaining, enthusing. Ellen's own efforts were greeted with praise and joy and helpful suggestions. Until she was seven, her existence was almost entirely given to the study and appreciation of art, carried on under the intimate supervision of an intelligent and talented adult.

When Ellen entered the second grade of school at seven, she amazed her teachers and playmates because she could read hardly a word, knew no childhood games or stories, could write nothing except her name—which she used in signing her "pictures"—and did not know a single number combination. But she could, and did, draw marvelous scenes on the blackboard. At recess time there was almost always a group of awe-struck youngsters watching Ellen draw. It was her one moment of success, for her recitations consisted of one failure after another. Because she hated being at the foot of the class and had reasonably good general ability, she soon improved in her schoolwork but she never excelled—partly, at least, because all her leisure time went into drawing and painting. At both home and school the one thing that paid dividends of praise and admiration was her artistic activity.

As Ellen progressed into adolescence, she began to realize how one-sided her development was, and made a few honest efforts to escape into a more normal existence. But her mother and, indeed, the entire community would have none of it. By that time she was labeled a coming young artist, her life was so related to her mother's by a multiplicity of shared interests and experiences that separation seemed hardly conceivable; the mother's small fortune made it easy to continue such an existence. ... Ellen is now a woman of fifty. She has never achieved any such position as her early talents seemed to promise. She does commercial illustrating, designing, and some painting. A few of her pictures have been exhibited but, while they show excellence of technique, they receive no prizes. Financially comfortable, she is a conventional, capable, but not outstanding artist.

Did Ellen inherit artistic talent, or was her skill the result of intensive, continued training? Did she have a "natural" artistic sensitivity and interest in art, or was her interest due to the fact that only by her artistic productions did she obtain the admiring attention of others? Why did she not amount to more? Would any girl of equal general intellectual capacity, in Ellen's place, have developed similarly? Certainly not. Obviously a colour-blind person could not have used colour as subtly as she did nor could a person with poor motor coordination have drawn as delicately. A girl of great physical energy would have rebelled against such a sedentary life. A very strongly sexed girl would probably have broken away more from her mother's companionship in adolescence. Perhaps Ellen had some special abilities. But such an assumption hardly seems necessary.

As this case suggests, special ability is usually the result of the combination of a great variety of factors. It is all too easy to posit some mysterious special capability or gift. Such an analysis as presented above seems much more adequately to describe most instances of special talent—and to be far more helpful in dealing with these individuals. Study of the biographies of great artists and musicians (to take two fields where special innate capacity might most be expected) seems to indicate four especially important factors in the development of these individuals: (1) Some had certain especially favouring physical traits such as the voice and physique of Caruso, and many probably had exceptional auditory or visual discrimination and neuromuscular coordination; (2) special circumstances developed an early and very strong special interest and drive; (3) special opportunities as regards instruction and practice furthered the growth of the special talent; (4) there was excellent general intellectual capacity. There may be (5) a certain special innate capacity or special combinations of intellectual traits. But in most instances the first four of these factors seem most important, if not entirely sufficient to account for the special abilities in question. Was Ellen's failure to achieve eminence due to lack of a real innate special artistic capacity? Rather, her economic security and her sheltered and restricted mode of life (also some lack of physical energy) seemed to have prevented the drive and the fullness of emotional experience needed for notable artistic expression.

> Different in his special ability, but not in the factors involved, was Will. His father was a carpenter, but the family lived in a "white-collar" neighbourhood and felt slighted. There were few books or magazines in the home. Although Will did not do well in school, he made the best ship models and was better at repairing things than any youngster in his class. His chum was another special misfit with similar interests. Both needed better social adjustment. But both boys had a genuine interest and adeptness in matters mechanical, and should be encouraged. However, Hugh's "special ability" in Latin was almost entirely undesirable in origin. Singled out by an unpopular teacher for praise, he was spurned by the other boys as a teacher's pet; however he worked extra hard on his Latin since this teacher's favour was the one social approval left him, and became a Latin major as a result of a social maladjustment. Mary's absorption in science seemed a refuge from her failure to make good with the other sex. A special ability may thus be a symptom of some maladjustment or handicap, and most cases of special ability present some adjustmental problems. All such cases deserve careful study.

Special Disabilities—How about individuals who seem to have some special disability or lack? Mary Anne was in the fifth grade but she had difficulties in reading. Frank was a college freshman, but his spelling was atrocious. Newton was considered by his teachers the most brilliant student in West High School, but he was extraordinarily poor at sports and was very inadept in using apparatus in the physics laboratory. Unhappy college student Henry had failed beginning German three times, although otherwise he was doing reasonably good work. Must the school throw up its collective hands and say that such youngsters, though reasonably bright in other respects, are constitutionally incapable of doing certain types of school tasks? The scheme of analysis used in the preceding section may be of help here.

> The case of Mary Anne, who had difficulties in reading, has already been mentioned in Chapter 3. Her trouble was due to visual defects which made it almost impossible for her to keep her eyes focused upon the page for any length of time in such fashion that she could see clearly. The poor speller also had a physical handicap. He was slightly deaf. Since he did not hear certain sounds clearly, he spelled in a peculiar fashion which was very understandable once the nature of his defect was known—and being known, it was possible to explain the difficulty to him. The extremely bright boy who had difficulty in sports and laboratory also suffered from physical handicaps. Partly because of nearsightedness and partly because he was not so well coordinated in movement as many youngsters, he had difficulty in the fine sensori-muscular adjustments called for in sports and in the use of mechanical devices. Also he lacked the exuberance of physical energy which many youngsters have.

In short, various physical handicaps or conditions may bring about what seems to be a special disability. Wherever such handicaps can be corrected, presumably the disability can in large part be remedied—though often not without special help. Thus the poor reader began to do better as soon as she obtained glasses. But she was so discouraged, and so out of touch with what the rest of her class was doing, that she required special help from the teacher to catch up. The deaf child required special explanation as to the spelling of words misheard. The clumsy bright child needed sports in which he could get along; as far as the rest was concerned, it had to be accepted that his abilities were verbal rather than mechanical.

But another factor was involved in the bright boy's clumsiness. Quick of speech, fond of reading, interested in history and English, only child of two highly verbal college graduates, as a child he had been reading and associating with adults when most youngsters were romping. The father was bookish and not mechanical. The family lived in a city apartment, and there were no opportunities to repair things, no basement shop, no pond upon which to sail model boats. All his life the boy had lived in a verbal and ideational rather than a mechanical world. His mechanical disability was in part due to his diversion of interest elsewhere and to lack of information and experience regarding mechanical matters.

A disability may have as a cause more than mere lack of liking; there may be emotional aversion or even panic. Well does one of the writers remember a very severe fourth-grade teacher whose class exercises in "mental arithmetic" he never could seem to keep up with, and whose sarcastic remarks, when he did not, caused malicious delight in the other children. Arithmetic remained thereafter a disliked, and his poorest, subject. In short, disinterest or emotional interference or blocking may result in poor work in a particular subject.

Henry's troubles with German showed a somewhat different pattern of causes. His college German class was taught by a grammatical method that referred frequently to grammatical terms. Henry had come from a very modern high school where formal grammar was largely omitted. Hence when the German teacher spoke of a conditional clause or a past tense or a demonstrative pronoun Henry was completely at a loss as to what was meant. He hesitated to admit this. In fact, he himself hardly realized that his knowledge of these grammatical terms was exceedingly vague. But the fact was that the instruction in German had a point of departure he had never reached. After his failures he became so discouraged that he made no effective effort to study his German. In short, a pupil may have difficulty with a subject because he lacks certain essential elements of prerequisite preparation.

Finally, there is the sad case of pretty Gloria. Gloria says that she cannot learn geometry. She is doing reasonably well, she says, in her other subjects. But a little conversation with her other teachers shows that she is having difficulties in French, English, and history also. She seems to have "special" difficulty in almost everything she undertakes. Gloria's trouble is primarily a lack of much general intellectual capacity and a scatterbrained inability to settle down to work at any task.

A special disability may be due to some physical handicap. It may be due to lack of interest in a subject or to emotional aversion or panic. It may be due to lack of prerequisite information and experience. Usually—as in the examples above—more than one of these factors is involved. What appears to be special disability may be a more general lack as regards methods of work or intellectual capacity. Perhaps, in a few cases, there are genuine innate special handicaps. But the trend of results is to the effect that these are rare. Neither teacher nor student should yield to easy temptation and assume a constitutional disability in reading or arithmetic or foreign language about which nothing can be done. Rather, an analysis should be attempted, such as has been suggested above, to see whether remediable factors may not be found. Usually much can be done. At least, the individual's distress can be alleviated somewhat, and educational programme and plans better adjusted to capacities. That is, *something* should be done; the disability should be either remedied or avoided and not become the rock on which the youngster's education is wrecked.

The Broad Practical Approach to Problems of Ability.—In short, a person's special disabilities or abilities, and his general effectiveness or general ability, are complex products of his total self and total experience. His physique and physical vitality, his equipment of information and skills, his ways of work, his integrations or conflicts of interests, as well as his constitutional intellectual capacity—all are involved in the ability he shows at a particular time to do a particular type of task. The last factor is obviously most important. But practically it can never be isolated from the others. The major thesis of this chapter is that only by keeping all these factors in mind can either psychological theory or educational practice regarding abilities be kept straight.

THE APPRAISAL OF ABILITIES

What contributions does this broad approach make to consideration of methods for the appraisal of abilities? It suggests first of all that any practical appraisal of the abilities of a particular child should not overlook any of these factors. And it aids greatly in understanding the nature and limitations of tests of abilities. First certain methods of appraisal may be noted which are sufficiently broad to include the various factors mentioned above.

Methods for Obtaining Judgements Regarding Ability—If appraisal is to be very broad, some method of obtaining the judgements of persons (such as teachers) who know the individual well may be used. Most informal is a general statement, such as the following report from a "progressive" school to the parents of a tenth-grade boy:

Ronald has been doing well in the industrial arts laboratory and has spent much extra time there. His more academic work is mediocre, however; his French in particular is unsatisfactory. All his teachers feel that his accomplishment is distinctly below his capacities. In class he is listless and often daydreams. He doesn't seem to know how to use time or study effectively. We would appreciate an opportunity to talk with you about your son's work.

This statement evidently sees the boy's abilities in something of the broad perspective suggested above. It pictures a lad with mechanical ability but (as a result perhaps partly of indifference and partly of poor preparation and work method) with inability in verbal subjects. His potentialities were sensed as distinctly above what he was doing. But when the principal went over a number of such unsystematic impressionistic reports, he was uncertain whether the same points had been considered regarding each pupil; he could hardly compare different students to see which ones presented the most serious problems of a given type. A rating scheme was therefore made part of the report on each youngster so that each pupil would be judged on the same general traits and the judgements expressed in somewhat the same fashion. Chart 4.1 shows the "profile" for two tenth-grade boys. The home-room teacher was asked to check, on a blank form, where Harry stood in academic work, in conduct, and so on. The ability profile was then made by drawing a line from one check to the next. On another blank she similarly rated Oliver. The

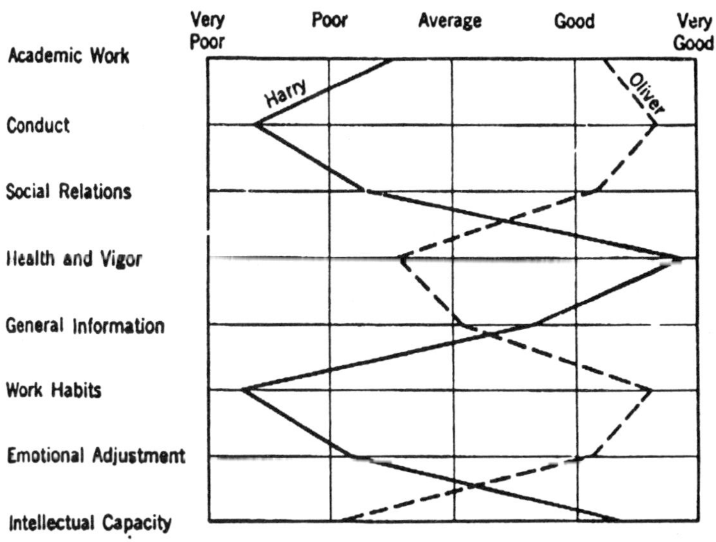

Chart 4.1—Profiles picturing the abilities and traits of two boys, as indicated by ratings made by their home-room teacher.

graph shows the profiles for these two boys on the same chart for contrast and convenience.

> The rating scheme requires that each pupil be considered not only as regards his academic work but also as to conduct, relations with other pupils, health and vigor, frustrations or furtherance of interests, general information, and work habits, as well as general intellectual capacity or potentiality. The chart shows Harry to be doing poor school work and to be a conduct problem. His relations with other people are bad; there is conflict in his home, he is not liked in the neighbourhood, and is shunned by other pupils. He has no real habits of work. His sour expression, surly manner, and erratic behaviour give constant evidence of the conflicts and frustrations in his life. But the teacher was inclined to believe that he really has good intellectual potentialities—though these potentialities are unrealized. In contrast, Oliver is doing good work, gets along well with everybody, is notably systematic and dependable in work, and enthusiastic about what he is doing. But his health is not of the best. The teacher feels that his intellectual capacity is really distinctly below Harry's.

The two cases shown in Chart 4.1 are extremes. But most cases are less clear, or the teachers do not know them well enough to make such an appraisal with any adequacy. A teacher may be prejudiced. She may rate the docile, well-behaved child too high and grossly under-estimate the too lively youngster who is impatient of books and a sedentary educational programme. Often an appraisal is wanted at the beginning of the school year, or regarding a new pupil, when teachers cannot thus judge. Also such judgments are hardly definite enough so that comparisons can be made from one school to another or from one year to another so as to compare schools or determine possible change as a pupil progresses through school. Clearly the most important and most difficult factor to get at is general capacity. To separate this last factor more clearly from the others and meet these various difficulties, the special devices known as intelligence tests have been developed. These must now be considered.

"Individual" Tests of General Ability.—Some tests of ability are so designed that they can be given to an entire class or other group at one time—quite as are tests in arithmetic or spelling or the usual class examination. But historically most important of the tests of "intelligence," and most distinctive and significant with reference

to problems in the field, are those tests planned for use with one child at a time. And of these the first and still by far the most important are the Binet scales. The French psychologist Binet issued the first scale in 1905. The form long best known in this country is the Standford revision of the Binet scale developed by Terman at Standford University. It was first issued in 1916 and has recently been revised so as better to measure ability in our culture.

The test is given to one child at a time, and consists of simple little questions and tasks which seem to him more like an interesting game or chat with the examiner than a test. For example, the child is asked what he would do if he were on his way to school and saw that he was in danger of being late, or if another child struck him without meaning to—such questions being put to find out if he has a sense for practical dealing with everyday minor emergencies. Absurd statements are made—for example, a man said a road from his house was downhill all the way to town and downhill all the way back home—to see whether the child can tell what is foolish about such statements. Certain pictures are shown him and he is asked what each one is about. If he merely names the objects shown in the picture, his response is considered relatively elementary; if he describes what is going on in it, his response is on a somewhat higher level; if he senses a story or situation back of it, his response is rated as still higher. He is given simple things to do, like making rhymes for certain words, repeating a series of numbers which are said to him, or reconstructing a sentence the words of which have been mixed up; he is also asked questions requiring practical generalizations, such as telling in what way wood and coal are alike or defining pity and charity.[1]

In short, the effort is to include in the examination ideas of things to be done which the child would know about from his everyday experience in play or general observation, or from minimal essentials of schooling which almost every American child might be supposed to have had a chance to obtain. In the effort to measure the last factor—constitutional mental capacity—the first factor, relevant information, is thus made unimportant by having the information called for such that all children have about equal opportunities to learn it. The second factor—methods of work—is in large part controlled by having tasks so short that systematic sustained work or study is hardly needed, by having interesting tasks which naturally hold attention, and by having the examiner constantly watch the youngster so as to keep him systematically applying himself to the work. The third factor—emotional blocking or facilitation—is controlled by having the test given to one child at a time, with special effort on the examiner's part to make the child feel at ease and confident, and by having materials and tasks so varied and interesting that the examination has the appeal of a game. The score which the child makes on the examination should in consequence be determined largely by his constitutional intellectual capacity, since the examiner is supposed to keep him to a maximum effort in an emotionally favourable attitude, and he uses material generally familiar.

> The student should, if possible, look over the Terman-Merrill book (54) and the blanks and materials for the revised scales so that he knows their general nature. It will be noted that the tests are in age group from age 2 to superior adult, each test having been put (in making the scale) at the age where half to two-thirds of all of that age pass it. The usual procedure is to give a child six tests in each group beginning with an age at which he can comfortably pass all the tests, and proceeding to one at which he can pass none. The score is then figured by considering the age where he passed everything as the "base" (it is assumed that all tests below this age could have been passed had they been given), and then adding to this "basal year" two months for each test passed in any higher year (each test of the six counting as one-sixth of a year, or two months).[2] The total score is the sum of these values or the "mental age," which is commonly abbreviated as M. A. Suppose a child passes all the 5-year-old tests, four of the 6-year, three of the 7-year, two of the 8-year, and fails all of the 9-year-old tests. The total score will be 5 years plus 8 months, plus 6 months, plus 4 months—or a total of 6 years and 6 months. This is his mental age, and it shows that his mental development is approximately that of the average child of about 6½ years. This concept of mental age is commonly used and its connotation should be thoroughly understood.

It was said that this child showed a mental age of 6 years and 6 months. But whether this indicates normal intelligence cannot be known until his actual chronological age is considered with reference to it. Suppose his chronological age is 6 years and 3 months; it is then clear that, in intelligence, he is approximately a normal or average child, since his mental and chronological ages are so nearly the same. Suppose, however, that his chronological age is 8 years. It is then evident that he has not grown mentally as much as he should have; he is mentally under par. The usual way of expressing a child's intellectual standing with reference to his age is to show the result in percentage. If a child is 10 years old chronologically but tests 7 years old mentally, it may be said that he shows 70 per cent of the mental growth that should be expected of him, or has an "intelligence quotient" of 70. This quotient is ordinarily referred to as the I.Q. If he is 10 years chronologically and tests 11½ mentally, he has an I.Q. of 115. In finding the I.Q., both mental and chronological ages are expressed in terms of months, and the mental age is divided by the chronological. For instance, if a child's chronological age is 8 years and 3 months and his mental age is 10 years 8 months, his I.Q. will be 128 months divided by 99 months, or 130.

Students often become confused as to the comparative significance of the M.A. and I.Q. It should be realized that the M.A. is a statement of a child's *intellectual maturity* without respect to the years he has lived, whereas the I.Q. is a statement of the *relationship* between the length of time he has been alive and the ability he has developed in that time—his brightness. A 6-year-old with an I.Q. of 150 and a 12-year-old with an I.Q. of 75 both have an M.A. of 9. They can do tasks of roughly the same difficulty. But their potentialities are very different. Four years later the mental age of the first child will probably be around 15, and of the second, about 12.

A child's M.A. increases as the years go by, at a rate usually indicated quite closely by his I.Q., until he reaches his adult level of ability.[3] That is, an individual's I.Q. tends to remain the same. But how constant is the I.Q.? Is it possible to predict with assurance that a 5-year-old boy with an I.Q. of 140 will show the same superiority at 15? Numerous studies of this issue have been made by retesting the same children at different intervals. The results seem to indicate that the I.Q. as determined by a Standford-Binet test given by a trained investigator is likely to vary an average of three points one way or the other on a second test within a few days; about one child out of five will vary more than six points. A retest six years later may be expected to show an average change of about nine points (33). Thus, if a child had an I.Q. of 90 when he was six years old, he will usually obtain an I.Q. between 81 and 99 if retested at twelve. Much larger changes are occasionally found. Variations are greater with the high than with the low I.Q.'s.

Presumably any one of the four factors mentioned at the beginning of the chapter as possibly affecting ability might cause such a change. That is, a low I.Q. might be made on one test because of emotional upset, for instance. It might even be that intellectual capacity changed. The question will be returned to later in the chapter.

The Standford-Binet scale is by far the most widely used and generally recognized individual "interview" test given to one child at a time. There are, however, various special individual tests for special purposes. The Binet examination has this limitation: it is largely verbal. For a child who has a speech defect, who comes from a home where English is not spoken and who therefore does not know the language well, or who appears to be much more "thing"-that "word"-minded, "performance" tests can be used—simple puzzles to be solved, or other things to *do*. The Pintner-Paterson and Arthur scales are perhaps the most widely known. They consist chiefly of various form boards and picture puzzles.[4]

The various tests which are given to one child at a time have important distinctive values. The examination not only yields a score; it affords excellent opportunity for the examiner to observe how the child works and to get acquainted with him. Interest can be maintained, any special circumstance affecting his work noted, and some adaptation made (within the rules) to each child. But there are important disadvantages. The examination of one child may take an hour. Methods of giving and scoring such tests are not simple; the manual for using the revised Standford-Binet scales is a book of 461 pages (54). Only after intensive study and experience can a person use these examinations adequately. Clearly it is not possible to give such time-consuming tests, requiring such expert testers, to anything like all the children regarding whom some measure of ability is needed. Tests which can be given to a whole class or other group at one time, and which also are simple enough in methods of administering and scoring so that the average teacher can use them, are clearly needed.

Group Tests of General Ability—The various group tests which have been devised to meet these needs are interesting examples of test-building ingenuity. A considerable number of these tests are now available. Those for the upper grades consist of blanks on which appear such questions as:

	Yes	No
Are apples good to eat?		
The day before Thursday is: (1) Wednesday, (2) Tuesday, (3) Friday, (4) Sunday.	(	)
Cheese comes from: (1) milk, (2) plants, (3) eggs, (4) butter.	(	)
What is iron never without? (1) coldness, (2) polish, (3) weight, (4) rust.	(	)
Head is to hat as hand is to: foot, glove, shoe, coat, wrist.		

The pupils are told to underline the answer to each question which they consider correct or, as in the second, third, and fourth of the above examples, to write the number or letter of the answer they think best in the parentheses to the right. Some recent tests have a separate sheet on which the answers are put. In any case, the directions are so simple that any teacher can give the tests; most tests now have the directions printed on the blank. Since the pupils answer by checking, writing a number, or some other easy method, a large number of questions can be covered in a short time—as many as 200 in 40 minutes—a scope very needful in any attempt to measure such a complex trait as general ability. And checking the pupils' answers against a key is so simple a matter that a 200-question test can be scored by a clerk in as little as three or four minutes. In fact, some tests are now being scored by machine.

It will be seen that the examinations require the ability to read (they assume that the child is at least above the threshold in reading ability, so to speak), but that the questions are, in general character, somewhat like those on the Binet. That is, they deal primarily not with material specifically taught in school, but rather with matters with which the child should be familiar from his everyday experience. It is evident that the examiner cannot control the pupil's attention so well as in an interview examination or make sure that each child's emotional attitude is favourable. However, the usual group examination has many more questions than the Binet, methods of administering and scoring are more clear cut, and it is sufficiently interesting so that it usually holds the pupil's attention well; consequently the results are, in certain respects, more reliable.

The group tests are even more verbal than the Binet. And they are somewhat "schoolish" in character, since they involve reading and information partly of a rather academic nature. Results may therefore be influenced somewhat by any reading disability. Inferences based on such tests as to probable success in a vocation must be made with caution. It might best be said that such tests measure general academic ability.

Group tests for the first two grades present a special problem because the children cannot read well enough to take examinations like those just described. Therefore pictures, geometrical forms, and similar materials are used. Thus a test in one such examination consists of a page showing 30 pictures, in each one of which one part is wrong (for example, one picture shows a letter with a stamp in the wrong corner); the pupil is asked to find this part and put a cross on it. Another test consists of a series of pictures, each showing several similar objects and one which is different from the others (in one picture are four dogs and a cat); the pupils are told to mark the thing that is different from the others. Here again the aim is to present familiar material and simple tasks so as to permit each child to show the extent to which he observes well, listens carefully to what is said, or sees the relationship between objects.[5]

The score on these group tests is usually the number of questions answered correctly. This figure can be converted into mental age by comparing the score for a given child with the average score for each age made by a large number of children. Suppose a total of 6000 children eight years old, who are tested to establish the norm, average 79 points, and about the same number of children nine years old average 91 points. If a given child scored 85, he would be considered to have a mental age of 8½.

It is, of course, then possible to find the I.Q. by dividing the mental by the chronological age, as explained for the Binet. However, because of special features of group tests which need not be gone into here, such percentage statements are not comparable to the Binet I.Q. and can hardly be considered sound. Rather, the results may be expressed as a percentile; or, instead of finding the mental age, a child's score may be compared with the grade norms. If the norm for the third grade is 68 and a child scores 69, he is considered to have approximately "third-grade intelligence." For such uses as grouping children into grades or sections, grade norms are more practical than mental ages.

Tests of Special Aptitudes—Tests of special abilities—mechanical, linguistic, and so on—are also available, although their value has not been clearly demonstrated. They usually present a youngster with typical problems involving the special abilities being investigated. For example, a test of mechanical ability may require the pupil to put together the pieces of a bicycle bell so it will ring; a test of musical ability may ask which of two chords played for him is more dissonant; a test of linguistic ability may present a sample vocabulary in an artificial language, which is to be used in various ways. The test may also include background needed in the field, such as the grammar necessary for the study of a foreign language.

The reader interested in such materials may well look over some paper test like the Detroit Mechanical Ability Test (Public School Publishing Company) or an assembly test like the Minnesota (the Marietta Apparatus Company, Marietta, Ohio), and try the revised Seashore musical discrimination records (R. C. A. Manufacturing Company, Camden, New Jersey). The Leverenz Test in Fundamental Abilities of Visual Art (Southern California Book Depository, Hollywood) may also be of interest.

Appraising the Tests—The various tests of general and special ability thus attempt so far as possible to determine constitutional, general or special capacity, since this is the basic limiting factor in abilities. They attempt to do this by using material with which everyone tested is presumed to have had equal opportunity to become familiar, and making all other conditions favourable. Roughly, for the general run of children, this is possible. But it must never be forgotten that control of all these various factors can be only rough, and that cases may appear where these suppositions are not met.

A 12-year-old girl whose family had just moved from an isolated district in the Kentucky mountains was once referred to one of the writers for testing. The school had tentatively put her in the fifth grade, and on the second day of school her class had been given a group test of general ability. But she read so stumblingly that she did almost nothing. When she was given the Binet, it was evident that sundry information which the examination took for granted a child would know had never reached her cabin home up the creek. She was so shy from her first experience in a city that it was almost impossible to get her to talk beyond monosyllables, or to handle freely and confidently the performance tests which were also tried. Moreover, she was badly malnourished, and vision seemed impaired. Clearly her low scores not only on the group tests but also on the Binet and the performance scale could not at once be constructed as due to defective intellectual capacity.

Under such circumstances the test may indicate rather well the individual's inability at the time; the scores made by the girl mentioned above showed how lacking in ability she then was to take her place in regular classes with children near her own age. But the result of intensive work with her in a special ungraded class and of medical attention to her health problems showed that though she was dull, she was capable of more than the test scores had suggested. As will shortly be seen, this distinction between realized ability and capacity or potentiality is of vital importance in the interpretation of important research regarding growth of "intelligence" and influences affecting such growth.

Relations of Ability, as Tested in School, to Later Success—A major practical question remains to be touched upon: the question as to what inferences may be drawn, from scores on tests of ability given in school, as to probable later success. Table 4.1 is of great interest in this connection and summarizes an investigation of unusual significance. All children in the sixth grade of a large city school system were given an intelligence test in 1923. Twelve years later, when these individuals averaged 24 years old, their careers up to that time were carefully investigated. Adequate information was obtained about 60 per cent of the original group. The table summarizes, in compact form, the outcome of this follow-up.

Of those who, when in the sixth grade, tested in the upper fifth on the "intelligence" test, 74 per cent graduated from high school, as compared with only 6 per cent of those who in the sixth grade tested in the lower fifth in general ability. Of those in the upper fifth in ability when in the sixth grade, 28 per cent graduated from college, as compared with only 1 per cent from the lower fifth. Clearly there is a relationship between ability as tested in childhood and later academic success. But this relationship is not absolute; a few even in the lower 20 per cent in score in the sixth grade later graduated from college. There may have been children who, perhaps because of some distraction or other special circumstance in the first testing, scored much below their real ability. It may also be true that an occasional dull child does later graduate from college!

TABLE 4.1

Relations of Ability as Tested in the Sixth Grade to Later Career; 4184 Cincinnati Sixth Graders Tested in 1923-1924, Their Academic and Delinquency Record, and Occupational Status in March 1, 1936[6]

Test Per-centile (1923)	*% Grad. High School*	*% Grad. College*	*% De-linquent*	*Percent in Each Type of Occupation* Profes-sional	Cleri-cal	sales	Skilled	Un-skilled	Unem-ployed.[a]
80-100	74	28	0.3	16	24	14	4	9	27
60-79	54	15	4	9	23	16	5	13	31
40-59	34	6	6	6	18	13	8	16	37
20-39	14	2	9	3	13	12	9	22	39
1-19	6	1	10	1	6	8	9	31	44

[a] "Unemployed" includes housewives; since 54 per cent of the "unemployed" group were married women these last figures clearly give an exaggerated impression of unemployment.

The inquiry showed that, of *all* the children originally tested, 7 per cent at some time got into the juvenile delinquency records of this city—presumably still more had delinquency records elsewhere which were not included in this investigation. More of the dull than the bright children had such records, but a few of those in the upper fifth did.

Finally the table shows the very rough relationship of tested ability to later occupational status. Most of those in professional work tested in the upper two-fifths when in the sixth grade. But most of the skilled workmen tested in the lower two-fifths. Clearly ability as thus tested in the sixth grade does not permit much inference regarding vocational future.

THE GROWTH OF ABILITIES

As pointed out at the beginning of this chapter, growth in abilities is really about as well recognized a phenomenon as growth in height; everyone knows that a 10 year-old child can do many more things, and more difficult things, than a 5-year-old. And a 15-year-old is still more competent. But there are many important questions regarding growth in ability which general observation cannot answer. Does ability grow at a regular rate and in a consistent fashion like height? Growth in height ceases around 18 or 20; does ability also stop growing, perhaps at about the same age? An answer in the affirmative might seem somewhat distressing! Height, weight, and strength showed an acceleration in rate of growth at adolescence; is there such an acceleration in ability? Are there sex differences? Do girls mature more rapidly in ability as they do in physique? Do men finally much exceed girls, as they do in strength? How do dull people differ from bright, in mental growth? Are dull people what they are because they grow more slowly in ability or stop growing sooner, or both? These are all questions of decided importance for education. And they are questions whose answers must quite clearly be obtained from the use of tests, in spite of their shortcomings mentioned in the preceding section. What, then, are the test findings regarding the general trend of growth in ability?

Growth of General Ability—Chart 4.2 shows typical results. Growth in ability apparently proceeds more or less regularly through childhood and adolescence; adolescence seems to have no clear effect on it. But the curves level off during later adolescence. At what age this level is reached is a matter of dispute. As already mentioned, Terman assumes a mental age of 15 as the mental level of the average adult. Other investigators have suggested that mental maturity is reached as early as 13 (giving the average adult only a 13-year mentality) or as late as 20. The present trend of thinking is toward these later years.

> Testing in the Army in 1918 indicated adult mental level to be between 13 and 14. This was about the average age of leaving school at that time. Now, however, average age of leaving school and findings regarding adult level have both gone up. Further, when the 1918 results were analyzed with reference to average test score in the different states, high correlations were found (.72) between these state scores and ratings of the quality of the schools in 1900—when most of these men were in school—in these states (Bagley).[7] In short, the level of ability finally reached, as measured by the tests, appears to be affected by schooling. But it must also be noticed that the general trend of the curve of growth of ability is very similar to the curve of growth in height. That is, a basic background biological growth factor appears to be involved here.[8]

These are the important findings regarding the growth of ability as measured by tests. But it is clear from the chart that different tests give somewhat different results and that findings must be regarded as rough. Thus there may perhaps be some effect of adolescence upon

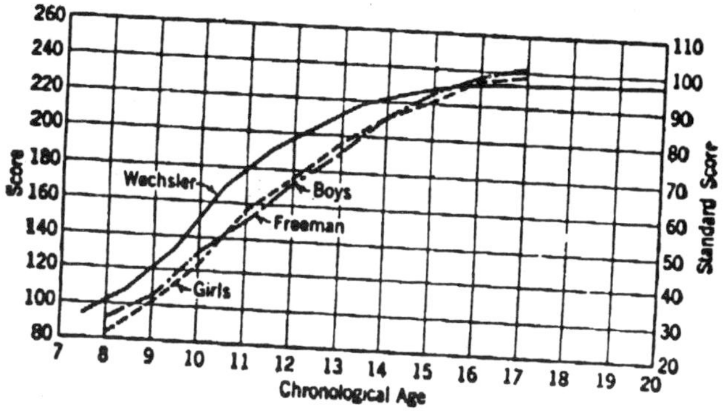

Chart 4.2—Growth in general ability as shown by an individual interview test of the Binet type (Wechsler), and a battery of group tests given to the same individuals at yearly intervals over a nine-year period. (Adapted from data of Wechsler [58] and Freeman [18.)

growth of ability which the tests are too inadequate to show. An adolescent lift for girls around puberty is often found, as in one set of data in the chart. There is no evidence for any general superiority of one sex over the other; apparently the sexes are equal in "ability in general."[9]

Individual Differences in Growth—Do dull children grow more slowly in ability than do the bright? Does their growth continue for a shorter time? Or do "slow" youngsters continue their development for a somewhat longer period and as a result tend somewhat to catch up? Evidence regarding these questions is admirably presented in Chart 4.3. It combines certain data from England and this country and is valuable because of both the consistency of the findings from these two sources and the relating of the test data to other evidences of ability. Thus the higher group is made up of persons who had demonstrated their ability by having won scholarships; the English group of mental defectives were, or had been, in special schools for mentally defective children. The American defectives had been diagnosed as of very low mentality on the basis of various evidence.

As will be seen, the chart shows the dull and bright cases growing further and further away from each other with increasing chronological age. Thus the difference between the English children who later won scholarships and those who were put in classes for the mentally defective was only about four years of "mental age" at age 6. But at 18 these two groups were almost twelve years of mental

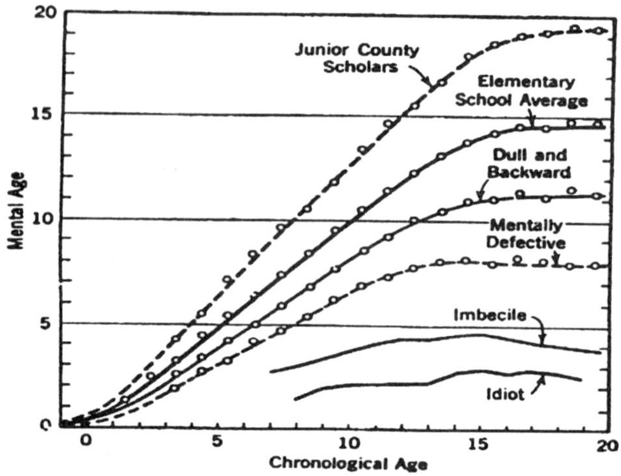

Chart 4.3—Differences in curves of mental growth of children with different amounts of abilities, from superior children who won scholarships, to idiots in an institution for the feeble-minded. (From Burt [8], p. 650; the lower two curves from F. Kuhlman. The results of repeated mental examinations of 639 feeble-minded over a period of ten years, *J. Appl. Psychol.*, 1921, 5, 195-224.)

age apart. Apparently the bright grow in ability more rapidly than the dull. And the mentally superior individuals also appear to continue growth somewhat longer. In fact, the curves for the most defective individuals appear early to go into a decline. Quite clearly, then, the problem of adjustment to individual differences becomes increasingly severe with increase in age. [10]

Do children usually grow in ability at a steady and consistent rate, or may one child show a spurt of growth while another lags and drops behind his fellows? Such variations in rate of growth would evidently involve changes in I.Q. As mentioned earlier in this chapter, the I.Q. of most children is relatively constant. That is, a boy who at 8 has a mental age of six is not likely to show any later period of rapid mental growth which brings him up to average. As shown in Chart 4.4 considerable shifts may occur, however.

When these five boys were all 7—0 years old chronologically, they all had the same mental age of 6—5 and hence the same I.Q. of 92. But ten years later one of these boys tested at only 13—6, whereas another was five and a half years further ahead according to the tests and showed a mental age of 19. "Since these cases were drawn at random and there was no selective factor

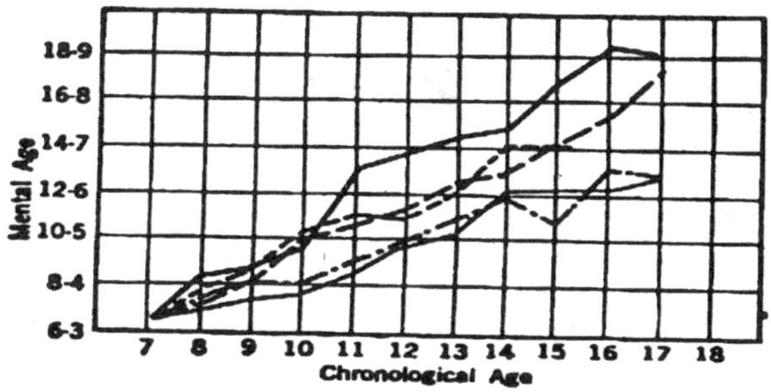

Chart 4.4—Variability in mental growth of five boys whose mental test scores and intelligence quotients were equilvalent at age 7.

other than identical mental ages at identical chronological ages, we may assume that such variability is a common occurrence—a fact which numerous other graphs corroborate and which further statistical studies have emphasized".

Growth in Special Abilities—Chart 4.5 shows growth curves for certain special abilities which are similar in general trend to the curves for general ability exhibited in the preceding section; growth is rapid and fairly consistent through the years of physical growth, and tends to level off with the approach to physical maturity.

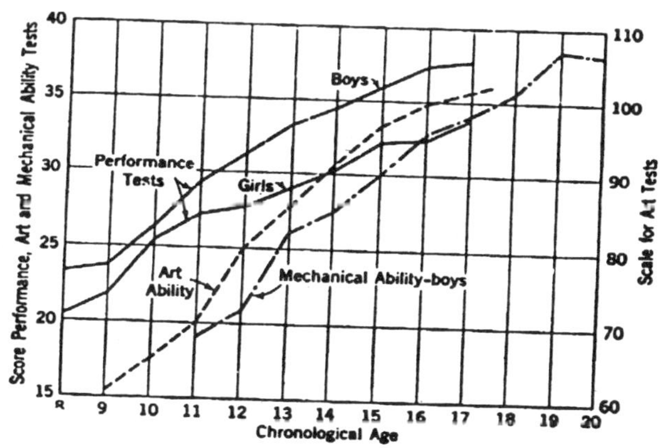

Chart 4.5—Growth in abilities as shown by *(a)* a series of performance tests (Ferguson Form Boards), *(b)* tests in abilities in visual art (Lewerenz), and *(c)* tests i mechanical ability (Minnesota Mechanical Test Battery A). (Adapted from data of Louise Wood and Edythe Kumin, A new standardization of the Ferguson Form Boards, *J. Genet Psychol., 1939, 54, 265-284;* D. G. Paterson, *Minnesota Mechanical Ability Tests,* p. 345; and the normative data of the Lewerenz tests.)

THE DISTRIBUTION OF ABILITY

As was mentioned at the beginning of this chapter, everyone recognizes that some people are more able than others. But how much do people differ in ability? Are the very stupid a distinct group like dwarfs or cripples? Are very bright children so rare that schools need ordinarily make no special plans with reference to them? How many very bright and very dull people are there? What differences in ability may be found between different occupational groups, neighbourhoods, or communities? Data on these questions will now be briefly summarized.

Range and Classification of Ability.—Chart 4.6 exhibits both the great extent to which individuals in any ordinary group differ in ability and the distribution of ability in such groups. It shows results of tests of general ability for the same children at three different ages. Clearly, at each age these children differ greatly in ability. Thus some of the 12-year-olds are no brighter than the average 8-year-old child, whereas some others are as able as the average 16-year-old youngster. In terms of mental age, these differences are evidently striking. It is also clear that ability is distributed, like height and weight, in a bell-

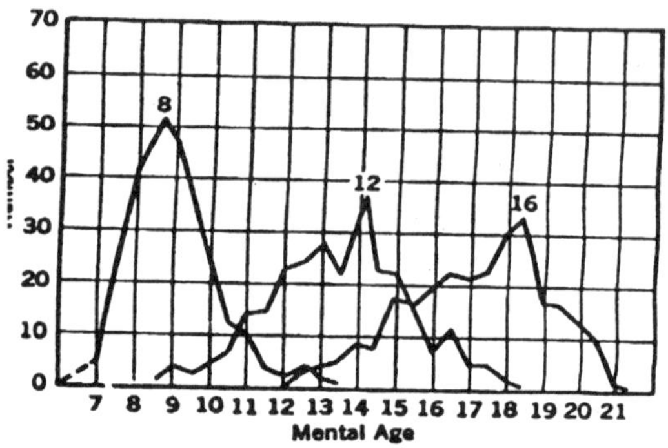

Chart 4.6— Distributions of mental ages of 167 girls at ages 8, 12, and 16.

shaped or "normal" curve. There are no separate groups of very bright or very dull. Most people are about average in ability. As one goes further away from the average, he gradually finds fewer individuals. But there are many who are sufficiently above or below average so that they present distinct educational problems. Thus there are many 12-year-olds whose mental ages are two or more years below average for their group, and many who are two or more years above that average in general ability.

It is clear there are no distinct breaks between individuals who might be considered feeble-minded or very superior and the great group of average persons, but it will be a practical convenience to classify individuals into groups according to ability. Table 4.2 shows a commonly used classification according to I.Q. Approximately 80 per cent of all children are put in the three "average" groups, with 10 per cent above and 10 per cent below. It will be clear from Chart 4.6 how arbitrary those divisions are. And the reader will understand that the statements about educational and vocational possibilities are even more rough, especially since many factors besides ability are here important. Not all children with I.Q.'s above 120 should attempt to enter a profession; some industrious fine personalities of relatively average ability may. But it is foolish for parents of a child with an I.Q. of 80 to try to send him to college and expect him to become an engineer. It is a waste of human resources if a poor child with an I.Q. of 140 leaves school for a "blind alley" job at 16.

TABLE 4.2

Classification of General Ability as Measured by the Revised Stanford-Binet Scale, with Approximate Academic and Vocational Possibilities of Each Group [11]

I.Q.	*Percent-age of Children[a]*	*Adult M.A.*	*Classifi-cation*	*Academic Possi-bilities*	*Vocational Possi-bilities*
140 and up	0.6	21 and up	Very superior	Graduate	Professional, executive
120-139	9.9	18-0 to 20-11	Superior	Technical	Professional, technical
110-119	16.0	16-6 to 17-11	High average	College	Technical, business
90-109	47.0	13-6 to 16-5	Average school	High skilled	Clerical,
80-89	16.0	12-0 to 13-5 average	Low	9th grade	Semi-skilled
70-79	7.5	10-6 to 11-11	Inferior	7th grade	Routine work
60-69	2.4	9-0 to 10-5 deficient	Borderland 5th grade	labour	Unskilled
50-59	0.5	7-6 to 8-11	Deficient	3rd grade	Simplest labour
Below 50	0.1	Below 7-6	Very deficient	Special class	Unemploy-able

[a] These percentages will be found to be approximate for white children of school age whose parents are native-born. They are calculated on the assumption of a normal distribution with a standard deviation of 16 points of I.Q. The adult "mental ages" are the Stanford-Binet mental age scores that these children will have to obtain to have the same I.Q.'s respectively that they had as children.

From the above comments it should be clear that feeble-mindedness should not be thought of simply in terms of score on a test. A total consideration of an individual's ability to get along in the world is involved. A feeble-minded person is one who cannot get along or "conduct his affairs with ordinary prudence" and is incapable of learning to do so. Tests will usually be a central means of determining such facts, but much more evidence than score on tests must be available if an individual is to be so classified.[12]

The feeble-minded are usually classified into three groups. Lowest are the idiots, who cannot even look after their own bodily needs but must be kept clean and fed and looked after throughout their whole lives. They never reach a mental age of over about two years. Imbeciles are a little better. They can talk and protect themselves from ordinary dangers and learn a few simple skills. But they cannot earn a living, have little grasp of the ordinary rules of conduct, may be almost without inhibitions. In school, they cannot learn to read or write—though a patient teacher may train one, somewhat as a parrot is trained, to read and write a little in mechanical fashion. Imbeciles never reach a mental age of over six or seven. Morons are the highest group of those who may be considered feeble-minded. Morons can learn to read and write, and may earn a living at simple tasks. However, they seem incapable of planning or judgment and cannot manage their affairs with "ordinary prudence"; they are easily taken advantage of, often slightly inhibited by social pressures, and thus frequently become delinquent. Usually they never develop in mental age beyond nine or ten.

Relations of Socio-Economic Status and Ability—Table 4.3 shows findings typical of many investigations regarding the relation of socio-economic status and ability. A large number of children who had been given the revised Stanford-Binet tests were classified according to the occupation of the parents, and the average I.Q. of each group was then found. Children of professional men average 20 points higher in I.Q. than children of day labourers.

It should be noted that the differences are about the same for the older as for the younger groups; if home conditions were the chief cause of the differences, they might be expected to increase with age—with the length of time the home influences had operated. As it is, these differences might be attributed to superior constitutional capacity in families of higher socio-economic status. Anyhow, the table shows only averages; there are nevertheless many bright children from poor homes, and dull ones from families of prominence. Chart 4.7 brings out the extent of such overlappings.

TABLE 4.3

Mean I.Q.'s of the Stanford-Binet Standardization Group Classified by Father's Occupation[13]

Father's Occupation	*Mean I.Q. by Chronological Ages, Years* 2-5½	6-9	10-14	15-18	*Un-Weighted Average*
Professional	116	115	118	116	116
Semi-professional and managerial	112	107	112	117	112
Clerical, skilled trades, retail business	108	105	107	110	107
Rural owners	99	95	92	94	95
Semi-skilled, minor clerical, and Business	104	105	103	107	105
Slightly skilled	95	100	101	96	98
Day labourers, rural and urban	94	96	97	98	96

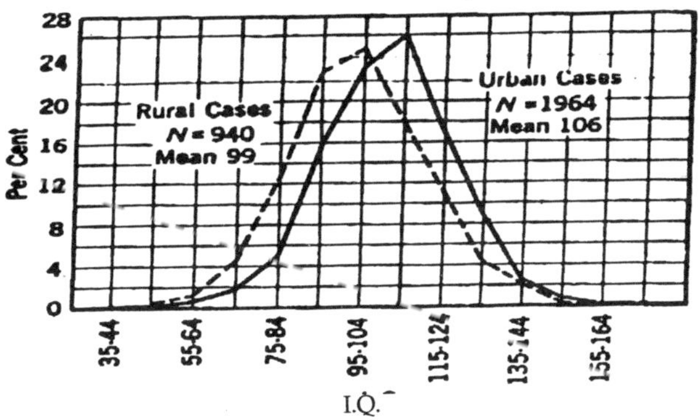

Chart 4.7—Distribution of I.Q.'s of rural and urban groups on the revised Stanford-Binet Scale.

Urban children (from any area with a population density of 1000 or more per square mile) average 106 in I.Q. as compared with 99 for rural youngsters. But the distributions overlap completely. Obviously the fact that a boy is from the country does not warrant his being forthwith dubbed dull. He may be right up with the brightest city boys; furthermore, some city boys are very stupid.

In fact, though very bright children may be found proportionally more often in city homes of professional or business parents, nevertheless most bright youngsters may not be in such homes. For these families are only a small proportion of all the families in the country, and they have even fewer children. There are, in total, many bright children in the country, and in poverty. The wise teacher will ever be on the lookout for them everywhere. They are her great opportunity; with them she can find great usefulness and joy.

Table 4.4 presents a commonplace finding of every school survey but nevertheless one of great practical importance. It shows results with a group test of general ability for the sixth-grade classes of two schools in the same city, and demonstrates how much two schools may differ in the abilities of the children attending them.[14]

TABLE 4.4
Variability in Scores in General Ability of Two Sixth-Grade Classes from Different Sections of the Same City

	Score												*Total*	*Median*
	40	45	50	55	60	65	70	75	80	85	90	95		
School A	2	4	5	7*	4	5	4	1	1		1		34	59
School B			1		3	5	2	11*	6	2		2	32	77

The unhappy young teacher in the first school was finding her class slow, stolid, and hard to teach, but in the second school the youngsters were living and learned readily. Observation of the neighbourhoods in which the two schools were located would lead one to expect what the result showed. The first school was in a part of town near a factory employing chiefly unskilled labour; the second, in a good residential section. The teacher in the first school was seriously handicapped by the poor "pupil material" in her school. Only one pupil in the second class scored below the median of the first. Actually the pupils in the sixth grade in school A were only as able as the students in the fourth grade in School B. No wonder her pupils did poorly on tests of reading and arithmetic and history. The supervisor had inferred she was a poor teacher. Rather it was the pupils who were poor. When this teacher saw the results of the tests of ability she almost wept from relief; she had thought herself a failure and had expected to lose her job.

Every teacher and every school official should keep in mind the possibility of such differences in the abilities of the pupils with whom he or she is concerned. Frequently the children in one school are found to average two years in mental age brighter than those in another school in the same community. Two first-grade classes may differ as much as 35 points in median I.Q. (54). Rural schools may differ almost as much, children in prosperous farming areas testing higher than those in poor rural districts. The teacher who does not recognize such differences and adjust her programme of work and her methods accordingly is bound to have trouble.

> One of the writers well remembers a one-room back-country school visited in a school survey, in which a third of the children tested as mentally defective; all these were siblings or cousins.

Children from better occupational groups and neighbourhoods thus average higher in general ability than those from less favoured situations. These differences might be due to more favourable conditions in the better socio-economic groups as regards health, diet, and living conditions, reading matter, and education of parents, which fostered the abilities of these children. Or parents with good constitution and intellectual capacity may tend to go into the better jobs, neighbourhoods, or farming areas—and have children who inherit their good native capabilities. In so far as this last hypothesis was true, the favourable conditions would be not the cause of the children's better abilities but only a concomitant circumstance. Data on this question will be returned to shortly.

Family and Ability—Many investigations have found that ability, or the lack of it, tends to run in families. Seventy years ago Galton reported that an eminent man was 130 times as likely to have an eminent male relative as was the average man. Terman made an intensive study of 643 "gifted" children with an I.Q. of 140 or higher, and found that in their family trees were six signers of the Declaration of Independence, two Presidents of the United States, and many other eminent people; these children "came predominantly from family stocks of decidedly superior intellectual endowment." The average I.Q. of the siblings (brothers and sisters) of these children with I.Q.'s above 140 was 123, or "almost exactly what would be expected if the correlation between siblings in the general population were in the neighbourhood of .45 or .50". At the other extreme, one investigator reported regarding a group of mentally defective mothers that 44 per cent of their children were mentally defective, or at least twenty times as many as in the general population. Feeble-mindedness as well as eminence seems to run in families. The history of such families as the "Jukes" and the "Kallikaks" is a sordid record of educational and economic failure and of illegitimacy, delinquency, and other evidence of mental defect.

Table 4.5 exhibits the increase in similarity as regards ability, in a family, with closer relationship. It summarizes results of twelve different investigations and includes correlations for physical as well as mental measures.

All these various studies show family resemblance in ability. But what are the important causes of these resemblances? An inherited constitutional capacity is at once suggested as the important factor. But identical twins in the same home who look so much alike that

TABLE 4.5
Correlations Found Between Related Pairs of Persons, Northern European Stock, in Twelve Different Investigations[15]

	Physical Measures	*Mental Measures*
Unrelated children		—.19 to .09
Cousins		.27
Parents	.00 to .15	.46 to .49
Parent-child	.42 to .53	.45 to .55
Siblings, same home	.42 to .53	.45 to .55
Non-identical twins	.58	.53 to .70
Identical twins	.91	.88 to .97

they are often mistaken for each other[16] are surely subject to such a similarity of influences that much similarity of abilities might be thus caused. All the people in the same home live under largely similar physical, socio-economic, and cultural conditions. Two children of the same intellectual constitution would certainly develop somewhat different abilities if one grew up with the best of care and schooling in the home of a California professional family and the other lived a half-sick, half-starved existence in the shack of an illiterate southern sharecropper. How much difference do such factors make? This is a vital question for education, and it must now be considered more closely.

THE EFFECTS OF VARIOUS INFLUENCES UPON ABILITY

The question may well be rephrased thus: To what extent may it be hoped that ability can be improved by improvement of children's health, living conditions, or schooling? Here is indeed a vital question for education.

Health and Ability—As was mentioned earlier in the chapter on physical growth, good ability and good physique tend to be found together. Intellectually superior children tend to be taller and heavier than average children and to reach puberty sooner, whereas dull and feble-minded children tend to be below average in size. Physical defects such as infected tonsils and malnutrition are somewhat more common among dull than bright children. Thus of over 14,000 children covered in one investigation, those with I.Q.'s of 110 or over averaged 1.6 physical defects of some sort, those with I.Q.'s in the 80's averaged 1.6 defects, those with an I.Q. in the 60's averaged 2.1 physical handicaps of some sort, and children whose I.Q. was below 50 had 3.1 defects (13). However, the correlations between either size or number of physical defects and ability are so low that no inferences regarding ability are warranted from an individual's physique.

Further, it must not be assumed from such association as does exist between physical condition and ability that improvement of physical condition or remedy of physical defects can be counted on to improve ability. Thus removal of diseased tonsils has not been found to cause any increase in I.Q. Nor has remedy of malnutrition been found thus to benefit. For instance, 25 underweight children were for six months given school lunches and health lessons and motivated to improve their physical condition. They gained in weight 26 per cent more than a control group that had no such programme, but intelligence test scores showed no corresponding gain. Investigators have, however, found improvements in school-work as a result of school health programmes. This apparently was due to greater energy, interest, and wide-awakeness (and to more interest in and consideration of the child on the part of teachers and parents as a result of their participation in the programme!) rather than to any increase in the children's ability (23).

Health records during the first six years have been reported as having no correlation with mental test scores. However, certain very serious or debilitating diseases may apparently have determinable effects. Thus those children most heavily infested with hookworm, of 117 pupils in three southern rural schools, averaged 14 points in I.Q. below the pupils without hookworm. Pupils with moderate infestation averaged 6 points below, and those with light infestation 4 points below the healthy pupils in these schools (50). But no evidence was obtained as to whether treatment for hookworm would increase I.Q.

Marked handicaps such as deafness seem to be related to ability, but just how is not clear. Tests adapted for use with handicapped children have shown I.Q.'s for deaf children to average around 80, for blind children around 90, and for crippled pupils about 85. However, the first two groups are hard to test, even with materials especially designed for them. Some of these seriously handicapped children are almost certainly cases of general constitutional inferiority, of which the inferior ability is simply another symptom rather than the result of the handicap. But blindness and deafness cut an individual off from so many experiences that every might well be expected somewhat to restrict the development of ability.

In short, the growth of ability may apparently be stunted somewhat by some serious physical handicaps and diseases, and perhaps restricted slightly by less serious physical conditions. But results are much less than might be expected, and improvement of physical condition has thus far not been shown to improve ability appreciably.

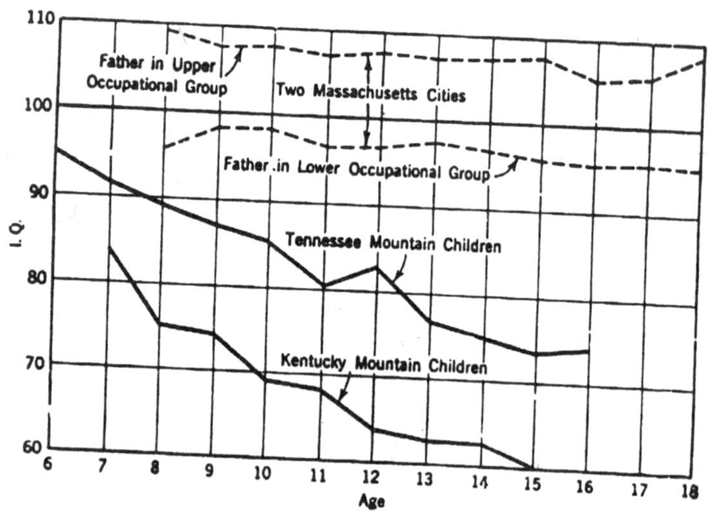

Chart 4.8—The effect of relatively slight and marked deficiencies in socio-economic conditions upon I.Q. (From data of Shuttleworth [48], Wheeler [61], and Asher [2].)

They Effect of Socio-Economic Conditions upon the Growth of Ability—Chart 4.8 appears to show an analogous finding as regards the effects of socio-economic handicap. In the grossly inadequate environment of the southern mountains, children apparently drop more and more behind the average child as they grow older.[17] But the boys in the two cities near Boston were all from a similar lively urban environment. And the possible "mildly stimulating" socio-economic status of the 53 boys whose fathers were in a profession or a good business position seemed to have no progressive effect upon the development of their general ability as compared with the possible "mildly repressing" home and neighbourhood circumstances of the boys whose fathers were semi-skilled or unskilled labourers.

> At the beginning (that is, at the age of 8) the two Massachusetts groups were different presumably because of differences in the constitutional capacity of their families, and possibly in part as a result of earlier childhood influences. But at least from 8 on, the differing socio-economic status of these two groups did not cause them to move further apart.

Similar conclusions are suggested by the fascinating and dramatic research regarding identical twins reared apart. Gladys and Helen were identical twins who were separated at 18 months of age and did not meet again till they were 28. Helen's foster parents were determined that she should have a good education; the girl graduated from college and became a teacher. But Gladys spent most of her childhood in an isolated district in the Canadian Rockies, never had an education beyond the third grade, and went to work as soon as she was old enough. When they were tested (as adults), Helen had an I.Q. of 116 but Gladys' was only 92. On the other hand, twin boys reared one in the country and one in a city, but in homes apparently roughly similar in socio-economic status, made almost the same mental test scores although one had had a little more education than the other.

Will marked change in a child's conditions of life change his tested ability? On the whole, the evidence is that it will—at least a little. Table 4.6 summarizes data from a typical study. A group of 74 children were tested shortly before being adopted and were tested again after an average of four years in the foster home. The average age at the first test was 8 years. The table shows (1) that children placed in good homes improved measurably more than those in poorer homes, and (2) that younger children benefited more than older children. Other evidence indicates that yet earlier adoption, as in the pre-school years, would probably have resulted in greater gain.

What is meant by a "good" home, in such studies? In the above investigation homes were judged on a rating scale which took account of the neighbourhood, the size and comfort of the building and the condition in which it was kept, the nature and amount of reading matter, the education and social life and the congeniality and kindliness of the foster parents. Other studies suggest the importance for a child of contact with and friendly attention from adults, a variety of toys to play with and of things to do, and friendly encouragement in and opportunity for a variety of stimulating experiences (57).

TABLE 4.6

Effect of Good and Poor Homes on the Measured Intelligence of Foster Children[18]

Home Rating	*No. of Cases*	*Pre-test (I.Q.)*	*End Test (I.Q.)*	*Gain*
Good	33	95.2	100.5	5.3
Poor	41	88.0	88.1	0.1

Relation of Age of Placement to Gains in Intelligence Made by Children Placed in Foster Homes

Age on 2nd Test	*No. of Cases*	*Pre-test (I.Q.)*	*End Test (I.Q.)*	*Gain*
Over 12 yrs. 4 mo.	37	89.7	89.3	—0.4
Under 12 yrs. 4 mo.	37	92.8	98.0	5.2

Is a good institution better than a poor home? Chart 4.9 indicates that it is. The plan of the investigation was simple. Fifty children, mostly between 8 and 12 years of age and considered high-grade morons or borderline defectives (with an average I.Q. of 67), were tested at intervals of several years prior to admission to an institution for the high-grade feeble-minded, and at intervals after admission. The chart shows that while in inadequate homes and presumably inadequate neighbourhoods the youngsters showed a progressive decline in I.Q. But after they came to the institution this decline was arrested and the trend reversed. Other investigations have indicated that a poor institution retarded the development of ability. But in this excellent institution for high-grade moron and borderland cases effort were made to stimulate constructive activity, to approve work, and to have available a variety of opportunities.

Fifty-one other cases who showed evidence of brain damage due to injury or to disease like syphilis exhibited less loss in I.Q. in the home and no recovery in the institution. But the cases shown in the chart were rather to be described as mentally retarded, and the poor home environment had apparently been a factor in the retardation.

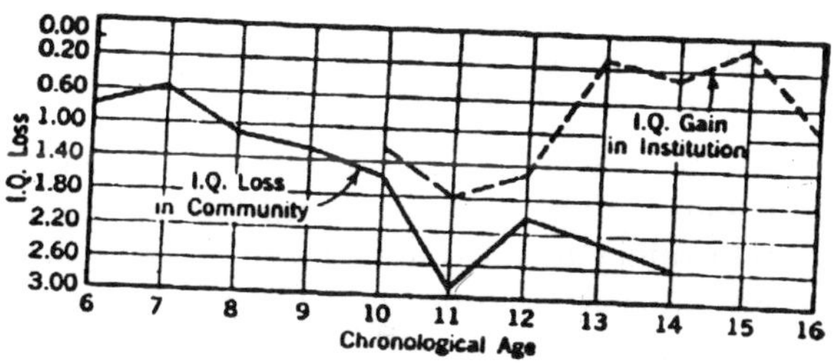

Chart 4.9—Gradual loss in I.Q. while in a poor home, and gain when put in a good institution, of 50 high-grade moron and borderline cases, as shown by repeated tests.

The Effects of Schooling upon Ability—Attention must now be turned to a question important indeed for teachers—the question as to whether schooling may raise ability. Again the problem is controversial and the evidence contradictory. The two investigations summarized in Table 4.7 may serve to illustrate both methods of research regarding the problem, and certain of the findings. Appar-

TABLE 4.7

Effects of Nursery School upon the General Ability of (1) Below-Average Children from a Poor Environment and (2) Above-Average Children from a Superior Environment[19]

	Orphanage			*University Area*			
	No.	*I.Q.*		*No.*	*I.Q,*		
	of Cases	*Begin-ning*	*End*	*of Cases*	*Begin-ning*	*End*	*3½ Yrs. Later*
Nursery school	17	92	113	29	112	126	129
Control	17	93	98	52	112	123	125
Difference		-1	15		0	3	4

ently the below-average orphanage children gained distinctly as a result of the nursery school programme. But for children already superior and from superior homes, nursery school made little difference as regards growth in ability, though gains in social adjustment may have been made.

> The orphanage group consisted of 17 youngsters just entering nursery school and 17 other orphanage children paired with them as to sex, chronological age, standing on the Merrill-Palmer scale of mental tests, and institutional experience. After the first group had been in nursery school about eight months all the children were tested again. Both groups scored higher on the second test—perhaps as a result of experience with the scale. But the nursery school group gained distinctly more.
>
> The method in the second study was essentially similar. The nursery school children entered at about 30 months of age and were tested then; they attended an average of about five semesters and were tested at various times up to about 8 years of age. They were paired with two control groups, totaling 52 cases, on the basis of I.Q. at the beginning and of parent's education. In contrast to the orphans these two groups were above average in ability at the beginning. Both groups gained in I.Q., presumably because of "increasing assimilation of the relatively high cultural levels" of their superior homes and the "intrinsic growth characteristic of an innately superior group," as well as experience with the tests. The extra gain of the nursery school children is so slight as probably not to be significant.

May the elementary or secondary school (or college) affect ability? The little evidence thus far available is contradictory. It has already been suggested that differences among states in the average intelligence of Army draftees may have been related to differences in quality and amount of schooling in those states, and that an apparent rise in average adult ability in the past twenty years may be a result of increased schooling. However, extensive data from three well-known private New York schools showed no consistent gain in I.Q. These schools served a superior group. It may well be—as suggested in considering the influence of foster homes—that the abilities of below-average retarded children might be increased slightly by schooling, though bright children from excellent homes would gain little.

The Interplay of Influences Affecting Growth of Ability in the Indi-

vidual Child—Up to now the effort in this section of the chapter has been to isolate the effects of some one factor—such as home or school—upon the development of ability. But actually various influences operate in various ways and at different times upon an individual. Only by intensive study of individual children over a period of time can something of the total dynamics of mental growth be appreciated. Chart 4.10 shows, in terms of variation from the average tested mental ability at each age, the mental growth of three children from infancy to 9 years of age. After an early superiority, Richard dropped more and more below average. From a poor start Caroline rose to the best status. From most able (on the tests used) Lawrence dropped to mediocrity. The life history of each appears largely to explain all these trends and shiftings about, and to make more understandable the total process of mental growth.

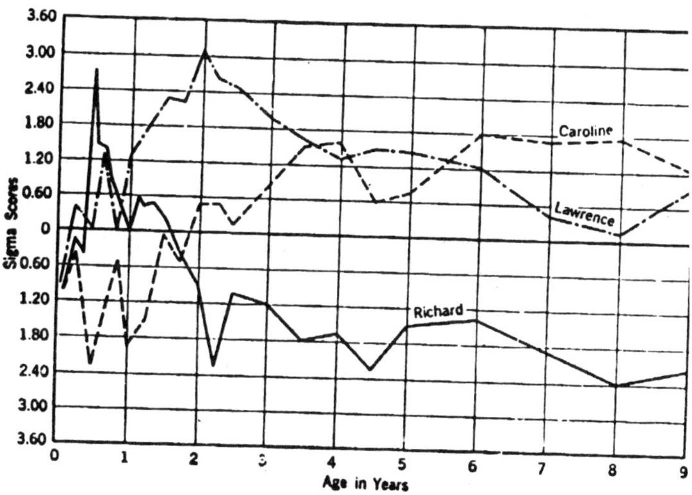

Chart 4.10—Individual trends in mental scores. (Adapted from Nancy Bailey Mental growth in young children).

Richard's parents had only an elementary school education. The father was a lumberyard worker who died when Dick was 9; since then the mother has been receiving public aid. Since Dick was a baby the family lived rent-free in a dilapidated overcrowded dirty house near freight yards, with only the street and a lumberyard to play in. The only reading matter in the house was a single book given the children by a teacher. Family life was noisy and quarrelsome; Richard was the youngest child and was alternately spoiled and spanked; his teacher has described him as nervous, inhibited, and shy. He was often ill, had double pneumonia when six, is under average in height. Clearly he has been handicapped as regards health, home, and neighbourhood; social and cultural experiences have been very limited; emotional experiences have been disturbing, and consistent motivations lacking. And constitutional capacity may not be good. Little wonder, then, that in spite of the good start the total trend is down.

In contrast, Caroline tested low at first; the examinations disturbed her and she often cried.[20] The parents are well educated and prosperous; the home is comfortable and well supplied with reading matter and other potentially educative materials. Since 4 she has suffered from asthma; this has required rest and thus she read a great deal. She has a very strong drive to excel, which apparently comes partly from jealousy of an older brother and perhaps also from feelings of insecurity with other children because of her restricted contracts with them as a result of her illnesses. In short, Caroline is a child, probably of good constitutional capacity, whose illness gives special opportunity for the development of verbal ability, and whose handicap and relations with an older brother combine to produce exceptional motivation.

Yet a third trend and pattern of influences are shown by Lawrence. The parents are highly educated and the home is beautiful and culturally stimulating. Presumably he has excellent constitutional capacity. Yet after a superior beginning his curve of ability steadily drops. His health was good during the first two years, but sundry illnesses then followed. The family is very artistic and musical; as early as two years of age Lawrence showed great interest in music, lying awake to hear his father play the violin. The boy early became adept at making costumes and toys, improvising dances, and painting. He enjoys performance tests but has little enthusiasm for predominantly verbal tests like the Binet. And he does not seem interested in getting adults' approval; hence he will not put forth much effort unless a task appeals to him. In short, Lawrence appears to be a boy of excellent constitutional capacity who comes from a fine home, whose development has been primarily along artistic lines which the tests do not measure.

The Comparative Importance of Various Factors in Determining

Realized Ability.—It should now be possible to evaluate to some extent the comparative importance of various factors in determining the ability and individual develops. Clearly most important is constitutional capacity; if that is lacking, all other factors avail little. Somewhat as some people are by constitution short in physical stature and others tall (and no amount of food or other favourable circumstance can make them taller than they were born to be), so people differ in their potentialities for intellectual stature and cannot go beyond them. But in both physique and mentality unfavourable influences may prevent that potentiality from being fully realized. Various influences operate in complex and sometimes even opposite ways in different individuals. Thus illnesses appear to have hampered the growth of Richard's abilities but to have furthered Caroline's mental development. A cultured home developed Caroline in one direction and Lawrence in another. An older sibling stimulated a strong drive to excel in Caroline but not in the other two. Clearly mental development is an exceedingly complex process affected by a multitude of factors and often in diverse ways.

THE SCHOOL AND ABILITIES

Somehow, the school should adjust to and further all the complex diverse upsurging abilities of all its pupils. Three types of problems may be distinguished.

Administrative and Supervisory Problems—As already mentioned, children in one school may average two years in age above children in another school in the same city. Fifth-grade children in one area of New York City averaged 74 I.Q., but in another area the average was 118. Obviously the teachers in the second district have very different problems from those in the first. Not only will the children in the second district learn much more readily, but almost certainly they will come from different types of homes and will have different vocational and socio-economic futures ahead of them. Both materials and methods of instruction, as well as standards, should differ greatly from one of these schools to the other. And if children from such different elementary school districts go to a common secondary school, many problems will be met there.

Obviously the work of every class should be adjusted in all these respects to the level in mental maturity of the children in it. Clearly the average 2-year-old child is just not mature enough in ability so that he can possibly learn to read, and it is futile to try to teach him to do so. Apparently "reading readiness" does not appear in the average child till around 6 or 7; not until then has he developed sufficiently in his capacity for such learning of symbols, or in his experience with words and meanings. Possibly many children's difficulties with fractions come in part from introducing that topic before they are sufficiently mature; they have not yet reached "fraction readiness."

Problems of Adjustment to Individual Differences in Abilities—Table 4.8 shows a situation that is found in most schools. Some of the first-grade children are mentally only 3 years old; obviously they are not yet sufficiently mature mentally to be ready for beginning reading. In contrast, the brightest first-grade child is up with the fifth graders in mental age, and the first-grade classwork probably seems to him unutterably infantile—somewhat like what the first grade would seem to an average fourth-grade boy. The brightest fifth graders are up with the high school ninth-grade average in mental age.

Table 4.8
Percentage of Children in the First, Fifth, and Ninth Grades of a School at Each Mental Age[21]

	Mental Age																	
	3	*4*	*5*	*6*	*7*	*8*	*9*	*10*	*11*	*12*	*13*	*14*	*15*	*16*	*17*	*18*	*19*	*Median*
First	3	15	21	34	21	4	1	1										6.2
Fifth					1	1	13	33	22	16	8	4	2					11.1
Ninth										2	7	23	23	21	14	8	2	15.8

Clearly a situation like this must not be dealt with by such radical measures as shifting a bright fifth-grade boy up to an adolescent ninth-grade group where physically and emotionally he would be greatly out of place, or humiliating the dull fifth grader by thrusting him into the company of first-grade babies. So far as possible each pupil should be studied and the school situation adjusted to his needs.

> As has already been mentioned, bright children tend to be taller and heavier, and reach puberty earlier than the average child; they also tend to be more mature in interests and social development. In every respect except birth date they *are* older. They should therefore be with children of the same developmental age rather than simply the same chronological age. Thus big, lively, self-confident Ruth, youngest of five children of a pro-

fessional man, started school in the first grade just before her sixth birthday. She returned home bursting with complaints: the other children were "such babies," the work was "silly." Quietly shifts to the second grade, she soon took a position of leadership, though still finding things too easy. But slight, anxious William, twice double-promoted by overambitious parents, is resented by the other boys in his class and can't hold his own in rough play. Soon he will move into secondary school where, a child among adolescents, he will be even more a misfit.

In the same first-grade class which Ruth scorned was little Jennie. Listless and thin, she took no part in what was going on either in class or on the playground, and became increasingly discouraged and out of touch with things as the weeks passed. She was clearly not yet ready for the work of the usual first grade and might better have spent the year in a kindergarten or pre-primary group. In the same sixth-grade class with William was a big sour fellow who was in the group but not of it. A 14-year-old lad among 11-year-olds, he had three times repeated a grade. Dull though he is, he is brighter than the educational system of which he is the victim. That is, he has sensed that the conventional school programme is not suited to him and has simply stopped trying. But the school system has *not* yet sensed that unsuitableness! However, the school did better with Joe, whose family has just moved to town. His I.Q. was found to be 86 and his scores on subject-matter tests rather low; the school nurse reported him under-weight and undernourished. Though he is a year older than the average boy in his class he fits in better with them than he would with his own age group in the next grade above.

In short, a school may make some adjustment to differences in ability by moving bright children through the conventional programme somewhat faster and dull children somewhat slower than average. But it must be careful that social maladjustment is not brought about thereby, nor feelings of conceit or inferiority. Furthermore, the school class in which the child is put may not be much better suited to him than that in which his chronological age would place him. Thus the work of the third grade is no better suited to big sour William than is that of the sixth; he needs a special programme, largely of pre-vocational handwork, to fit him for the kind of simple job to which he will go before long.

Instead of the rate of movement through the school programme being varied all pupils of the same age might be kept together but the work individualized, each child so far as possible doing what is best suited to his abilities and interests at his level. But this procedure also runs into difficulties. Children *do* develop at different rates, and chronological age is a crude basis of classification which neglects this fact. The burden on the teacher is great.

> Miss Jones is working early and late, trying to individualize the work of her sixth-grade pupils. She has an "enriched" programme of special reading for brilliant Jeannette. But the girl is unappreciative. "Why should I be asked to do a lot of extra work just because I'm bright!" she says angrily. She is big for her age and has already reached puberty; she feels out of place and wants to be in junior high school, where most of her friends are. Little Marie is not so dull that she does not uncomfortably sense how things are being made especially easy for her; much of the time she feels uncomprehending and left out; when she can, she plays with younger children.

A compromise of sorts regarding these various difficulties may be reached by ability grouping. Thus there may be slow, average, and fast sections or classes. The first group has "minimum essentials" and may take seven years for the first six grades. The fast section may do these same grades in five years with an enriched programme. But unfortunate attitudes may be set up in both children and parents by this grouping, the bases for which may be recognized. And marked in individual differences will still remain within each group. Nevertheless, different classes and programmes may make possible a more adequate meeting of different needs than would otherwise be possible.

For best adjustment to ability, the following seem required: (1) Total development in physique and social status as well as ability must always be taken into account. (2) Flexibility should be great, and adjustments of various kinds so common as to be taken for granted. Thus some acceleration of children of all-round superior development should be common enough not to arouse comments; extra time and help and a somewhat different programme for those having some difficulty should also be a common and accepted thing in the school. Flexibility is especially important in view of the recent evidence that individuals may differ in rate of mental growth from time to time (see charts 4.4, 4.6, 4.10). (3) Not simply differences in amount or rate but rather differences in type of education according to need is the most important consideration in adjusting education to abilities.

Twelve-year-old Sam (I.Q. 78) is on of the large family of a factory worker just moved into a ramshackle house on the edge of town. Sam reads only very slowly, is dirty, frequently truant, and tough; as soon as possible he wants to leave school and get a job. Raymond (I.Q. 128) is also 12; he is an only son of the town's leading lawyer, finds school too easy for his own good, and is a little slick; he plans to enter his father's profession. Sam needs tactful help on care of his person and on manners and conduct. He needs companionship with other boys not so different from him but that he can be comfortable with them. He needs special help on reading. Planning with reference to pre-vocational courses in junior high school is in order. Raymond's personal and educational needs are very different. It will be much easier to help Sam in a small "adjustment" class made up mostly of other children of war industry workers recently come to town than in a heterogenous group that throws all these pupils together.

The Nurture of Abilities—It was argued at the beginning of this chapter that the abilities which an individual showed in dealing with problems depended most upon his constitutional capacity and also upon his fund of relevant information, his efficiency in attacking problems, and the extent to which his emotions stimulated or interfered with his efforts. Experiments were cited to indicate that unfavourable conditions might limit the growth of abilities and that improvement of those conditions might bring about more growth. Growth of ability, as of any organic entity, depends upon both heredity and environment. In the last section detailed case studies suggested that more adequate knowledge of these processes of growth might make it possible for the school still more to further them.

> Thus 12-year-old Sam mentioned in the preceding paragraph might gain nothing and even be antagonized and discouraged by a conventional school programme. But if his reading difficulty were remedied, his confidence restored, and his interest stimulated by work which he felt he wanted to do, his abilities might grow appreciably (perhaps his I.Q. might go from 78 to 85, or from "inferior" to "low average")—somewhat as he might grow in physique if given an adequate, vitamin-rich diet instead of the greasy fried stuff which was his usual meal at home. In

neither physique nor ability could he exceed his constitutional potentialities, but in both respects there was room for decided improvement.

Chapter 2 mentioned that, presumably as a result of better nutrition and conditions of living, college students of today are over an inch taller and several pounds heavier than their parents. As mentioned earlier, adult "intelligence" in this country seems to be higher now than twenty years ago, possibly as a result of the increase in time and resources devoted to education and the rise in the general level of culture in this country over that period. Surely, further gains in average ability may be expected in the future.[22]

SUMMARY

The topic treated in this chapter is complex and the materials presented do not always permit clear-cut conclusions. But when the material is reviewed, certain general trends and conclusions appear with some clearness. They may be briefly summarized as follows:

1. In everyday life the meaning of ability is fairly well understood: an individual's abilities are shown by the extent to which he can deal effectively with situations and problems in his daily life. Four major factors affecting ability can be fairly well distinguished. Some individuals are more and some less informed about the problems with which they have to deal. Some tackle those problems with more and some with less effective methods. Some are stimulated, but others are distracted or blocked by emotional situations. And—most important of all—some individuals constitutionally are more and some less capable. These four factors are fairly generally recognized as involved in ability in general. Similar factors are involved in special abilities or disabilities. Thus the person with great artistic ability has usually had much acquaintance with art, has artistic "know how," has great interest in art, and also innate capacity possibly of a somewhat special nature. The individual who is especially lacking in mechanical ability usually has had little opportunity to become familiar with mechanical devices, has not learned how to "take hold" of mechanical problems, feels hesitant and timid about dealing with machinery and tools, and perhaps may lack some special aptitude in such matters—though usually the first three factors account for the difficulty.

2. Appraisal of a pupil's abilities may be made by a teacher on

the basis of her total acquaintance with him. But such judgments (even though guided by the use of rating schemes) are subject to errors of prejudice or inadequate information and are at best rough and hardly comparable from one teacher to another. Various tests have therefore been developed. Interview examinations like the Binet are given to individual pupils by specially trained examiners; their results have comparatively high accuracy. There are also group tests which can be given to entire classes at one time, and tests of special abilities or disabilities as in arithmetic, reading, music, or mechanical aptitudes. Such tests have great value. It must be realized, however, that persons in some respect especially handicapped (for instance, by deafness or by living in some extremely isolated section of the country) cannot be measured entirely satisfactorily by such instruments.

3. Abilities grow and reach an adult level, much as physique grows and matures. There are great individual differences in growth. The feeble-minded have a slower growth rate as well as a lower level of maturity, whereas brilliant children's abilities usually show both rapid and early growth. During the school years the abilities of pupils are thus constantly growing but at different rates in different children and with great individual differences at any given age.

4. People vary enormously in ability— from the idiot to the genius. In general, people in better socio-economic groups are apt to show better ability. And, as a rule, ability appears to run in families.

5. In general, ability appears to be relatively unaffected by health. But early and debilitating illness or accident probably does hamper the growth of abilities. A very inadequate home or neighbourhood environment or inadequate schooling may handicap the development of ability somewhat. However, the major factor in mental growth is quite clearly constitutional capacity or potentiality. Favourable circumstances may assure the realization of the individual's potentialities but those potentialities can hardly be increased.

6. Different schools show differences in the average ability of the children. In a given class the children vary greatly in ability. Different grades markedly overlap; thus some third-grade children may be above the average sixth-grade child in ability. Such a child cannot be advanced in school in proportion to his ability for fear of social maladjustment. But maladjustment will also follow if each child's ability is not recognized. A flexible system of progress through school

which will take account, with the best compromise possible, of each child's total stage of development seems best. It must be recognized that children of different abilities have different futures to prepare for. A bright child is headed perhaps for a profession; a dull child, toward some type of unskilled work. Though constitutional capacity cannot be increased, by bringing it about that children will more adequately realize their potentialities an increase in the general level of abilities is possible.

REFERENCES

1. It is strongly urged that the instructor demonstrate giving the revised Stanford-Binet tests and have a sufficient number of the complete blanks so that each student may have a copy while the examination is going on. The examples above are of items that are in both the revised and the original Stanford-Binet, and thus illustrate the nature of both forms. The content of the revised form is distinctive especially in the amount of material for ages 2 to 5 (six tests for each half-year) and the use of toys and other materials at these early ages both to interest the child and to escape excessive verbal material.
2. As a matter of detail, in the lowest years the tests are in half-year groups in order to give more adequate testing in those first years of most rapid growth. And there are three "superior adult" groups for better measurement of very bright older children and adults. The month equivalents of each test at these two extremes will thus be given different values than "two months." For such details, the Terman-Merrill book (54) should be consulted.
3. Terman now considers the average adult level of ability to be 15 (not reached till 16) and therefore uses 15 as the chronological age in calculating the I.Q. of persons chronologically 16 or over. For details, the Terman-Merrill book (54) should be consulted. The problems of adult mental level will be returned to later in this chapter.
4. Tests of very young children are necessarily largely individual performance tests—handling a cup, piling blocks, playing peek-a-boo, and so on. The reader interested in nursery school will find of distinct interest the little stunts of the Merrill-Palmer scale (Stutsman), the Minnesota Pre-School tests (Goodenough), and the California Pre-School schedule (MacFarlane). As already mentioned, the revised Stanford-Binet goes down to two years, making use of sundry performance items in these early ages.
5. The student should procure or look over two or three sample group intelligence tests such as the series of Detroit Intelligence Tests, Pressey's Classification Tests (both published by the Public School

Publishing Company, Bloomington, Illinois), the California Test of Mental Maturity (California Test Bureau, Los Angeles), or the Otis Quick-scoring Mental Ability Tests (World Book Company, Yonkers, New York). The McCall, Herring, Loftus Comprehensive Battery (Laidlow Brothers, Chicago) may serve as an example of a test of ability in combination with tests of other types.

6. Adapted from material in *Sixth Graders Twelve Years Later*, a bulletin of the Regional Department of Economic Security, Cincinnati, Ohio, 1938, 81 pp. The delinquency figures cover all cases in the original group having juvenile delinquency records (7 per cent). The remainder of the data covers only the 2485 cases still alive in 1936 and for whom information was found (60 per cent of the original of all sixth graders tested twelve years before). Median age of this last group was 24 years 3 months on March 1, 1936; 6 per cent were coloured.
7. W. C. Bagley, Do good schools pay? *J. of the Nat. Ed. Assoc.,* 1923, 12, 211-216.
8. Beyond the scope of this volume but nevertheless of great importance both theoretically and practically is the question as to what does happen to abilities through adult life. Quite clearly ability does cease to grow, somewhat as height and strength cease to grow. Through adult life the individual continues learning and understanding and doing, but he does not *increase* in his ability to learn and understand and do. In fact, as he gets over into the older ages, his abilities may decrease—somewhat as his strength and vigor do. But again the various factors involved in ability must be kept in mind. Not only decrease in intellectual capacity but also failure to keep broadly informed and to maintain effective work habits and motivations are probably involved. Obviously attempts should then be made to maintain adult abilities at a higher level than most older people do. For a discussion of these last questions the reader is referred to (43).
9. Tests of special ability tend to show that boys and men are more mechanical. But this fact may be due to more contact with and expected interest in mechanical matters among boys rather than to any constitutional greater mechanical capacity. Girls usually score higher in verbal tests.
10. The curves for the English data show mental growth as beginning slowly; "to assume that growth ... starts suddenly at birth with maximum speed seems scarcely plausible" (8, p. 644). For an excellent technical treatment of the growth curve the reader is referred to (8), pp. 643-657.
11. The table is adapted from material in M. A. Merrill, The significance of I.Q's on revised Stanford-Binet scales, *J. Ed. Psychol.*, 1938, 29, 641-651; M. Teagarden. *Child Psychology for Professional Workers*, Prentice-Hall, New York, 1940, p. 405; and Douglas Fryer and E. J. Sparling, Intelligence and occupational adjustment, *Occupations*, 1934, 12, 55-63. The writers

wish to express their obligation to Dr. Francis N. Maxfield for his aid in the preparation of this table.

12. There *should* be as broad a consideration of the very capable children. They should be differentiated as not only high scorers on tests but also individuals of special balance and good judgment. And they should receive as much careful study and have as many special efforts made to develop *their* full potentialities as is at present the case with the feeble-minded and the delinquent. The returns from such special efforts to deal adequately with the very able would be many times as great as from such investment in the most stupid.
13. Modified from (54), p. 48.
14. The table shows that two pupils in the first class scored between 40 and 44, four children scored in the 45-49 group, and so on. An asterisk marks the group in which the median falls, in each class.
15. Adapted from (21, p. 716)
16. Dr. F. N. Maxfield tells of a number of instances where one identical twin, catching a glimpse of himself in a mirror, has thought that it was the other twin and spoken to him or advanced to meet him.
17. It might be argued that the decrease is due to the undoubted fact that the tests were less satisfactory for mountain children (and more generally for rural children) at the older ages. Such considerations must not be forgotten, but the findings can hardly be dismissed on such grounds. The range of material in this interesting chart must be emphasized. The 339 Kentucky children were given the relatively simple straightforward Myers Mental Measure, the Tennessee children the more varied Dearborn group test, and the Massachusetts boys a variety of group tests of general ability. Different mountain children were tested at each age, but the same Massachusetts boys were tested every year for ten years. The variety of the data here compressed into a single chart, all bearing on the same problem and yielding a nice balance of conclusions regarding it, would appear exceptional. What this balanced conclusion should be is a matter which will be discussed shortly.
18. Adapted from (18).
19. Adapted from (3), and from (39), Part II, pp. 207-222.
20. Examination of infants is of course difficult and subject to many hazards of cooperativeness and special circumstance—as in this case distraction by the presence of an older brother during some of the early tests.
21. Adapted from L. M. Terman, The use of intelligence tests in the grading of school children, *J. Educ. Res.*, 1920, *I*, 20-32.
22. For an interesting discussion of this question, see the material on "Nature and Nurture" in W. S. Monroe (ed.), *Encyclopedia of Educational Research*, Macmillan, New York, 1940.

5

Development of Interests

As emphasized in Chapter II, the school years are a time of extraordinary upsurging growth; from 6 to 18 the youngster triples his weight, increases in strength still more, is physiologically made over in proportion and tissue. It is inevitable that such a dynamic expanding organism should have strong wants and desires, and be exuberantly active, like a puppy. What are these wants and desires, and what directions do these activities take? These questions might seem relatively simple. But education has shown an amazing capacity for either neglecting them or assuming wrong answers—or even doing both things at once!

The problem is a very practical one for every teacher. She wishes to find the interests of her pupils and to relate the school work to those interests. She wants her pupils to be active in the work of the school. If she bores them or tries to get them to do what is not natural to them (or, worst of all, tries to make these wriggling human puppies be still), there will be trouble. The pupils will not learn. They are likely to be unruly. Here are the difficulties which most commonly cause teachers to fail.

A careful empirical inquiry as to children's interests and "natural" activities would thus seem worth while. The children may be asked what they like to do, or they may be watched to see what they do when they are free to do as they wish. Data may be gathered as to what they read, or say they enjoy reading. Similar data may be gathered about radio programmes or moving pictures. An apparatus may be used that literally measures which movies stir their pulses most. The topics they choose for school themes may show what concerns them. The investigator may even go straight up to them and ask in so many words what their interests are. The result of these various inquiries must now be looked at.

> Like the shrewd little sinners they are, children will often deceive the investigator. They will check Shakespeare as much liked and never mention *True Romances.* The blunt investigator may find few high school girls checking "sex" on an interest questionnaire. Often the investigator will be puzzled as to whether an activity is to be considered a basic interest or only a fad or fashion. Many children seem to have no interests of their own but simply go along with the situation in which they find themselves—playing whatever games others may suggest, reading what may come to hand (and is easy), seeing whatever is showing at the local movie house, tuning in whatever may be on the radio at the moment. But from careful sifting of the total mass of all such data information of great value may well be hoped for.

PLAY

If play is defined as what a person does because he likes to, a survey of play might be expected to suggest something as to what those likes may be, and what activities are natural and pleasant. Such surveys may be made in various ways. Children may be watched when at play to see what they do. They may be asked to list things they like to do, or to check, on a list of play activities, what they like or do frequently. Play of different individuals, neighbourhoods, communities, nations, or races may be compared to see what characteristics seem universal and presumably basic, and what factors influence it. From the total of such data, valuable understandings of child nature should come.

> The topic is a fascinating one for retrospection upon one's own childhood. The reader will find it interesting to go back in memory and list those things he did at various ages, in the country and city, on the school playground and in the neighbourhood, in the winter and during the summer vacation. These reminiscences may well go back to an obscure memory of the pleasure, at the age of 3 or 4, of blowing a whistle or digging in the sand or scuffling through autumn leaves or wading, the later joy of running with a wagon or coasting on a sled, the satisfaction of shooting with bow and arrow or slingshot, build-

ing a hut, or inconsequential ranging through the woods. Simple games gradually appear—hide and seek, anty-over, or run-sheep-run. Later, team games, such as baseball and football, come to have a dominant appeal. And there is the new embarrassing, exquisite pleasure of companionship with the other sex. The making and scanning of such a catalogue of childhood and youthful delights will doubtless bring no little amusement and reminiscent pleasure, with which there will be mixed a certain wistfulness and lingering nostalgia.

Changes in Play with Age—A natural first question regards the changes in play which come with age. The baby's play will obviously be very simple. Playing with hands and feet (and seriously contemplating them) is common at 4 months. By about 6 months the youngster begins to pat the table with his hands and bang with spoon or rattle; by about 9 months he has learned that objects fall when brushed aside—and for some reason takes delight in hearing them fall (25). At about one year of age there begins to appear activities of types more commonly spoken of as play, such as manipulation of blocks. By 3 years of age the nursery school youngster dabs paint on large sheets of paper to make blobby "pictures," hammers at a nail in a piece of board, climbs in the jungle gym, and may earnestly enjoy riding nowhere, round and round, on a tricycle.

Elementary or secondary school youngsters, however, rather than nursery school babies are probably the concern of most readers of this volume. What are the outstandingly important features in the development of play through the school years? Table 5.1 should be of service here; it is from an extensive study of play based on 26,056 reports of play activities, from children in the primary grades to students at a state university. The little tots below the third grade were each asked individually to mention what he or she liked best to do; from the third grade on the pupils checked the three activities they most liked, on a carefully prepared list of 200 play activities (39). The table shows, in order of frequency of mention, the ten activities most often preferred by each sex at ages 5, 10, 15, and 20.

Some of the activities, like reading the newspaper, might not be thought of as play; but a merit of the inquiry is that it was broad and included a great variety of leisure-time activities. The data were gathered mostly in Kansas in 1923-1926; doubtless a similar inquiry now would show the girls listening to the radio more and playing the piano less, and if made in New York or Cali-

TABLE 5.1
The Ten Most Popular Play Activities at Ages 5, 10, 15, 20[2]

Boys	*Girls*
5 Years	
Playing with a ball	Playing house
Playing with blocks	Playing with dolls
Playing with a wagon	Playing with a ball
Playing house	Playing school
Playing horse	Drawing
Hide-and-seek	Mulberry bush
Palying tag	Playing with blocks
Drawing	Skipping
Playing school	Making things
Playing in sand pile	Jumping rope
10 Years	
Football	Playing the piano
Baseball	Going to the movies
Boxing	Looking at the "funny" paper
Just playing catch	Playing with dolls
Riding a bicycle	Roller skating
Basketball	Riding in an automobile
Wrestling	Reading books
Paying cowboy	Playing school
Roller skating	Jacks
Marbls	Listening to the victrola
15 Years	
Basketball	Reading books
Football	Going to the movies
Baseball	Social dancing
Driving an automobile	Playing the pinao
Tennis	Riding in an automobile
Watching athletic sports	Having dates
Hunting	Watching athletic sports
Going to the movies	Going to parties, picnics
Boxing	Basketball
Reading books	Doing gymnasium work
20 Years	
Having "dates"	Social dancing
Watching athletic sports	Playing the piano
Football	Having "dates"
Basketball	Going to entertainments, etc.
Listening to the radio	Just "hiking" or strolling
Going to the movies	Going to the movies
Driving an automobile	Reading books
Reading the newspaper	Watching athletic sports
Tennis	Card games
Baseball	Riding in an automobile

fornia it might include swimming rather than hunting. Differences from one locality and time to another will be returned to later. But in general the lists remain valuable evidence of the trend of leisure-time interests through the first 20 years.

As already mentioned, 5-year-olds like to play with blocks. They also like to imitate adults in simple ways such as playing house,[1] and to play simple games like tag. Much of the 5-year-old's play is such that he can play by himself. By the age of 10, boys prefer play recreations like playing football, riding a bicycle, or playing cowboy. At 15 active team games continue to head the list, but passive amusements such as watching athletic events, going to the movies, and reading books appear among the ten most popular recreations. By 20 the sex-social interests of having dates and watching sports hold first and second places—and much of the interest in such sports as football is of the watcher rather than participator type.[3] Five-year-old girls play in much the same simple fashion as boys of the same age. In middle childhood and adolescence they differ from the boys in the less active and less competitive nature of their play activities and the earlier appearance and greater prominence of sex-social interests (a fact which might well be related to earlier physical maturing in the girls). By 20 these sex-social interests are outstanding.

If all these data regarding play over the first 20 years are reviewed, two phases of its development seem to emerge: (1) Over the years of rapid physical growth (roughly from babyhood through 15 to 18) there is a parallel growth in the vigour and the complexity or metal level of play. (2) With adolescence and the slowing down of the vigorous onrush of growth, sex-social interests tend to dominate leisure-time activities, and participation in very active sports is less general.

The decrease of interest in active and relatively simple sports and its increase in social affairs which involved companionship with the other sex, also the earlier and more marked appearance of this last type of interest in the girls, are shown in the Chart 5.1. Students from the sixth grade through college were asked to go over a list of 90 amusements and recreations, checking those in which they were interested and double-checking those which interested them very much. The curves show total number of checks per 100 students, thus combining in one "score" the number of individuals interested and the degree of their interest. Whenever the score goes above 100 it is clear that some were very interested (double-checked) in that item.[4]

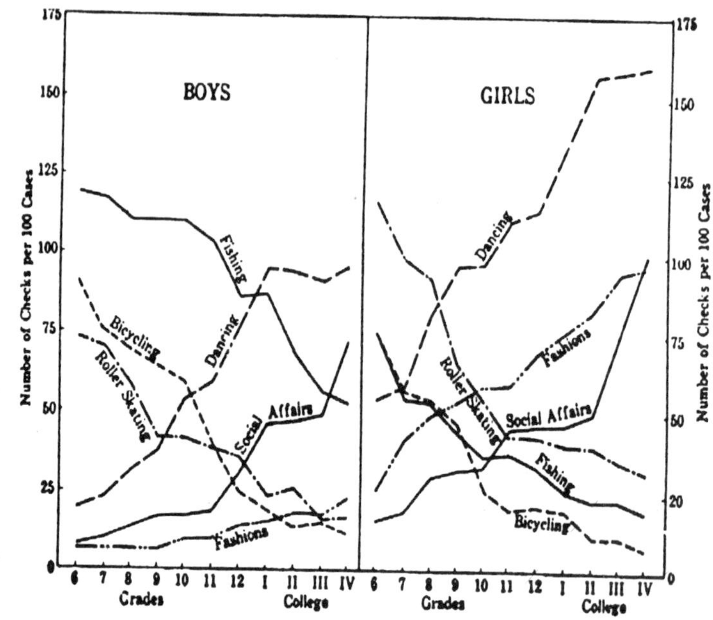

Chart 5.1—Changs in certain interests with age as shown by number of checks for each interest per 100 students at each grade from the sixth through college. The students were directed to check those items in which they were interested, and to double check those in which they were very much interested. (From unpublished data, 4187 cases, obtained with the Pressey Interest-Attitude Tests.)

The extensive investigation of play first referred to in this chapter showed that the number of different play activities which each youngster checked as those "in which he had engaged on his own volition during the week preceding" dropped from a median of about 40 for the 8-year-olds to 18 by the age of 20. As shown in Chart 5.2, the change was gradual. The great differences among the younger children are also to be noted; thus the 25-75 percentile range is 28 at 8 years as compared with 11 at 20. Apparently children 8 or 9 years old engage in a variety of relatively simple activities. Gradually some games and amusements are dropped, some centered upon, until by his last years in high school the average individual's leisure activities have been largely conventionalized to a relatively few generally popular (almost socially necessary) habits of recreation. These recreations are also conventional topics of conversation and become part of the American way of life; baseball and golf and bridge and movie-going are part of American culture.

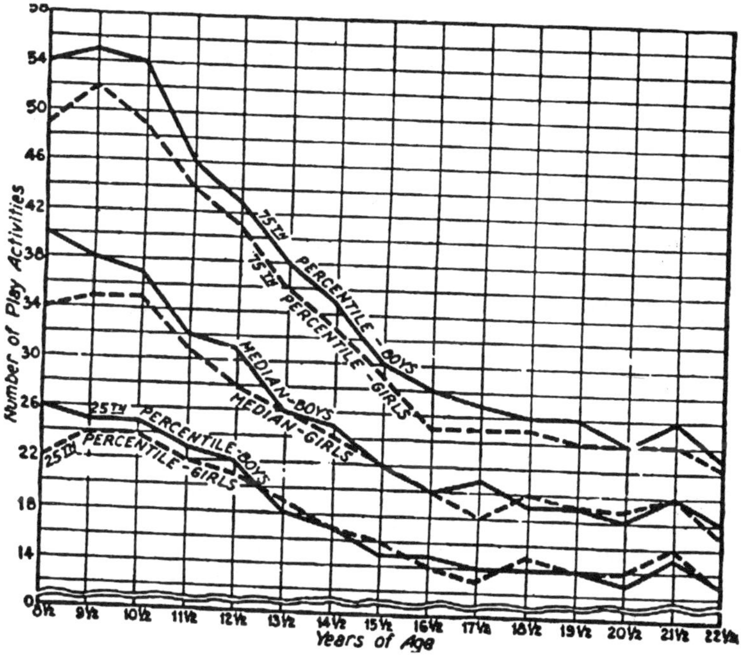

Chart 5.2—Change with age in the number of different play activities engaged in. (From Lehman and Witty [39].)

Though usually not a matter of consideration, teachers should be concerned as to the leisure-time activities of out-of-school youth. These activities are a further development of the trends so far presented. And they exhibit problems which the schools should face. The data in Table 5.2 are from an investigation in which over 13,000 Maryland young people between the ages of 16 and 24 were individually interviewed, asked questions, and given an opportunity to express themselves.

The paucity of interests of those with sixth-grade education or less—largest portion of the time spent in loafing—is the most striking item. Presumably with the low educational status there tends to be associated low intellectual ability, low socio-economic status, and low family morale. But surely the situation shown in the table need not be thought of as inevitable. Sample replies may make the situation more concretely real. An 18-year-old farm labourer said his spare time was spent "piddling around visiting, and reading." Another boy said, "I play cards, loaf, eat, and sleep"; another, "I sit in the barber shop." A 22-year-old unemployed boy of ninth-grade education spent his time "reading and sitting around home and listening to the radio. I try to be as little expense as I can to my mother". Apparently the development of leisure-time activities and interests, which went on more or less satisfactorily through the school years, is for many blocked off after leaving school. Especially do sex-social opportunities appear to be lacking.

TABLE 5.2

Principal Leisure-time Activities of Out-of-school Youth According to the School Grades They Completed[5]

	6th Grade or Less	*9th 10th 11th*	*4 or More Years Beyond High School Grad.*
Loafing	22%	8%	4%
Dancing, dating	13	16	8
Individual sports	12	16	18
Reading	11	23	43
Team games	10	9	4
Movies	9	13	8
Hobbies	9	8	10
Other activities	9	4	2
Listening to radio	3	2	1
Quiet games	2	1	2
Total	100	100	100
Number of youth	1483	2569	396

Aptitudes, Abilities, and Play—By now it should be clear that the development of play is affected by various factors. A natural first question is as to the relation of intelligence to play. It is often supposed that bright children tend to play much less than "normal" youngsters. Research does not show this to be true. Children who are ahead of the average grade for their age do not as a group show either fewer play activities or more solitary play; in short, a moderate acceleration of healthy bright children in school seems to do no harm to their play life.[6] Exceptionally intelligent children read more and, apparently largely as a result of this fact, engage somewhat less frequently than average children in social and very active games, but they enter into about the same total number of play activities. Duller children and children behind in school grade read less and engage more in social and active games (39). All this very understandable. They are poor readers, and finding little success in school they turn to activities where they can to a greater degree "make good."

Special aptitude as in music naturally will affect the direction of play activities; almost inevitably special aptitude in athletics will do so. Very important but little studied is the effect of special handicaps on recreation. The boy who cannot see a ball well enough to hit or catch it will play little baseball; glasses are something of a nuisance in rough-and-tumble games. The play of children lacking in health or vigor will be less vigorous. Recreational programmes should be adapted to such youngsters much more than they usually are.

The Influence of Environment on Play—The effect of different types of environment on play is a matter of great practical and also great theoretical importance. Certain contrasts between town and country children shown by the Lehman and Witty investigation are of interest here. In general, country children play games of a less highly organized and team character, presumably partly because there are fewer children in a given age group to make up a team and less opportunity for different groups to compete, and partly because in a play group of mixed ages the games have to be simple enough for the younger children to play. Thus, 41 per cent of the rural children between the ages of 10 and 15 played "Blackman," as compared with 7 per cent of the town children; 35 per cent played "Teeter-totter," as compared with 10 per cent of the city children. Country boys naturally hunt more than city boys; country children of both sexes indulge more in mildly boisterous behaviour such as whistling and singing, they more often climb things, they ride horseback more but bicycle less. An average of 40 per cent fewer of the country children between the ages of 8 and 15 went to the movies in a week than did city children; the distance of the country children from the movies is the obvious major explanation. In view of the manifold influence of the movies (to be discussed shortly) in giving vicarious compensatory experience and in modifying attitudes, ideals, and standards of living, such differences are of decided importance.

Other factors of physical environment or circumstance are important. Thus if streams or lakes are nearby, swimming, canoeing, fishing, skating, and building rafts and making precarious journeys thereon are likely to be common activities, but otherwise they are hardly possible. The exhilaration of skating and skiing, the thrill of bobsledding, and the sociability of the sleigh ride and obviously not possible in a southern climate. The lack of such winter sports would seem, to anyone who has grown up in the enjoyment of them, to make the total character of child life in the South a bit different from childhood in a northern state. Other factors are more special. Play, both at school and at home, is varied according to the nature of the play space and according as various facilities such as sandpile or baseball diamond are available. It should be noted that these facilities have multiple effects. For example, it has been observed that, with younger children, the sandpile or the seesaw tends much more to bring children together sociably in their play than do dolls or a blackboard.

Fads, Fashions, and Conventions in Play—Play thus varies with the physical and intellectual development of the child, and with physical environment. A third important influence is social. Here it must first be noted that there are fashions and fads among children as well as in the adult world, and also that games and other play activities may be handed down from one child generation to another;[7] in short, that in their play children are greatly influenced by one another.

> In the boyhood of one of the writers it was the fashion (he has not found it in any other community) for boys in middle childhood to build what were known as lath tracks on which a peculiar form of railroad was played. It was also the fashion to build "cubbies," which were simply holes in the ground roofed over with planks covered with dirt, with a fireplace in a corner, the use of which made the hole almost uninhabitable., Sometimes a vigorous child leader has an important effect on play, carrying a group to dramatic Indian raids or the construction of a nondescript "club house."

Fads and conventions may operate either to extend or to limit the variety of play. Thus Lehman and Witty found that in certain schools many of the younger girls enjoyed turning handsprings; this activity was traced to the influence of a private class for aesthetic dancing which some of the girls had been attending. A study of children in summer camps showed that upon arrival they checked baseball and other conventional pastimes on the camp "interest-finder," but after they had been in camp, awhile many of them became greatly interested in handicrafts. Children old enough to regard sand play as "baby stuff" became interested in it when a camp counsellor showed them possibilities which challenged them.

Certain larger cultural influences upon play also deserve mention. The organized team game seems to be largely an Anglo-Saxon product. American collegians prefer football, whereas the youthful intelligentsia in Germany before the war had a special fondness for dueling and the French preferred tennis to play between groups. But all this was presumably not because German or French youths lacked some mysterious instinct or ability which tended to make English and American boys peculiarly fond of team games. Rather the explanation was to be found in differences in climate, in the size and character of the leisure class, and especially in the largely unknown development of the conventions of amusement. It must be further observed that these differences are being rapidly modified. American baseball has no very long history, and its amazing popularity in Japan before the war came about in a short period of time. The great interest in golf in the United States is comparatively a recent phenomenon. In short, there is every evidence that the form which the play life of a community or a nation takes is determined by influences which are best described as cultural; certain conventions are developed with respect to sport and amusement.

> The writers are inclined to believe that the competitive character of much American play is to be regarded as such a convention: After all, many recreational activities, such as fishing, canoeing, hiking, dancing, and singing, are not competitive. The tendency to identify play with competitive games and sports may be partly a product of our highly individualistic and competitive socio-economic mode of life. It is probably more a result of newspaper publicity for sports, advertising of sporting goods manufacturers and bridge system authors, and exploitation of sports by schools. The present emphasis on the competitive in recreation seems to be relatively recent[8] and, on the whole, unfortunate.

Sex Differences in Play—The various ways in which environmental influences may work are well illustrated by the development of sex differences in play. Dolls are given to girls but not to boys, and girls are commended for playing with them, whereas boys who do so are made fun of by both adults and other children; parents even go so far as to take dolls away from boys who enjoy such inappropriate amusement. Boys are given carpenter's tools, mechanical toys, footballs, guns, and books about science, war, travel, sport, and adventure. The father enjoys baseball and he takes the boy—but not the girl—to watch games; he plays catch with the boy. For a boy to engage in rough-and-tumble sports in considered only fitting and proper. But girls may be scolded if they indulge in rough tomboy play. However, increasingly in recent years—and with accelerated pace as a result of the war—these influences are changing. New freedom as regards dress and manners, and opportunities for girls in sports, are making girls more active. New occupations for women may affect the play of girls. And it will increasingly be apparent that sex differences in play, except as they are the product of a slightly earlier puberty and a slightly smaller physique and strength among girls, are primarily a product of convention.[9]

Play and Adult Life—Extremely important and much neglected is the extent to which the play of children is an imitation of adult activity. Children play doctor or soldier or policeman; they play store; they are interested in dramatic activities like aviation. Prominent events such as war may greatly influence their play. Local adult life has its immediate effect upon child play, as in the imitation of local industries or episodes. Such play can obviously be made educative. It should be noted that this play usually mimics not only adult activities out also the attitudes, prejudices, and moral code of the adult group concerned.

Finally, both child and adult play are greatly influenced, more or less directly and obviously, by commercial attempts to make a profit out of amusements. Yo-Yo and Chinese checkers have a vogue for a while; kiddie cars, roller skates, and Pandas have become almost standard appurtenances of childhood. The ubiquitous newspaper and radio publicity for sports, moving pictures, and night clubs modifies youth and adult alike.

> Because these social determiners of play have been so much neglected but are so important for an understanding of the educational potentialities of play, the reader should make a special effort to make real to himself in recollection of his own experiences the importance of such influences in determining amusement. The analysis of one boyhood showed the following: Fads for stamp collecting and for the catching and imprisonment of grasshoppers in small screen-covered boxes had their vogue. The popularity of the air rifle and of that pestiferous concealed weapon, the rubber-band slingshot, played a large part in boyhood episodes. An international boat race once set every boy to making model boats; the building of a new railroad bridge nearby caused the erection of numerous miniature derricks and

bridges. The war set all the boys to soldiering; the reading of Scott's *Ivanhoe* in school led to the brandishing of wooden swords and lances throughout the neighbourhood.

Individual Differences—The preceding pages have outlined general trends in the growth of interests as shown by play activities, and discussed major factors affecting that growth. But, as always, the reader must keep in mind that individual differences and variations from these general trends are great.

Thus Lehman and Witty (39) found that most games were indulged in by less than half the children of a given age. Differences in the number of games or amusements engaged in were great; for example, some 5 per cent of the children between 8 and 9 years of age reported 10 or less different play activities in a given week, while, at the other extreme, about the same percentage checked more than 80 different kinds of play engaged in by them during the week. Children differ greatly in the extent to which they play with other children. These same investigators found that through the ages from 7 to 19 slightly over half of the average individual's play activities were with other people. But 7 per cent of the 8-year-old children and 10 per cent of the 15-year-olds showed less than a quarter of their play activities to be with other youngsters, as against 26 per cent of 8-year-olds, and 13 per cent of the 15-year-olds who reported three-fourths or more of their play as activities in which other children took part.

In the secondary school, as interests become increasingly sex-social and socio-recreational status claims attention as never before, such individual differences often present difficult problems. Athletics bring some a heady prominence. Recreations are largely competitive and society is sophisticated. Those who "belong" live in a feverish little world of games, dances, dates, and other activities. Though often little noticed, however, the number of students who are outside all this, starved and miserable socially and recreationally, is great. One sample investigation showed 67 per cent of boys and 62 per cent of girls in the freshman year in a high school who never attended dances, and 46 and 40 per cent respectively in the senior year (45).

In college and university the diversity may be even greater. An investigation at the University of Minnesota showed half the freshmen participating in no activity, but 2 per cent participating in four or more activities (11). By the senior year a quarter of the students were still not taking part in any campus activity. At

Ohio State University 22 per cent of a large group of seniors reported that they had not during the past year engaged in any sports, 33 per cent had not played any indoor games (such as bridge), 25 per cent belonged to no social organization; of the senior men, 27 per cent had been to no dance and 24 per cent had had no date during the previous month. Here clearly are problems for a constructively guided socio-recreational programme.

All such material suggests that data regarding an individual's recreational activities should yield valuable information about him. Especially should such information be indicative as regards his social adjustment. This will be returned to in the next chapter.

RELATIONS OF READING, MOVING PICTURES, AND RADIO TO INTERESTS

So far the chapter has dealt broadly with the various things people do when they do what they want to, as evidence of interests. Stress has been on the more active uses of leisure time. Now attention must be turned to certain topics which have already appeared in the catalogue of uses of leisure but which are passive amusements and are both sufficiently special and sufficiently important to deserve separate treatment.

Such interests can be investigated in various ways. Simplest and therefore most widely used is direct inquiry; pupils are asked to list books they have read, movies seen, or radio programmes listened to or most enjoyed, or to check lists of such books or programmes, or to tell why they like the books or movies or programmes they prefer. Reading preferences may be determined by the use of books in libraries or the circulation of magazines; movie interests, by attendance; radio listening, by telephone inquiry or by an apparatus which records when a family's radio is on. Each one of these methods has its limitations. Pupils tend to report what they think the teacher will like. They read what they find at the neighbourhood library, see what is booked at the neighbourhood movie, and listen to what the local radio station carries but they might enjoy other material if it were available. Magazine purchases are determined chiefly by adults. In spite of such difficulties, from the total of all the findings a fairly consistent picture of the nature of interests at various ages emerges.

Here once more the reader will find it interesting to retrospect.

In reading, memory will very likely go back to certain charming tales printed in large type and with line drawings, telling of other little children at the mountain or seashore or in friendly games together; there will be a lingering recollection of the satisfaction which was obtained in reading about the good times had by other children and somehow identifying oneself with them. Soon came, for the boy, a fascination in stories of adventure. Perhaps *Tom Sawyer* was read and reread; the *Tarzan* series received their full share of attention. Still wilder tales may have had their surreptitious place, such as Superman or other ten-cent dreadfuls. Perhaps the Henty books took the boyish reader in courageous adventures to the most daring times of history. Or possibly the major interest was in tales of football heroes or triumphs in the ninth inning. With adolescence came a shift to the romantic story and perhaps also to the surreptitious reading of by no means respectable romances. Reminiscence of movie interests will probably show a gradual development from the primary interest in adventure and the comics to more and more sophisticated, as well as romantic, presentations.

Reading Interests—First of all, what types of books do children prefer at different ages? Children just beginning to read (about 6 or 7 years old) show special delight in short, profusely illustrated, rather fanciful stories about animals or fairies or other children. Gradually there is a certain emergence from fancy to fact, and for three or four years, beginning with 9 or 10, the boys are interested in tales of active adventure, in invention and mechanics, in the lives of famous men, and in material about hobbies. A typical study (33) showed that 32 per cent of the books dealt with war and scouting (such as Altsheler's *On the Plains with Custer*), 29 per cent with school and sport after the fashion of Barbour's *The Half Back*, 16 per cent with Boy Scouts, and 23 per cent with strenuous adventure as in Mark Twain's *Tom Sawyer.* Around 12 or 13 there may be a "reading craze" when the boy reads more books than ever before or after. Entire series, such as the Tarzan books, may be devoured. Meanwhile the girls read stories of home and school life, and show some interest in boys' stories of adventure. A typical study of the books read by girls 10½ to 13½ showed that 37 per cent were studies of home life such as *Little Women*, 15 per cent stories of school life like *Peggy*, 6 per cent fairy stories such as *Alice's Adventures in Wonderland*, 7 per cent love stories; another 6 per cent had a historical background, and 29 per cent were miscellaneous. Relatively early, girls become addicted to romances and love stories and sentimental trash (a level which many of them seem never to leave); and by the middle teens they are reading adult fiction. Chart 5.3 summarizes the situation.

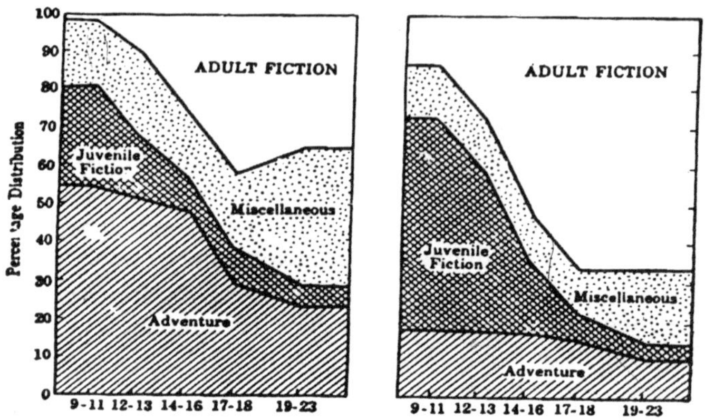

Chart 5.3—Percentage distribution of best-liked books classified according to type, by age groups and sex. (From Shuttleworth [47], Fig. 308. Based on Jordan's data.)

However, books are not the most universal form of reading matter; first come newspapers and then magazines. Thus in a mid-western city 89 per cent of the pupils in Grades 5 to 11 reported having read one or more books during the previous month, but 98 per cent had read magazines and 99 per cent newspapers.[11] Analysis of magazine reading shows much the same trends. A survey as to magazines read regularly yielded results shown in Table 5.3. Most often read by eighth-grade boys is the mechanics-hobby magazine; there is a shift to western adventure in the tenth grade and to the miscellany of *The Saturday Evening Post*[12] in the twelfth. First with the girls at all three ages are the movie magazines, with *True Story* second in the last two groups.

Interest in various sections of the newspaper is summarized in Chart 5.4. For both sexes and all ages the most frequently looked-at section is the comics. Next comes the miscellaneous headline news of the front page. Interest in the children's page and in puzzles drops with age. Distinctively prominent is the sports page for the boys and the society page for the girls.

That there are great individual differences in reading interests and amount of reading done need hardly be said. A hobby may lead

TABLE 5.3

The Five Magazines Most Often Mentioned as Read Regularly by 2500 Pupils in 21 Communities, March, 1937[10]

	Grade					
	8		*10*		*12*	
Magazine	*B*	*G*	*B*	*G*	*B*	*G*
Popular Mechanics	1		5			
Boy's Life	2					
Western stories	3	5	1			
Detective Magazines	4		2		2	
American Boy	5					
Movie Magazines		1		1		1
American Girl		3				
True Story		4		2		2
The Saturday Evening Post			3		1	
Liberty			4		3	
The American Magazine					4	
Literary Digest		2		3	5	
Ladies' Home Journal				4		3
True Confessions				5		4
Good Housekeeping						5

to avid reading along some special line. A high school survey showed that one boy read 23 different magazines regularly, while many other youngsters read none. Gifted children read two or three times as much as the average child, and their reading is more likely to be informational. The nature and amount of a child's reading will almost always be greatly affected by the amount and variety of reading matter available to him—and not only families but neighbourhoods and communities vary enormously in this respect. Thus the circulation of twenty leading magazines per 1000 population varied from 488 in Nevada to 105 in Mississippi (48). In Maryland, over half the rural white young people reported no public library available to them (1).

> Dramatic were the results of comparison of a "good" and "poor" area in Chicago. In the good area there was a sprinkling of professional people, business men, clerks, and a large number of labourers; delinquency rates were low; English was the dominant language in 97 per cent of the homes. In general appearance the district was prosperous. The poor area appeared shabby; population density was twice that of the good area; a large proportion were foreign born, and only about half the

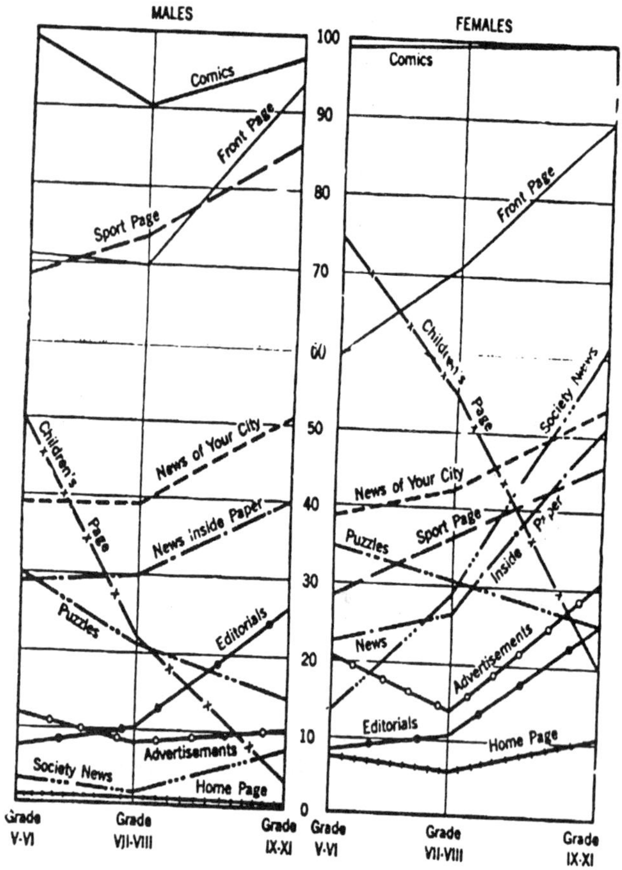

Chart 5.4—Percentages of Duluth children of different ages (in succeeding school grades from 5 through 11) who in 1929 usually read various sections of newspapers.

families used English as the dominant language. Most were Catholic. Educational level was low; delinquency rates were high. Now as to the reading in these districts. People in the good district were found to be reading 2.68 times as many magazines, 2.06 as many books, and 1.58 times as many newspapers as people in the poor district. Further, the better area read about five times as many reputable books (in terms of approved book lists or the investigator's judgment) and about sixteen times as many of the better type of magazines, but the poor area read about twice as many pulp magazines.

Evidently both the quantity and still more the quality of the individual's reading depend not only on age and sex but also on the total social-cultural milieu in which he develops and lives.[13] This is true of all interests.

The findings regarding reading interests are thus essentially similar to the data regarding play. First there is interest in simple little stories of childhood and home. In later childhood boys are interested in mechanics and adventure, girls in fiction stories of home and school life such as *Little Women*. First girls and later boys become predominantly interested in adult romantic fiction. But the nature of an individual's reading may have a significance beyond what his play activities show. That is, his reading may indicate not only what he likes to do, but what he would like to do and cannot. The slight sickly boy may revel in stories of football heroes and thus obtain vicariously certain feelings of accomplishment and prestige which in real life are most conspicuously impossible to him. Success stories may bring brief specious thrills to commonplace uninspired folk who in reality can anticipate nothing but drab mediocrity or failure. The poor and homely and unsought-after girl may in "the pulps" find social and romantic satisfactions which in real life are conspicuously absent. Reading choices thus not only show the direction of an individual's major interests; they may also indicate something as to which of those interests are most lacking of realization.

> More generally, happenings and characters in preferred fiction show what the reader would like to do and be. The characteristics of the heroes and heroines in the stories most enjoyed by readers at different ages are therefore of distinct significance. Boyhood admiration is for strength, skill, courage, self-control; the hero comes through sundry crises to success and general recognition. Gradually in adolescence the romantic element is added to these characteristics, the hero being the strong handsome individual who wins the charming girl. The younger girl's heroines obtain the esteem of worth-while friends; this esteem usually involves an element of social position. Opportunities are described for the wearing of fine clothes and for pleasant social gatherings. There is the display of certain admirable social characteristics such as friendliness. The heroine of the adolescent girl may still show such traits, but others become more prominent. She is attractive—if not beautiful, it is at least finally evident that she has sex appeal. She suffers bravely certain vicissitudes of love, and ultimately she is wooed by a most desirable young

man. Usually either hero or heroine has wealth and social position, or prosperity is at least glimpsed around the corner.

Reading may also stimulate interests, may shape and direct them. For example, one teen-age boy read everything he could about a much-publicized criminal and determined to emulate him; another reentered high school and went on to a scientific course in college as a result of reading a biography of Pasteur. Such episodes are of course exceptional. Presumably millions of boys have played Indian or cowboy as a result of reading stories about such persons. Probably as many young people have been thus stimulated to unwise vocational ambitions, extravagant leisure-time interests, sentimentalized and irresponsible impulses and ideas as regards the other sex. But all this is only inference; strangely enough, there has been practically no research on the effects of reading. For research regarding the effects of such ready-made imagining and thinking it is necessary to turn to the moving picture and the radio.

Interests and Moving Pictures—Certainly the movies are a major interest; attendance in childhood and youth is almost universal, with about 70 per cent of youngsters between 8 and 18 going at least once a week and about 25 per cent going twice a week or more, and almost a fifth of them seeing the feature through twice (14). What types of movies are preferred? Table 5.4 summarizes data which are representative. As with reading, the chief interest in middle and later childhood is in active, swashbuckling tales. Comedy is also liked. The loss of interest in "Westerns" from grade to high school on the part of both boys and girls, and the girl's increased interest in romance, are the most marked changes with age. The lesser interest in adventure and greater interest in romance are the most marked characteristics of the girls as compared with the boys.

The development is from the melodrama (in which the characters are readily classifiable as either good or bad, the plot is stereotyped, conversation unimportant, and action everything) to the romantic story that unfolds usually against a background of wealth (with characters and plot nearly as stereotyped as before and conversation concerned mainly with lovemaking) toward the adult story of conversation and characterization. In childhood boys prefer actors and girls actresses. In adolescence the girls shift over the devotion to the current "great lover" of the screen and the boys shift less strikingly to interest in women stars. Interest in the movies, as in reading and daydreaming, gives vicarious desired experience. By identifying themselves with the hero or heroine the audience tend to feel the satisfaction of being such a splendid person, having such exciting experiences, and receiving the attention of such delightful individuals as the identifiedwith character meets on the screen.

TABLE 5.4
Percentages of Grade and High School Boys and Girls Who Selected as Their First Choice Certain Types of Movie, with Increases of High School Over Grades and Sex Differences at Each Level [14]

	Boys			*Girls*			*Differences Girls over Boys*	
	Grade	*High*	*Gain*	*Grade*	*High*	*Gain*	*Grade*	*High*
Western	34	7	—27	20	6	—14	—14	—1
Adventure	14	14	0	7	6	—1	—7	—8
Comedy	11	13	2	16	10	—6	5	—3
Historical	2	13	11	5	11	6	3	—2
Sports	5	12	7	4	8	4	—1	—4
Mystery	6	9	3	7	9	2	1	0
Romance	5	7	2	13	23	10	8	16
Tragedy	2	6	4	8	10	2	6	4
War	5	4	—1	2	2	0	—3	—2
Educational	1	3	2	1	2	1	0	—1
No. of Cases	702	1153		765	2180			

Analysis of the content of sample motion pictures shows something further as to what interests people—or what the realistic movie industry thinks interests them, and in any case what the public gets. Analysis of 500 feature pictures shown in 1930 indicated that 7 out of 10 dealt with love, crime, or sex (15). Of 115 pictures selected at random in 1932, 45 included killings and 21 had attempted killings. In 78 per cent there were liquor situations and in 43 per cent intoxication. Another analysis of 142 pictures showed 741 scenes of kissing and caressing, 52 of treatment of children by parents, 313 of treatment of employees and subordinates. In scenes of the last two types, it was found that children, employees, "inferior" races, and persons of "inferior" social standing tended to be treated better in the movies than in the real world. In the movies girls are more aggressive in lovemaking than is generally approved in real life. If a major appeal of moving pictures is the fact that vicarious satisfactions

> are thus obtained for desires not adequately met in real life, here is evidence as to what those unsatisfied desires are: hunger of children and humble folk for status, sex hunger, and hunger for activity, variety, excitement, and letting oneself go.

Now as to the research, referred to above, of the effects of movies on children. Records of pulse, breathing, and electrical changes in the body were obtained from certain children while they watched various types of movies. Melodramatic scenes were found strongly to excite 9-year-old children, but older persons sensed the unreality of these episodes and were little affected. Erotic scenes stirred a few children as early as 9 years, had greatest effect (in heightened and irregular pulse and breathing) around 16-18, stimulated yet older persons less, probably because of "adult discount" (18). A device under children's beds which recorded every movement showed that youngsters frequently were more restless in sleep after seeing a moving picture (as restless as two cups of coffee made them) (46).

Movies thus have demonstrable effects on the child's physical being. Other effects are also important. Movies even more than reading have an effect on play. Roles of hero and heroine are widely imitated in games. In most cases the victorious character assumed by the child in the play situation is a "good" character and the criminal is vanquished. Children seem largely to imitate those situations in the movies that fit in with interests already somewhat established; the imitation is not of any or every scene but is highly selective in character.

> The lively 10-year-old boy already fond of frontier stories starts a cowboy and Indian game imitating an episode in a "Western" film—much as his father did the same thing after reading a dime novel. A boy already started toward a delinquent career may get further stimulus toward crime from a movie, but the average youngster will hardly be so affected. Thus a young burglar told how "when we came out of the show a couple of the boys suggested that we try to rob a store, the way we had seen in the picture ... We bought a crowbar and screw driver and went to a clothing store and sprung the lock".

Far more important for the average youngster are the suggestions he or she receives for furtherance of social interests. Thus one girl "kept my hair just like" an admired actress, "plucked my eyebrows in her way," imitated ways of holding her hands and of glancing down. Other girls reported that from the movies they had learned "what to do when in a crowd," ... "how to act with boys ... to make love, to smoke, and to wear swell clothes." Desires are stirred: "When I see movies that show snappy clothes and wealth I want these things also"; "passionate love pictures ... make me want to be loved."[15] That along such lines the movies do have influence there seems little doubt. They conventionalize interests and standards as to their satisfaction, and do so at levels of luxury and self-indulgence which are highly undesirable.

The Radio—There are radios in over 90 per cent of American homes; data indicate that in the average city home the radio is on over three hours a day.[16] The average child goes to the movies about once a week for about two hours, but he listens to the radio every day; his listening time for a week totals several times longer than his time in the moving picture theatre. Further, the radio is an extraordinarily subtle and pervasive influence. It literally enters the home and becomes part of the life there. Favourite programmes may be regularly turned to, as part of the accepted routine of the family existence together. Much of the time the radio is a background accompaniment of study, entertaining, or housework. On occasion famous men speak, right there in the living room, to the family, and events in the world of sports or politics or war are recounted as they are in the making. In total the radio is the most extraordinary instrument for entertainment, education, and propaganda ever devised. Data regarding radio listening and radio programmes should be of significance to every teacher.

As with reading and movies, the programmes may be thought of as both interest-indicating and interest-forming. Certain reports indicate that two-thirds of the younger listeners tune in blindly, about 5 per cent of all listeners tune in regularly to only one station, and three-fourths restrict their listening to three stations. However, even the most indiscriminate tuners-in have preferences. Programme-makers check upon and adjust to these preferences. All the time these preferences are responding to fad and fashion and perhaps somewhat to education; they are also developing all the time along the directions set by the essential characteristics of human nature.

Chart 5.5 is a sample of findings regarding sex and age differences in radio preferences. The major trends are similar to those already seen in movies, reading, and play. Grade school children most enjoy dramatic action and humour. By the senior year these programmes are much less popular, and popular dance music has shot up to first place. From grade to high school there is a marked increase of interest in news and sports, but by the senior year these programmes attract

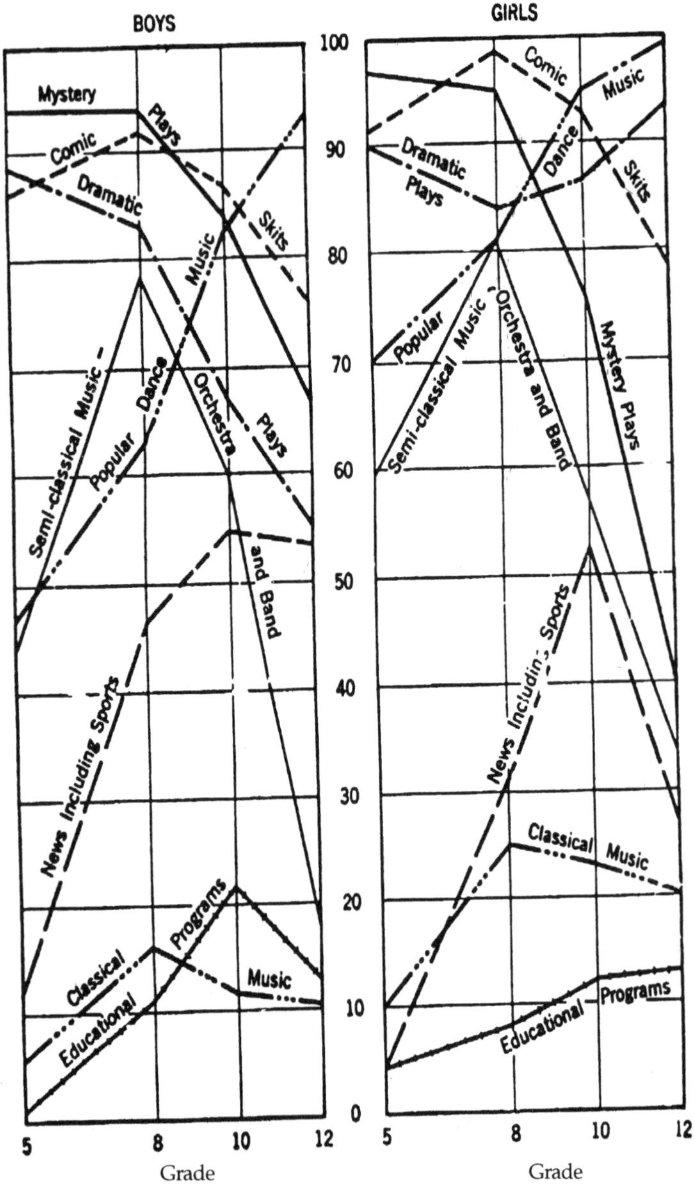

Chart 5.5—Percentage of 2500 boys and girls in Grades 5, 8, 10, and 12 who checked different types of radio programmes as types to which they enjoyed listening. (Adapted from data in Brown [8], p. 328.)

less, especially the girls. Semi-classical music for orchestra and band appeals to eighth-graders but then drops off strikingly. Classical music and educational programmes have little vogue at any age for either sex.

> Obviously a programme may be liked—or disliked—for various reasons. The New York City eighth-grade children above referred to mentioned "comical and funny" most often (25 per cent) as a reason for liking a programme; next most often mentioned (16 per cent) was that a programme had music and singing, next (14 per cent) that it was exciting and thrilling. Most common reason for disliking a programme was that it was "silly" (26 per cent). Says one of these pre-adolescents, "There is one kind of programme that I dislike and that is a love story... My sister likes to listen to them. I think these programmes very silly." But the term is of broad connotation. A girl writes that she doesn't like the Skippy programme because "he talks very silly for a boy of his age." It must be remembered that back of any individual's interests are very complex circumstances determining what *he* will like. Wrote one boy, "I like comedy programmes because after my mother scolds me for doing something wrong I go upstairs, turn on the radio, and end my worries".

Evidence has been mentioned that movies may measurably stir a child's pulse or disturb his sleep. The radio also produces physiological changes (17). Of the New York children referred to above 27 per cent reported lying awake in bed thinking about what they have heard over the radio, and 36 per cent said that they sometimes dreamed about what they had heard.[17] The majority of these dreams were unpleasant or frightening, though a quarter concerned more or less pleasant things. Statements made by the children about other results should not be overlooked. Forty per cent thought they had got help for their history from the radio; 44 per cent thought the radio had led them to be good, honest, and obedient. Songs, games, stories, jokes and learned from the radio, say 15 per cent of the children; 20 per cent learned to eat good food, 18 per cent to drink Ovaltine! To the question, "Do you think listening to the radio makes one do bad things?" 11 per cent answered yes. Of all wrong acts mentioned, stealing comes first, then disobedience and mischievousness. Catch phrases are learned, like Red Skelton's "I dood it." Nineteen per cent of the children had joined a radio club, 13 per cent had entered one or more radio contests, 16 per cent had visited a broadcasting station,

21 per cent had written a letter to some radio star, 11 per cent had had their names broadcast. Clearly the radio plays a considerable part in the lives of most children.

The Escape of Interests from Reality—In reading, movies, and radio, an individual's interests may thus escape his limitations of circumstance and ability and take flight in whatever direction fancy may choose. The directions which interests naturally take should be shown with special clearness. Features of human nature might appear which in the real world have little opportunity to show themselves. What features do stand out?

In association with age, the same characteristics and changes are seen as have already been noted. Young children are involved in the task of making acquaintance with their immediate world of home and neighbourhood, and the things, people, and animals to be found there; their interest in reading and radio is in such things. Coordinate with upsurging physical and mental growth in later childhood is a restless interest in adventure and travel and invention; pre-adolescent youngsters delight in movie and radio serial thrillers whose outstanding characteristics are action, excitement, variety, novelty. With puberty romantic interest in the other sex appears and soon dominates the situation; the fiction which appeals to the adolescent is almost completely sex-social. Boys are more interested in adventure and novelty, and girls more in stories of pleasant social happenings, with sex-social interests appearing earlier and showing more strongly. These are the same basic trends which appeared in play. They are clearly a part of the processes of growth which were outlined in the chapter on physical growth.

But in these worlds created by the imagination, those desires which are most feverishly strong *and* most unsatisfied show themselves more clearly than in the real world. The school will do well to pay attention to them. Healthy boys should have games and trips, and shops in which to tinker and make things; because the old-fashioned school did not provide such opportunities, vigorous boys left or became "disciplinary" problems. Slowly, modern school are learning to provide such experiences. Healthy adolescents have as their chief concern acquaintance with the other sex. Slowly, secondary schools are learning that one of their two or three outstanding tasks is the healthy guidance and furthering of such acquaintance. Throughout it is evident that achievement of status—of regard and respect from one's fellows—is *the* major underlying human craving.

Much of the next chapter will be concerned with this problem.

It is also evident that these pseudo-worlds of the heart's desires stir and stimulate interests, often in heady fashion. They fix the direction in which satisfaction will be sought, and suggest how it may be found. Within wide limits they set the expectation and the standard as to what will satisfy, in social and economic status, vocation, and mate. For the most part they do these things in irresponsible, impractical, unrealistic, socially undesirable fashion. But these influences—of reading, radio, and moving picture—in total are tremendously influential. If only schools were even a quarter as effective in thus molding interests and setting goals!

CONVERSATIONS; AMBITIONS

Interest may be shown not only by what people like to do or what they like to see or hear or read, but also by what they talk about or want to be. Brief inquiry regarding these matters should be of significance with reference to the topic in hand—and of more special value to the teacher, as in considering topics in oral English or issues in vocational guidance.

Conversational Interests—Conversations should contain just about the best possible evidence as to what people are thinking about—and what they want others to think. They should be simple to investigate—all one need do is eavesdrop on people and keep a record of what they say. Yet there has been little research on conversation, and astoundingly little systematic inquiry as to what children talk about among themselves. What data there are were mostly gathered at school, and possibly affected as to topic by that circumstance. The findings are nevertheless worth brief mention. A study of children's chatter at recess as recorded by teachers in 24 schools in 7 states showed youngsters in Grades 3 to 6 talking about games and sports, personal experiences, trips, family and friends, accidents, school, and parties. That is, in general these younger children talked about doings rather than persons or ideas. The older children tended to focus their conversations on fewer topics than did the younger children, and to ramble less (16).

> Stenographic reports of daily free-conversation periods in the schoolroom yielded largely similar findings. Less spontaneity might be expected; however, the children were accustomed to these "free" periods. It was found that 27 per cent of their

conversation related to home play, 14 per cent to animals, the same amount to school, 13 per cent to auto trips (56).[18]

Studies of the conversations of secondary school pupils seem unfortunately lacking. However, a study at the college level may interest college student readers and also indicate something as to the probable trend of conversations as youngsters grow into adolescence, as well as the factors influencing these trends. Reports were obtained from certain college students of the conversations which took place in certain fraternity and sorority houses and women's dormitories. Table 5.5 is a summary of the results.

TABLE 5.5
Major Topics Discussed by College Students and Percentage of Total Conversations on Each Topic in Different Student Groups, also Differences between "Organized" Men and Women, and between "Unorganized" and "Organized" Women[19]

	Fraternity Men	*d*	*Sorority Women*	*d*	*Dormitory Women*
Sex interests (dates, dancing, clothes, sex problems	22	0	22	8	30
Campus affairs (organizations, campus politics, gossip, studies)	28	2	26	1	25
Culture (music, debates, literature, travel)	6	5	11	4	7
Morals (drinking, religion, smoking, public affairs)	10	1	9	1	8
Recreation (sports, trips, shows, stories, games)	15	0	15	8	7
Money and work (money, summer employment, vocations)	9	3	6	2	8
Home (home and relatives, home town)	3	1	4	2	6
Differences, fraternity-sorority and sorority-dormitory		12		26	

The table shows sex-social interests and campus affairs clearly heading the list. In short, the results are in harmony with the gross trends already indicated earlier in the chapter. Ideas (culture, morals) now appear as topics of some frequency. But there is a further feature of these data which is of decided significance. Differences between "organized" men and "organized" women are less than differences between sorority and dormitory women. And the more talk in the dormitories about sex and recreational interests appears due not to greater experience in these respects but to less; it apparently is a deprivation phenomenon. The influence of what might be called socio-cultural circumstance is dominant.

Vocational Interests—So far the data have dealt primarily with recreational and leisure-time interests. What are the findings as regards vocational interests? The usual procedure here has been simply to ask youngsters what they would like to be or do, or have them check on long lists of occupations those which appeal to them most. Vocational choices of older children and young people in high school or college may of course be based not merely on interest but also on consideration as to possibilities for realizing these ambitions. The ambitions, attitudes, and circumstances of the family will also in various ways probably influence their choices. But in so far as such factors do affect interests, the outcomes should be here counted in.

Table 5.6, which presents typical findings, shows the occupations liked best or preferred most by boys from 8 to 18 years of age. The occupation most frequently checked was "aviator" (the study was made shortly after the Lindbergh flight and this outstanding preference was presumably somewhat a product of that event). For 8-year-old boys, however, "cowboy" had first place. At 8 and 10 "soldier" also stands high. Yet by 16 "cowboy" and "soldier" were mentioned by too few boys to have a rank assigned! At 12 and 14 "civil engineer" and "electrician" push up into prominence, and by 18 "architect" and "lawyer" have risen to second and third place.

Evidently the findings are consistent with what has already been said about the development of interests. The younger boys are interested in active and dramatic occupations like "cowboy" or "soldier". In middle childhood many of these interests continue; but in accord with the fascination which mechanical things have for many boys of this age, there emerge ambitions toward engineering and invention. As a boy moves into adolescence these last interests may continue, but other interests appear. He may desire to enter a profession, such as law or medicine. The social prestige of an occupation begins to play a part.

TABLE 5.6
Rank in Frequency of Occupations Liked Best by Boys of 8½ to 18½ Years of Age[20]

Occupations	*Ages*					
	8½	*10½*	*12½*	*14½*	*16½*	*18½*
Aviator	2	1	1	1	1	1
Cowboy	1	2	2	16		
Lawyer	6	10	7	10	4	3
Civil engineer		8	3	2	3	7
Physician or surgeon	11	10	11	11	6	6
Musician	20	14	10	7	9	5
Electrician or Electrical engineer		20	5	3	2	4
Architect			17	4	5	2
Physical director or athletic coach				23	11	4
Soldier	3	4	20			

Girls show throughout an interest in teaching. The little girl's interest very likely is based on the fact that the teacher is the most important woman in child experience outside the home. With older girls various other considerations enter. Teaching is felt to be a genteel and proper occupation for a woman; there are more opportunities in it for women than in most other occupations; it may also be regarded as an occupation from which the transition to marriage is readily made. Interest in and liking for children may be a factor. But other occupations have an appeal. A childhood fondness for painting or writing may, especially if there is much adult admiration of the productions, lead to a more or less permanent artistic or literary ambition. Younger children may show interest in the dramatic occupations of actor or opera singer; in adolescence, occupations which permit great display and attention-getting have a tremendous appeal to some girls. Matter-of-fact girls may, from their home or school experience, develop a special interest in home economics or nursing. In the background of most girls' thinking is doubtless the possibility of marriage, and this consideration operates in various ways to bring about the choice of an occupation which will be likely to effect acquaintance with a satisfactory mate. The appeal of work as a private secretary combines these factors of feminine interest and usually meets with home approval. In short, once more the girls' interests are less active and adventurous; they are more social. Here specially do the conventions influence girls in various and often subtle ways.

Table 5.7 showing vocational desires and actualities in Maryland youth, well exhibits the above-mentioned trends and sex differences and also the comparatively more realistic nature of the girls' ambitions. As will be seen, six of the ten most preferred jobs among the young women were among the ten most frequently entered by them, while none of the boys' most desired positions actually were among the ten most often attained. Apparently the girls are vocationally more realistic or less ambitious than the men, or conventions regarding desirable women's occupations are more sensible.

TABLE 5.7

The Ten Occupations Maryland Youth Most Frequently Desired, and the Ten Most Frequently Entered[21]

Male		*Female*	
Desired	*Entered*	*Desired*	*Entered*
Engineer	Farm labourer	Nurse	*Housewife*
Mechanic	Industrial labourer	*Teacher*	*Family domestic*
Farm owner	Inside salesperson	*Stenographer*	*Inside salesperson*
Aviator	Unpaid family worker	*Housewife*	Textile operative
Physician	Textile operative	*Secretary*	*Stenographer*
Lawyer	Clerk	Beautician	*Teacher*
Electrician	Truck driver	*Family domestic*	Waitress
Teacher	WPA	Artist	*Secretary*
Musician	Helper	Musician	Clerk
Machinist	CCC	*Inside salesperson*	Clothing operative

Both girls and boys show in the high school and college periods the great extent to which the influence of admired individuals may operate. Frequently the youngster decides to specialize in a given subject because of his liking for or admiration of a teacher of that subject. All too often an enthusiastic teacher urges a student who shows such interest (which she mistakes for interest in the subject itself) to continue in that field even though he has little real aptitude and the opportunities are not great. A father may push a pupil toward a certain line of work because he himself had an unrealized ambition in the field. Finally, accidental circumstances may determine the choice.

Studies of vocational interests thus repeat what was said in preceding sections of this chapter. A survey of the data, as one compares choices of young children, youngsters in middle childhood, and adolescents shows a movement from the active and dramatic toward the more intellectual and the socially furthering; conventional attitudes pay a large part, and vocational fashions are evident.

CONCRETE REALITY: THE LIFE HISTORY OF INTERESTS

The preceding pages have indicated the general characteristics of interests as shown in play, in reading and movies and radio, in conversation, and in vocational choice. But the discussion so far has been general, and in that respect false. Interests are always the interests of a particular person and are extremely personal; they are relatively specific, often highly so. Ruth likes chemistry, hiking, and John; Madge loves dramatics, dancing, and Tom. Further, interests are the product not of general influences, but of highly specific influences in the life of each individual. In fact, a given interest may be the out-working of an underlying urge or circumstance which does not appear in the interest as seen by the outsider at all: John's great interest in chemistry is really a major factor in Ruth's interest in that subject. Harry's interest in travel books is a product of his desire to escape a restrictive and unhappy home. Homely Helen's absorption in romantic movies and the lack of all romance in her own life have their obvious relationship.

Sample Interest Biographies—To see the concrete reality regarding interests, the interest biography is highly useful, in many ways it remakes the whole picture and gives insights unthought of otherwise. As a sample of such an approach the following two interest biographies may be of value. The first is that of a young man, a graduate student in psychology.

> Earliest play recollections are of ringing a handbell which mother had hung up so it would ring when he pulled a string, and of digging in the back yard with a toy shovel. A little later (around 5 years of age) much interest in playing train following a train trip and in playing horse following a trip to the grandfather's farm.
>
> When the boy was 6 his family moved to a more nortnern state. The novelty of a long winter season led to great interest in coasting and such activities as building snow forts. In summer, playing soldier was frequent, this play being led by a neighbour

boy whose father's war record was a matter of much pride to his sons. A frequent indoor winter amusement was gathering at some boy's home to compare stamp collections and trade stamps; how this interest began is not now remembered. The gift of *Swiss Family Robinson* led to fascinated reading of this story and then of *Robinson Crusoe* and sundry other stories of adventure. A Christmas present of an air rifle and trips with the father squirrel hunting developed some boyish interest in "hunting." However, because of undetected nearsightedness he was a poor shot, and was also poor in baseball; in consequence his interest in these sports was slight.

In his ninth winter the boy was frequently ill, went to school only irregularly, seemed to have no energy, ability, or interest in active play. His mother bought him some water colour paints for home use and he greatly enjoyed painting and drawing. His teacher visited him at home and encouraged him; some of his work was displayed at an exhibit of pupils' work. He was much set up by this and as a result thought of being a designer or illustrator. But with spring came a return of health, and then sedentary interest were forgotten in the returning zest for vigorous outdoor play.

Beginning when the boy was about 10 years old it became the regular practice of the father to give his son certain carpenter's tools for Christmas. This interest in making things had also been fostered by stories which the father told of a little mill which he himself had made when he was a boy, like the real sawmill which the grandfather owned. A workbench was made for him in the basement. At about this same time a new bridge was built near by; all the boys watched the steam shovel and derrick, then with fascination began making model steam shovels and derricks. With a little help from the father the boy was able to make a better Derrick than the neighbour boys. And he looked up in his father's encyclopedia about bridges and as a result made a different and better bridge than those the other boys were making. He thus received admiring and even jealous attention from his friends and a great accession of self-esteem. Increasingly he read widely on mechanical topics and became much interested in being either a skilled mechanic or an engineer.

When he entered high school his father urged him to take a college preparatory programme. The boy insisted, however, on including a course in manual training. But the first two weeks of this course disgusted him. He had been making complicated objects, but the manual training instructor insisted that everyone make a whisk-broom holder. The youngster abandoned the course in disgust and became so busy with his high school work that the mechanical interest was dropped.

For a while in high school he was without any definite vocational objective. He became greatly interested in a girl. He took it for granted that he was going to college and that vocational choice could be made later. However, in his senior year of high school he was much influenced by his history teacher, one of the few men teachers in the school. As a result he decided to major in history in college. He had also joined the high school debating society and he became further interested in the governmental problems there discussed.

He went to a small residence college and there found adjustment rather difficult to a different place and different type of student from those with whom he had associated before. He also found himself increasingly dissatisfied with his major in history; history seemed just one episode after another, whereas work in science (he was now taking both chemistry and biology) with its experimentation and its progressive advance to new understandings seemed to have greater potentialities. Further, happenings in history seemed to need explanation in terms of the ideas and emotions of the human beings involved. And his college history professor was stodgy! The combination of concern with personal problems of adjustment, impatience with history and the local historian, and thrill at the potentialities of the scientific method all seemed to come together in a new interest upon taking a vigorous course in social psychology. The major interest was thus changed to this subject. And this individual is now taking graduate work in this field.

It will be seen that this biography begins with very simple play activities and follows through with progressive changes due partly to underlying slow processes of growth in intellect and physiological urges and partly to circumstances such as a train trip, moving to a colder climate, and the gift of tools. Ill health changed the nature of the interests for a time. The influence of parents and teachers was frequently important. So were success and recognition, and also social maladjustment. Both good and poor teachers had their effects.

The final outcome is highly individual and personal, but also very understandable once all the main factors are known.

The second biography is that of a young woman, a college student majoring in home economics.

> As a small child her sole companions were boys. She enjoyed their games as pranks, did not like girl's more sedate amusements.
>
> As she advanced in the primary grades she slowly fell away from male companions and took to dolls. She enjoyed treating them for sickness, bandaging their wounds; she came to think that it would be wonderful to be a nurse and help the sick. At about this time an illness took her to the hospital where she remained over a month, becoming even more interested in and acquainted with a nurse's life and duties. After finishing her sophomore year in high school she declared this ambition to her parents. They objected and refused to give their consent to her entering nursing training. She acquiesced in their decision.
>
> In grammar school and the freshman year of high school her teachers had told her that she was talented in painting and drawing. When she gave up the idea of nursing she turned with vigorous reaction to painting as a possible career. She visited galleries and museums, went sketching, and dreamed of a trip abroad for training. This she felt was certainly her vocation. But she gradually came to realize that to be famous would take years of toil and hardship. She therefore put aside this ambition as impractical. However, she liked to cook. And she said frankly that the old adage, "The way to a man's heart is through his stomach," was also a factor in this thinking, as one of her ambitions was to marry. She therefore decided to major in home economics, still keeping in the back of her mind the thought that perhaps sometime she might return to her interest in painting.[22]

This biography shows the importance of playmates as initially affecting interests, the effect of a time in the hospital upon vocational choice—especially strong because of the already present interest in nursing—the influence of parents, and the hope of marriage as a factor in a girl's vocational thinking.[23]

The reader should find it illuminating to write an autobiography of his own interests and to compare it with similar accounts of other students. Clearly interests show certain very general trends, as already described earlier in this chapter, from the younger to the older ages. Generalizations may be made about influences affecting interests—physical environment, economic status, conventions. Such generalizations, however, are very inadequate for understanding a particular individual's interests at a particular time. His interests are a complex resultant of his total history. They cannot be understood from generalities but must be seen in the perspective of his total life experience.

Interests and Feelings—The first impression one obtains from the interest biography is the extent to which each person's total interest pattern is an individual thing. But consideration of such biographies —and especially of one's autobiography with all the vividness that one's own life has to oneself—emphasizes a further point. A generalized treatment of interests leaves the topic objective and cold. To the person concerned (to oneself), however, an interest is a dynamic and feelingful matter. Surely one's interest in high school in a certain high school girl was stirring and had feeling-tone aplenty. But those boyhood October afternoons—what with the sharp weather and abounding health one's whole body seemed to hunger for activity. To run and jump and shout was a highly desired and delightful thing to do, whereas to be still made one restless and miserable. To be mentally active (in one's own boyish fashion) was also natural and interesting for the healthy nervous system, and there was a restless urge to talk, ask questions, solve puzzles, make things.

The vicarious experiences of reading, movies, and radio similarly involve feelings. As has already been seen, objective physiological evidence shows that melodramatic or romantic moving pictures get right down into a youngster's vitals, stirring his pulse and undoubtedly his impulses and emotions. To have an interest is to feel a hunger, an urge, a craving, a restlessness. And when one is in the grip of an interest, he has excitement, thrill, satisfaction, and a sense of expanding well-being—or letdown, discouragement, frustration—according to whether the interest is satisfied or not. Obviously his interests—and their gratification or denial—are a matter to which he is acutely sensitive. Some interests may be superficial and relatively unimportant. But back of and giving energy to the total complex of interests there appear to be basic organic drives. What happens to a person's interests appears vital to his organic health; if they suffer serious injury his feelings are touched to the quick. Since different people have different interests and those of adult differ from those of children or adolescents, it is easy for a teacher to be uncomprehending of a pupil's interests or to treat them lightly or even with impatience or scorn. She is surprised or angered at the strength of the pupil's reaction to this slight. She should keep always in mind how interests and feelings are thus part and parcel one with the other, and let her tact be guided by a study of her pupils' interests.

Interests and Success—Mention was made a few sentences back of the feelings of expanding well-being which come with satisfaction of an interest, or of letdown and discouragement if the interest is frustrated. Here is a second major point that emerges from the biographies: an interest grows and flourishes if it is satisfied and if it is approved and brings recognition, but trends to weaken if such consummations are not obtained. The boy's craftsmanship and the girl's painting were recognized as good and these interests became strong. Baseball had slight interest for the boy because he was poor at the game, and the girl's interest in nursing dropped when the parents disapproved. Interests feed for success and on the attention-getting and approval which are social success; they starve if success and approval are lacking, and either die or manifest themselves in desperate or morbid fashion (facts so important that they will be given treatment in a later chapter).

THEORY AND APPLICATION

Understanding of interests has been sought by study of play, of such amusements as reading and radio, of talk and vocational choice, and of development of interest in the individual. The question now is whether from this overview the basic elements in interest may be determined, the important influences shaping them noted, and suggestions for their nurture derived. The writers suggest that the total situation may be interpreted with reasonable adequacy as follows.

Basic Urges—Back of particular interests, and the source of their energies, are certain physiological tensions or pressures or urges. Of broadest and greatest importance is the urge toward activity normal in any healthy organism. That dogs should run about and bark or children run and jump and shout requires no special explanation; such a "going off" of the healthy organism is simply the normal and inevitable product of structure and organic constitution (failure to be active *would* call for explanation). Such activity is not limited to mere physical exuberance but also includes mental activity, *i.e.*, curiosity, playing with ideas, imagining. During the years of growth this basic urge or pressure to be active is strongest; restless energy is recognized as characteristic of childhood and youth. In adolescence appears the powerful urge of sex. This causes a lift in the total energy of the organism and gives a sex-social direction to it. This redirection is the basic background phenomenon during adolescence. These two physiological urges, the pressure for activity and the pressure of sex, are (the writers contend) the two major drives behind human doing and thinking. Other physiological pressures or tensions are in the background, however, such as the urge of hunger and appetite. The discomforts of heat or cold make the individual seek more pleasant conditions. The total of all these physiological stirrings, restlessnesses, and urges is the force back of any interest or activity.[24]

> Into the complex urges and tensions of the normal organism may come the special peculiar tensions and discomforts of physiological malfunctioning, pain, or illness. If these discomforts are strong and the individual is weak, he may be preoccupied with them largely to the exclusion of other urges. The sick child has little attention (or vitality) for other interests.

These are the background physiological pressures that are the driving power behind human interests and activities. To these "elements" must be added one major derivative. The one most evident, most useful fact learned in helpless infancy and dependent childhood is the importance of favourable attitudes on the part of other people. The competitions of middle childhood and the sex interests of adolescence enforce this social sensitivity. Little wonder, then, that hunger for attention and for approval of others appears very early and, enforced by the sex urge, grows until (once the most elementary physiological demands are somewhat satisfied) it is the most powerful of all drives. The drive is not easily satisfied since the various groups from which the growing child wishes to obtain acceptance—home, school, gang, and community—tend to set up still higher goals as he attains initial status.

The strength of these basic drives is very different in different people. Thus in some children the urge to activity is almost feverish, whereas others are listless. Sex is much stronger in some persons than in others. Some show hysterical craving for the approving attention of others, but a few people seem almost indifferent. This, very briefly, is the concept regarding the basic urges behind the interests of children and young people. What inferences and implications valuable for education follow from this concept?

In the first place, any educational programme which involves an effort to block one of the basic urges or drives is sure to cause conflicts and disciplinary problems and to lack vitality and interest for the pupils. The old-fashioned school which asked children to sit still and be quiet was contrary to nature. The conservative secondary school (or college) which separates boys and girls at just those adolescent ages when they are most interested in each other and might be going through processes of healthy acquaintanceship is contrary to nature. The school at any level which rules it wrong for pupils to talk together and work together is ruling against the most established and pervasive of all human tendencies and one of the most desirable.

In the second place, if vigor and liveliness of interests have their origin in physiological pressures and urges, a first step in stimulating a pupil's interests should be to see that he is vigorously healthy. Undernourished ill children usually have sluggish dragging interests. They may be docile in the sedentary programme of a conventional school. Genuine and effective interest in play or in the undertakings of a modern school must stem from the energy in a sound physique—the neuromuscular system in good tonus and quick to respond, the ductless glands all making their proper and balanced contributions to the internal chemistry, nourishment reasonably adequate, sleep sound and long enough, and the system not burdened by injury or disease.

> Up to now Harry had been interested in his school work and active in play. But this September he was listless in school, seemed bored with his work, participated little in the doings of his neighbourhood gang, did little with his stamp collection. Investigation showed that the family had just returned from a trailer trip in which sleeping quarters had been cramped, hours of rest irregular, diet poor; constipation had alternated with diarrhea, and Harry had suffered from a chronic cold. His teacher's efforts to interest him in his schoolwork proved entirely futile, but with gradually returning health his interests slowly returned.

Limiting and Stimulating Conditions—Taken for granted, but its pervasive importance usually missed, is the fact that interests are highly adaptable and responsive to the conditions and circumstances of each youngster's life. His playthings and play places, the resources of the family as regards a car and money for amusements and clothes, the resources of the community as regards recreation and vocation—these factors in total are for the average person largely definitive as to what his interests are.

> Mr Thompson grew up on a farm forty years ago As a boy he hunted and fished, enjoyed helping his father look after the farm machinery but did not like the farm, work, was fascinated by the trains on the railway which ran along one side of the farm. There was little reading matter in the home except a farm journal and the newspaper from the small city up the line, no school or village library, no radio or moving pictures or automobile, no organized team games because of the small number of boys of the same age who could conveniently get together. Social contacts were restricted to the immediate neighbourhood and social affairs centered around the church; there was no dancing or card-playing, no money or time for vacation trips, parties, shows. Mr Thompson left school at 14 to help on the farm, married a neighbour girl at 19, and moved to the nearby small city to work for the railroad which had so fascinated him as a boy. Now he is a locomotive engineer.
>
> His son Tom, growing up in the comfortable suburban home, has had no farm or other work to do, no occasion to tinker with machinery. Instead, sports (fostered by both the schools and the city playgrounds) have absorbed his energies, and he has been a Boy Scout. Parts of two summers have been spent in a camp. In comfortable circumstances, the family has all such modern conveniences as an automobile and radio; magazines and movies are commonplace, as are also week-end trips which would have been the event of the year in his father's boyhood. Tom is now a high school senior and is on the basketball team; dances and dates are a taken-for-granted part of his active social life. He rather looks down upon his father's rough heartiness of manner and also feels a little apologetic about his father's job. Tom plans to go to college and enter business or perhaps become an athletic coach. Constitutionally he and his father are much alike. But the different circumstances of their lives have developed very different interests

However, conditions which either limit or stimulate interests may be found in the individual as well as in his environment. Obviously a deaf child is likely to have little interest in music, or a crippled child in active sports. Such factors are of much more frequent importance than these extreme examples would suggest.

A big strong boy has the energy and strength to initiate and foster an interest in athletics for which the puny lad has neither vigor nor capacity—though the latter's inadequacy might find compensation in fiction about athletes. The girl with the lovely voice would be strange indeed if she did not like to sing. The dull boy will hardly enjoy chess or debating or mathematics but the bright youngster may. In general, interests and capacities go together.

> Tom (discussed above) was a husky active lad for whom athletics was as natural as the tussling of two puppies; the admiring regard from his associates which his athletic powers brought him accentuated that interest. The total pattern and development of his interests was very different from that of his classmate William, who was short, slight, and bright. William longed with a great longing for physical strength and status and tried to make the track team, but without success. His urge to achieve some sort of recognition frustrated at this point, he put himself with special vigor into debating. And he tried extra hard to be agreeable since he could not muscle his way into popularity.

The practical applications of the above facts are so obvious that there is danger they will be neglected. A playground creates different play interests from those which grow in slum alleys. Having the schoolyard open for after-school and summer play and the school "industrial arts laboratory" open evenings for the hobbies of both boys and their fathers will affect the interests of the neighbourhood. Playthings are a subject deserving discussion by teachers and parents as interest-making materials. A community hall or church may foster active games, socials, dances, and dramatics, and be a major influence is shaping the interests of the community. Yet in a city known to the writers the largest church would not permit young people to have social gatherings in its big basement room because the carpet might be damaged, and the school board would not open the schools at night for the same purpose because it would add to the heating bill! But a night club just outside the town limits *was* open and not grudging in its welcome. The high school in one small city had only an academic programme, but a nearby school of about the same size offered practical industrial arts, secretarial, commercial, and home economics courses, and had a vocational counsellor in touch with the community's business and industrial life. Various feasible vocational interests were thus stimulated and furthered, and brought fruition in jobs after graduation.

One high school the writers know about had no athletics except for its interschool teams and no music except its much-featured band with its much-photographed drum majorette. Another big school had football teams for boys of different weight groups, included such simple and inexpensive games as paddle tennis in the programme, and aimed at an athletic programme broad enough to include something for everyone. It had not only a band but orchestras and glee clubs and informal sings. Obviously this school stimulated a greater variety of athletic and musical interests in a far greater number of pupils than did the first.

The Anthropology and Sociology of Interests—The preceding section stressed how a person's interests are shaped and limited by the physical conditions and circumstances of his life, and by his physique and capacities. It must now be pointed out that important as are these potentialities of the environment and the self, even more important are customs and conventions, fashions and fads which bring it about that in a particular group certain things are accepted or admired as *the* things to do, but other interests are considered inappropriate or even taboo. In the example above, hunting and fishing were interests every country boy of the father's generation was expected to have, whereas football and basketball were expected interests in the son's group. Dancing was expected of the son but taboo in the father's boyhood. Railroading had glamour and status in the father's boyhood group but was somewhat looked down upon in the son's more sophisticated society.

But the total culture and way of life in which this father grew up were more different from the interest-moulding culture of his son's youth than the above examples show. The competitive urge to beat someone—to beat the rival classmate for the place on the team, to help the team beat the rival school—is pervasive in the life of the present-day high school boy but was largely absent from the rural boyhood of his father. Similarly an investigation by one of the writers showed girls in a mid-west community to be distinctly less interested in athletic team games. As will be pointed out in a later chapter, high school social life is far different today from social life in the father's youth; now a dominant desire is to be among those who "belong," but such social striving and climbing were slight among the father's boyhood associates. Now sex-stimulating association with girls is more frequent. Going to church and interest in religion are less part of the accept and expected way of life.

If the differences in one mid-west family over one generation can be thus great, how much greater are differences over longer periods of time, or from one nation or race to another. Organized team games were an Anglo-Saxon development, until recently not popular on the European continent. For a boy to have mechanical interests is part of the American tradition but less an approved and fostered interest among boys in Europe. Vocational interests are different here than there. And if interests in non-European cultures are examined—the development of interests among young people in India or China or Samoa—then indeed are striking differences found.

Great differences in interests between one time and place and another may thus be found. But all the time, flickering over the surface of these larger movements, there are less important changes in interests, Mah-jongg and the Big Apple and the Bunny Hug have their vogue and then are forgotten. Sleek sloe-eyed vamps and swarthy sheiks are the movie rage; then curvesome blonds come in. Lindberg and Al Capone and J. Edgar Hoover in turn are in the spotlight; publishers and movie producers feature aviators or gangsters or G-men; boys' play and ambitions run the same way. Handies or Little Audry stories are all the rage and then forgotten. A particular school or a particular high school crowd may have its own little fads and fashions.

In sum, the total society in which the individual grows up has an enormous influence upon his interests; within the limits set by his capacities and the gross circumstances of his life, a person's interests are primarily the product of the culture and the society in which he lives. It *is* possible, by persistent shrewdness, to modify and even direct these influences. A vigorous teacher can make it the thing to belong to the glee club or the Latin club or the home economics club. A school can easily stimulate interest in the basketball team but it can also arouse much interest in a Red Cross Drive. Its policy with reference to secret societies will have an important influence on the nature of the social interests of its pupils. A single enthusiastic community leader can make music a major interest of the young people in the town.

> The European dictators have given frightening examples of the extent to which the interests and ideals of an entire nation can be controlled. But moulding of interests by national leaders can be more admirable. Interest in strenuous activity, and in honest public affairs, was strengthened by Theodore Roosevelt. Now there is stimulation of interest in conservation, welfare, democracy. Leadership can thus do a great deal in school, community, nation.

The Nurture of Interests—An interest must, then, have its roots in the basic urges. It must be reasonably adapted to circumstances and abilities and the local culture. If it meets these prerequisites it may grow with such vigor that almost overnight the individual seems possessed by it to the exclusion of all other concerns. Or it may languish and die like something that has received a mortal injury. What are the powerful influences that may thus operate? They are two in number (but fundamentally one). An interest grows with tropical lushness in the warm sun of success and approval. It withers if not so nourished and stimulated, may even be blighted by only one devastating experience if instead of success and approval it meets ridicule or contempt and failure. An interest is essentially a thing alive. It is alive with feeling. It feeds on success—and on the attention-getting and status-achieving which are social success. It cannot be nourished otherwise.

Now the application to teaching. It is really very easy for a teacher to control the interests of her pupils, to stimulate desired interests and eliminate the undesirable (of those interests which meet the prerequisites mentioned above). All she need do is see to it that her pupils succeed with the desirable interests and achieve status with their fellows and her in so doing, but do not obtain success or recognition from interests which are not to be fostered.[25]

> A certain small boy in grade school loved to sing. One day the singing teacher was testing the voices of various pupils. This youngster, too eager, sang with uninhibited boyish vigor. With an annoyed look which the child did not miss the music supervisor said, "At least he has volume." The other children snickered and the boy was never interested in music again. Contrast this episode with the way in which interest in drawing was stimulated in the first case mentioned in the preceding section of this chapter. Both the boy's teacher and his mother helped him so that he made great progress in it. They approved

and admired his work. The exhibit of some of his sketches at school gave him status with the other pupils and his interest was much stimulated by that outcome.

SUMMARY

The chapter attempts, by a survey of recreations and amusements and preferences as to work and pleasure, to determine the nature of interests and the factors which shape them.

1. Play develops, in step with the growth of the organism, from simple and individual to more vigorous, complex, and social activities, then becomes dominated by sex-social interests in adolescence. Great individual differences are found in the nature and variety of play activities as well as in the extent to which they are social. Physical and mental ability, circumstances, and especially the attitudes and customs of the group in which the individual lives are the important factors involved in differences from age to age and within any age group.

2. Data on reading, movies, and radio make still clearer the development from simple and active interests in childhood to the sex-social interests of adolescence. They show also how the ready-made vicarious satisfactions of fiction may take the place of real consummations when major interests are blocked or starved in real life. And they show how amusements in turn may modify or stimulate interests.

3. Study of conversations and vocational choices once more point out the fundamental development from the simple and active to the more complex and sex-social. Again the importance of social and economic circumstance and of conventions is enforced.

4. Interest autobiographies emphasize the fact that interests are perhaps the most modifiable of all human traits. They are at the source of feelings—are vivid with feeling. They change, grow, or wither according as they achieve success and approval or are blighted by frustration and loss of status.

5. Interests are held to draw their energies especially from three basic urges: the urge to activity, the sex urge, and the urge for attention and approval. They develop within the limitations of the individual's physical and economic environment and his physical and mental capabilities, and according to the patterns set by his culture. Within these limits their development depends upon the

extent to which they reach the consummation of success. From these considerations, applications to education can be made which should be of distinct help in efforts to direct and control pupil's interests.

REFERENCES

1. As a matter of fact, this interest of young children in adult activities was even more important than is shown by the table. The investigators mention the frequency with which young children spoke of liking to "help mama" do this or that, or "put coal in the furnace if allowed." Because of difficulties in classifying such reports, they were not included in the table.
2. Modified from (39).
3. This is clearly shown by the data in this same study on the frequency with which various activities are engaged in at different ages. At 15, football is seventh in rank in the frequency with which it is played, but by 20 it has dropped to twenty-eighth position.
4. The data were gathered in 1931-1932; since then bicycling has become more popular. Fads and fashions in recreation will be returned to shortly. The general trends of the findings are believed to be of general significance.
5. Adapted from (1), p. 166.
6. A marked acceleration which puts a bright child far ahead into a class where the children are bigger and stronger than he and socially more mature (as when a preadolescent boy is put in among adolescents) is of course another and most unfortunate matter.
7. This continuity of child life is a fascinating and important thing; it is also illustrated by the way in which certain vulgar words are kept current among children in spite of adult disapproval.
8. One of the writers has recently been going over copies of *Our Young Folks,* a magazine published in 1867 for young people, and also some diaries of that period. The absence of formalized sport or competitive amusements is striking. A charming story by Harriet Beecher Stowe of an adolescent girl going to the "Academy" describes bobsled rides, and a candy pull from which the young people did not return home "till almost nine o'clock." But a competitive game is never once mentioned.
9. As a matter of fact, some younger boys do play with dolls, and there are plenty of boydenish girls. Analogous cases in adult life are also interesting. One of the writers knows of a star college halfback whose hobby is embroidering, and a woman whose favourite girlhood amusement was tinkering with machinery and who now owns a

garage; the late George Eastman's two favourite amusements were hunting big game in Africa—and cooking. At all ages, marked sex differences in play may soon largely disappear. And it may be added in this connection that sex differences in vigor and physique may then be lessened. Surely the extraordinary activity of the healthy boy must affect his physical development. Healthy girls seem about as active, if they are not restrained in such ways as have been mentioned.

10. From (8), p. 344.
11. This study included excellent data on adult reading, gathered by personal interviews. Only 27 per cent of adults had read a book during the month, whereas 82 per cent had read magazines and practically all had seen a newspaper (32).
12. The investigator states that the prominence of the *Post* and the *Literary Digest* may be due to emphasis in school on current events and large home circulation rather than outstanding pupil interest.
13. It would be pleasant to be able to say that school programmes in literature were an important influence upon the reading interests of young people. But unfortunately such programmes seem usually out of touch with the young people they might serve. Significant here is an article reporting that the average data of publication of material college students read of their own choice in 1934 was 1934, but the average date of first publication of books used in literature courses was 1673 (52).
14. Adapted from (44), pp. 111, 113.
15. The books of Blumer contain illuminating firsthand reports, from school youngsters and reformatory inmates, of incidents and actions illustrating the effects of the movies on them.
16. This total of course need not mean that any one person listens all this time. One careful investigator has found New York City children in Grades 6 to 8 to average about 6¼ hours per week. These children stated that they would rather listen to the radio than read an adventure story or book. They did, however, prefer a movie or reading the "funnies" to listening (21).
17. Declared one junior high school youngster, "The *Witch's Tales* is on at a pretty late hour when everything is still and somtimes I think a witch could walk right into the room, grab me, then take me to an underground den. ... After the *Witch's Tales,* which ends about ten-thirty P.M., I try to fall asleep. If I do, I dream of ghosts, goblins, and witches" (quoted in [21], p. 109). But many children, it should be added, early develop a certain sophistication. Said one, regarding the plight of the hero in a serial, "Of course the shark won't get him, because he has to be back for the broadcast tomorrow" (quoted in [30], p. 450).
18. Possibly of some interest in this connection are the results of an analysis of some 3000 actual letters written by children in Grades 4 to 6. The following topics predominated: (1) "activities and experiences of life,"

(2) objects, (3) school, (4) animals, and (5) weather. J. A. Fitzgerald, Children's spontaneous writings, *Peabody J. Educ.*, 1932, *10*, 172—178.

19. Adapted from (50).
20. Adapted from (38).
21. Adapted from (1), p. 134. The jobs italicized appear in *both* desired and entered lists and show some congruency of desire with attainment.
22. The above is a summary of a case study presented in (23), p. 377. The reader may find it interesting to look over the series of interest autobiographies presented in Chapter 11 of Fryer's volume.
23. Though aside from the topic of this chapter, it should be noted that in neither of the above cases was there informed consideration of probable opportunities in the vocations chosen, or of aptitude for them. In short, both cases well illustrate the haphazard way in which the average young person deals with his vocational problem, and the need for guidance and the lack of it.
24. Perhaps it need hardly be said that the above statement grossly oversimplifies the facts. Nothing less than the entire organism of the healthy child is back of the urge for activity; any attempt to give adequacy of treatment must call for mention not only of tonus in the neuromuscular apparatus but also of nutrition, the functioning of the various ductless glands—all the various organs and functioning in organic coordination.
25. The critical reader may well feel that the above discussion overemphasizes the modifiability of interests and gives too little recognition to biological determinants. Very likely so. Constitutional sex differences in interests may be subtly important; surely sex differences in total physique, ductless gland balance, and strength are such as might include or cause differences not only in aggressiveness but in the direction of interests. As will be seen in the next chapter, sex differences in social behaviour appear very early. Perhaps the pendulum of professional thinking has swung too far away from the concept of innate behaviour patterns. But the statement in this chapter seems reasonably in accord with empirical observations. If it errs a bit on the side of euthenics it at least takes the more optimistic and effort-stimulating point of view regarding human nature and its possible betterment.

6

The Development of the Emotional Life

Thus far children and adolescents have been pictured as having a great variety of interests and eager for their fulfilment—for recognized accomplishment and companionship and approval. It was stressed that the development of an interest depended upon the extent and nature of that fulfilment; an interest might grow greatly if nourished by success experiences, or wither if meeting only failure. Such outcomes must now be given more detailed consideration, with special reference to the cumulative effects of repeated experiences of one type or the other. What are the effects of continued failure and frustration of interests, of chronic neglect or disapproval from teachers or associates, or of continuing uncertainty and insecurity? How much difference does it make if, instead, a youngster usually has reasonable fulfilment of his interests, is usually approved, and feels that his world can be depended upon to act consistently in these respects? Here is a problem of outstanding and pervasive importance, on which much important work has recently been done. For teachers, the problem is central as regards their relations with their pupils—and their own success.

> Shy, shabbily dressed Jim had been "carried along" into the fifth grade, but it was obvious to everyone that he could not do the work there. He was chronically scolded by an impatient teacher, either disregarded or teased by the other children, clumsy and unskilful in games, criticized and bullied at home.

The boy was in a chronic state of bewilderment and fear because in most of the situations he had to meet he did not know what to do and was in constant dread of failure or rebuff. Largely similar in the nature of his difficulty but not in most other respects was a highly intelligent college freshman doing night work to earn his way. Because of lack of leisure and inconvenient hours of work he had made no friends; irregular and inadequate meals had disturbed his digestion; fatigue and loneliness and poor health had finally so upset him that he had failed a course. He was bewildered and on the verge of panic because he did not know how to meet the manifold problems presented by his first college year.

In contrast, plump Polly found her high school lessons easy. Youngest in a large family well known in the little town, she was popular with both students and teachers. Confident, active, smiling, a picture of health, she well illustrated how consistent success experiences (including satisfactory social adjustment) foster effectiveness, pleasant emotional tone, and physical well-being.

A FUNCTIONAL CONCEPT OF EMOTION

The basic concept is, then, that the nature of a person's emotional experiences depends on the extent to which his interests and urges are satisfied. If his interests and drives are frustrated, he will be unhappy and either timid and withdrawing or angry and aggressive. In fact, results of frustration may be varied indeed, and will depend upon a great variety of factors such as the individual's stage of development, health, previous experiences, present status, and the way in which the immediate situation is handled. But it often seems forgotten that habitual success experiences also have important and largely opposite effects upon the personality; there is not frustration but furtherance. These various features and types of emotion must now be considered in more detail.

Physiological Effects of Emotion—Certain physiological involvements of strong emotional episodes are well recognized. A person may tremble from either rage or fear. In fear or embarrassment (as before an audience) the mouth becomes dry from constriction of peripheral blood vessels including those to the salivary glands. In excitement the heart rate and blood pressure go up. The digestive system may be markedly affected. It is common to hear a person say, after some emotional experience, that he was "too excited to eat." It is a well-known experimental fact that emotion reduces the normal digestive movements and the secretion of digestive juices. There may be either constipation or diarrhea; the "examination diarrhea" of some students is a well-known college phenomenon.

These are the effects of strong emotional episodes. More important but less generally recognized is the fact that chronic emotional distress causes chronic conditions of these same types. The timid, often-rebuffed youngster may not actually tremble, but he is likely to be hesitant and awkward in his actions and to stammer in his speech. Appetite and digestion are likely to be poor, and he may be underweight. Disturbances of sleep are frequent—restlessness or nightmares in sleep, and trouble in getting to sleep or frequent working. Because sleep is not restful, there is chronic fatigue.

The extent to which children presenting emotional problems show various symptoms such as have been mentioned above is illustrated by the following tabulation. It gives the percentage of children brought to a clinic in the first instance because of fearfulness, who showed other difficulties.[1]

Sleep disturbances	65%
Feeding problems	45%
Temper tantrums	34%
Nail-biting	33%
Enuresis	29%
Crying and whining	18%
Masturbation	8%
Stuttering	6%

In contrast, the child who has reasonable satisfaction of his interests, and the social satisfactions of companionship and status, is likely to be ready of movement and of speech, to have good appetite and to sleep soundly.

Possibly the reader may have had this experience: The imminence of an important examination or interview or other critical occasion so worried him that he had trouble sleeping, dropped things and stumbled on the stairs, started and stammered when spoken to, found food less interesting, was constipated. Then if the crisis was passed successfully he found himself perhaps a little too active and talking even a little too readily, eating very heartily, and having an almost immediate marked restoration in the tonicity of the bowel.

Effects of Emotion upon Intellectual Efficiency—As was mentioned in the chapter on abilities, emotional distresses and frustrations interfere with intellectual efficiency. The unhappy individual seems abstracted, has difficulty keeping his mind on a task, and may become so emotionally blocked as to be unable to do anything at all. But as was also mentioned in considering the growth of special abilities, interests which come through and which bring approval and status make abilities grow.

One student, who was supposed to be taking a final examination, spent most of the time staring at the paper or out of the window. Occasionally she moved restlessly and wrote a few sentences, then relapsed again into inactivity. The girl had up to this time done fairly satisfactory work. Upon investigation it was discovered that her parents had decided to obtain a divorce on particularly unpleasant grounds, and that for about a month both had been pouring out their difficulties to her. All her feelings and affections for them were now thrown into confusion. She was fearful of what people would say. Gradually she became more and more unable to concentrate and more fatigued, until finally she came to this blocked condition in which she could remember nothing or make any progress whatever on the examination.

In contrast was a music student. She had not been doing outstandingly well. But to her delight she was chosen for a solo at a recital. She practiced as never before under the stimulus of this recognition, did well, applied herself yet harder, became one of the best musicians in the school, and chose the teaching of music as a career—all largely because of the emotional stimulus of these satisfactions to her desires to achieve status and to do well.

These two cases were somewhat extreme. Even mild frustrations, however, are likely to interfere somewhat with intellectual efficiency, and mild success make it more effective. A somewhat unusual experiment with 24 high school seniors is of interest here. At the beginning, each boy was asked to wait a few moments in a comfortable reception room where he thought himself alone, but really was being secretly observed as to whether he played with some games placed there, looked at pictures and other objects or sat and daydreamed. Then the experimenter came in and had the boy sort a pack of cards 15 times. With half the boys the investigator was bored and contemptuous of their work and faked a record showing them to have done far below the "norms." With the other lads he was congratulatory and enthusiastic, and faked a record showing very superior work. Then again the boy was left alone, and the concealed observer watched what he did. On the second day card-sorting was done again in the same way with each boy, with concealed observation again following. But after that, both groups were given a somewhat different task, and all were praised and "made to feel as phenomenally successful as possible"—then secretly observed again. Table 6.1 shows some of the things these boys did when alone after these experiences of "success" and "failure."

TABLE 6.1

Effects of Success and Failure upon General Behaviour When an Individual Thinks He is Alone and Unobserved (24 High School Senior Boys). Change from Initial or Pretest Observation, in Number of 5-Second Intervals Spent in Three Different Ways[3]

	"Failure" Group			*"Success" Group*		
	First Day	*Second Day*	*Final Success*	*First Day*	*Second Day*	*Final Success*
Daydreaming	3	8	1	—6	—2	1
Looking at record	2	1	0	9	5	4
Unfinished sortings	26	11	5	0	0	0

The first line shows changes from the initial observation in number of 5-second intervals spent in daydreaming or just sitting. The second line shows similar intervals looking at the norm sheet and record sheets. The third shows total number of times in each group that a boy, when alone, started sorting the cards again of his own volition—but never finished the job. Clearly failure caused these boys to turn away from their record and either withdraw their minds from the task or fumble in discouraged and inefficient fashion with it. But the boys who were happy with success examined the records closely, put their minds more to the immediate situation—and never once tried sorting the cards without finishing (23).

This experiment is an interesting demonstration of a phenomenon commonly observed. If such outcomes can be obtained on only two days of experimentation, it can well be appreciated that months or years of continued failure might establish habits of turning away from work, or of discouraged inefficient fumbling with a task, which would be of great characterological importance. Or success might increase competence.[2]

Effects of Emotional Conditions upon General Attitude—Emotional strain and frustration may cause attitudes of timidity and withdrawing or of irritability and aggressiveness. Such attitudes may appear significantly only in certain situations or in the presence of certain people. Thus a high school freshman was surly and aggressive in his attitude toward his Latin teacher; her sarcastic criticisms of him in class had affronted his pride. But he was shy and apologetic in an after-class discussion of his troubles in algebra with the teacher of that subject, since no such injury to his status before the other pupils had occurred. The attitude may be more general, appear elsewhere than at its source, or show only where it is safe; for example, a child may be irritable and aggressive at school because of a brutal father, or a father may be irritable at home because of a domineering foreman. It may become general; a sensitive child who has been criticized and humiliated for failing a recitation may soon come to dread reciting, then teachers and school, may play truant, have trouble at home—and become a runaway from all authority. Moodiness due to distress at home may become the habitual emotional tone.

It has been shown experimentally that frustration makes attitudes in general less favourable to other things and persons. Thus, boys at a summer camp were prevented by a tedious examination from attending bank night at a local theater. Before and after this frustration they indicated by a rating scale their attitude toward Mexican and Japanese (half rated Mexicans before the frustration, and half afterward, so that initial attitudes would be balanced). The attitude toward either set of foreigners was less favourable after the frustration (18). The attitudes of poor and frustrated southern whites toward Negroes may show an analogous displacement. It has also been found that voters in rural districts are likely to vote office holders out after a season of poor rainfall, though it was obvious that they were not responsible for the weather.[4]

In contrast, the person whose interest has found fulfilment is friendly with the people and circumstances about him, since they are fostering satisfactory experiences. If he is receiving the satisfactions of recognition and felt accomplishment in school, he comes to participate readily (perhaps too readily) in class discussions, likes teachers and school, and may from his satisfactory school experiences develop a general attitude of friendly confidence in his relations to those in authority.

A word frequently used nowadays is morale. One psychological dictionary defines morale as "the individual attitude in respect to confidence, perseverance in work, and adherence to ideals." Clearly the extent to which the individual habitually has success or failure, and so develops confidence or hesitancy in his efforts, is a major factor in morale. Also morale usually involves an identification of oneself with some group purpose—involves "belongingness." And this belongingness can hardly develop except where the youngster has a status and feeling of security as a result of reasonable success in his social relations.[5]

The Sociology of Emotional Development—The above point of view would make home and community conditions important factors in emotional development. Evidence stresses that this is so. Thus in one city it was found that there were only 86 maladjusted[6] school children per 1000 school enrolment in approximately 1800 square city blocks having residences of the single-family type. But in approximately 750 square city blocks of the multiple-family type of dwelling such as rooming houses and apartments, there were 183 maladjusted children per 1000 enrolment. Fathers of maladjusted children were classified occupationally as follows: 67 per cent were unskilled labourers, 22 per cent semi-skilled or skilled, 8 per cent clerical, and 3 per cent professional. Ninety per cent of the families of maladjusted children had inadequate income (less than $800 per year for two or more persons). Of the maladjusted group, 15 per cent were found to be lining with neither parent, 20 per cent with one parent who had been divorced and remarried, 62 per cent with their mothers alone, and 3 per cent had neither of the parents living. Whereas in the community studied there were 1.8 children in the average family, the maladjusted children came from families averaging 2.5 pupils enrolled in school. Almost 5 per cent had moved more than seven times within a single year. Sixty-six per cent of the homes were rated poor or very poor by welfare workers.

> Somewhat aside, though a product of the total socio-economic circumstance at least in part, are these further facts, that 35 per cent of the seriously maladjusted school children were 10 per cent or more underweight, as compared with only 5 per cent of the total school enrolment. When the seriously maladjusted boys were taken to a mountain camp for three weeks, they averaged a gain of eight pounds during the first two months of the new school term. None came before the school authorities for serious problem behaviour during the two months' period in the autumn. Of the seriously maladjusted cases, only one was a boy scout and he was not in good standing.[7]

Changes in Emotion with Age—Being thus a function of his interests and the extent of their fulfillment, which in turn are a product of his growth and the circumstances of his life, the individual's emotional nature should show a consistent development in congruence with all these facts. Nicely illustrative of this development is Chart 6.1. It is based on results from over 5000 cases and shows changes in worries or anxieties from Grade 6 through college.

The chart is based on unpublished data obtained with the "worries" test of the "interest-attitude" tests. This test consists of a list of 90 common topics of anxiety such as money, clothes, morals, appearance; and the directions are to put one cross before matters about which the individual worries or feels fearful, and two crosses before items about which he has been very fearful or worried much.[8]

Most obvious is the marked anxiety about physical dangers in the younger years and the way in which these are almost completely replaced by what might be called socio-economic worries by the end of college. But the sex differences must also be noted. The girls are apparently more timid about physical dangers such as fire. They show an earlier and (until the last two years of college) much greater concern about appearance and also about examination. Presumably the earlier sex-social maturing of the girls is here evidenced. Perhaps the falling off in these anxieties in the later years of college is a result of assurance (or acceptance) regarding these matters by that time. The boys worry more about ability and money. Clearly emotional development is a complex phenomenon, interrelated with all the other phenomena and factors discussed in this book.

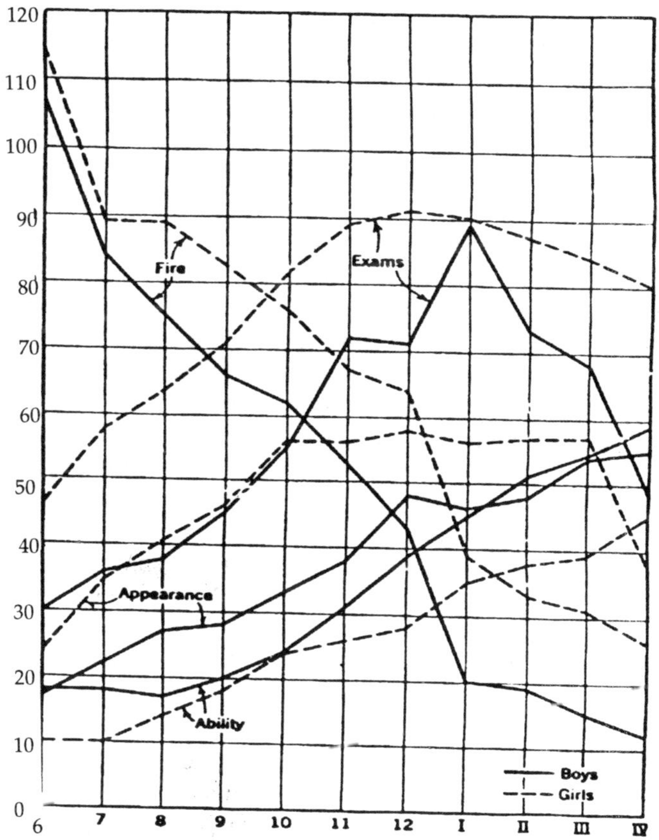

Chart 6.1—Changes in worries with age, Interest Attitude Test. (Numer of crosses for each word per 100 cases.)

It is often said that a person is or is not "emotionally mature." Presumably the expression refers not alone to such development as was mentioned above, but also to the extent to which emotional responses are under control. A 2-year-old in a temper tantrum may be thought of as not immature for his age. But a similar display in a 12-year-old would be regarded as a demonstration of immaturity. For a discussion of the concept, see (40), chapter 7

COMMON CAUSES OF EMOTIONAL STRESS IN CHILDREN AND ADOLESCENTS

From the above discussion it is clear that almost any situation may cause emotional distress if it is so hampering or so unfamiliar to an individual that he does not know how to satisfy his interests or desires. However, certain such confusing or frustrating situations occur so frequently during the school years that they deserve brief mention. As will be stressed shortly, the first step in dealing with an emotional problem is to find the cause.

Adjustment to a New School or Neighbourhood—Emotional distress may be acute as a result of transplanting a child or adolescent from one environment to another, if circumstances interfere with his ready fitting into the new one. Every nursery school, kindergarten, and first-grade teacher knows that the first day or two of school is a time of great perturbation for many children because they do not know how to get along with the other children or to behave in their strange new surroundings. A somewhat similar difficulty appears upon entrance into junior or senior high school or on going away from home to college. Each time the young person may feel so uncertain as to be greatly excited and distressed. Moving to new neighbourhood, especially if it is distinctly different from the old, may cause similar upset. The boys in a neighbourhood expect a newcomer to make good his status with them; thus freshmen are hazed. As was mentioned in the preceding section, maladjusted children often come from families which have frequently moved about.

> A friend of the writers as a boy, because of the itinerant nature of his father's work, went to 22 different grade schools. He never had a chum or felt secure enough in any neighbourhood or school to indulge freely any of his boyhood interests and desires. His most vivid boyhood memory is of a teacher who understood his problem and, in the five months he was in her room, helped him really to participate in the school life.

Adolescent Social Adjustment to the Other Sex—Adolescent boys and girls trying to satisfy their desires for companionship with the other sex are often acutely distressed. For instance, a high school boy calling on a girl for the first time did not know how to leave, nor did the girl know how to suggest his departure. Two embarrassed and miserable adolescents sat in the front parlour until well after midnight, talking of the same things over and over again, until at last the girl's father intervened and none too tactfully started the lad on his way. The next day the story was circulated by the father as a joke; but it was no joke to the boy and girl concerned, both of whom developed antagonisms and fears that remained with them for years.

> Anyone can remember incidents of a similar painful nature involved in efforts at heterosexual adjustment. Who has not known a boy who secretly worshipped some girl for weeks but did not know how to approach her? Or the girl who was introduced to a most charming young man—and then could not think of a thing to say? Or the boy who takes a girl out for the first time and does not know which show to see, whether or not to buy her a soda afterwards, or if she expects to be kissed when he leaves her? Who can forget the distress he or she went through, at one time or another, in regard to the suitability, in the eyes of the opposite sex, of one's clothes and appearance and manners? Such adolescent crises may be amusing to adults, but to the adolescents concerned they are potential or actual tragedies.

School Failure as a Cause of Emotional Problems—Continued failure in school, as has already been stressed, is another common and potent cause of emotional disturbance. The extent to which frustration of a youngster's desire for success and status in class and consequent regard at home may torture him is often not realized by adults. Every year there are newspaper reports of young people who have killed themselves rather than face further such agony. The number of youngsters who run away from this distress by truancy or who leave school at the first opportunity is large.

Social Conflict or Handicap—Children and adolescents are subject to far more varied and often conflicting social pressures at home, in school, at church, and in their own group than are most adults. Desires stimulated in adolescent groups may be disapproved by church or home, and school-fostered interests derided by companions. The girl who wants to make a high school social group may find herself snubbed because of her father's occupation, her mother's social ineptitude, or her family race or poverty. Such blocking or conflict of desires may have lifelong effects in warped personality; all too often the real cause of the emotional attitude is concealed because of hurt pride.

Vocational Problems and Emotional Distress—In later adolescence especially, there may be conflicts between the vocational desires of the youth and of the family for him, or handicaps which prevent the following-through of vocational interests. The drawn-out emotional strain of attempting an impossible vocation, then giving up but remaining dissatisfied in some other work, is only too common. But even this may be preferable to the longer stress of pressing on because of family influence to a goal not desired, obtaining a job not wanted, and pursuing uninteresting tasks day after day for a lifetime. A realistic and carefully considered vocational plan, taking sensible account of the individual's abilities, resources, and probable opportunities, is a major contribution to emotional well-being.

> One man, now over 40 years old, wanted to be a doctor. He attempted in vain to meet the requirements of several medical schools. His friends tried to discourage him, but to no avail. Even after his marriage and the birth of his first child, he returned to college for one more trial, as a result of painful saving for several years in his teaching position. He was only then finally convinced of the impossibility of this goal. And in spite of this experience he wants his oldest boy to study medicine, although the boy does not desire to do so and does not have sufficient general ability.

Level of Aspiration and Emotional Development—Very significant in connection with these problems are certain investigations regarding what is known as "level of aspiration." For instance, college students were given certain simple tasks, and before each trial each one was asked to indicate how well he expected to do. The task might be working problems in arithmetic for five minutes; before starting, each student would be asked how many problems he expected to do correctly in that time. Then his level of aspiration was compared with the accomplishment actually attained, and his reaction noted to his success or failure to do as well as he had stated he would do. Some students were overcautious and really did better than they had estimated, some were overambitious or boastful, some appraised themselves well. What a person says he will do, whether he does it or not, and how he reacts to his success or failure—all these features of these apparently simple little experiments may be significant regarding his emotional development.

> Thus, one student's prediction was always set lower than his performance. An interview showed that this attitude coloured his every action in life situations. He wants very much to go ahead but so fears failure that he systematically sets his goals low (thus "hedging" against failure). Another student who feels that he cannot really attain a certain goal tries to convince himself that he can by loudly declaring that he can. And yet a third sets a high goal and then tells people about it so he will work harder to avoid the shame of failure. In general, a goal too low or too easy causes decreased interest; the individual might stop work on the task entirely. A good success was likely to bring about a higher declared goal for the next trial. Motives might be various and complex. When asked why he tried to do better, one student said that he thought maybe he "wasn't doing as well as others, and therefore wanted to do better." Another student wanted to do better each time "because I didn't want to appear dumb, I guess. But [immediate cover-up] I'm not particularly worried whether people think I'm dumb or not."
>
> Failure usually caused the level of aspiration to go down; only rarely did it stimulate to a still higher level. Often it caused the task to be dropped. Said one student, "Sometimes I get sore, at other times I'm just discouraged. As a general rule, failure does not tend to spur me." Said another boy, "Failure makes me moody. Rather than spur, it probably acts as an anchor. I probably contrive an excuse for the failure. Success, I always think, is my own doing." And another boy said that, after failure, "I bust around the room and want to break everything."

Clearly, the individual's levels of aspiration are a product of his emotional development to date and a major determinant of his emotional reaction to a given experience. Obviously, a major contribution of the school to emotional development can well be an attempt to adjust levels of aspiration to reality as regards ability, socio-economic status, and personality so that emotional development may go forward without undue stress.[9]

THE PATHOLOGY OF EMOTION

If an individual suffers from continuing strong emotional stress and frustration, various results may follow, depending upon his vitality and ability, his previous habits, and the total situation. These results of continued emotional stress are so common, often have such serious consequences, play so large a part in classroom problems such as discipline, put such serious responsibilities upon the teacher, yet are so often completely misunderstood that they must now be carefully considered.

Emotional Exhaustion— The first of these results occurs when the individual remains face to face with his difficulty and is worn out by it. The outstanding symptoms are those enumerated above, only in more acute form; the individual is abstracted inefficient in work, unable to concentrate, irritable, sleeps poorly, is restless, has indigestion, and show marked and chronic fatigue. This condition is known technically as neurasthenia, and if a general collapse ensues is usually referred to by the popular phrase, "nervous breakdown." Such people have carried an emotional maladjustment until it has exhausted them. They have neither solved their fundamental problem, escaped from it, nor become adjusted to it; they have merely gone on and on living with it until it has overwhelmed them. The nervous breakdown may occur at practically any age but is most common in adolescence and early adult life.

> Some years ago one of the writers knew a girl who became a neurasthenic invalid. She was an only child. Her mother died when the girl was born, and the child was "brought up" by her father, of whom she was very fond. She was physically not vigorous and had a quiet and retiring disposition. During her first year in high school her father married a woman who had a daughter also in the first year in high school. The stepsister was a bright, vivacious, attractive person who soon over shadowed the other girl socially and academically. The girl's father was so in love with his new wife that he did not sense his daughter's difficulty, and she felt that she had lost her previous close companionship with him. The situation both at home and

> at school became unbearable. Her work went to pieces, she lost appetite, slept only irregularly, began to complain of headache, backache, indigestion, eyestrain, and attacks of dizziness and faintness. Eventually she took to her bed, where she stayed most of the time for over a year. There was no evidence of physical disease, although her physical condition was not good. But the emotional invalidism did have these two advantages: it kept her away from the situations where she could not successfully compete, and it brought her (as an ill person) more attention from the family than she could otherwise obtain. She could not really solve her problem and was continually hurt and exhausted by it; she stayed in the place where it was most acute—her home.

The neurasthenic is finally worn out because he neither solves his emotional problem not finds any emotional relief. Other individuals, although failing to solve their difficulties, manage nevertheless to avoid them in some degree. Such pseudo-solutions will next be discussed.

Escapes and Pseudo-Solutions—Perhaps the most obvious thing a person can do when faced by an unpleasant situation is to run away from it. Sometimes the escape is actual—the child leaves school, the man resigns his job, the wife leaves her husband, the mother abandons her illegitimate child, and the adolescent joins the Army or Navy as an escape from home supervision or a disastrous love affair.

> A man obtained a good position as chief clerk in a business office. It was soon apparent that he could not get along with his office force. Actually his failure to control the situation boiled down to the two facts that he did not give adequate directions for what he wanted done and that when annoyed by an error he shouted at the offender, making a public display of what could have been settled quietly. His subordinates were generally efficient workers, and they resented having the mistakes made through inadequate guidance aired so conspicuously. The man sensed the attitude of hostility readily enough, worried about his failure, was unable to sleep, lost his appetite, and became more crotchety than ever. One day he did not come to work. Inquiry revealed that he had left town during the night. He is now living on the family homestead in the country, his defects not only unremedied but intensified by the

bitterness of failure.

His difficulties might have been dealt with rather easily, for he needed to give more adequate directions and to speak quietly. But instead of analyzing his troubles and solving them, he ran away from the entire situation and wrecked his whole future career. Such "escapists" are more common than most people realize.

Some individuals cannot or will not run away, in the sense of actual flight to a new locality. However, they may still escape almost as completely by other behaviour. Perhaps the most common type of compensatory reaction is daydreaming. To be sure, everyone daydreams a bit, because everyone meets obstacles to the carrying-out of his desires. If the desires are not especially vital or the daydreams not so habitual that they interfere with the youngster's real work and play, such imaginings give some emotional relief and no harm is done. The trouble comes when a child settles back to habitual daydreaming instead of trying to "make good" in his work or play. Such a condition may arise when a youngster who is not very aggressive or sure of himself is faced day after day with a total situation that seems utterly unsolvable. He cannot run away permanently, although he may make the attempt. Since he is not vigorous or assertive, outbursts of indignation and resentment are not likely to occur; but a retreat from the whole unbearable situation is both possible and comfortable—he can simply not notice what is going on around him but substitute daydreams in which he plays with imaginary companions, is liked by them, dominates them, and can do as he wishes. If the maladjustment to child society, schoolroom, or home continues long enough, he will build up a habit of running away from reality, and probably, in later crises of his life, he will again resort to fantasies instead of trying to meet and solve his problems. While it brings temporary relief, habitual daydreaming is an escape mechanism that leaves the individual without any real, lasting solution.

If such symptoms as have been described are indulged in long enough, the individual concerned may develop dementia praecox, may become insane. The essential characteristics of this disease are a complete withdrawal from reality and a concentration upon a world of fantasy. Such a person has so entirely substituted his fantasies for the actual happenings of the world that he on longer distinguishes his daydreams from reality. As implied by the name, dementia praecox starts relatively early, usually during the years of adolescence. It thus presents a very serious problem. Case histories of dementia praecox almost invariably show that the beginning can be traced back to odd behaviour long before the child completed his schooling. Parents rarely appreciate the danger in the early stages of this condition; unless the teacher does, no preventive steps are likely to be taken.

> The unhappy, socially isolated youngster who finds relief in reverie is a rather common problem in the schoolroom but is often overlooked because he is so quiet and well behaved. For instance, one girl moved from the country and went to a large city high school. There her somewhat boisterous, unsophisticated efforts at friendliness were met with rebuff. She was at first hurt and bewildered, then irritable and defiant. Her classwork slumped badly. But gradually she seemed to become reconciled to the situation, and would sit for a period of time apparently deep in thought, occasionally smiling to herself. A little later she dropped out of school. She tried to hold a job but was too abstracted and absent-minded to be employable. Gradually she lost contact more and more with the real world, and lived completely in her imagination. She sat for hours apparently in a daze, smiling oddly from time to time, developed queer mannerisms which appeared to be related to her imaginary experiences, and occasionally became suddenly excited or exhausted, apparently without reason. In the end she had to be sent to a hospital for the insane.

These extreme cases are not common; but the possibility of this outcome should make the teacher consider carefully any pupils who show such symptoms. The final collapse rarely comes while the individual is in school. However, the teacher should realize that the disease has its start in the conditions of frustration and withdrawal into an imaginary world described above, and she should appreciate the school's responsibility for getting such youngsters back into a normal existence before their isolation is so complete that nothing can be done.

Other less complete retreats from reality are shown by those who find emotional satisfaction through the movies, reading sentimental stories, or in a highly emotionalized religion. Some people lose themselves so completely for a time that the movie or story becomes reality for them, and they themselves live the scenes in imagination. Often the incidents of the story are embroidered by the reader with brief daydreams. In any event, he becomes identified emotionally with the characters of the play or story, and is oblivious to reality. It should also be mentioned that the type of reading matter often reveals the nature of the unsatisfied longings. The physically weak boy not only dreams of being an athletic hero but also reads fiction or sees movies of heroic events. The homely and unpopular girl dreams of being popular and sought after, and finds a wistful pleasure in romance and in stories of girls who were happy in their home and school lives. The compensatory nature of these activities is obvious.

Rationalizations—Thus far, two common and unfortunate results that may be brought about by a persistent "obstacle situation" have been presented. The person may struggle along until he is worn out, or he may avoid the problem either by running away from it or by retiring into a false world of imagination. The third inadequate reaction which the individual may make is this: he may falsify the situation to himself so as to minimize the problem.

Extremely common are certain mental mechanisms called "rationalization," "projection," and the "sour grapes" type of response. Suppose, for instance, that boy wants to belong to a certain gang but is for some reason unacceptable to them. He is constantly faced by the exceedingly uncomfortable fact of social rejection by a desired group. Suppose further that he is too vigorous to become exhausted or admit he is licked, and that he either finds no compensation in daydreams and reading or else does not happen upon that particular form of escape. He may "rationalize" his failure by saying that his parents do not wish him to play with the gang because it is composed of undesirable boys. If he is successful in this rationalization, he no longer feels the unpleasantness to the same degree. Or he may project the blame for his exclusion on some boy in the gang, saying that this boy has always disliked him without reason. Having done this, he becomes much more comfortable. Projection is, in essence, merely a particular form of rationalizing in which the individual shifts the burden of his own maladjustment to someone else. Again, he may explain to anyone who will listen that the gang is not really worth belonging to—after the fashion of the fox in the fable who could not reach the grapes he wanted and so said they were sour and not worth reaching. This is another form of rationalizing an unbearable situation so that it becomes more tolerable.

> If the reader wishes to observe these mechanisms in action, he or she should talk with students who have desired beyond all else to join a fraternity or sorority and have not been asked to do so. These students may wear themselves out with their distress over the situation, they may leave college, they may use some form of rationalization, or they may go on at great length, upon all possible occasions, about the pernicious character of secret organizations. Or there may be still other reactions, to be described next, to the situation.

Overcompensation—Overcompensation, another reaction to frustration, is the result of feelings of inferiority. However, it takes a quite opposite form from that shown by nervous breakdown and exhaustion, for the individual seems to take on an excess of self-confidence and desperately starts out to make himself appear adequate when he really is not. He pushes himself ahead and into everything, brags about his achievement, is generally obnoxious, is usually resistive to discipline, and tries constantly to "show off." But a little close observation will usually show the condition for what it really is. The bewildered and unhappy youngster is frantically trying to conceal his difficulties and to bluff through, somehow, the situations with which he is having trouble. Sometimes such extroverts succeed and emerge with a real adjustment and a truly self-confident personality. Sometimes, their bluff called, they collapse utterly, with courage gone and spirit broken. The boy in the illustration below was able, because of good native ability and the considerable assistance given him, to achieve a partial adjustment; his case demonstrated the type of symptoms that appear in the schoolroom.

> William Nelson came to the university from the farm. His education had been gained in a small township high school and before that in a one-room country school. His whole manner, dress, and speech showed the sort of background he had. Upon entering the university he went into pre-medical work and was getting along fairly well when he was sent to one of the writers because of personal difficulties with his instructors and with the assistants in his laboratory courses. They reported that this boy was often extremely conceited, that he talked back to the teachers in an aggressive manner, that he domineered, over the other students in such a way as to irritate them, that he talked

> continually about his cleverness, and generally conducted himself in a manner that was most unpleasant to those about him.
>
> He appeared for his interviews dressed in "clothes, talked in a loud and familiar manner, and in general seemed to be trying to give the impression that he was a sophisticated and very self-sufficient collegian. The picture presented by this student is familiar to those who deal with problems of emotional maladjustment. He had as the basis of his trouble the much-talked-of "inferiority complex" which is common among students who come from small places and find themselves unprepared to compete socially with most of the students at the university. This boy's grammar and dress immediately gave him away as a farmer, and he therefore adopted an extreme manner and clothes to overcompensate for the inferiority which he actually felt. His impertinence and his talking back to his instructors were to be thought of primarily as efforts to appear to them a competent individual who could handle any situation with a debonair and confident manner. His occasional efforts to domineer over his associates were, similarly, frantic efforts to assert his adequacy and thus conceal his inadequacies from both them and himself.

It is evidently vital that the teacher should understand these conditions for what they are and help the youngster to a real adjustment, instead of adding to his already intolerable burden by well-intentioned but ill-timed disciplinary measures which, at the very best, can serve only to eliminate certain symptoms and can never solve the underlying situation.

Hysteroid Reactions to Emotional Distress—There remains one other relatively common but odd and hard-to-understand reaction which children may make when frustrated and in emotional distress. Some peculiar, inadequate response may be hit upon and used because, for the time being, it seems to work—or at least to give some release to the stress.

> A dull third-grade boy, who was failing in school, chronically scolded by his teacher, and looked down upon by the other children, one afternoon vomited his lunch—partly because of indigestion and partly because of emotional distress from a scolding. To his utter astonishment, his illness caused sympa-

thy from teacher and children, and he was for the first time in his life the centre of attention. Thereafter, whenever he was scolded or his desires were blocked in any way, he would vomit. In another case, a little girl had been told some smutty stories that had greatly disturbed her, especially because she was assured, on what she considered undebatable authority, that her adored mother and father had indulged in the practice so lewdly described to her. She could not reconcile what she had heard with her previous estimate of her parents' moral infallibility. The conflict continued to disturb her, causing general restlessness, careless schoolwork, and sexual fantasies. Finally she struck out at her problem and discomfort by stealing a sum of money from the cash register in her father's store. This act seemed, by some obscure reasoning, to bring relief. Of course it solved the situation only temporarily, and her vexation soon returned. Presently she again stole because it made her "feel better"; inasmuch as she never made any use of what she stole, this explanation seems likely. Several of her thefts followed directly after she received more sex information from an older child, thus precipitating the fundamental problem once again.

These special devices for getting attention or one's own way range all the way from the small child's simple tantrums to almost unbelievably bizarre, hysterical episodes. But they all have this in common: they originate in frustration and emotional distress and are devices for relieving that distress and achieving in some form the frustrated desire. In handling such cases, therefore, it is exceedingly important that one should seek the cause and not merely the symptoms. Obviously, to expose the girl for her unconscious subterfuge or punish the boy for his gastric gymnastics might or might not suppress the particular symptoms in question; it would only increase the emotional distress, and almost inevitably other similar devices would soon appear.

In both cases, the hysterical symptoms disappeared after their cause was understood but, unfortunately, not until after both teachers and parents had punished the children severely. There is usually nothing more senseless than punishing a hysteric. For the boy, the treatment consisted in his removal into a class where he could progress and where he was as capable and acceptable as the other children. During the period of his readjustment any vomiting was disregarded as far as possible. When he could gain formal attention and satisfactions in other ways, his vomiting ceased. The girl was quietly talked with until her deep conviction as to the nastiness of sex relations had been replaced by an attitude of understanding. The stealing has since disappeared. Both children are at the moment free from their previous troubles, but their freedom may not continue. The dull boy will undoubtedly meet with failure again, and the girl will probably find heterosexual adjustment and marriage difficult. Both children have already set up hysterical modes of response, and these reactions have been ground in by punishment, reproof, and misunderstanding. It is possible that in another crisis these or other hysterical actions will be resorted to.

These two examples illustrate a number of points in regard to the hysterical type of response. The response is often irrelevant to the stimulus and, indeed, is in many cases a veritable accident. It is almost always dramatic, explosive, and attention-getting. It often turns the situation from something distressing to something pleasurable by the simple expedient of playing on the sympathy of others. It offers a temporary dishonest solution of the underlying problem which, however, remains virtually untouched and in readiness to set off another explosion in the near future.

Stammering and Other Incoordinations—Among the unfortunate effects of prolonged emotional stress is stammering. A few unfortunate children thus afflicted have actual anatomical defects or dysfunctioning as the basis of their difficulty, but most stammerers have on physical handicaps; the entire cause is emotional distress. Nothing shows this more clearly than the fact that the stammerer usually has trouble only in certain situations. When he feels relaxed and comfortable he speaks normally, but he stammers when embarrassed or excited. School obviously involves numerous opportunities for embarrassment to a stammerer, and he is therefore likely to grow worse as his schooling continues. Most cases largely clear up early in adulthood after the stresses of adolescence and schooling are past—leaving, however, unfortunate residues of shyness and reticence.

The child with a speech defect is almost always ridiculed and made fun of, at least by the other children if not by the teacher. It is therefore to be expected that a stammerer will develop various secondary emotional attitudes, such as shyness or irritability. The teacher should always be on the lookout for children who are beginning to show a speech defect or already have one. In only rare instances is there anything wrong with the speech mechanism; usually the difficulty is wholly emotional. As one expert has said, "Stammerers can always sing, swear, and soliloquize." Fluent speech under some circumstances and a stammer under others make it clear that the defect is not physiological.

Instead of or in addition to stammering there may be other incoordinations such as tics, peculiarities of movement or posture, or clumsiness. Again there may be a physical basis; thus the tic or clumsiness may be a residual of chorea. But more often the cause is emotional.

Belligerency—A person who is too vigorous to admit defeat, too pugnacious to run away, too clear-headed to fool himself by pseudo-solutions may fight back at a worled that is so uncomfortable. Naturally, this type of behaviour leads to acute and stubborn problems of discipline in the school or at home.

> Illustrative is a high school boy who had almost terrorized his companions and teachers. This lad's father was in the penitentiary—unjustly, according to the boy. For a time after the commitment the boy remained in a somewhat dazed condition, was publicly humiliated by comments from the other children, and ignored when invitations for social gatherings were being issued. Presently, however, he began fighting back. He knocked down anyone who twitted him about his father when a little girl ignored him he twisted her arm until he had forced her to kneel and apologize; he threw rocks, with deadly aim and intent, at others. Sometimes his cruelties were practiced on children too young to resist, presumably because he could get release from his emotional strain in proportion to the pain he inflicted. Gradually his bellicose attitude spread to adult society. On one occasion he tinkered with the brakes on a teacher's car so that they would not hold; the teacher was nearly killed. At another time he entered a neighbour's house and fixed a heavy weight over the front door; when the woman of the house returned from market the weight fell on her head and stunned her. Twice he set fire to valuable property. This blind striking-back at society was his method of response to intolerable humiliation.

Aggression may manifest itself in various ways. Most obvious is aggression against the cause of the frustration—the adolescent is angry at the parent who objects to his late hours and other efforts at escape from childhood restraints. But there may be displacement. Thus a brilliant college girl had all her life been dominated by her brilliant and very dominating mother. She admired her parent too much to rebel but became a great espouser of causes to aid the oppressed, her latest episode being leadership of a student strike against a faculty rule. The aggression may be turned toward a scapegoat. For example, a teacher in difficulty with her principal developed a strong antipathy toward one of the most capable boys in her room. Aggression toward the principal was hardly safe, but this boy seemed to have become a symbol of her instructional trouble and she vented her irritations on him.

Clearly, aggression is almost always difficult to deal with, and belligerency such as was illustrated by the delinquent boy may become very dangerous.[10] How should one deal with such cases? To try to stop aggression due to frustration by attempting to frustrate the aggression would seem to run the risk of compounding the psychological pressure. Yet this is the first impulse. These aggressive cases are often frustrating to the teacher's efforts to carry on the schoolwork as she had planned; a mounting aggressiveness on both sides is the result. Others are drawn into the situation; there are punishments and recriminations, and lifelong personality trends may thus be established. Many criminals seem to have such a background. Evidently early calm understanding of the real situation and alleviation of the frustrations or a finding of substitute responses by which the individual can make good are here especially important.

> Efforts were made to help the belligerent boy described above. Other pupils were asked to be considerate of him and accept him. He was helped to make good in athletics. His escapades were disposed of out of court, and one teacher who understood him had many friendly talks with him. But unfortunately things had gone too far; most of the other students and teachers, and the boy himself, were all too bitter to permit reconciliations. He was helped just enough to keep him out of trouble and show him how to get by, and he came to take pride in his ability thus to get along. After leaving school he became notorious as a man who engaged in shady business practices and with whom the law never quite caught up.

The strikeleader was talked with in considerate fashion by a teacher who knew her very well, and when she had calmed down a bit she was asked quizzically if her difficulties with her mother might not have something to do with her crusading zeal. After a moment of spluttering protest she laughed and admitted that it might be so. The strike was soon cleared up. But the girl is chronically an agitator and leader of causes. And in all fairness it should be added that often the cause is good and she renders a real service. As mentioned earlier, many famous people seem to have obtained their drive from psychological backgrounds such as have been described above. Benjamin Franklin in his autobiography that his lifelong desire for liberty may have had its origin in his boyhood resentment at the domination of an older brother.

Factors Determining Mode of Response to Emotional Strain—Why one person reacts in one way to persistent emotional strain and another person reacts in very different fashion, while a third seems hardly affected at all, is often not clear. It is generally recognized that individuals suffering from illness, fatigue, or lack of sleep are especially subject to emotional upset. Differences in physical vigor might affect mode of response, physically strong individuals tending more toward belligerency and the physically weaker to escape or exhaustion. Stage of physical development is almost certainly important. One investigator found a correlation of .94 between aggressiveness in boys and evidence of onset of puberty.[11]

Social and cultural factors are also important. Thus aggression is a more approved reaction for boys than girls. A repressed New Englander seems more likely to become neurasthenic than a Southerner. A person from a lower social class is perhaps more likely to overcompensate. The family "culture pattern" is undoubtedly very important. The reader probably knows some families in which children rarely cry when hurt and other families in which crying or hysterical outbursts are the expected form of response to any difficulty. But within each family there may be great differences in reaction to emotional strain. Presumably each individual's response to stress must be understood in terms of his total personality and development.

The Frequency of Emotional Distress—It remains to emphasize that emotional distress of a considerable degree is by no means rare. In fact, it might well be called the more usual thing, somewhat as most individuals have some physical handicap. A very careful and intensive study of the emotional life of a group of college students, selected more or less at random, showed that 68 per cent had either a past or present persistent inferiority feeling. One-third had experienced rejection in childhood. One-third had had a marked guilt reaction. A concluding paragraph of the study may well be quoted:

> "Most of our subjects were carrying . . . a heavy load of crippling anxiety, inferiority feelings, guilt feelings or dejection. Many of them, of course, were troubled by thoughts of financial insecurity, but the majority were more concerned about their general social status. They doubted that they could live up to their own standards or to the expectations of their parents. Frequently, they suffered from memories of stinging humiliations, and when they went to their books in the evening, overriding apprehensive thoughts of future failure or depressing feelings of separateness and forsakenness prevented concentration. A basic sense of insupport aggravated by dissensions with one or both parents was a frequent finding. This was commonly accompanied by moral conflict."[12]

In fact, most people, knowing little of other folks' emotional distresses, overestimate their own. It is a sorry but perhaps helpful thought that probably one's own troubles are not so unique or so great as, lacking that perspective, is likely to be assumed. Increased considerateness for others and a gain in one's own comparative self-confidence may well result. The need for much more helpful consideration of these so frequent and so distressing problems in school is also emphasized by all these facts.

> "The patterns of affective behaviour shown by children are certainly as important as number knowledge, eye-movement habits, and language skills; yet they are widely ignored by school people. Tantrums, daydreaming, fighting, shyness, teasing and bullying, bidding for the attention and approbation of the teacher, masturbation, impertinence, and a host of other ways of behaving are the patterns by which pupils try to relieve tensions or work out their personality needs. To recognize these behaviour patterns for what they are, to understand their causes, to know the manner in which they were learned, to find more mature ways of behaving appropriate to the particular child and to evoke that mature behaviour—these are not easy tasks for school people."[13]

THE DIAGNOSIS OF DISCIPLINARY PROBLEMS

Chronic or severe conditions of emotional strain have thus far been emphasized because in a young person's development these are far more important than the occasional outburst of talking back, uncontrollable laughter, fighting, swearing, or crying, and because, being more extreme and persistent, they show more clearly the important phenomena involved. Furthermore, the discussion was not restricted to emotional problems as they appear in the school, because it is vital that emotional distress be understood as a whole, with reference to the child's total existence. With this background, the question now arises as to what understanding may be obtained concerning episodes of conflict in the school. Since disciplinary problems are usually reported as the most difficult with which the young teacher has to deal, insight into such problems should be of great value.

Chronic Emotional Distress and Disciplinary Problems—First to be considered are situations in which the chronic emotional conditions discussed in the preceding section may cause disciplinary crises. Belligerency and overcompensation are usually irritating to both the other pupils and the teacher. Hysteroid behaviour is likely to be both disturbing and puzzling. The daydreamer and the neurasthenic usually present no classroom police problems, except as the first type may resent the teacher's efforts to break in upon his reverie, or an unsympathetic teacher may push a neurasthenic so far beyond his strength that he becomes desperate (that they especially need her help has already been stressed). In view of all that has been said in the preceding two sections, it should not be necessary to elaborate further upon the extent to which children suffering from persistent problems of emotional distress may present persistent problems of classroom management. If a teacher will locate and carefully study such cases, she will be on the way to a solution of her most baffling disciplinary problems. A pupil not emotionally "sick" may nevertheless present disciplinary difficulties. These cases must next be considered.

Disciplinary Problems Due to Conflict with an Unsuitable School Programme—The most common difficulties of this sort come from the reaction of healthy children against an unsuitable school routine or programme of work. Significantly, such difficulties are more common in a conventional school than in schools of a more progressive type, for in the conventional school the pupils are expected to be quiet and not to move about or *do* things. But healthy children are active and restless and find being still for any length of time almost intolerable. Inevitably, in a conventional school, healthy youngsters come in conflict with its methods and with the "drillmaster" teacher.

Furthermore, as is emphasized again and again throughout this volume, school-age youngsters are highly social. But the conventional school has a routine which is anti-social. Conversation between children is forbidden, and for children to help each other is considered wrong—it is each child for himself. Inevitable the friendly, sociable child finds himself in conflict with the perverse moral code of the classroom.

Moreover, the curricula of the average school are all too often out of contact with the pupils' interests. The youngster in the manual training class who would like to make a model place is required to make a whisk-broom holder. The girls who would enjoy, and who would be helped to a discriminating acquaintance with, good modern literature are required to read Shakespeare or George Eliot and write character studies of Lady Macbeth. Modern-minded youngsters who would read avidly about current events must consider instead the state of the Roman Empire under Augustus or study the weary details of the Hundred Years' War. Millions of children still plod wearily and resentfully through the intricacies of Latin grammar. Little wonder that an alert and questioning younger generation, hungry for knowledge about the manifold problems of the modern world, should be chronically rebellious against the inanities still present in the average high school course of study. And the teacher who must force such a programme upon her pupils must expect to have continuing difficulties of discipline in holding her charges to these tasks.

Finally, in the average school there are numerous instances of maladjustment between work and ability. It has been reiterated that success experiences are essential for healthy mental hygiene. The boy in the algebra class who cannot learn algebra is a frustrated, unhappy, resentful youngster who is almost certain to cause the teacher trouble. The daughter of the local grocer who is being made to wade through *Hamlet*, though without the slightest understanding, is more than likely to pass notes or whisper to her neighbour. The highly intelligent girl in the first-year class who can read French better than the average third-year pupil is almost certain to show periods of inattention which are irritating to her teacher.

In the conventional school, then, there are many conflicts between pupil and teacher which are the fault of the school, not the pupil. It may almost be said that the more healthy and intelligent the pupil, the more disciplinary problems are frequent in her room, to consider whether such factors may be the real cause. To be sure, she is largely helpless to remedy certain of the faults above mentioned, as in the course of study. Yet if she understands the situation she will at least be more tolerant, and perhaps, on some curriculum committee, she can do her bit toward making things better. In numerous little ways she can do much to bring the work into more vital contact with the needs and interests of her class.

The Analysis of the Specific Disciplinary Episode—The above discussion has been general. Actually, any real disciplinary episode is a concrete, specific affair, born of a variety of obscure influences which may include all the factors mentioned above. A consideration of the following episodes should make this clearer.

> In a certain school Miss A was one day asked to take over a group of tenth-grade youngsters who were completely out of control of the young teacher who had been in charge. The class had started on its downfall in a curious fashion. In the middle of the room there were two small columns that supported the ceiling. One chronically failing boy whose seat was behind a column evidently became exasperated and proceeded to "shinny up"the annoying post. The inexperienced teacher unwisely shouted at him and he, being well out of reach, proffered some replies. In a few moments another lad had climbed the second column. Someone suggested a race between the climbers; in a moment there was a group at the foot of each post, thus preventing the teacher from laying hands on either boy, and an elimination tournament was in progress. The teacher shouted, scolded, and even cried, all to no avail.
>
> At this point Miss A entered the room, reassuringly sent the younger woman to the teachers' rest room to regain her composure, then calmly sat down at the desk and began

correcting themes. Not the slightest attention did she pay to the students, who presently discovered that climbing dustry posts was not much fun. When the groups had dispersed of their own accord, Miss A took a hand. First she asked the two boys who started the trouble what had ailed them. They replied that the posts were a nuisance. She then asked if there were not some more sensible solution than climbing them. In a few minutes the class was at work moving the desks around the room until difficulties of seeing and hearing were reduced to a minimum. By this time the school day was at an end.

On the following Miss A entered the room to find a couple of lads climbing the posts again, but she simply smiled at them and went on with the interesting lesson she had prepared. Soon they went back to their seats. The childish boy who had started the trouble returned to his gymnastics two or three times, but Miss A paid no attention. By the next day his antics began to be greeted by adverse comment from the other pupils. Miss A smiled to herself and knew the crisis was over.

In this case, the outburst was clearly a reaction of irritation, on the part of a failing boy, against the chronic handicap of having the post in the way; and this reaction was elaborated and continued because the lad found that it made him the centre of attention and interest and hence was in delightful contrast to the legitimate class activities in which he could never make good. The class gleefully aided and abetted him because the episode gave them welcome opportunity to shake free for a few minutes from a conventional school routine and get up, move about, talk. The incident was successfully handled by eliminating the immediate cause (the seat behind the post) and by bringing it about that the proscribed activity (post-climbing) brought social disapproval rather than applause.

In another instance a bright, nervous, high-strung third-grade child refused point-blank to read aloud a simple story about animals that talked, because she regarded it as silly. The order was repeated, the stubbornness increased, and the exasperated young teacher told the child she could not leave school until she had read the story aloud. At five o'clock the deadlock was broken by the principal, who required merely that the girl read a passage from any book, whereupon the youngster proudly pulled from her desk a copy of *David Copperfield* and read a passage with gusto. Once again the underlying causes of the trouble were multiple and of long standing. In the first place, the child was not well. The work was far below the level of her interests and her ability; the episode was the climax of an accumulated exasperation at work which she considered beneath her. And she craved the satisfaction of showing what difficult material she could and ordinarily did read.

In the background of all these episodes one sees a gathering rebellion against a series of stupidities on the part of the school. To be sure, the school is not always wrong! The moral is that one should stop and study a situation before acting. The reader should recall disciplinary episodes he has observed and attempt to analyze them in similar fashion. Obviously, such episodes can never be understood without understanding the children involved, and the social situation. Even where the fault is the pupil's, analysis is still needed if the treatment is to be effective.

The Teacher's Attitude as a Cause of Emotional Stress and Disciplinary Difficulty—Very often indeed, a teacher's attitude toward her pupils arouses in them feelings productive of disciplinary problems. Significant here is Table 6.2, which shows the teacher characteristics best-and least-liked by high school students.

TABLE 6.2

Four Most Frequently Mentioned Characteristics of Best-Liked and Least-Liked Teachers, as Reported by 3725 High School Seniors[14]

Best-Liked Teacher	*Mentions*
Helpful with schoolwork, explains lessons clearly	1950
Cheerful, jolly, can take a joke	1429
Human, friendly, companionable, "one of us"	1024
Interested in and understands pupils	1024
Least-Liked Teacher	
Cross, crabby, nagging, sarcastic, loses temper	1708
Not helpful with schoolwork, work not planned	1025
Has favoured students and "picks" on others	859
Haughty, overbearing, does not know you out of class	775

Clearly the teacher who loses her temper, has favourites, and is overbearing is likely to stir up resentful emotion in her students and to have disciplinary clashes.

THE HANDLING OF PROBLEMS OF EMOTIONAL DEVELOPMENT

It remains to bring together the implications pervading this chapter regarding the handling of problems of emotional frustration and fulfilment. The following suggestions appear of most importance.

The Importance of Going Back of Symptoms to the Underlying Situation—It is first of all fundamental to recognize the inadequacy of simply treating symptoms without consideration of the underlying situation and the possible effect of the treatment upon it. The pupil who is belligerent, morose, daydreaming, or truant is not adequately dealt with if punished for his aggression, berated for his moodiness, rudely interrupted in his "wool-gathering," or pursued by the attendance officer; instead, the treatment may in each instance aggravate the basic difficulty. The important questions are: What frustration or confusion is causing the aggressiveness or moodiness or the real or imaginary flight from the schoolroom? How may that situation be cleared up? Can a reasonable satisfaction of the frustrated interests be somehow secured? Or may the interests need reconstitution, and the level of aspiration need to be changed? These problems, not the symptoms, require attention.

Where there is not frustration but furtherance, the background situation must nevertheless be considered. Mabel seems particularly interested in history and is doing notably well, but a crush on the history teacher turns out to be the key factor in the situation. Ruth writes so well that her delighted English teacher hints at a possible career as an author, but Ruth is a shy little girl whose interest in literature is almost as unhealthy a substitute for real experience as daydreaming. Bill's long hours and beautiful work in the industrial arts shop are in part an escape from and compensation for his poor work in his other subjects. Mary's interest in preparing to teach turns out to be more her mother's interest in having her do so; Mary's good work in normal school is motivated by her loyalty to her parent, not her eagerness for her prospective profession. John's enthusiastic good work in mathematics is really enthusiasm at beating Algernon, son of the community's toplofty social leader. Whatever the nature of the emotional experience, if the background situation is not considered, the teacher may make some sad or even ridiculous mistakes.

> The puzzled mathematics teacher found that when Algrenon dropped out of the class John's work slumped badly. Ruth's interest in literature evaporated after she acquired a boy friend. When Mabel's crush came to its inevitable disillusionment, she "hated" history.

The Importance of the Teacher's Being "Objective" and Having Insight Regarding Possible Involvement of Her Own Emotions—In the second place it is of prime importance that a teacher should not let her own emotions become so involved in her relations with her pupils that she acts to satisfy her own feelings rather than their needs. A pupil's inattention, stubbornness, or insolence naturally arouses irritation and countering aggressive responses in the teacher, and to indulge her own feelings by sarcastic remarks and yet other aggressive responses is a release and satisfaction to her. But it usually only adds to the tension. Instead of reacting subjectively in terms of her own feelings, she should maintain an objective attitude of calm, friendly open mindedness and desire to understand what the trouble really is. Often nothing more is needed to handle a disciplinary situation that easy good nature and refusal to take a bit of excitement seriously.

> All that the experienced teacher did in dealing with the post climbing boys was to maintain an easy placidity that calmed the class and made it evident that she could not be "razzed" into making a Roman holiday for them. On another occasion in her own class, a boy put his feet on his desk, while watching her covertly. The young teacher would have been irritated or hurt and ordered the feet down. But this experienced teacher, wise in such matters, seemed to have a blind spot for those feet. After a while the lad put them down. Then she thanked him for doing so, but went on to explain blandly that if he simply could not work in any other posture she would certainly not let the conventions of the classroom interfere with his education. The feet remained off the desk for the remainder of the semester.

"Objectivity" means further that the teacher will not be shocked or upset by various types of distressing information which may come to her. For instance, a desperate youngster may blurt out to her a story of some sex episode which seems to her very disgusting. But she must not show that feeling, any more than a physician should show disgust when he sees a sick person. Nor should she go into a dither of sympathy for the unhappy youth, any more than a physician should exhaust his feelings in sympathy for his patient. An important contribution of a good physician is his calm unemotionalized cheerfulness in the sickroom— the implication he gives that things after all are not so bad as the patient thinks, that many people have been ill before and recovered, that one shouldn't worry, that if the patient will only keep calm and follow the doctor's directions everything will be better before long. Similarly the distraught young person needs calm reassurance, understanding of his problem, and commonsense suggestions as to what he should do. The well-informed teacher will know that various episodes and habits not uncommon among children are not so abnormal as was once supposed.[15] She will not be prudish or moralistic; she may give directly, or in suggested reading, information which will be helpful; she will have helpful suggestions or suggest where they may be obtained (perhaps from physician, nurse, or psychologist).

Very important but little mentioned is the fact that a teacher should be objective and on guard as to possible involvement of her own emotions in connection with her pupils' likes and accomplishments as well as their antagonisms and wrongdoings. Mabel's interest in history (mentioned in the preceding section) was at first greatly encouraged by her teacher in large part because this teacher much enjoyed the girl's admiring attentions. The English teacher encouraged Ruth's ideas of becoming an author and helped her obtain publication of a story in the local paper, because it added to the teacher's own self-feeling and reputation as the one who had discovered and developed this girl's "unusual talents." The mathematics teacher did not like Algernon much better than John did, and encouraged John in part for that reason. In fact, probably most of the time, the average teacher, being human, deals with her pupils' emotional problems on the basis of her own feelings rather than theirs.

Deep-seated and long-established attitudes present especially difficult problems here. Two teachers in the same school, who may be called Miss Wright and Miss Frank, had both come from very strict homes. Miss Wright was a repressed sensitive woman who was so shocked and upset by student delinquency as to be worse than useless in dealing with such cases. But she did much to encourage and help shy sensitive girls such as she had been. Miss Frank was a big hearty rebel who was impatient with sensitive people but rather admired pupils with "spunk" even when they got into trouble. Pupils who liked one of these teachers usually disliked the other. As faculty adviser, each was good (in fact, sometimes too sympathetic) in dealing with the emotional problems of some pupils but only stirred up trouble in contacts with others. In assigning students to advisers the shrewd principal kept these facts in mind, and the two teachers nicely supplemented each other, each handling especially well youngsters the other disliked.

The teacher's as well as the pupil's emotions are thus involved in most emotional problems arising in school—and to keep thinking straight is indeed a task for all concerned. Perhaps the greatest single help in this matter (beyond understanding it) is a sense of humor. If a teacher can laugh at herself—and laugh with but not at the pupils—in considering these problems, then tensions are released and perspectives gained.

The Importance of a Devlopmental Rather Than a "Police" Point of View, and of Fostering Desirable Emotional Experience—All too often administrators (and visiting parents) consider a teacher capable in proportion as she keeps order. And the teacher approves those pupils who never upset the order in her room, but extends herself especially to restrain those lively youngsters who "disturb the peace." This is a police point of view.

However, if a vigorous outgoing development of each child is considered the main objective of education, criteria for judging both teacher and pupil will be very different indeed. The quiet repressed child will be regarded as a problem—and also the repressive teacher who tends to make children so. The good teacher will be recognized as one in whose room the pupils feel so secure and unrepressed that legitimate activities can be undertaken without hesitation. She will try to free them of frustrations, fears, and resentments, and resolve any impasse causing unpleasant emotion.

But she should do more; she should foster desirable emotional experiences. It was suggested at the beginning of this chapter that pleasant emotions were the result of the satisfaction of interests—in contrast to emotional distress which was caused by their frustration. In the preceding chapter, however, it was emphasized that interests are a complex product of many factors. They have their roots in biological urges. But specific interests are largely determined by the total socio-economic and cultural environment in which the individual develops. The present chapter has stressed the importance of level of aspiration as determining the extent to which a person finds it needful, for his selfesteem and status, to carry through a particular interest. A school can thus make a first contribution to a young person's happiness by giving sensible direction to his interests so that they are congruent with his abilities and by keeping his goals so that they are feasible for him.

In the second place, a young person's interests and aspirations at a given time being what they are (and assuming that they are good), the school can help him realize them. As was emphasized earlier in this chapter and in the discussion of special abilities in Chapter 4, the satisfying of interests can be as pleasant and as upbuilding as their frustration is distressing and destructive. It is to this constructive task that the teacher's chief efforts should be directed, and in which she can find her own greatest satisfactions.

SUMMARY

The chapter his stressed what has been called a functional concept of emotion. Emotion has been defined as a condition of heightened feeling which may be pleasant or unpleasant according as the interest involved is satisfied or frustrated. If frustrated, the individual may draw back, or he may become aggressive and drive forward with increased and angry effort. Where there is success, there is furtherance of the activity—a tendency to continue it, with heightened vigor. The total organism responds to this total biological situation. With frustration there is interference with normal physiological activities, but a heightening of them with success. The failing person tends to give up what he is doing, but with success he applies himself more. With frustration there is an attitude of irritability or fear, but success brings confidence and agreeableness. Emotional experiences are naturally affected by age and by socio-economic circumstances.

Some frustration and emotional distress are likely to occur whenever a particularly difficult problem is met. A child or adolescent is especially likely to have difficulty when he enters a new school or neighbourhood; when his development, as in adolescence, carries him into new interests; when he has trouble with schoolwork, social ambitions, or vocational plans, or has aspirations not congruent with possibilities. When such crises seem to be occurring, a wise teacher will especially try to help.

If frustration becomes acute or chronic, abnormal psychological conditions may result. The unhappy person may become exhausted by his struggle. He may try to run away or escape from his problem, or deceive himself about it, or adopt a pseudo-solution. He may become angry and aggressive. Such conditions are symptoms of emotional illness and call for careful study and treatment.

Emotional problems are particularly difficult to handle because pupils often dissimulate, and the teacher's own feelings are often involved. It is therefore very important to get back of symptoms to underlying causes, and to be objective. Most important of all, the teacher's effort should be to foster success and desirable emotional experiences, rather than simply to prevent emotional distress.

REFERENCES

1. Adapted from Kanner (35), p. 289.
2. A section in chap. xii will develop further the effect of emotions on learning in school.
3. Adapted from R. R. Sears, Success and Failure, a Study in Motility, in (23), pp. 235-258.
4. Amusingly illustrative of shifts in general attitudes with frustration is the case cited by Murray (46) of the boy who had recently had a falling-out with his girl. When asked to give an estimate of the state of the world in general, he wrote: "I believe the world is going socially and morally to destruction. Society is on the downgrade now, even as that of Rome." It would be interesting to know what his attitude toward the world in general would have been if the two had made up.

5. It must not be inferred from the above emphasis on the desirability of success experiences that the individual should have *all* his paths smoothed and efforts made successful. It is only desirable activities which are thus to be fostered; but they must be so fostered if they are to develop and if there is to be good morale. However, a point shortly to be stressed must here be anticipated. Frustration may cause increased effort—sometimes mere fruitless anger, but sometimes (as in the lives of many famous individuals) a drive that accomplishes more than might otherwise have been expected. If his last is to occur, there must be no collapse of morale. The individual must find a way in which he can succeed—into which he puts himself with increased satisfaction and vigor because frustrated elsewhere.
6. The question may be raised as to whether "maladjusted" here means "emotionally maladjusted." The writers believe that essentially it does, in the sense in which these items are used in this volume. That is, these were bewildered or frustrated, the fulfilment of their interests was hampered. They were considered maladjusted because of evidence to that effect.
7. James F. Bursth, Home and Community Conditions Related to Pupil Maladjustment, *Fifteenth Yearbook*, National Elementary School Principals, 1936, 15, No. 6.
8. The tests are described in the *Journal of Applied Psychology*, 1933, 17, 1-16.
9. For instance, of aspiration to enter a profession, there may be built up an interest in a skilled trade or agriculture in youngsters whose abilities and circumstances best fit them for these latter occupations.
10. Hitler and Mussolini may well be considered cases of long-continued frustration producing exceptional aggressiveness. Social groups like the Ku Klux Klan may be formed of frustrated elements in a society and operate in fashions described above. Even whole nations, like Germany, may become frustrated, then aggressive, turn on a racial scapegoat, and strike out savagely in all directions. For an interesting discussion of such matters, see (18).
11. Sollenberger, quoted in (18), p. 103.
12. From H. A. Murray and others, *Explorations in Personality*, Oxford University Press, p. 730. By permission of the author and the publishers.

    A further finding of this investigation may be mentioned. An emotional stress may be determinative in life plan. Thus a student who stuttered chose philology as his major field, and another, who had a frequent fantasy regarding the death of his parents in an automobile accident, became a salesman of automobile insurance and consequently had frequently to go to the scene of accidents.

13. Prescott, *Emotion and the Educative Process,* American Council on Education, p. 202.
14. Adapted from F. W. Hart, *Teachers and Teaching,* Macmillan, *1934,* as quoted in (49), pp. 273-274.
15. Well worth reading in this connection is Hugh de Selincourts's remarkable story *One Little Boy* (Boni, 1924, 266 pp.) Good general discussion of such problems will be found in P. M. Blanchard and C. Manasses, *New Girls for Old* (Macaulay, 1930, 281 pp.); Dorothy D. Bromley and Florence Britten, *Youth and Sex* (Harper, 1938, 303 pp.) J. K. Folsom (ed.) *A Plan for Marriage* (Harper, 1938, 299 opp.) and Butterfield (15).

7

The Social Psychology of the Child

The preceding chapter showed how within very wide limits interests are determined by social influences. More than that—increasingly interests *are* social until in adolescence they are predominantly so; the drive for social recognition and status becomes the most pervasively important of all. Later chapters will show how character traits and ideals result from the subtle conditionings of social psychology, and how delinquency may be an outcome of psychologically unhealthy homes and neighbourhoods. Emotional stress will be found largely a product of social conflict or maladjustment, and various types of mental abnormality the resultant of such distress long continued. Disciplinary problems in school usually have such backgrounds. In the pupil's social development is thus to be found the key for understanding many of the most difficult problems with which a teacher has to deal. The guidance of this development along healthy and desirable lines might well be considered the first concern of modern education, and the almost complete neglect of this problem the outstanding weakness of the traditional school. An adequate treatment of the social psychology of the first 20 years should thus be essential and central in educational psychology.[1]

It must never be forgotten that development is continuous and cumulative; how a child gets along with other people at 10 or even at 5 may be of great importance in understanding his social difficulties at 15 or 20. Nevertheless, it must be stressed that changes in child nature plus changes in the circumstances of life combine to make the social psychology of different age periods very different.

Three such periods may here by profitably differentiated: the "pre-school: years, up to 6; the elementary school or middle childhood period, from 6 through about 12; and the adolescent period, from puberty to about 18. The social psychology of adolescence is in fact so distinctive and so important that a separate chapter will be devoted to it. A concrete description of a typical boy and a typical girl at each stage may make the differentiation clearer.

First, Jimmy at 5. Much of the time he plays happily by himself, often talking to himself. Even when with other children he may pay little attention to them. At most, play groups are small—not over five other children. Play (a already described in Chapter 5) is usually largely random running about, tricycle riding, block building, or sand-pile digging. He is still very much a home body. His parents are the all-important people in his social world. He plays with children of either sex and even in a group in which all the others are girls; he is not yet conscious of sex. Nor is he modest about physical matters when in the company of girls; he will fight physically with girls and is not embarrassed by physical contact with them. And Betty of the same age is similarly home-oriented, still somewhat of a baby, and as yet also undifferentiated as regards the fact of sex.

Jim at 10 is a different boy. He is very insistent on the fact that he is no longer a baby; the neighbourhood rather than the home is his social habitat. A chum of his own age and sex is now at the centre of his social interest and he is much in the company of seven or eight other boys of his own age. Jim's mother is afraid the group may take on the character of a gang, but the association is too casual and the composition of the group too variable with circumstance to be so designated in any unfortunate sense. Jim's family is now somewhat on the periphery of his social world. Games are social and loosely organized like marbles or cops-and-robbers; Jim plays little by himself. He pays little attention to girls, plays mostly with boys, will not take part in a game or join a group in which he is the only boy. He is sufficiently conscious of sex to be modest around girls and to avoid touching them. And Betty for her part, now 10, has pulled off into her own sex group, sits with other girls, whispers and giggles with them, plays with them, is modest with boys. She is more conscious of her sex than Jim, partly because she is a bit older physiologically and emotionally, partly because society emphasizes sex to her more by stress upon modesty and the proprieties and restraints of conduct which parents and teachers think appropriate for a girl.

At 15 James is socially a different person again. He now participates in highly organized team games. He will not take part in games with girls, but he does begin to show an interest in such social activities as dancing with them; he is interested in them but self-concious and embarrassed where they are concerned. Whereas previously the chum of his own age and sex was socially central and the gang of seven or eight other boys the social group, now a member of the other sex is at the centre of social interest (his choice as yet varies from time to time, however) and the social group is the crowd of both sexes. His parents are yet more out of his social world and are often regarded with impatience because of their "old fashioned' notions about hours and behaviour. He will not tolerate any sort of physical attention from adults or others of his own sex. Elizabeth is very much interested in boys, but she does not engage in their games. Instead she likes to dance with them, sit next to them, have their attention; she spends much time primping when she is to be with boys. In contrast to James, she indulges in physical affection with other girls of her own age.

In short, it is clear, if one only stops to think of it, that there are marked changes in the social life of children at different ages. These matters must be now looked at somewhat more fully.

THE "PRE-SCHOOL" YEARS

The pre-school years might at first thought seem no concern of school or teacher. But study of this period shows major personality trends often already clearly evident in these first 6 years; habits of social adjustment or maladjustment formed at this time may determine the course of the individual's social relationships for the remainder of his life. So important indeed are these years that the nursery school movement, aiming to guide children's development better than is possible in the average home, has become one of the most distinctive and scientifically productive movements in modern education.

By the age of 3 or 4 some childhood personalities are already clearly recognizable—some as fretful, others gleeful, some placid or quiet, and others restless or assertive. By these ages some babies have so well learned to get their way by temper tantrums that years later they use similar techniques in managing their mates. Spoiled 4-year-olds grow up to be willful adults. A child who has lived in a quarrelsome home or been constantly shouted at and yanked about for the first 6 years of his life is likely to have established attitudes of cringing timidity or callous, noisy self-assertion which continue for years thereafter. In almost all such cases, wise handling during the pre-school years could have largely avoided the unfortunate outcomes.

Social Trends During the First 6 Years.—The newborn infant is a squalling little animal. But response to social stimulation begins surprisingly early. Around 2 months a baby may begin to smile in response to a human voice even though at this age he does not smile at other stimuli. By 7 or 8 months he will stretch out his hands toward an adult, pull at an adult's clothes, cry when an adult stops talking to him. If at this age another infant is placed nearby, the baby may touch him, coo, and smile; otherwise his behaviour might be described as socially blind—the partner is treated about the same as are play materials. But around 18 months the interest gradually shifts to include the partner. From 2 years on, the way in which both solitary and parallel play (play where two children are together but pay practically no attention to each other) rapidly decrease is shown in Chart 7.1 Associative play, already fairly common at 2, increases somewhat, and cooperative play most of all.[2]

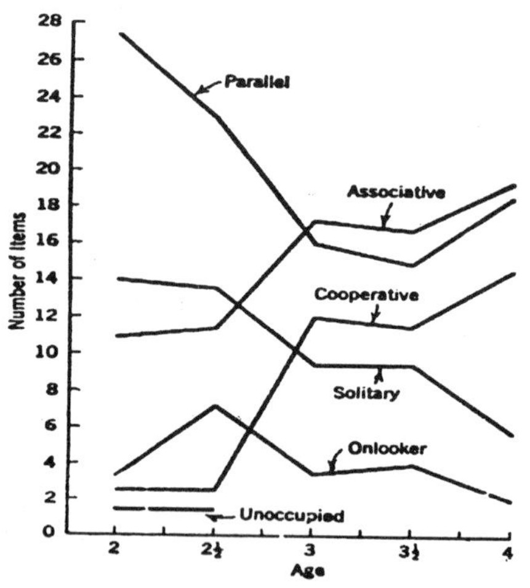

Chart 7.1—Mean number of times each activity was engaged in at different age levels (6 children at each level; 600 observations on each child). (Adapted from Parten [50].)

This development of social behaviour may be reported in various ways. Another nursery school investigation showed that in free play situation 2-year-old children spent 41 per cent of their time in social contacts, 3-year-olds 64 per cent, and 4-year-olds 77 per cent (41). Further, social play for 2-year-olds is likely to be some relatively unsocial act (like mutual admiration of mud pies) with one other child, whereas a 4-year-old will engage in the cooperative making of sand pies with four others. Further evidence of the increase in amount and complexity of social behaviour is shown in Chart 7.2. Social withdrawings and mishaps decrease; efforts to secure attention and status grow.

Older nursery school children respond to social contacts by laughing and smiling more often than younger children. But through-

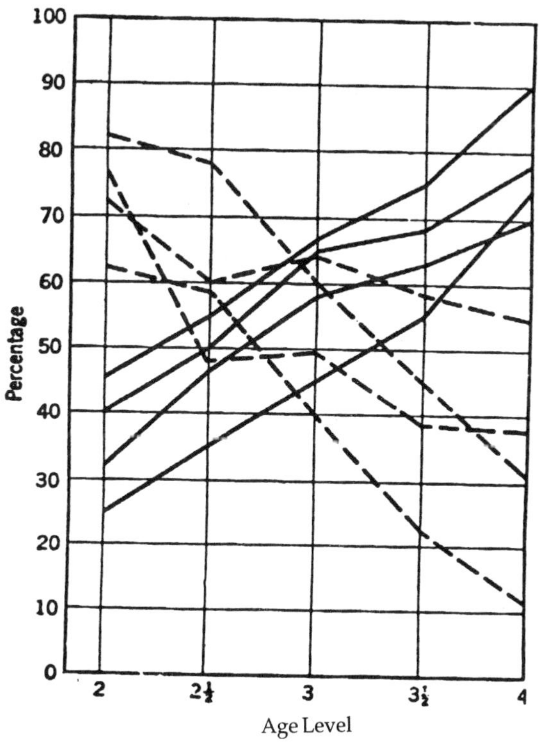

Chart 7.2—Developmental course of certain types of behaviour (555 children) (Based on Hattwick and Sanders [28].)

out these young ages laughing and smiling occur more often in connection with general motor activity than in purely social contacts (15). One investigator found over these ages a laudable decrease in percentage of pronouns referring to the self (a trend which unfortunately seems not, by many, continued into adulthood!). With increasing age, other children are more frequently referred to by name. That the social world of young children is still greatly home-centered is evidenced by the finding that of the total number of word concepts used by children aged 2 to 5, one-third referred to mother, father, sibling, or home (57). Very interesting are the following percentages of children at each age from 2 to 7 who exhibit competition (23):

Age group	2—3	3—4	4—5	5—6	6—7
Number of cases	8	15	11	20	11
Percentage showing competition	0	43	69	75	86

Seemingly indicative of a growing social understanding of sorts is the summary of records of behaviour presumably involving anger that were kept for a month by certain mothers. With advancing age the forms of behaviour displayed during anger become more definitely directed towards a given end—presumably often social. The following figures show the percentage of the outbursts at each age involving undirected energy and retaliative behaviour :

Age	Under 1 yr.	1-2 yrs.	2-3 yrs.	3-4 yrs.	Over 4 yrs.
Undirected energy	89	78	75	60	36
Retaliative behaviour	1	6	11	26	28

Individual Differences in Social Development—Intensive observations of 20 infants from birth showed differences in "personality" (in irritability, in tone and timbre of the cry, in tonicity of the muscles, as well as the quality of reactions to the test situations) apparent in some from birth and in all within the first 3 months (57). In a nursery school group one child played alone only 1 per cent of the time, whereas four other children played alone 33 per cent of the time (50). In a kindergarten some children made twice as many social contacts as did others (65). Even in the nursery school some children seem to be "born leaders" whereas others are passive and easily led.

Certain sex differences in social behaviour appear even in these early years. Boys quarrel more. Girls talk more! Table 7.1 summarizes some of the data regarding sex differences in nursery school.

An intensive study of a group of 20 children from birth until about 6 years (56) showed vividly the differences in total personality and especially in social reactions and attitudes which children may exhibit. The children were seen at home, at play, at the nursery school, and in neighbourhood play, the investigators becoming well acquainted with these children and their families and being accepted by child and family as a friend. Even in the earliest weeks these children showed differences. A boy and girl who were twins were in many respects oddly contrasting. The boy was active, expansive, smiling, constantly seeking the attention of other people; but the girl was more quiet, serious, thoughtful. Yet this little girl even in the nursery school took a somewhat protective and slightly condescending air toward her twin brother. In another family, the boy was, from the earliest weeks, exceptionally strong and adept in movement; on the playground he became something of a problem because his great vigor and skill made him dominate all too easily; and literally run over other children. But in social relationships he was relatively silent and shy. And in all these respects—physique, strength, skill, and reticence—he was very like his father. Another girl was wiry, tomboyish and very active, like her mother in physique and behaviour when she was a child. This little girl preferred play with boys, was more competitive than the average girl, more assertive, Yet another girl was described, even in diapers, as petite and with a certain air about her which some people never attain. She had a way; with her; clearly the social personality showed early.

TABLE 7.1

Sex Differences in Behaviour; Percentage That Certain Types of Behaviour Occurred[3]

Behaviour More Common with Boys	*% Occurred* *Boys*	*Girls*	*Difference*
Attacks others	60	44	16
Asks unnecessary help	79	66	13
Laughs, squeals, jumps around	68	51	17
Rushes into danger	48	27	21
More Common with Girls			
Stays near adult	41	67	26
Twists hair	37	57	20
Avoids play	40	52	12

The Child's Social Nature and His Home—The preceeding section has indicated that constitutional factors are important in determining a child's relations with others—his social personality. Constitutionally some children almost from birth are energetic, quick, attractive in appearance or manner, responsive to the presence and behaviour of other human beings; other children are passive, unappealing, shy. But almost from birth, the baby's responses begin to be modified by other people's responses to him, and more broadly by the total circumstances of his babyhood.

> Quite obviously the child of a half-sick harassed mother in a crowded noisy slum home develops different reactions to others than does the only child of doting parents in a quiet suburb. Many other factors operate. The youngest in a large family may be babied and the oldest be early neglected for the next child, with important consequences as regards the social personality in each instance. Personalities in the home may interact in many ways. Thus the father of an exceptionally strong and vigorous boy was strong and active and delighted to play with his son; he also enjoyed having the youngster in his basement workshop—but the father was shy and there were few visitors in the home. Shyness on the part of the boy, and development of mechanical and athletic interests, were natural outcomes. A little girl was high-strung and tended to have temper tantrums. The mother was also high-strung and indulged in emotional outbursts. The father was reserved, dreaded such outbursts, and almost invariably gave in to whatever was wanted. Presumably the child was constitutionally more excitable than average. More important, however, are the further facts that she was frequently excited by her excitable mother and that she found she could get her own way by such means.

Numerous investigations have shown that homes of different types tend to develop distinctive social characteristics in young children. Children who live in overattentive homes tend to be too dependent on adults, avoid aggressive play with other children, dawdle and leave tasks incomplete, cry easily and lack emotional control. Children who come from homes where the mother is irresponsible or negligent tend to seek attention by showing off, telling fanciful stories, crying easily. Children whose parents share work and play experiences with them have better understanding of property rights, are more cooperative, get along better with other children

(26). Nursery school children who come from homes where there are tension and conflict between the parents are more likely to show problems of social adjustment than youngsters from reasonably harmonious homes (7).

Discipline is a matter of obvious concern to both parents and children. How do different types of discipline affect the child's social adjustment? Table 7.2 shows that the more frequently "natural result" is used the more desirable is the personality trait.[4] But discipline based on temper or on what happens to pop into the parent's head at the time tends to be associated with undesirable outcomes.

TABLE 7.2

Correlation Between Types of Discipline Used by Parents and Personality Traits of Their Children[5] (Positive correlations appear throughout only for "natural result" and correlations are all negative for the last four types of discipline)

Type of Discipline	*Sociability with Other Children*	*Attractiveness of Personality*	*Tendency to Face Reality*	*Independence of Adult Affection and Attention*
Natural Result	.19	.33	.33	.37
Rewards	.30	—.11	—.14	—.15
Physical	.05	—.17	—.35	—.20
Isolate	—.28	—.06	—.07	.01
Worry	—.07	—.21	—.30	—.44
Pops into head	—.40	—.54	—.52	—.40
Temper	—.33	—.42	—.61	—.10
Penance	—.15	—.19	—.44	—.08

Child specialists also agree that consistency of discipline is exceedingly important. Demoralizing to anyone would be inconsistency such as the following: An 18-month-old baby refused to take his nap; after he kicked and screamed for five minutes his mother gave in and the nap was omitted. That night when he was put to bed he repeated his tantrum, but this time he was spanked. A day or so later he refused to take his nap without being rocked, and after five minutes of screaming he was rocked. Next day he again demanded rocking and was spanked.

Perhaps it need hardly be added that consistency does not mean unreasonable rigidity. Reasonable compromises between parent and child often avert clashes. Thus a small child who wanted to carry a pan of potatoes which his mother would not let him have because it was too heavy, was quite satisfied when she gave him two of the potatoes to bring along. Sometimes a tantrum may be a largely justifiable device. Thus a 2-year-old repeatedly made a reasonable request for help in getting upon a davenport, but was completely ignored. Finally, in desperation she began to kick and scream and was then lifted up.

As intimated by various of the above illustrations, not only what is done, but the "home atmosphere" in which everything goes on, is exceedingly important. Calmness, tolerance, humour, a voice unexcited and manner unhurried, a perspective such that the parent is not unduly disturbed when a nap is not taken or one child pinches another, calm and prompt application of corrective methods if called for without nagging afterward—such an agreeable home atmosphere prevents many problems from rising and facilitates the handling of those which do appear.

School for Babies.—The little everyday happenings in the life of a 3-year-old baby may seem very unimportant indeed. Yet (as mentioned at the beginning of this section) they may determine the direction of the whole social development of the individual. Adults who are complaining or petulant or irresponsible or subject to emotional outbursts are often what they are because of habits learned in this pre-school period. These problems of social adjustment in infancy are subtle and difficult, and few parents are "professional" parents! In fact, most mothers and almost all fathers have had no education whatever for parenthood. And though most mothers won't admit it, the small child about the home is not always an unmitigated joy; he is sometimes a burden or even an exasperation. Further, many modern homes give no contact with adults other than the parents—aunts and grandparents and friends are less often in the home than used to be the case. The modern small family may contain no other children. How splendid it would be if there were places to which a mother's spoiled brat might go for part of each day to be under the eye of adults who *did* know about small children, and in association with other babies who might themselves teach the brat a thing or two. The nursery school might well seem an answer to prayer.

The nature of nursery schools has already been briefly described in Chapter 4. Here it must be emphasized that the nursery school is most of all a school for social development; it might be called the beginning school for the process smugly supposed to be completed in the private finishing school but almost entirely left out of the usual elementary school programme. The nursery school sees as its most important and explicitly recognized task the guidance of the child's relationships with other people, especially through two critical phases of such relationships—the achievement of a first independence of parents and friendly acceptance of adults outside the family, and the debut into the society of other children of the same age outside the family group. For these new contacts the small child must learn the appropriate manners and the ways of holding his own and getting along with all these new associates. Here is a task indeed for child and school.

> The careful nursery school knows much about the child and his home before the school year begins. Parents have been interviewed. The child has visited the school with his mother. Perhaps it was arranged that several mothers visited the school at the same time, with their offspring. For half an hour, while the children played and the mothers visited in comfortable chairs at the edge of the playground, the teachers could observe and make some acquaintance with both babies and mothers.
>
> If a child is timid or unused to being away from home, the mother may be asked to stay at school the first day or so. But she must be to one side, with knitting or reading, and must not encourage the toddler to stay with her. Instead attractive play materials are placed at a little distance, and a teacher encourages him to play with them. Usually after a day or so the child pays little attention to the mother.[6] She then remarks to him casually that she is going on an errand but will return shortly. If her absence has not disturbed him she can, from then on, leave as soon as he has become interested in some activity. Thus dexterously and without the infant's awareness has an event of tremendous import to him been brought about. He has left his home and his family and ventured out into the wide world by himself.
>
> Usually he finds this new world delightful. Very possibly the teacher's calm, imperturbable "know how" with children is something of a relief from a home not always imperturbable. There are many things to do: blocks to pile, easels at which to paint, an aquarium with fish to watch, picture books to look at, a piano which the teacher will play. No less interesting are the other children; to an only child they are the greatest novelty. Watching them is an important aid in social development. The

shy child is not hurried into participation. The teacher finds play which interests him and, as he becomes accustomed to the school, soon has him playing near other children, as in the sandbox. She may have him and another child help move the teeter-totter and then suggest that these two children play on it, or show him how to do something special which he then shows another child and thus acquires importance and self-confidence.

If two children are too much together she arranges activities so that they join different groups. If in social difficulties a child regresses to mere crying the teacher may say, "Tommy doesn't understand what you want when you cry. Talk to him." And both talking and social cooperation are furthered. Friendly acts are publicly commended. A tease or bully is kept busy at activities which bring him legitimate satisfaction. A contagious good humour eases through social crises which might otherwise cause conflict. The able nursery school teacher regards such guidance of each child's social development as her major function, and her outstanding trait is tact. She is not so much a teacher as a hostess. Would that teachers above the nursery school put even half as much emphasis on such development or had even half her sensitivity to each child's social nature and needs!

When an attempt is made systematically to determine the outcomes of such programmes as regards social development, what is found? In the first place, it is clear that nursery schools do foster social contacts between children. For example, two groups each of seven children average 3½ years old were carefully observed in the fall and again in the spring with reference to the number of half-minute intervals in which they engaged in some sort of social interchange with other children. The first group had not been in nursery school before, but the second group had been there for a year or more. Table 7.3 summarizes the results.

TABLE 7.3

Percentage of Half-Minute Intervals During Which Social Contacts Occurred[7]

	Fall	*Spring*
Children without previous nursery school experience	21	54
Children in nursery school one or more year preceding	47	58
Greater sociability of second group	26	4

Those children without nursery school experience rapidly (in fact, even during the first few weeks) gained on the "veteran" nursery school children. Analysis showed that social interchanges in the latter group in the fall consisted in considerable part of contacts with close friends from the preceding year, but over and above this there was a greater readiness to enter social enterprises.

However, more happens than simply an increase in sociability; a positive personality develops. A nursery school is a lively place; one study has reported the average nursery school child to get into some conflict with another twelve times an hour (conflicts of brief duration, of course, and far outnumbered by contacts friendly in nature).[8] Independence grows, as shown by a count of the number of times a child refuses, by word or deed, to carry out the demands of others or to give ground. Children who had been in nursery school six months were rated higher than youngsters new to the school in sympathy, independence, and self-reliance (64). Careful comparison of over a hundred children who had been in nursery school only six weeks with others who had been there nine months showed the latter group less likely to grab toys or attack others. Table 7.4 compares two comparable groups and well shows the social gains of those in nursery school.

TABLE 7.4

Gain Over a Six-Month Period in Certain Personality Traits of Children in a Nursery School Compared with Children Not in Nursery School, as shown by Ratings on the Bonham-Sargent Scale of Personality Traits[9]

Trait	*Nursery School Gain*	*Control Gain*	*Difference in Gains*
Sociability: Talks	1.0	0.2	0.8
Sympathy: Shows sympathy when stranger feigns weeping	1.4	0.0	1.4
Contentment: Plays quietly with toys given him	1.0	0.4	0.6
Good nature: Cheerful when toys are taken away	0.0	—0.5	0.5
Pride: Shows satisfaction in achievement with toys	1.2	0.5	0.7
Orderliness: Arranges his toys in an orderly way	1.4	0.1	1.3
Lack of initiative: Waits to be told what to do next	—0.9	0.5	—1.4
Suggestibility: Pliable to suggestion with regard to toys	—0.6	—0.1	—0.5

Gradually there are being systematically tried out various ways for developing desired traits. Thus several children who were shy and unassertive (non-ascendant) were helped until they could especially well do certain things of interest to the other children—such things as fitting together the parts of a picture puzzle, making designs with blocks, telling an interesting story. These formerly shy children were then paired with other youngsters while they were dealing with these materials, and they now showed a much greater tendency to lead and assert themselves (49). Clearly the nursery school may serve as an invaluable laboratory in applied social psychology.[10]

THE ELEMENTARY SCHOOL YEARS

The nursery school has bountiful possibilities for constructive social education. Unfortunately, few children go to nursery school. During the first 5 or 6 years most youngsters have little contact with adults other than their parents, and have few associations with other children, except if there are brothers or sisters, or neighbour boys or girls of about the same age. Social life is so very simple: the parents are the all-important centre of regard and prestige and they, with any other members of the home group plus a few neighbour children and perhaps a pet or two, make up a single compact primary social group, as the sociologists would call it.

With entrance into school a new adult, Teacher, takes a place of great importance in the child's life, and the new pupil becomes a member of a new child group, his class. As he gets about more he may become a member of other groups—Sunday school, Scout, Y.M.C.A., club, or gang. Initiation into each—even the most hospitable—presents to the new member certain problems of adjustment. Between these groups there are certain disjunctions and incoordinations; there may be acute conflict, as between home or school and a delinquent gang. In each group each individual is faced with certain questions as to his status in it. Truly the problems with which the child is faced soon become bewilderingly complex. And truly marvelous is the extent to which most youngsters in the few short years from 6 to 12 do find their place in these various groups and get them more than reasonably well coordinated. For around the age of 12 many persons are better adjusted than at any other time in their entire lives. It is the age of happy confident childhood to which adults look back with longing.

The Class as a Little Society—and Teacher—Most children start to school at 6. All at once (usually there are no first visits and gradual acquaintings such as the good nursery school uses to ease the child into his new experience) on a bright September morning the small child finds himself facing not only a strange new adult in a strange new place but also a while roomful of strange children. For a timid or a sheltered only child the situation may be bewildering indeed.

> It will be difficult for the reader, who after at least 12 years of being in school takes the routines and the manners and customs of education for granted, to have any conception of that bewilderment. A college freshman from the country is a sophisticate by comparison! The little first-grader must learn about the comings and goings and when things are done and being on time. There are numerous details of manner and custom: when it is appropriate to speak to another child and when not; when it is commendable for one to help a friend and when it is considered wrong to do so (a most puzzling matter); when and how Teacher may be addressed. Sundry crises may occur. Thus when in the presence of this strange adult and in this great crowd of children a physiological need becomes insistent, there may be embarrassing episodes—as every primary teacher well knows.

The teacher is far more important in this little society than the reader might assume, after a dozen years of habituation to the breed. To the small child her size, adulthood, strangeness, authority, similarity yet difference in status as compared with the parents, all combine to give her an influence far greater than she usually appreciates. The children watch her closely, and they are often far more sensitive and more keen in understanding her attitude toward them than she realizes. A smile and word of praise may make a little girl exquisitely happy. Sarcasm, public ridicule, and especially unfair criticism or punishment may determine an attitude which remains for years.

> Strikingly illustrative of this fact is the true story of Grace, as told by herself and *also* by her teachers. A sensitive only child, she entered the first grade with great anticipation of the joys of school. But the first-grade teacher humiliated her by saying that she was behind the other pupils in her reading—and she had difficulty in getting used to the other children. The second-grade teacher was young and pretty—but never recognized children on the street. The next teacher was ill and irritable and jerked children about. In notable contrast the fifth-grade teacher was

friendly and her room quiet and restful. But in the seventh grade was one of those big teachers who shouted.

Meantime the teachers were reporting that the child was anxious to please but shy and nervous. In junior high school a brief success as a leader in a student activity built up her confidence greatly, but again things returned to the old level. In college, a brief note of encouragement from an English teacher thrilled her so that she could hardly keep back the tears, but she lost confidence again when criticized. She enjoyed it greatly when a teacher put her on committees, and she worked very hard, saying it was the first time she had had a chance to take part in social activities, as a leader. These teachers reported the girl as "shy, almost like a frightened animal, very responsive to kindness."

Grace is now teaching in a one-room country school, beloved by her pupils and their parents perhaps because she knows how to give the encouragement and kindness she so much desired. It might well be said that her life had been formed by the inconsiderateness and obtuseness of her teachers, especially those in elementary school (63).[11]

An exceedingly important, rather obvious, but nevertheless often overlooked characteristic of a successful teacher is thus the elementary social virtue of considerateness, and more generally the "psychological atmosphere" of the classroom. If she is friendly, fair, and encouraging—not impatient, impulsive in discipline, or critical and sarcastic—she will have met the first requisite of successful social leadership. The social atmosphere thus brought about may largely determine the personalities which the children exhibit there. Miss Brown is a calm, friendly young woman; an unhurried composure is typical of her room, and in it Johnny is friendly and cooperative. Miss Thompson is anxious and suspicious; in *her* room there seems to be always an undercurrent of restlessness and resentment, and when there John is irritable and full of mischief. But there may (and should) be much more involved than teacher temperament and good will; basically more important is the nature of the social structure and procedure in the group. What is meant here can be best made clear by a famous investigation both illustrating and evaluating such factors.

Three groups or "clubs" each of five 10-year-old children undertook mural painting, mask-making, model airplane construction, and other like activities calling for planning, cooperation, and working together. A graduate student took charge of one group in autocratic fashion, telling each pupil one step at a time just what to do, how to do it, and with whom to work, bestowing praise or blame in personal fashion, but remaining aloof and not participating in the work of the group. In short, he behaved very much like an old-fashioned teacher. A second graduate student dealt with the second group in *laissez-faire* fashion. He let it do as it pleased, did not participate in discussion or work, and made only infrequent comments. The graduate student associated with the third (democratic) group discussed the total project with the pupils, gave them suggestions when requested but let them decide among themselves who would do which portion of the total project and with whom each would work and which method of doing this or that might be best. He tried to help them in their planning and clarify their thinking, was "objective" in criticism or praise, and worked with them. Each group met twice a week for 50 minutes, and observers kept a careful record of what went on at each meeting. After six weeks leaders and methods were changed about; that is, the leader of the autocratic group moved to another group and there used democratic procedure; the democratic group was handled by a second leader in an autocratic fashion, and so on. It thus could not be charged that results for a given method were due to peculiarities of a particular group or leader.

> Two differences between these societies, and particularly between the autocratic and democratic, may here be stressed. The pressure of the frequent directions and demands of the autocratic leader maintain a state of *tension* in his group. He made about six times as many "directing approaches" as the democratic leader. And (the second difference) since he determined the goals, methods, work companions, and tools, the children's *space of free movement* was much less than in democracy. This tended to cause trouble in somewhat the same fashion that trouble arose when a group worked in too small a room. In *laissez-faire* there was also little space for free movement because the children got in one another's way. These two concepts of *tension* as a result of *pressure*, and of *space of free movement*, are very important.

A detailed record of what each group said and did showed that there were about thirty times as many episodes of hostility in the autocratic as in the democratic groups. Sometimes the children handled dictatorially were apathetic; but if their leader left the room, work quickly fell off and displays of irritable aggressiveness toward others in the group were marked. In other autocratic groups the youngsters were markedly aggressive toward one another even when the leader was present, though subservient to him. In the democratic group work went forward much as before if the leader left. The *laissez-faire-group* children "ran wild" whether the leader was present or not. The average number of aggressive action per 50-minute period was as follows: *Laissez-faire,* 38; autocracy (aggressive reaction to restraint), 30; democracy, 20; autocracy (apathetic reaction); 2. Working by himself instead of cooperatively with one or more other boys was twice as frequent in the autocratic regime. Twice children in an autocratic group ganged up on a scapegoat and forced him out of the group; their repressed feelings apparently were thus relieved. Toward the end of the experiment the democratic group voted that they would like to continue the work, but the autocratic group did not wish to do so. Informal talks with the children showed that they liked the democratic leaders best. At the end, the democratic group either kept the results of their work or gave them to the leader, but some of the children in the autocratic group threw their work on the floor and jumped on it (36).[12] The bearings of such experiment and such findings on methods of classroom management are obvious.

> Under the pressures and restraints of the autocratic "society" conversation tended to be resistant, attention-demanding, hostile both to the leader and to the other members of the group. In the democratic society conversation was more friendly and matter-of-fact, objective rather than personal; the children had more of a "we" feeling and thus more readily cooperated, gave constructive suggestions, asked information. Chart 7.3 shows these differences.

In summary, then, if a teacher is to meet successfully the socio-psychological problems of her classroom, she should maintain a "psychological atmosphere: and an attitude of considerateness, fairness, and friendliness. She should appreciate the importance of the total situation in her class and have some ability to construct situations which guide without putting such pressure on the children as to cause undue tension or hamperingly restrict the space of free movement. If she is at all sensitive to the happenings in her little classroom society (many teachers are not) she is aware that a great deal is happening "off-stage". In certain respects the children live in a society of their own; when they are not in school, this becomes increasingly the important society for them. Much that happens in the classroom has its origin in child society. This topic must now be considered.

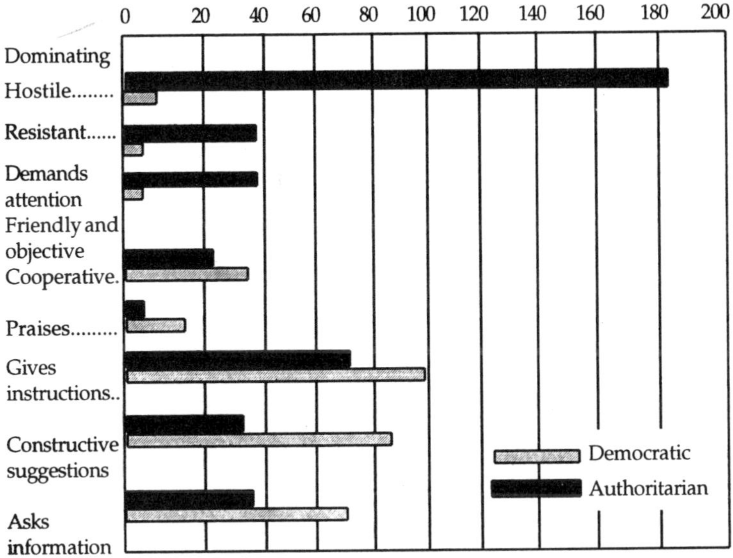

Chart 7.3—Components of conversation behaviour in autocratic as compared with democratic experimental child societies. (Adapted from Lewin, Lippitt, and Ecalona [36].)

Child Society: Problems of Belonging and Status—Going to school is the distinctive school experience that for the average child distinguished the years after 6 from those before. But the outstanding social change through the years from 6 to puberty is the escape from the family into the society of other children, primarily of the same sex. The great questions with reference to each child in relation to child society are: Does he "belong"? What is his status? Here are the central problems of these years.

That these years are indeed a time of rapid change from family to other child companionship is suggested by Chart 7.4. The scene opens, so to speak, with the change already rapidly under way. That is, the curves begin at the age of 8, but from direction of the curves from 8 to 9 it seems evident that much escape from the family has already occurred. From 8 to 14 going to movies with the family drops from being the average occurrence to being relatively rare, and going with one's own friends becomes the most common procedure. The rapidity of the escape from the family up through 10 is especially to be noted.

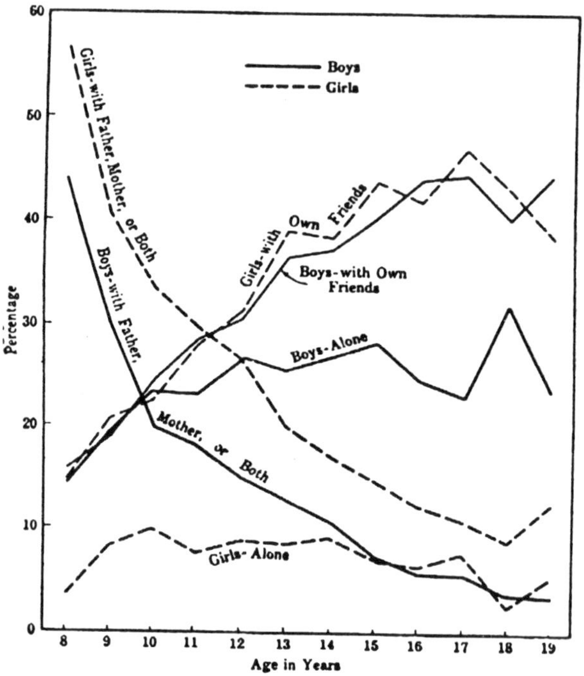

Chart 7.4—Change with age in children's companions at movies. (Adapted from Dale [14], pp. 19, 22.)

What is the nature of child society? For the average child at entrance to elementary school it hardly yet exists. He probably already knows two or three neighbour children, and he comes to know others in the neighbourhood from going to and from school with them (times when socialization goes forward more rapidly than in the conventional classroom). Child groups spontaneously formed are small—they rarely consist of more than five youngsters—and even these small groups do not stay together more than 15 or 20 minutes. First-grade children have no sense of belonging to the whole class, and they are unable to designate those they like or dislike outside their little circle of acquaintance. They are also little aware of any code of social behaviour though they soon learn such elementary requirements as waiting one's turn, not tattling on other children, and playing simple games according to rules.

By middle childhood (roughly 7 or 8 to 11 or 12 years of age) the groups have grown in size to six to ten children and tend to be unisexual. But these groups are still not hard and fast as to membership; and though group undertakings are by now fairly frequent, they are often not completed because the group does not hold together long enough. And the group increasingly has its codes of conduct—one must play fair, do one's share in any group undertaking, divide the spoils evenly, and so on.

In later childhood or pre-adolescence (11 or 12 to 13 or 14) the social coalescing goes yet further. The group is likely to contain ten or fifteen youngsters and to be much more explicit as to membership and activities. It may call itself a club or gang, and as such have a definite membership with a badge or other sign by which a belonger is known; it may have an element of secrecy, specified times and places of meeting, special activities, and leaders or officers.

However, the observer who notices only the gross fact that there are groups is socially almost as blind as an individual who can distinguish only the outlines of large objects but cannot see their structure of the details of which they are composed. Perhaps first to be noticed is the fact that there are some individuals who do not belong to groups. They are isolates. The wise teacher will see them as more serious problems than the child who fails his arithmetic or throws spitballs. They are bewildered and miserably unhappy over their unpopularity, and are establishing habits of timidity or resentment toward others which may continue throughout life.

> Sometimes the causes of the isolation are fairly obvious. Thus Harry was slightly deaf and James very nearsighted; the sensory handicap in each case hampered play with the other boys. The Rabinian family were French-Canadian Catholic and stayed by themselves. But sometimes these problems are more subtle. Thus a playground activity record begins with 7-year-old Ralph wandering aimlessly along the edge of the playground looking bored and ill at ease. Two other boys run up to him and grab him—apparently it is a "cops and robbers" game. Ralph pulls away. He goes over and watches children swinging, but they say nothing to him and he wanders off dejectedly. He sits down at one side of the playground and watches the other children. The whole race was taken up with such withdrawings, attempted approaches, and failure to participate. The situation was explained in part by the fact that Ralph was an only child of

> strict parents and was without social resource or initiative in child society.

At the other extreme is the leader. What characterizes the leader? Sundry studies have been made of him. He has interests common to the group and is very much of the group, not apart from it or too markedly superior to it. He is above the average in certain traits which the group regards highly: among boys, the leader is more active and successful in games; among girls, more friendly and able to girls' undertakings. In either sex the leader is characterized by initiative and fertility of ideas—suggests things to do and gets things going.

> Various circumstances may play a part. One of the writers remembers the accession to his boyhood popularity one summer when a relative gave him a fine "patrol wagon," and for some weeks he was leader of the group which wished to play with his unusual new toy. The son of an ex-governor of the state was chronically a neighbourhood leader; he combined natural vigor with confidence coming from the status of his family, and was ever ready with ideas for war-like games based on his father's stories of military experiences.

Leader and isolate—these are two extremes. But in middle or later childhood there is another figure who is very important—the chum is an individual of the same sex and approximately the same age. He is likely to be in the same school class and from the same neighbourhood and of the same socio-economic status. That is, geographical, educational, and socio-economic propinquity brings youngsters together and in total may often seem personalities is also involved—not all neighbour classmates are chums. Some similarity of interests and coordinateness of traits are also needful. Sometimes an active child may have associated with him a relatively quiet youngster who is a complement in personality. In any case, the chum relationship is usually much worth while. Each gains in confidence, adaptability, and resourcefulness. It is the distinctive social relationship of middle childhood; the focus of social interest has now shifted from the parents to another of the same age and sex. Literature has many stories of the chum, such as *Tom Sawyer*.

Chum, leader, and isolate—these are the three major type figures in child society. But it must not be assumed that except for the relationships thus implied child society is without structure. On the contrary, the structure is often complex. Yet the average teacher is often blind to these facts. Some concrete experimental data may here be of value. The children in a fifth-grade class were told that the seating arrangements were soon to be changed; each was asked to write on a sheet of paper his first and second choice of classmate to whom he would like to sit next in class,[13] and also to give in each instance the reason why he would like to sit next to that person. Chart 7.5 shows something of the complexities of social interrelationship revealed by the simple, practical inquiry.

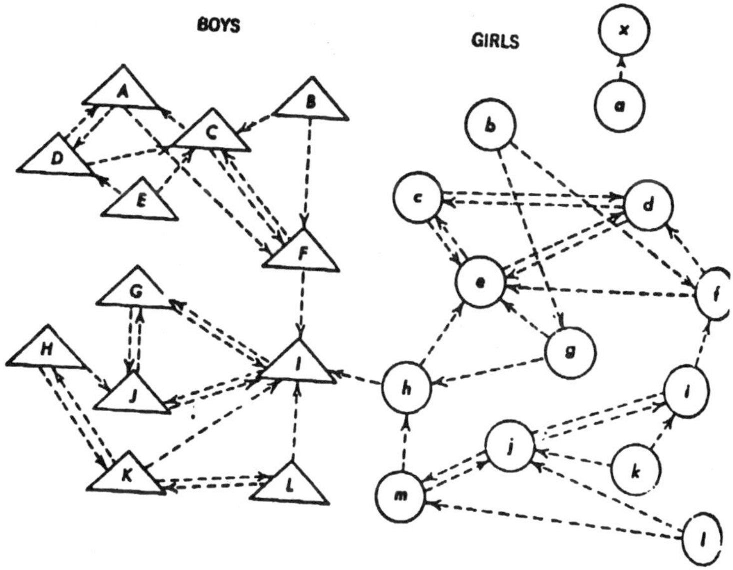

Chart 7.5—Social structure of a small sixth-grade class, as shown by results of the request that each child name the two classmates whom he would like best to have sit next to him. The chart shows that Boy *A* chose *D* and *F* and was chosen by *D* and *C*; Boys *B* and *E* and Girls *a, b, k,* and *l* were unchosen or isolates but *I* and *e* were very popular, being chosen by six and five other children (Method modified from Moreno's [43].)

Six children (*B, E, a, b, k, l*) were not chosen by anyone, even as second choice. They apparently were isolates. Girl *a* was herself so little acquainted that she made only one choice and that of a girl *x* in another turn. In contrast, Boy *I* was chosen by six and Girl *e* by five other children. But the larger structure of the little society is here especially to be heard. The boys are in two distinct groups, the lower one having as its are the close-knit triangle *I-G-J*; the accessory chain is *H-K-L*, with *I* quite ocurly the leader. The teacher considered that the character of

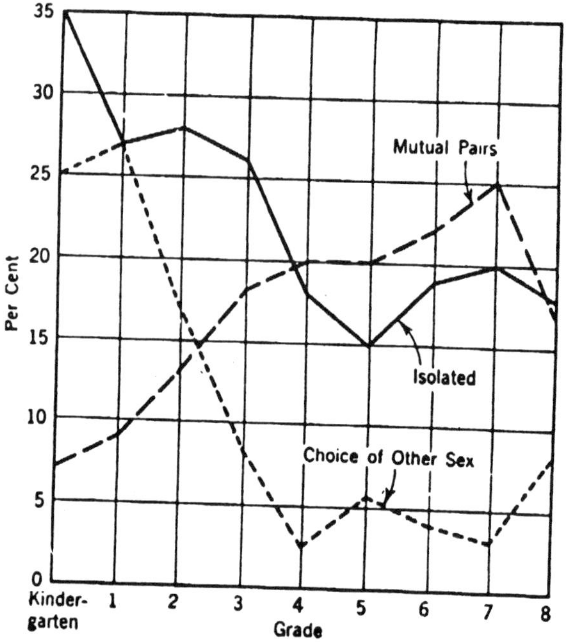

Chart 7.6—Social structure in public school classes. Each child was asked to name his first and second choice of the children he would like to have sit next to him. The chart shows that in the kindergarten 35 per cent of the children were not chosen; they were isolates. A quarter of the choices were of the other sex. In only 7 per cent of the cases did two kindergarten children choose each other. (1053 children in a Brooklyn public school, three months after school began.) (Inn from Moreno [43], p. 26.)

the group was not entirely healthy; the boys seemed on the way to becoming a mischief-making gang. The girls also formed certain groups, such as triangle *e-c-d,* but these groups seemed on the whole desirable in nature; the top problem among the girls was to take care of the isolates.

On the basis of the chart and the children's explanations regarding their access plus her other knowledge of them the teacher then proceeded with her change in seating plan. Boys *F, I* and *A* were put together to foster other groupings. Isolates were put with their choices if there was some compatibility of interest. The teacher tried to be the tactful hostess in fostering the relationships initiated by these classroom propinquities. As a result, she changed her class from two cliques, two other loose groups, and sundry outsiders into a much more friendly total group.

What, more generally, are the findings of such "sociometric tests?" Chart 7.6 summarizes results from 1800 children from the kindergarten through the eighth grade, obtained three months after the beginning of school—that is, after sufficient time in the school year for the children to become acquainted with and appraise each other. Isolates are most common in kindergarten simply because the children are too young to know each other well, but even in the upper grades about a fifth of the children are "unchosen." Mutual pairs (these may be called chums) grow in number, but a majority of the children in every grade are without such friends or at least without a chum in the same class. Choice of the other sex practically disappears in the middle grades but appears again in the eighth. Here is indeed a perspective in social trends and problems.

The remarks of the children in explanation of their choices often gave exceedingly valuable insights regarding levels of social development and values in child society.

> Ist grade (age 6-7 yrs.)—Marion chooses Claire: "I like her because she always gives me some candy when I eat with her. She lends me crayons when I have lost mine."
>
> 6th grade (ages 11-12 yrs.)—Madeline chooses Marietta: "She is about my size and age. I like to walk with her cause I think we look nice together. She isn't noisy or rude. She is willing to play games that are gay and with a lot of action. She is truthful. Also if you ask her to bring you something, she will bring it even if she has a lot of other things to carry just the same."
>
> Joel chooses Gunther: "I keep tropical fish, and I collect stamps, and Gunther likes to see my things. That's what I like about him. He isn't only always wanting to play baseball. I don't see very well so I like to do other things than play sports."
>
> 8th grade (ages 13-14 yrs.)—David chooses Marie: "She's better looking than the majority. Curly brown hair, blue eyes, same height as I am. She's my idea of what a girl should be like."

Clearly a child's problem in finding his place and status in the society of his fellows is not simple or easy. A teacher must study both the children and the group. She must help each child make good in some way, as suggested in the preceding section. She must see each class as a total social pattern, into some parts of which a given child may fit well but into others not at all. If she can help him find his place and status she can hardly render him a greater service.

The immediately preceding paragraphs have dealt with child society as it shows itself in the schoolroom for the obvious reasons that it is there both most readily available for study and most a matter of concern for the teacher. But it should never be forgotten that child society exists chiefly outside the classroom, and that status and structure may be different in different groups and situations.

> When one the writers was in the fifth grade his chum (this because be lived next door, had similar mechanical interests, and lived with kindly grandparents who indulged both boys in numerous minor ways) was in the grade above. A second frequent play companion went to another school, but the families were friends and the children became well acquainted through family and church gatherings. A third pal was in the same school class, but the companionship was based more on the friendship of the two families. An occasional fourth companion was an older slightly lame boy who was Red for his good nature and his pluck and who, because of his physical handicap, found his play level with younger boys. If to the fifth grade in the Murray school so many years ago the Moreno sociometric test had been applied, this somewhat heterogeneous boy group might never have been found.
>
> Further, choice of any companion depends on the situation. Harry was a good person to have sit next you since he was very good in his school work and was anxious to obtain the regard of other children by helping them. But being stout and clumsy, he was no person to choose on your side in a game. Art was biggest and strongest; Jim had the best stamp collection; Will's athletic older brother gave him prestige and taught him athletic dolls; Sidney was bests in certain handicrafts.
>
> Isolates were rejected because of factors similarly diverse. John was Catholic and Ralph coloured; parental prejudice was operative here. Henry showed off in the classroom and was considered teacher's pet. Algernon was affected in manner and sissified. The children in the big Jones family stayed by themselves. The Smiths had recently moved into the neighbourhood; nobody seemed to know them, and their only son was quiet, shy, and offish.

Clearly such larger understanding of child society requires knowledge of home and also of community resources—church,

YMCA, boys' club, playground, summer camp—in dealing with any problems which may be discovered. The influence of the first factor mentioned above, the home, upon the elementary school youngster must now be more specifically considered.

> It is first desirable, however, to stress that such means as club and camp should more often be explicitly used as part of a total programme for dealing with problems of child society. Suggestive of possibilities here is an experiment in which thirteen 6- to 10-year-old children who were shy and socially maladjusted spent several weeks in a small camp where there were no other children. At first each played alone, but gradually they became acquainted, asserted themselves more, achieved confidence in this group. When they returned home they showed distinct improvement in poise and status (38). In a child group one child—boaster or crybaby or cheat—may be disciplined to good purpose by the others. Or the group may tease or ignore in a way which accentuates the social maladjustment. In such an instance the playground or camp director may perhaps find and feature some ability the misfit does have and thus raise his status, or get some other child to befriend him (48). In any case, constructive social thinking is called for.

Home—Up to the time of going to school the child has lived in only one social world, the home. In that home there may be conflict, or at least disharmony. But when he goes to school he moves into two other social worlds, school and child society. There may be conflicts or disharmonies between these worlds, and he becomes gradually aware of any conflicts which may exist between his family and the adult world in which they live. Examples will make clear each type of difficulty.

> After much bitter quarreling and charges against each other, often in the presence of their only child Mildred, her parents have obtained a divorce. Mildred lives part of the time with one parent and the remainder of the time with the other. Being part of the time in one neighbourhood and school and part of the time in another, she makes few friends in either place. In no one of her three social worlds—home, school, or child society—does she feel established or secure.

> Mediocre Marjorie's younger sister is brilliant and exceptionally attractive. In a mistaken effort to urge Marjorie to do better work

she is chronically compared in disparaging fashion with this sister. In school this younger sister is now in the same grade with her; an unwise teacher in a moment of irritation threw this fact up at Marjorie, and the other children have shown that they sensed the situation. Marjorie's lack of status makes her shy, timid, seclusive, and she is so upset that she works even less effectively than she might.

Mary's ignorant Kentucky mountain parents are puzzled and defensive regarding the school's efforts to help her. Well-meaning but blunt suggestions from the school nurse regarding better diet for her children are resented by the mother, and a visit from the nurse antagonizes still more—it is sensed as critical. Mary's schoolwork is poor; a note from the teacher, asking the mother's help in improving it, is painfully without awareness of the parents' near-illiteracy and poverty; the mother's scrawl in reply is shown to the principal with a comment which Mary overhears. The girl is increasingly absent, and inquiries from the school are met with evasion and antagonism, Home and school societies are in conflict. Further, the family is on relief. Some of the other children know it. Mary senses that her family lacks status in the community, and she in child society.

After six months of pathetic struggle Mrs. Johnson's oldest son died as the result of being struck by an automobile while at play. Albert is now her only child; he is frail and frequently ill. Lest some misfortune come upon him he is allowed little opportunity to play with other boys, is kept from school at the slightest sign of bad weather or indisposition—has become a amid little hypochondriac. In contrast, the red-haired little minister's son Lester reacting against the dreary decorum of his home, has become the neighbourhood brat, leader of his group in mischief. And Henrietta, trained by her once stage-struck mother in elocution, is featured for every visitor and school or church affair—and is scorned by the other children as concerted little show-off. In each instance the home has failed to understand child society.

Perverse is one "home" consisting of father, three children by a divorced wife, and a stepmother. The stepmother dislikes the children as a constant reminder of the former wife, and the children are bitter against her. A conservative neighbourhood regards the divorce and remarriage with disfavor and ostracizes not only the two adults but also the children; neighbour youngsters are not allowed to play with them. The children lack affection and security in their own home and are social outcasts in the community; in class they are emotionally preoccupied and indifferent. No wonder they are suspicious in attitude toward teachers and other adults, defensive and irritable in relations with other children in school, and consort with a delinquent gang "across the track"—it is the only group which will receive them.

What generalizations may be drawn from such instances? This should be obvious: children cannot be understood without some knowledge of their homes. Yet the average teacher knows nothing of the homes of most of her children. More particularly, what are the essentials of a psychologically good home? Two seem outstanding. First, the home should give the child affection and security. Second, it should not hamper— it should rather help—the child's achieving belonging and status in child society. Whatever its other shortcomings, if a home does these two things it is almost certain to be a psychologically good home.

Interesting evidence that the treatment a child receives at home has its persisting and various effects on what he does in school is summarized in Table 7.5. These children were rated, in the second grade and again in the fifth as to their social adjustment in school and also their work habits there. At about the same times their homes were visited and the way in which they were treated there was observed. Approximately three times as many children who were handled in well-adjusted fashion at home were socially well adjusted and had good work habits at school as was the case with youngsters who were babied or pushed at home. The babied children were worse at school in the fifth grade than they had been in the second.

Perhaps it should also be made clear that a home which is psychologically good may materially be very modest—even poverty-stricken. Poverty makes it harder to give the child a sense of security and it otherwise handicaps; but kindly and sensible parents may make an economically poor home an admirable place for child development, whereas a domineeringly successful business man and butterfly mother may make a wretched home.

TABLE 7.5
Relation of Treatment of Child at Home to Social Adjustment in School and Work Habits There, in the Second Grade and in the Fifth Grade[14]

Treatment of Child at Home	*No. of Cases*	*%Good Social Adjustment in School*		*%Good Work Habits in School*	
		2nd grade	5th grade	2nd grade	5th grade
Babied	51	24	16	27	20
Pushed	22	18	23	18	18
Well-adjusted	73	70	73	75	77

Relevant here is a depression-year study of 112 children, half from a community of superior economic status and the others from an inferior urban area. The two groups showed no significant differences in personality development. Such items as poverty, broken home, foreign-born parents, illness appeared to have little effect *on their own account*. The most important influence upon the children's development seemed to be what might be called the psychological climate of the home. Its neatness, the parents' knowledge regarding playmates and willingness to let the child go away from home to play with other children, given the child an allowance (all factors helping the youngster in child society) were items of some significance. In one family on relief for two years and always near the hunger zone the children showed excellent social adjustment with a wide circle of friends and a fine school record. The parents in another family were in the same financial condition but were constantly worrying about ways of getting more relief; there was constant strife and discontent, and the children were tending toward delinquency. It was also noted that when, if a child was ill, the parents too a matter-of-fact attitude and showed him how to help himself, the illness did not seriously affect social adjustment (19).

It must also be emphasized that influence of the home is pervasive and often shows itself in ways having no apparent relationship to the home situation. Thus a recent careful study compared children whose parents were decidedly fond of them with children whose parents showed lack of affection or rejection. The first group much more often slept soundly, kept clothes neat, worked well with others, were attentive and popular, liked school; the "rejected children smoked, sought attention, boasted, were classroom nuisances, had younger companions, were emotionally unstable and antagonistic. Children of dominating parents were neat, courteous, docile; children of overindulgent parents had food fads and poor table manners, were aggressive and disobedient, and lacked interest in school, but were self-confident and expressed themselves well (61).

The Social Triumph of Later Childhood—The child entering the first grade is little more than a baby. He must learn his way about in school. He must get along in his home, but socially and emotionally escape from it. He must find his place and status in child society. What an overwhelming set of problems! Yet such is the vitality and adaptability of these years that the average person attains in later childhood what is probably the most adequate social adjustment of his entire life. About teachers and school he has nonchalant sophistication. He associates with easy confidence with others of his own age and sex. His family his come to accord him the independence of boyhood, and he has not yet asked for the anxiety-causing freedoms of adolescence. The socio-economic stratifications and stresses of adult life have determined the neighbourhood in which he lives, and he is not unaware of such matters; but among those with whom he has contact he associates more freely and democratically than he ever will again. The other sex does not trouble him; for it he has scorn. This is the time of happy, self-sufficient, carefree childhood. In another three or four years, how things may change! It is with these next turbulent years that the following chapter is concerned. But first the material of this chapter must be reviewed with reference to certain practical applications—needful because many children do *not* thus become adjusted, and most might be better.

THE APPLIED SOCIAL PYCHOLOGY OF CHILDHOOD

This is social development through the first dozen years. Two questions remain: As one looks back over these years, what seem to be the major factors in this development? And what might be done, especially by teachers, to prevent maladjustment and bring more children to the well-adjusted later childhood described above?

Major Factors in Childhood Social Adjustment—What, first of all, are major background traits and circumstances, and psycho-social influences and factors, that determine a child's social development? As was said early in this chapter, some children seem constitutionally to have much greater social potentialities than others. Some are certainly far more attractive than others in appearance, and probably in disposition—some seem naturally friendly and good-natured and others shy or cross. Some are more alert, quicker, stronger, healthier than others. All such factors play their part in a child's social relationships and status.

As has been mentioned, even in childhood the socio-economic status of the family counts somewhat, democratic though most children are. It determines the neighbourhood in which the family lives and the companions which have family favour, as well as such material childhood social assets as size of allowance and attractiveness of toys.

> Also, even in childhood, the subtle, pervasive effects of the prevailing culture begin to affect the individual. Boys are expected to be rough and ready, but little girls demure and proper. All are growing up in a competitive and acquisitive culture in which one tries to beat one's opponents in games, get good marks, and do better than someone else.

Each youngster thus has certain social assets or liabilities of biological constitution and of socio-economic and cultural circumstance. But how, with these potentialities, he actually does develop socially seems to depend especially on three further factors.

The first is elementary indeed: Other things being anywhere near equal, children learn to get along with other people in proportion as they are with other people and have experience in so doing. The only child in the city apartment whose chief companion is his mother does not develop socially as he should (nor is the situation healthy for her). In this day of small families and decreased neighbouring with the folks next door, special provision for a child to have association with other adults and other children (in nursery school, playground, church or community social center, summer camp) becomes increasingly important.

In the second place, a child gets along in a group and finds a desirable status in it in proportion as he can do the things that others in the group are doing, and do something well enough to obtain recognition. Even a nursery school baby needs to learn certain social skills—how to climb in the jungle-gym, go down the slide feet first, ride a tricycle. An elementary school boy should be able to play softball and the girl to roller-skate. In proportion as a child can do many of these things he can participate widely and thus extend his social experience. In proportion as he can do some of these things better than most he is likely to become a leader. If he is incapable in all the activities of the group he is a social blank and can hardly "belong."

Finally important is what has been called the "psychological atmosphere" of the home, class, playground, or other group. If the mood is good-humored, friendly, relaxed, and operates in a reasonably cooperative and democratic fashion, the social development of everyone in the group is furthered. But if the mood is irritable, suspicious, tense, and there is confusion or inhibiting domination, social development is inhibited or even becomes perverse. If children have many social contacts, if in these contacts they have things they can do together, and if the social atmosphere is such that they associate freely and with mutual facilitations, then childhood social development is almost sure to go forward in satisfactory fashion.[15] Certain practical suggestions for bringing all this about remain to be considered.

Toward a Programme for Better Social Adjustment—From all this discussion, what practical suggestions are there of help to a teacher? Four seem especially important.

The first comes directly from the last item in the analysis above. Every teacher should try to make the "psychological atmosphere" of her classroom good-humored, friendly, relaxed. Further, her management of the class should be such that the situation is democratic, cooperative. This is the first step, a prerequisite for any other constructive social measures.

In the second place the teacher should, from consideration of each child's behaviour in classroom and on playground and from such other relevant information as she can obtain, come to some evaluations of the way he gets along with other people—especially with his fellows. Such an appraisal is far more important than marking him in arithmetic or deportment. If she does not thus study her pupils' social problems she may not really understand the children at all and may with blundering perversity deal with many of them in just the wrong way.

A typical class anywhere from the elementary grades to college (the reader should consider the students in his classes to see whether this is not true) has a member who is too anxious to have the teacher's favourable regard; he raises his hand too often, takes part too much. Another is a smart aleck, trying to get laughs and attention from the other members of the class. Yet another is overactive, restless, mischievous. A pretty little girl plays up to the boys, and some boys pay too much attention to her. One girl is able, but never participates in what is going on unless asked. Another does little but sit, apparently daydreaming. A fourth girl is sensitive, critical, unsocial. In a given class hour only eight or nine out of the class of thirty really take much part in things. Three or four are disturbers. They may be impertinent, cheat, play truant. There are about a dozen ordinary, somewhat colourless, reasonably well-behaved youngsters who have so little classroom personality, good or bad, that the teacher tends to forget them.

It is only natural for the teacher to encourage those youngsters who act in accord with the school programme, and to call little upon those who contribute little. The persistent seeker of her attention she bluntly snubs. If she is a vigorous person she may counter the aggressive youngster with aggressive behaviour of her own. If she is kind, she may hesitate to disturb the shy, sensitive child; anyhow, he presents no obvious classroom problem. In all of these instances she may be doing exactly the wrong thing. The boy too persistently bidding for Teacher's attention is compensating for failure to make good with the other boys outside of school; he needs to be helped with that problem, not cut off from the one source of favourable attention he has found. The overactive boy needs to be given responsibility and things to do, not challenged to yet more aggression. The daydreamer and the sensitive girl are really the most serious problems in the class; somehow the teacher should get them out of their isolation and into the social group. The colourless non-participators are the ones who most need experience in participation.

Evidently such insightful understanding of these so various social problems presented by these so different youngsters requires some appraisal of their social liabilities and assets, their position in their homes and their play group as well as at school. Special attention should be given to those quiet, commonplace school children so often overlooked because there is nothing special about them to catch attention. Not very attractive, not very vigorous, from drab homes, socially isolated or with a chum like themselves, they lead a socially half-starved existence. They are the forgotten children.

The third step is obviously to act on the basis of such information. All too often the teacher will have to depend entirely on her own social ingenuity and good dense; her superiors and her books in psychology and education will seem to offer little aid. They will tell her more about how to help children in arithmetic than in getting along with people. But research is gradually being done that will help her. As already mentioned, it has been demonstrated that if a shy child is helped to gain some special skill he may then show more confidence and thus achieve status in the class. That is, consideration of the second factor in the above analysis—the child's equipment of socially valuable skills—may give some hint as to a fruitful means of dealing with his social problem. Or the teacher may find that he already can do something well or has some special characteristic and by playing this up gain him prestige. Thus two girls of foreign-born parents who felt shy and out of place became looked up to when the teacher featured discussion of their parents' homeland and had them bring interesting handicraft from their home. Different children present very different problems, and the teacher must be clever in social maneuvers. But if she will thus carefully study each pupil and base her dealings with him upon this understanding, she may expect numerous benefits therefrom.

Now the fourth and last suggestion. At the beginning of the preceding section it was emphasized that children learn to understand other people and to get along with them by actually having varied social contacts and experience. In present-day America, with its small families, frequent moving about, less visiting and neighbouring, absence of parents from the home, and social affairs in which the children are not included, special efforts are needed to bring about many and varied social experiences. The quiet commonplace youngster mentioned above may not know any other woman besides his mother (he does not feel really acquainted with his teacher) and in addition to his father the only other man he knows is the school janitor. There are few other children in the neighbourhood, and he has little to do with them. Summers are dreary indeed. Elementary schools as well as high schools need a social programme. They need to consider the resources—playgrounds, community centres, churches, camps, organizations like the Boy Scouts and Camp Fire girls—with which cooperation is such a programme might be worked out. Social planning is a major need in elementary schools.

SUMMARY

In summary it may be stressed that this chapter deals with what is in many respects the central problem of development over the school years—the problem of learning to get along satisfactorily and effectively with other people—and with the first phase of that problem from birth to puberty.

In the pre-school years the child's major problem is adjustment to his family; his parents are at the centre of his social world. In the home, sundry factors of physical constitution, health, home atmosphere parental attitude and discipline combine to develop in him attitude of timidity or assertiveness, good nature or irritability. The few children so fortunate as to go to nursery school have "professional" guidance in first adjustments to adults and children outside the home.

However, not until they enter elementary school do most children come to know and have continuing relationships with an adult outside the family. The prestige of Teacher as parent-surrogate, source of knowledge, wielder of authority, bestower of favours, is enormous. The social atmosphere of the classroom and the social structure (autocratic, democratic, or *laissez faire*) which she there—perhaps all unconsciously—sets up, are of great influence on the child's social behaviour and development. But even more important for his future is his debut (which for most children really begins in the elementary school) into the society of his fellows. There he seeks belonging and status and though associates and status may change, it is of great importance that he does find a respected place among his peers. Although the important people in his social world are now his fellows of the same sex and approximately the same age, and the most important person as his chum, the family continues as an influence able greatly to help or hinder him in thus finding his place in the world of his own kind.

Certain factors are of special importance in affecting social development. Some children almost from birth are favoured by greater physical attractiveness, vivacity, vigor (all traits having social value) than others. The family socio-economic status may help or hinder. Within the limits roughly set by such social assets or handicaps a child's social development seems to be determined in particular by the amount and variety of social experience which he has, his equipment of socially desirable social skills, and the social atmosphere of the groups of which he is a member. His conformity to childhood's code of conduct (not to tattle, not to be a crybaby, etc.) is also important. Schools can aid social development by creating such a favouring social atmosphere, studying each child's social problems, aiding him on the basis of such understanding to make good socially, and providing a rich and varied social experience. There is every reason to believe that the schools could increase greatly their effectiveness in thus furthering the development to desirable social personalities.

REFERENCES

1. It follows that such social sciences as sociology and ethnology should receive more consideration by educational psychology than is usual.
2. It is much to be regretted that this investigation, like so many others dealing with the period, stops at 4, leaving a distressing gap, as regards both science and child guidance, from here to the elementary school. Why is it that even genetic psychologists cannot see a problem or carry through an investigation with a long-time perspective!
3. Adapted from (28).
4. The following episode may serve as a sample of the application of the "natural result" method in a social situation: A 3-year-old and his 5-year-old brother were having an argument. The 3-year-old's patience gave out and he used his fists. The 5-year-old struck back, and the topic was changed by mutual consent (20).
5. From (5).
6. Sometimes much to her distress she discovers that she is not so essential to the happiness of her offspring as she would like to believe. The mother is sometimes more of a problem than the child. She stays morning after morning when she should go, or departs tearfully at thought of separation from her baby. Parent education is an important phase of an adequate nursery school programme.
7. Adapted from (32), p. 222. The more detailed date show even in the second group at the end of the year one child with social contacts only 12 per cent of the time as compared with 84 per cent for another, and two in this last group show a decrease from fill to spring. As always, individual differences are a notable fact which must never be lost sight of.
8. It may be some comfort to the parents of a lively youngster to know that

within bounds all this is healthy. The more a child "gets around" the more he is likely to bump into others. One investigator has stated epigrammatically that "mutual friends are more quarrelsome, and mutual quarrelers more friendly than the average" and that "quarreling is part of friendly social intercourse at these ages" (22).

9. Adapted from The nursery school and behaviour, studies in child welfare, *Soc. Sci. Mo.*, 1929, I, 43-51, as quoted in (46, 1931 ed.) p. 316.

10. Perspective with regard to the nursery school and its values must not be lost, however. As has will been pointed out in a notably careful resume of the total topic of this chapter (46), present concepts regarding development over the first 4 years have been based all too exclusively on results from nursery schools. Not only are these schools relatively rare, but the situations they present and the behaviour patterns they call forth are relatively special as compared with the variety of situations in which children of this age may ordinarily be found. Like every institution, the nursery school has developed certain conventions as regards not only equipment but things to do and daily routine. Children of wealth playing in a park under the supervision of a nursemaid would presumably develop a more limited and surely a different repertoire of social behaviour. Slum children with swarming companions and a yet younger child to care for might in their own way show greater social maturity and responsibility. Country children would be in a still different social and "play equipment" situation. Most of the research comes from nursery schools with children from professional homes predominating, with whatever this fact may mean as regards verbal readiness, home surroundings, and parental attitudes. The greatest need at present seems to be not for more research from the university-affiliated nursery schools but for systematic study of children from other socio-economic classes, in street or country-yard play, with whatever equipment and social situations appear there.

    Also, the nursery school enthusiast should be careful not to attribute to the nursery school social development which would come about anyhow, as a result of maturation and the ordinary experiences of everyday life. For the time being, the social development of the youngsters in the nursery school may be hastened but by the age of 8 there may be little difference as compared with non-nursery school children. Perhaps the chief result will be a little more social confidence—an outcome of importance, but possibly obtainable more practically in the great majority of children by other means. In short, it might be charged that the great need as regards understanding of the pre school child is to get the investigators out of the nursery school!

11. This case may be considered extreme. But time and again college students have reported incidents from their own childhood showing how over many years they have vividly remembered similar episodes,

often their feelings about them are still so strong that they cannot bring themselves to tell the incident to the class. The reader may well go back in his own memories and see whether he does not have poignant recollections of some kindness or slight from a teacher when he was a small child.

12. The description has taken this liberty with Lewin's work that it has combined results of two experiments to give a more adequate picture of the outcomes of democratic versus autocratic procedures.
13. This is, of course, the "sociometric test" of Moreno. His unusual monograph is interesting reading (43).
14. Adapted from (29).
15. The above is of course a gross oversimplification, but it seems nevertheless of value for purposes of clarification and emphasis. A fourth factor might well be the extent to which a child has learned certain rules of conduct the breaking of which makes him *persona non grata in a* group. Not to be a crybaby, not to be always losing one's temper, not to tattle, to keep to the rules of the game, to share, to acknowledge a favour—a "job analysis" of social relations in childhood would probably show that the rules whose breaking really counts seriously are relatively few in number. Morons can learn them, but some bright children don't. Undoubtedly more children could be taught to observe them than how do—to the benefit of all concerned. But if the above three prime needs are all met, usually children will teach each other such rules.

8
Development of Understanding

At the close of the preceding chapter a distinction was made between memory-level, understanding-level, and reflection-level teaching and learning. However, no attempt should be made to draw extremely fine lines between these levels. Memory-level learning, at times, can contribute to understanding or help provide a background for reflection. Likewise, understanding-level learning unquestionably fosters learning of individual facts—though seen in a related fashion—and may easily merge into reflection-level learning. Furthermore, it is inescapable that students will learn large numbers of facts and understandings whenever they become involved in reflection-level learning. If they do not learn many facts in the process of "reflection-level learning," such learning really has not occurred—only some pseudo version of it. Accordingly, we may safely conclude that the three levels of learning may—although not necessarily do—interact and blend so that it would be a mistake to attempt to draw sharp lines of demarcation between them.

However, it would be an even worse mistake not to make a reasonably clear distinction between the three levels; each is quite distinctive. Virtually all educational psychologists consider memory-level learning which seeks nothing else—neither understanding not reflection—a waste of time on the part of both students and teachers. Nevertheless, teachers sometimes get caught in a bind of pressures and distractions which make it temporarily impossible for them to do much else than resort to memory work of some kind. Since educational psychologists think that memory-level learning *per se* is not worth striving for, we do not devote a chapter to it as we do for each of the other levels.

To the extent that memory-level learning ever can be justified, the problem of teaching on this level takes care of itself; a teacher needs only teach as he himself usually has been taught. However, there are a few general considerations worth noting about memory-level learning. Some persons, for reasons not yet understood, have better memories for unrelated facts than do others. An occasional individual has what is known as a "photographic memory", that is to say, he seems able to retain almost indefinitely even the most meaningless of the mass of potpourri which he encounters. Other individuals are notably forgetful concerning all matters with which they are not deeply involved.

There is little or no evidence that either of these traits bears any significant relationships to a person's ability effectively to solve the problems which arise in his life. (In short, a person with a "photographic" memory is not necessarily either more or less—"intelligent," as we have defined the term, than is a forgetful person. We have described the real-life case of Polly, the idiot-savant who could remember virtually everything with remarkable precision. Another case in point is that of the late John von Neumann, one of the greatest creative mathematicians ever to live in the United States. He had great difficulty remembering not only all the commonplace small routines of life but even some of the larger ones. The story may be apocryphal, but it is told that when he was required to travel away from home—even to some important conference where he was scheduled to deliver a paper—someone (his wife, we assume) pinned a sheet of paper to the outside of his coat explaining which airplane flight he was supposed to take, at which hotel he was to stay, and other necessary information so that people along the way could help him arrive at his destination and meet his commitments.

Teachers would be well advised to remember that students who seem unable to remember lists of facts, even until the next day's quiz, may have a much higher functional intelligence and a much greater potential contribution to human culture than do some other students who make a perfect score on every quiz. Accordingly, when testing is pitched on a strictly rote-memory level, test results should be given very little weight in one's trying to estimate a student's potential. In fact, there probably is little point in giving memory-level tests at all except to fill in times when a teacher is working under conditions of such desperation that he can't think of anything better to do.

We now turn to the major theme of the chapter—understanding-level teaching. We open our discussion with a theoretical treatment of the meaning of the term understanding.

WHAT IS UNDERSTANDING?

The term *understanding* has been used so ambiguously by psychologists and educators that teachers are likely to use it rather glibly, without being able to define it clearly. For example, a teacher may ask his students, "Are you sure you understand this?" and himself not know the meaning of his question. One may be fairly sure his students do not know it either. Also, the word's everyday, layman's meaning, such as is intended when one says, "Yes, I understand you" (That is to say, "I know what you are talking about"), is inadequate for our purposes. Understanding, as a product of the learning process, involves much more than this.

Understanding as Seeing Relationships

This definition of understanding is implied in the first category of dictionary definitions; namely, to perceive the meaning of, to grasp the idea of, or to comprehend. One meaning for *comprehend* is "to take in or embrace", the Latin root is *comprehendere*, meaning "to seize." In other words, we have here the idea of reaching out and gathering individual items. As they are pulled together, they are understood. However, the definition implies still more; it involves inclusion or embracement of a group of particulars under a single overarching idea. If this definition seems too abstruse, perhaps the following illustration will help.

John M. is a beginning teacher. He has had little experience working with children and none with a group so diverse as his sixth-grade class. He notices that some of his students steal and others seem scrupulously honest. Some come to school dirty and unkempt, others are always well washed and groomed. Some speak ungrammatically, others consistently use "school teachers' English." Some use "dirty language," while others seem to use only language which would be approved in a Sunday school class.

For a long time, these differences in students puzzle John. But, as a result of back-to-school nights, occasional contacts in the community with parents, and information received from other teachers, he finds that the habits of his students are very much like those of their parents, or, if not that, like the prevailing pattern of behaviour within the socio-economic group to which the parents belong. John gradually begins to form some generalizations to explain the individual students in the class; he restructures his life space.

One of these generalizations is that "Much in the behaviour of children can be explained by the nature of the social class in which they live." A number of corollary generalizations, of which the following three are illustrative, also are helpful: "Almost without exception, 'lower-class' children use 'rough' language." " 'Middle-class' children do not reveal as great an overt interest in sex as do lower-class' children." "On the average, 'middle class' children get better marks than 'lower-class' children."

Note how John M. has changed the way in which he perceives his students. He has come to group or classify them in a more meaningful manner. He understands little Mary better because she is a member of a general classification: lower-middle class, suburbia, U.S.A. There are other little Marys who exhibit the same habits and who can be placed in the same classification. Because of certain things they have in common, John M. has grouped these students into a "class"; he has "pulled them together." As is illustrated in the foregoing paragraph, he sees each individual child in relation to appropriate generalizations.

Seeing solitary facts in relation to a general principle is the essence of understanding, as implied by our first definition of the term. Although we are about to suggest that there is significantly more to understanding, teaching probably would be much more effective than it now is if all teachers grasped even this limited definition. Too few teachers realize that any item of factual knowledge is quite meaningless unless students see how it is embraced by a general principle.

Understanding as Seeing the Tool-Use of a Fact

Now let us look at a second definition of understanding. We may say that a person understands something if he sees how that thing can be used to fulfill some goal. (*Thing* is used here in its broadest sense of any existent object, process, idea, or fact.) As soon as a person sees what something is for, he understands it. Of course, the degree of one's understanding is always relative. If I know that a camera takes pictures, I have begun to understand a camera. But if I am going to use a camera successfully, I need to know the details of its operation. I need to know the consequences of using different types of lenses, film emulsions, lighting, and picture compositions.

Note that, according to this second definition, *purpose* always is involved in understanding. The understander must have a goal, and he must see that which he seeks to understand in relation to that goal. Moreover, he must see how what he is trying to understand can be made to help in achieving the goal, or how it can be kept from hindering such achievement. It is as important to understand things which get in our way as it is to understand things which help us along. A rattlesnake may be understood as something to be avoided just as a good steak may be understood as something to add savor to life.

This second definition of understanding harmonizes well with the cognitive-field outlook. According to this outlook, each individual, when behaving intelligently, is trying to reconstruct his life space in terms of how its various functional regions—objects and activities—can better be made to serve his purposes. The chief of these purposes we labeled in an earlier chapter "maintenance and enhancement of one's self," *i.e.*, progressive improvement of a person's ability to structure and use his psychological person and environment for his own purposes.

It is from experimentation that understanding grows. One continuously experiments in that one tries first one course of action and then another, preserving only those which work. Thus, through experience, the features of each person's environment progressively develop a "pointing quality"—dark clouds "point" to rain, Johnny's outthrust jaw and angry squint "point" to a poke in the jaw for Freddy. This pointing quality which we give to features of our environment permits us to behave intelligently—we can act with foresight because there are signposts along the way. The pointing quality of things tells us the probable consequences of using them, which is to say, how to use them with maximum effectiveness.

Understanding as Seeing Both Relationships and Tool-Use

It is important to realize that understanding as seeing the relation between particulars and generalizations and understanding as seeing the tool-use of things are not incompatible. Not only are they compatible; it would appear that, in order to have a fully adequate definition of understanding, we need to consolidate the two definitions.

Because it ignores the role of purpose, understanding as merely seeing relationships is not an adequate concept. Suppose one sees the relationship of certain specific facts to the principle of flotation, as we portrayed in the example of a Herbartian lesson plan. A student reaction to a forced acquaintance with such relationships might simply be, "So what" and no attempt would be made to delve deeply into the implications of the principle, to remember it for future use, or to transfer it to new situations. In other words, understanding which confines itself to seeing relationships between particulars and a general is a fragile and superficial achievement. But suppose a student is a boat hobbyist. He builds boat models and operates them upon a local lake. He is involved in developing a design and needs to know how much of the boat will be submerged when it is carrying four persons whose average weight is 130 pounds. To this student the principle of flotation, and the concrete facts subsumed under it, will seem of vital importance.

Thus, what we may label "full understanding," true understanding," or, even better, "functional understanding" is much more likely to occur if a learner, in learning generalizations and the specific facts pertinent to them, sees how some purpose is served thereby. In effect, we cannot divorce the problem of teaching understanding from that of developing motivation.

If understanding is best achieved when we want to use that which is to be understood, it is equally true that, when motivation toward understanding is present, what is understood will inevitably consist primarily of principles derived from a pattern of specific facts. At this point, we must restate an assertion made about the nature of insights. Among other things, it will be recalled, specific insights tend to be generalized. As soon as one achieves an insight, the thought comes to mind, "Possibly this idea will work in other—or all— similar situations." Accordingly, the insight's general value is tested through its repeated use in similar situations. If it fails to work, it will be discarded as having extremely limited worth. If it seems always to work, it will become a valued possession. Of course, most insights are valid in degrees of predictability; they fall somewhere between the two extremes just suggested.

We now have pushed our analysis to the point where we can offer a third definition of understanding. *Understanding occurs when we come to see how to use productively, in ways which we care about, a pattern of general ideas and supporting facts.* This is the definition which we use throughout the rest of the chapter. Furthermore, when we use the verb *mean* and the noun meaning, we intend them as equivalent to *understand* and *understanding.*

Understanding as a Noun

So far we have been discussing what the verb *understand* means. In the literature of education, we also regularly encounter the noun *understanding* or *understandings.* The noun form refers to the product of acts of understanding. We go through an experimental process of trying to see how certain relationships may be put to use. We find a relationship between something done and the consequences of doing it. This is our *understanding.*

An understanding, then, is a generalized insight. Often it may be put into words but not always. The understandings a person achieves about a golf swing, running the high hurdles, or casting a fly may lie, in part, in a "feel for the act" which would be difficult to verbalize. On the other hand, most persons who have thought about such achievements are able to make statements about the probable consequences of attempting them in alternative ways. Other names for understandings are *generalized insights, general ideas, concepts, principles, rules, laws, generalizations, and theories.*

A word of warning about the use of the word *generalization* is in order. Whenever we use the word in this book it is used synonymously with *generalized insight.* However, in other places generalization often refers to a statement based on inadequate evidence. For example, "You are only generalizing" sometimes means that we should not take the statement seriously. This is a very imprecise use of language which students should avoid. What people really mean by such statements is not that a person has "generalized" but rather that he has been vague or unclear. Since generalization is the only possible basis for intelligent behaviour, the highest possible quality of generalization should be demanded in all situations.

KEY FIGURES IN DEVELOPING UNDERSTANDING-LEVEL TEACHING-LEARNING

Johann F. Herbart, Charles H. Judd, Henry C. Morrison, and Jerome S. Bruner, have provided perhaps the most significant leadership in the development of understanding-level teaching, based upon their respective conceptions of the nature of understanding-level learning. Many others, too, have made important contributions, but these four stand out as perhaps the most prominent innovators with respect to understanding-level teaching and learning. Then in succeeding major sections we develop Morrison's and Bruner's respective positions in some detail. We trust that it will be useful for readers to review briefly the contributions of these four key figures, the latter of whom currently is doing outstanding work in studying understanding-level teaching and learning.

Herbart and Apperception

Johann Friedrich Herbart wrote no treatise on the meaning of understanding, yet his approach to the teaching-learning process indicated that he was aware of one aspect of understanding—*i.e.*, relating the isolated fact to the general principle or rule which gives it meaning.

In steps 3 and 4 of a Herbartian lesson plan as developed by American Herbartians, students are asked to identify *common elements* in a body of factual material and to make a general statement which will link them; *i.e.*, they are asked to take an assortment of related facts and formulate the relationship into a rule, principle, or law. Then in Step 5 students are expected to demonstrate that they see clearly the nature of the principle by applying it in novel situations. A number of school subjects today are taught with essentially the same aims. These are the subjects in which the crux of the subject matter is the learning and application of principles. English grammar and mathematics are usually taught this way. In contrast, foreign language, history, geography, and many other subjects often are taught on a strictly memory-level basis.

Judd and Generalizations

Charles H. Judd (1873-1946) demonstrated the crucial nature of generalizations in his celebrated experiments related to the transfer of learning. Judd and Edward L. Thorndike conducted a running debate as to whether the basis of transfer of learning is identical elements (Thorndike's position and that of associationists in general) or generalizations (the position of Judd and his followers). For the purposes of this chapter, the significance of the great discussion over transfer lies in what it contributed to our understanding of the process and products of understanding.

Perhaps Judd's major contribution, in addition to his concept of transfer—advanced for that time—was simply the emphasis he placed on generalizations as the only subject matter worth learning. (By generalizations, he meant theoretical statements, or, it you prefer, rules, principles, or laws.) For emphasis, we shall repeat here a quotation from Judd which appeared in Chapter 18.........".generalizations which epitomize great numbers of experiences are the highest products of racial and individual intellectual effort." We might construe the expression "experiences" in Judd's statement to mean "individual facts which relate to one another." In short, Judd saw no point in formal education except as it acquainted students with general, or theoretical, statements which could be applied widely in out-of-school situations. To him, memory-level learning which remained as such was completely pointless because of student's inability either to remember or use it except for immediate test-taking purposes.

HOW DID MORRISON'S IDEAS PROMOTE UNDERSTANDING-LEVEL TEACHING?

Henry C. Morrison (1871-1945) was an influential figure in American education during the 1930s and devised a unit plan which at one time was in rather widespread use. Like Herbart and Judd, Morrison is now considered outdated and his books no longer are required reading except in a few schools of education. Nevertheless, some of his ideas still are too avantgarde for many educators of the 1960s to accept.

Within an idea-centered frame of reference, Morrison describes various types of learning, including conditioning, "bonding," and trial and error.[1] However, the kind of learning he felt schools should promote is not any of these as such, but a special form which he referred to as *personality adaptation*. In developing his position, he borrowed freely from various schools of thought, yet to call him an eclectic would be an oversimplification. Because of his emphasis upon *personality adaptation*, to some degree he developed a synthesis of prevailing outlooks on learning. Personality adaptation, we take it, is essentially the same as permanent personality change—*or change in insight*. It refers to revised attitudes, values, beliefs, knowledge and whatever else makes up the psychological person.

Biological adaptation in its most general sense means both a process and a product. The process occurs whenever an organism achieves a better adjustment to the conditions of life. The adjustment itself may be called an adaptation—a change in an organism which throughout the future will enable it to cope with its environment more effectively. Adaptations may be in both structure and function. An animal's eye is a marvelous example of a structure adaptation. Structural adaptations tend to make functional adaptations easier. The latter are changes in behaviour, either instinctive or learned, which help an organism cope better with its environment.

According to Morrison, each of the various types of learning is an adaptive mechanism. But remember that Morrison was interested primarily in human beings and their formal education. Thus, he felt that it is the business of teachers to produce in students a special kind of adaptation. Here we must distinguish between what he called an *adaptive response and true adaptation*. An adaptive response is a habit learned more or less by rote which its bearer does not understand and therefore uses blindly. Morrison thought that much human behaviour is on this level. But he deplored any kind of teaching which leaves students only with adaptive responses instead of personality adaptations.

The proper task for education, said Morrison, is the creation of true adaptation, which is a *permanent change in outlook* as indicated above. Or, put in language which Morrison frequently used, it is *personality change.* To him, the term *personality* meant a total person in its psychological and sociological sense, not those superficial aspects of a person's make-up which we sometimes signify when we say, "John has a nice personality." Specifically, Morrison said personality is the "sum total of what an individual has come to be by learning the cultural products of social evolution."[2]

Adaptive responses, as just defined, do not involve true but rather only pseudo learning. In Morrison's words.

> All down through the ages, from Greek times at least and probably earlier, the one consistent meaning found in the writings of those who have been and are trying to think straight about the matter [*i.e.*, what learning is] is the notion that *learning is becoming* and that the product is a new birth in the individual, a changed point of view, a new taste or set of values, a new inward ability ....
>
> Thus, *every step in the development process for which we use the term education is a piece of learning, or a learning product, and the learning process is the change in personality which constitutes a new insight, or sense of value, or ability.*[3]

Evidently the kind of learning Morrison envisioned is quite similar to the gaining of generalized insight, which gives the generalized position of the Gestalt-field family. Although Morrison's theory of learning is not the same as that implied by cognitive field theory, it is clear that he did regard learning as insightful. In fact, he used the term *insight* with some frequency (as, for example, in the second paragraph quoted above).

One of Morrison's key contentions has met with considerable objection. It is that true learning results in permanent learning products—that is, when true learning has occurred the consequences are never lost. "The ultimate test of a product of learning which has involved a genuine adaptation is that it is not lost, otherwise than through its transformation into new adaptations or through the rise of pathological inhibitions. It is never lost by simply fading out."[4] This view of the permanence of learning harmonizes with the thinking of most contemporary cognitive-field psychologists. Furthermore, it contrasts with the view of most S-R associationists, who hold that the product of learning is conditioned actions which tend to disappear when they are practiced and not reinforced (the process of "extinction"). Morrison would say that a learning which has to be reinforced to prevent its extinction was not a real learning in the first place.

Let us see how these ideas might apply to some common school practices. If a student is able to pass an examination at the end of a course, most teachers would say he has learned something. If he makes a perfect score on the examination, they would say he has learned a great deal and they would be delighted at their own effectiveness and at the student's capacity and diligence. However, it is almost always the case that if a student takes the same examination a year later he will do poorly on it; ten years later he probably will fail it miserably. What is the usual interpretation? Most teachers and administrators take this outcome for granted. They say it is to be expected that much learning will be forgotten.

It contrast, Morrison and many contemporary psychologists would say that a student actually learned little, if anything, in such a process. Morrison stated repeatedly that it is possible for students, in spite of high grades and "graduation with honours," to go all the way through school without really learning anything which was intended. He personally felt that no more than about 10 per cent of students achieve much true learning from their school courses; and those who do, achieve it in spite of their teachers and textbooks rather than because of them.

Morrison's Concept of Understanding

To be able to recall something does not mean to understand it. Often just the contrary is the case. A person might be a "walking encyclopedia" and not understand any of the vast content of his memory. Morrison distinguished sharply between education and erudition. People, he observed, typically have held that "knowledge and information are synonymous with education, that the more an individual knows in the sense of erudition the better education, that the more an individual knows in the sense of erudition the better educated he is."[5] He then took several pages to scoff at this point of view, ending his criticism with the observation that the confusion between education and information-collecting leads schools to try merely to inform students instead of giving them the "insights upon which intelligence is founded."[6]

What are these insights, or understandings, with which Morrison was concerned? To him, understandings were generalizations, rules, principles, concepts—whatever we choose to call them. They suggested an "if-then" relationship—if I perform action A, then action B, is likely to follow. Morrison clarified his position with an illustration of how a person might come to understand the function of valves in a pump. In ordinary instructional practice, a student might be asked to memorize the location of valves in a particular pump. But this is not understanding; "all pumps are not alike." To achieve understanding, a student must learn the principles governing operation of valves. If he knows what valves *do*—not in one pump but in all pumps—he will understand the valves, no matter what kind of pump is involved. When he is confronted with a pump situation and asked to describe action of valves, what he then does is not a matter of recall but one of prediction.

In this pump-valve situation we have almost all the elements of understanding, as set forth earlier in the chapter. We have particulars—facts—in the form of specific pumps with specific valve arrangements. But the specifics are made meaningful by generalizations of principles. Furthermore, the principles sought are cause-effect relationships. They describe the habitual consequences of a given action. Thus, an understanding is not only a generalization adduced from specific facts, but insight into how it may be used in future situations.

Morrison interpreted the role of motivation in a fashion different from that of contemporary cognitive-field psychologists. He appears to have assumed that students will understand the operation of valves just as well whether or not they have a feeling of personal involvement with valves. However, it seems more reasonable to suppose that a generalization is always more meaningful, and hence more useful, if a learner feels a personal urge to master it. It is difficult—perhaps impossible—to teach children genuinely to understand something about which they do not care. However, Morrison took care of the problem of motivation—to his own satisfaction—by suggesting that learning, tends to generate its own appeal. No doubt there is an element of truth in this, but motivation is not something which can be taken for granted and isolated from involvement.

Nonteachable Subject Matter

Since it is impossible to deduce principles or rules from some kinds of subject matter, such as most collections of "descriptive facts," evidently some kinds of subject matter can never be understood. Such subject matter intrinsically is lacking in any basis for understanding—in other words, it is inherently meaningless. Morrison refers to such subject matter as "non-teachable material" and cites examples in textbooks. He had this to say, for example, about some history textbooks:

> Perhaps the most striking example of non-teachable material is to be found in the older texts in history. Nearly all of them were made up of this sort of content from beginning to end. They were chronicles of a meager sort but not histories. They recorded events in chronological order of occurrence, but they failed utterly as a class to interpret the past as an intelligible evolutionary process. *There was nothing to be learned because there was nothing to be understood.*[7]

Perhaps Morrison was unnecessarily kind when he said "older texts." Within a frame of reference to teaching for understanding many of the newer texts in history also are largely unteachable, as are many newer texts in other fields. Furthermore, the psychology of meaning has been so poorly understood by teachers and administrators that they find it difficult to judge whether text or other material is teachable. Consequently, our schools have spent a substantial amount of time, and continue doing so, trying to teach children that which cannot be taught.

Morrison's Recommended Teaching Procedure

Fundamental to comprehension of Morrison's teaching procedure is an understanding of his concept *mastery*. The outcome of all teaching is mastery—not mere memorization of facts, but mastery. Mastery is reached only when planned understandings have been grasped thoroughly. An understanding, as we have seen, is a generalization seen in relation to the pertinent facts and to the uses to which it might be put.

Each subject field, according to Morrison, is to be divided into units. Each unit should present a specific understanding with such thoroughness that mastery is achieved by most students. Note that Morrison did not mean by a "unit" what is commonly meant today. In contemporary parlance, a unit usually is a block of work which, to a teacher or textbook writer, comprises a logical work-task. A unit, therefore, is typically conceived as simply a piece of work, based upon a certain quantity of related facts in a textbook or other source. Morrison's conception of a unit of work was *psychological.* To him, a unit was a generalization and its related facts, *as a student should come to see them.* A unit was never "covered" until all or almost all students thoroughly understood the generalization—its factual origins, its probable reliability, and the kinds of situations in which it could be used in the future.

Some subjects contain many units, each of which may be grasped by most students in a fairly short time (as algebra). Others contain only one unit, i.e., the whole subject must be mastered before a student has anything worthwhile (as a foreign language). The point is, a unit represents an insight which is relatively complete in itself. This insight may be relatively simple and readily grasped, or it may require years of study. Hence, a unit, as Morrison conceives it, may require anywhere from a class period to many years to be mastered.

Each unit is developed according to a sequence of steps, which, although Morrison disclaimed their relationship to the famous five steps of the Herbartian method, are nevertheless reminiscent of the Herbartian steps. No sufficient purpose would be served here by describing a Morrison unit. Students who may have a further interest in Morrison should refer to his books, where the steps of a Morrison unit are described in detail. His contribution was major and most current teaching would undoubtedly be greatly improved if Morrison's thinking were more widely understood. His notion that mere collections of descriptive facts have no meaning, provide no basis for understanding, and therefore constitute unteachable subject matter is of especial importance.

HOW DOES BRUNER EMPHASIZE UNDERSTANDING THROUGH CONCEPTUALIZATION?

Jerome S. Bruner (1915-), now at Harvard University, is

a cognitive psychologist. Although some of his later writings do not seem to be wholly consistent with earlier ones, clearly he is in favour of understanding-level teaching and learning. However, he uses a different vocabulary and manner of describing his view than do others within the same general frame of reference. Furthermore, Bruner does not limit his position merely to advocating teaching for understanding. At times he appears to slide over into supporting reflection-level teaching.

Bruner asserts that, if he is to be categorized, he prefers to be labeled a "functionalist." He rejects "purposivism"—by which he means something akin to vitalism—by saying it has nothing to offer but "cheap-solutions."[8] Since he considers it a hopeless task at present to try to *explain* many psychological phenomena, he sees his role as primarily that of a *describer* of psychological concepts and operations. Because of Bruner's impact in the 1960s, and his probable influence for sometime to come, we treat his position in some detail.

It should be understood that what follows is an attempt to pull together certain aspects of Bruner's thought which seem to represent a contemporary, sophisticated statement of the nature of understanding-level teaching and learning. Accordingly, it does not purport to be a summation of "Bruner's psychology," which is far-ranging and broaches many subjects in addition to teaching for understanding. Students who wish to study the totality of Bruner's thinking should delve into his books and his articles in various journals. The chapter-end references include his major books.

Bruner thinks that highly effective teaching will emerge only from an understanding of the learning process. His *A Study of Thinking* deals with what he considers the most important aspects of thinking (and learning)—persons, by conceptualizing or categorizing, making sense of a hodge-podge of perceived facts. (Bruner uses the terms *conceptualizing* and *categorizing* interchangeably.) The object of his research is "... to describe and in a small measure to explain what happens when an intelligent human being seeks to sort the environment into significant classes of events so that he may end by treating discriminably different things as equivalents."[9]

Bruner first points out that human beings have a fantastic

capacity to discriminate objects or processes in their environment. He then observes that, for a person to make any sense out of his environment, he must be able to select, from an almost infinite number of discriminable objects and events, those which appear to have something in common, and to treat these either as a single category or as a manageable number of categories. Accordingly, we categorize all discriminable colours into one thing, "colour," or into a few things, like the "primary colours," or "the colours most fashionable in clothing this season." Similarly, we try to categorize people by social class, common personality traits, religious affiliation, nationality, size, or age. Unless we can reduce the phenomena of our environment to a manageable number of categories, we are unable to think at all.

Two Basic Types of Categories

Bruner's two basic types of categories are those of *identity* and *equivalence*. An *identity category* is formed by putting into one intellectual barrel a number of different variations of the *same* object. Bruner points out that the moon goes through a series of phases ranging from a barely visible crescent to a full orb—yet we classify each phase of the moon as "moon." We would add that a group of thirty 5-year-old children may each differ conspicuously from the rest, but we still classify them as, depending upon circumstances, "kindergartners," or "lovable darlings," or "little monsters."

An *equivalence category* is one in which different kind of objects are seen as related to one another. Equivalence categories take three forms: affective, functional, and formal. Since there is no hard-and-fast line between identity and equivalence categories, it seems that identity categories also have affective, functional, or formal characteristics.

1. *Affective equivalence categories.* If certain objects or processes in the environment evoke the same affective (emotional or feeling) response in a person, he tends to classify them together. For example, a person might have a category which he labels "the most terrifying experiences I have ever had" within which he would include certain nightmares, being lost in a wilderness, facing surgery with only a small chance of survival, and hallucinating the devil.

2. *Functional equivalence categories.* A functional category arises when one puts *different objects* into the same barrel. "Fruit" is a functional category even though it contains such diverse objects as breadfruit, tomatoes, apples, and pomegranates. "Food" is a functional category even though it contains such diverse objects as snakes, wheat, dogs, beefsteak, grubs, squash, and locusts. All objects discriminated as having the *same function* are placed in the same category.

3. *Formal equivalence categories.* Formal categories arise when a person deliberately specifies the intrinsic properties which an object must have for him to place it in a given category. Formal categorizing uses symbols—mathematical perhaps—and is widely done in the sciences. It may involve highly abstract concepts, such as "force" as it is defined in physics.

Bruner recognizes an affinity of the three types of conceptualization when he says "It is obvious that there are close relationships between affective, functional, and formal categories and ... they are often convertible one into the other."[10] Let us think of an example of such an affinity. A person might invent a category such as "all men who weigh less than 110 pounds." Note that this sort of formal category, based on intrinsic properties of the objects themselves, might also be based on both functional and affective factors. Suppose 110 pounds is the maximum weight at which a man can be employed as a horse racing jockey; then the category obviously becomes functional because a heavier man would be more difficult for a horse to carry. Further, suppose a person *likes* small men for emotional reasons of his own—perhaps he feels more secure associating with them. Then affective factors are clearly operating.

The Process of Categorization

Running through all of Bruner's works is the theme that a thinker rarely can describe the actual process by which he attains his thought-goal. However, he may be able to describe it in a fragmentary and often misleading way, or he may not be able to describe any part of it. In the latter instance, an answer seems to emerge in a flash—what is commonly labeled "Aha learning." Inability of a thinker to verbalize the process by which he has learned does not mean that nothing describable has occurred.

There may have been a lengthy series of acts of weighing evidence and making decisions which the thinker performed on an unconscious level. Various psychologists, particularly Bruner and his associates, have devised a number of ingenious tests aimed at discovering the structure of this largely unconscious—unverbalized—process.

Whether thought processes are formal and susceptible to verbalization or largely unconscious and indescribable, any sequence of decisions purposefully undertaken to attain a goal—such as concept attainment—is labeled by Bruner as *strategy.* Accordingly, a *strategy is any sequence of decision requiring mental events which is goal-oriented.* Thus, it is through the use of strategies that conceptualization occurs. According to experimentation which Bruner reports, selection of a strategy has its own goal: namely, an evaluation which weighs three dynamic factors against each other. These factors are *(a)* the informational situation, *(b)* the cognitive strain, and *(c)* the risk. We consider each in turn.

1. *Informational situation.* Bruner seems to assume that everyone begins a thought task with a certain amount of information in his possession, but the task at hand may require a great deal more. The subject decides just how much more information should be gathered in relation to the strain and risk elements involved. Hence, if the total situation warrants, much time may be spent in data gathering. A classical example of meticulous and extended data gathering prior to conclusion-making is to be found in the work of Charles Darwin. Apparently, he was reasonably sure he could stand the strain, but the risk of announcing an indefensible conclusion was so great that much of a lifetime was spent in data gathering. On the other hand, under very different conditions a person may spend little or no time gathering data, either because the strain is too great or the risk of failure too inconsequential.

2. *Cognitive strain.* Anyone who has been around students, especially those of high school or college age, is familiar with expressions like, "I sure poured sweat studying for that last chem exam." The student may have sweated in a literal sense, but what such a statement really refers to is some degree of mental torment. If a student spent a night doing nothing but rotememory work, the example might not apply. But, if the student's aim is to categorize specific instances and so emerge with new concepts,

the example fits very well. Thinking may be a most arduous activity. It not only may take time, but it also may require numerous frustrating attempts to grasp that which is just beyond reach. Furthermore, a thinker's uncertainty about the reliability of his thought may produce states of high anxiety. Nevertheless, virtually everyone who is living on higher than a vegetable like mental level will frequently set for himself very difficult intellectual goals—often more difficult than he can achieve.

3. *Risk.* If failure would have highly unpleasant consequences, a person tends to put more effort into data processing and is willing to endure more cognitive strain than if the consequences of failure are negligible. Also, individuals vary greatly in the amount of risk they are willing to assume. This variation is probably a function of experience. Persons often make poor estimates of risk, especially long-term risk.

It is apparent that with experience students learn increasingly effective strategies. *Why* a person tends to balance against each other the above three factors in strategy making. Bruner considers an unknown. But that they do, he is reasonably sure. Furthermore, individuals work at improving strategies and again the *why* of this is a matter of speculation. About all we can say is that in some situations people have rather impelling reasons for wanting to improve performance.

The time-consuming work of devising and improving strategies appears to lie in the selection of information (or *instances,* as Bruner would say) which will "fit" a category. This involves learning to identify the cues which distinguish the relevant from the irrelevant. The more accurately and rapidly one can identify cues, the faster he can sort instances into categories. This is probably only another way of saying that the more readily a person can learn to put together significant data—in contrast to amassing mere intellectual junk—the more effectively he can think. Bruner is convinced that whatever processes are at work in achieving this kind of learning, we don't know much about them; but we can be fairly certain that acquiring ability to "think straight" is a matter of learning and, except in the case of those who are conspicuously genetically defective, this prowess is not innate.

We turn now to what we interpret as the next step which a person takes after initial concept-learning. This is stringing concepts together into cause-and-effect genralizations—*coding.*

Coding

Most of Bruner's essay in the report of the Cognitive Symposium held at the University of Colorado in 1955 treats the subject of psychological coding.[11] Bruner states, "A coding system may be defined as a set of contingently related, nonspecific categories."[12] His meaning becomes clearer when he says that the problem of instruction "... concerns the best coding system in terms of which to present various subject matters so as to guarantee maximum ability to generalize."[13]

It appears, then, that Bruner views the process of coding as one by which concepts are combined into generalizations. Further, such generalizations permit both "backward and forward" predictions of what particularized statements are most likely to be either true or false—or, in Bruner's words, ".. a good theory—a good formal or probabilistic coding system— ... should permit us to go beyond the present data both retrospectively and prospectively"[14] (A *formal* code takes the form of, or is subsumed under, some principle of logic; a *probabilistic* or *informal* code is a generalization acquired inductively, perhaps even intuitively.) For our purposes, a code may be regarded as a generalization, commonly of the if-then form, by which we can infer the consequences of previous actions and thereby forecast the consequences of future ones. A code is either stated in, or implies, the present-tense verb form, as when we say, "When a mother bear is cornered she is likely to attack," (probilistic) or "If object A is located on spot X, then object B cannot be placed on X at the same time" (formal). When a code is regarded as a generalization, principle, rule, or law, we see the relatedness of Bruner's thinking with the discussion earlier in the chapter on the role of general statements in the achievement of understanding.

Codes can be related to other codes, *ad infinitum.* Thus, we come to have *systems* of codes. A system of codes relating to a particular subject provides the *structure* of that subject. History has a structure, as does mathematics, a language, industrial arts, physics, music, or football strategy. Later in the chapter, we have more to say about the significance of codes and structure for learning and curriculum making.

Since the ultimate process in learning anything is coding, if a student stops with the memorization of unrelated facts he has achieved nothing of worth. When he categorizes facts and thus invents concepts, he has achieved considerably more. But it is only when he gains command of theory (codes) that the real payoff comes. He now has something to think with. However, the term *theory* must be construed very broadly. It may mean a highly formal code which can be stated in the shorthand of mathematics, such as $S=\frac{1}{2}gt^2$; contrariwise, it may mean an unverbalized "feel" for something—a "sense of pattern." Perhaps, if we return again to spelling, we not only can better illustrate what we mean but also suggest something useful about how spelling should be learned.

To learn spelling on an understanding level, one may learn the so-called rules of spelling. For example, " 'e' precedes 'i' in all words in which the ei' combination is pronounced as a 'long a' or 'long i'." But there is another way of learning to spell which involves probabilistic coding: *we develop a sense of which letters are likely to follow a given letter within a certain context.* This kind of coding is probably done quite unconsciously and could not be explained by those who do it. To use the language of cognitive-field psychology, it involves getting a "feel" for spelling.

Bruner cites a significant experiment conducted by Miller, Postman, and himself. They arranged some fifth-grade children into two groups—those who fell in the lowest quartile of a standard spelling achievement test and those who fell in the highest quartile. In short, they identified a group of poor spellers and a group of good spellers. Bruner and his colleagues first confronted these students with a set of pseudo words (*i.e.,* letter combinations which are not real words) which only slightly resembled English words. Both groups identified the words as English to about the same degree. But when both groups were presented a group of pseudo words which resembled English very closely in letter patterning (and which, as Bruner says, "... but for the grace of God, might have been in the dictionary") the good spellers much more likely than the poor to identify the words as English.

Bruner suggests that the good speller had learned to code the English language with respect to typical letter patterning. He concludes, "The difference between the two groups is in *what* they had been learning while learning to spell English words. One group had been learning words more by rote, *the others had been learning a general coding system based on the transitional probabilities that characterize letter sequences in English.*"[15]

Bruner also provides additional evidence pertinent to coding by citing his and Robert Harcourt's experiment in which they presented both English and foreign-speaking persons with pseudo words which resembled closely the letter patterning of several foreign languages as well as English. Subjects tended to be able to reproduce those pseudo words which had a letter-patterning, or code, similar to most words in their language, whereas they had great difficulty reproducing pseudo words coded in a foreign tongue.

It would appear that, if children are taught spelling by rote, some will learn it that way and others—for reasons not yet known—will learn to code as they progress. The first group may do very well on weekly spelling quizzes, but be unable to spell accurately when using the same words in themes, letters, or any other context. On the other hand, the second group—the coders—tend to spell correctly any word which they have learned, in any context in which they need to use it.

Structure

As code is built upon code (or generalization upon generalization) a learner achieves increasingly "large" grasps of a subject. That is, he sees an ever increasing number of concepts and generalizations as related. The more generic or generalized a coding system is, the more useful it is to a learner. It relieves him of any need to learn and try to remember a large number of facts. As Bruner suggests, successful coding produces a situation where "...new instances can be recognized with no further learning and the memory of instances already encountered need no longer depend upon sheer retention. *For now, knowing the code, the subject can reconstruct the fact that all positive instances encountered were all marked by certain critical attributes.*"[16] It is obvious, therefore, that the more extensively a subject can be encompassed by systematic coding (or, if you prefer, by linked generalizations), the easier the subject is to be understood and utilized. This leads us to the concept of structure, of which Bruner has made a considerable point.

Bruner suggests that the ultimate aim of teaching in any subject or group of related subject is "... general understanding of the structure of a subject matter."[17] But, when Bruner applies the word *structure* to a subject matter he does not use the term in the sense in which it often has been used. "Grasping the structure of a subject is understanding it in a way that permits many other things to be related to it meaningfully"[18]

In *The Process of Education,* Bruner gives some interesting examples of what he means by structure. One, from the field of biology, involves coding that is relatively formal and can probably be verbalized all along the way. He says:

> Take first a set of observations on an inchworm crossing a sheet of graph paper mounted on a board The board is horizontal: the animal moves in a straight line. We tilt the board so that the inclined plane or upward grade is 30°. We observe that the animal does not go straight up, but travels at an angle of 45° from the line of maximum climb. We now tilt the board to 60°. At what angle does the animal travel with respect to the line of maximum climb? Now, say, he travels along a line 75° off the straight up line. From these two measures, we may infer that inchworm "prefer" to travel uphill, if uphill they must go, along an incline of 15°.[19]

At this point, Bruner observes, we have discovered the meaning of *tropism.* This is not an isolated fact, but a concept with broad applicability. From this concept we can demonstrate regularities among simple organisms with respect to regulation of locomotion, preferred levels of illumination, of temperature, of salinity, and so on. When a student comes to see the fundamental relationship between external stimulation and locomotor action, he has a code whereby he can understand innumerable other events in biology. Presumably, the student can then relate this genre of code to other biological codes until he finally sees the whole field of biology (or what constitutes the "whole" field at that particular stage of learning) in a related way. The more relatedness he sees, the more able he is to think about biology in terms of broad abstractions. This saves him the bother of trying to retain in memory a clutter of detail; the detail can always be reconstructed when needed because the code is there.

Bruner also offers an example from the field of language which illustrates informal, nonverbalized coding. He puts the example this way:

> The often unconscious nature of learning structures is perhaps best illustrated in learning one's native language. Having grasped the subtle structure of a sentence, the child very rapidly learns to generate many other sentences based on this model though different in content from the original sentence learned. And having mastered the rules of transforming sentences without altering their meaning-- "The dog bit the man" and "The man was bitten by the dog"—the child is able to vary his sentences much more widely. Yet, while young children are able to *use* the structural rules of English, they are certainly not able to say what the rules are.[20]

Space permits only a few more words about teaching a subject as a structure. Many persons think that it is only the "bright" student who can conceptualize and generalize, and build concepts upon concepts and generalizations upon generalizations until a subject is seen as a related whole. Not so, Bruner insists. Dull students appear to profit even more than do bright ones from teaching which has structuring as its aim. Presumably, this is because bright students can do much of their own structuring. In any case, the worst possible way to teach dull children is by rote.

Another of Bruner's points of significance is that learning achieved through structuring tends to be permanent. It is not subject to "extinction." Morrison, as we pointed out earlier in the chapter, contended in similar vein that if anything is truly learned the learner's total personality has undergone change; he will not forget unless some future personality change gives him good reason to reject the original learning.

Purpose and Motivation

In all of Bruner's works with which we are familiar there seem to be the underlying assumption that when a teacher confronts students with a learning task all that is necessary is to explain carefully what the learning goals are and students will, *ipso facto*, be sufficiently motivated to see the task through, with the qualification that motivation will be aided if the cultural milieu is exerting a pull favourable toward intellectual exertion.

There is no question that Bruner's psychology is purposive in the sense that he sees learning as always goal-centered. He makes such statements as: "Anticipatory categorizing, then, provides 'lead time" for adjusting one's response to objects with which one must cope", [21] and "It is this future-oriented aspect of categorizing behaviour in all organisms that impresses us most."[22] But, he is hesitant in hypothesizing what lies behind purposing. After discussing various historical researches and assertions that have been made on the subject, he concludes that, on the basis of earlier theories, not much advantage is served by trying to go beyond such statements as "the person strives to reduce the complexity of his environment," or "There is a drive to group things in terms of instrumental relevance......"[23]

Bruner then goes on to suggest that there is some experimental evidence to suggest that tensional states up to the point of frustration may be the key to understanding motivational states. Further, he seems to show some sympathy for postulating a primary need other than the "animal drives," which might be called "curiosity," and which keeps an organism active even in the absence of tensional states. He points out that our cognitive activity is not dominated at all times by concerns for such things as food and sex—after all, we do have to try to explain in some way why a person may want to learn to play chess.[24] However, after asserting what *seems* to be true in the words, "Cognitive frustration, within tolerable limits, helps keep search behaviour going. The 'insight' experience leads to new bursts of testing activity," he seems to negate this whole line of inquiry by saying, "We are completely without evidence for such assertions or even without proposals as to how one might gather evidence."[25]

Bruner's most interesting comments on motivation have nothing to do with the origins of motivation or techniques for producing it, but with the most desirable *level* of motivation. In discussing this topic, Bruner has data of research to draw from and evidently feels on fairly sound ground. His chief contention is that there is a kind of "golden mean" for which a teacher should strive. "Somewhere between apathy and wild excitement, there is an optimum level of aroused attention that is ideal for classroom activity." In answer to his own query as to what the optimum level is, he says. "Frenzied activity fostered by the competitive project may leave no pause for reflection, for evaluation, for generalization, while excessive orderliness, with each student waiting passively for his turn, produces boredom and ultimate apathy."[26]

Later in the paragraph he introduces an issue which is of great significance for Bruner's own position. He distinguishes between day-by-day motivation and "the long-term establishment of interest in the broader sense." Short-run motivation can be induced by various means without much imagination or long-term sense of direction on the part of a teacher. This kind of motivation emerges from the "bag of tricks" approach to teaching. If a teacher has a large bag of gimmicks for inducing attention and short-span activity he can keep his classes going for an entire school year and a casual observer might be fooled into thinking that something worthwhile had occurred.

Bruner rejects any kind of gimmickry intended for short-run motivation. In an entertainment-oriented, mass-communication culture, there is grave risk that students will come to expect this and nothing else from their schooling. Instead, Bruner would emphasize only long-range goals, the ultimate goal of any subject area being structurization as described previously. Motivation to achieve this sort of goal does not require a "full head of steam' but is rather analogous to a slow-burning fuse or a smoldering forest fire that resists all efforts to be put out. It involves a kind of dogged persistence which is slow moving but not too slow to prevent a student from seeing that he is making progress toward something of real import. It is this relatively tuned-down motivation which permits careful thinking and accuracy of results. Research suggests that if organisms are stimulated—or coerced—to learn something quickly they tend to rely on what they see as the quickest solution: the memorization of particulars. Translated to human terms, they see high-pressure drill as the quickest or surest way to get the job done. Generic or coded learning necessarily is a leisurely process.

Significance of "Intuitive Leaps"

In his use of the concept *intuitive leaps* Professor Bruner seems, at times, to move from advocating mere understanding-level teaching to hint that teachers should teach for understandings or insights through reflective means. Whereas early proponents of understanding-level instruction had nothing to say about anything like "intuitive leaps," Bruner gives the concept a good deal of importance.

When Bruner uses the concept of intuitive leaps, he is referring to unverbalized (or, in his language, unconscious) thought processes, sometimes very rapid, sometimes long and drawn out, which lead in a flash to an insight which can be verbalized and treated as a hypothesis. He reiterates the value of this kind of thinking, reciting various major breakthroughs in human thought which occurred this way. Furthermore, he advocates that teachers encourage students to play hunches and propose bold and even improbable ideas. He also warns that in no case should "answers" so reached be thought of as valid conclusions. A next—and oftimes difficult—step is analytic testing of the hypothesis. This is pursuit of the sequential steps which we associate with open or public verification.

WHAT SUGGESTIONS MAY BE MADE FOR IMPROVING UNDERSTANDING-LEVEL TEACHING?

As now organized, many courses are built around concepts and generalizations. This is true of languages, provided the "rules" are taught. It also is true of mathematics, which is one of the courses par excellence so far as generic learning is concerned; it is practically all rules, once the fundamentals or arithmetic are taught (by rote, all too often). Home economics, too, rises to the level of coding when a student learns generalizations about nutrition, cooking, baby care, housekeeping, etc. Readers can name the remaining school subjects which commonly are focused on concepts and generalizations, rather than on the memorization of discrete facts.

Unfortunately, there are certain regularly required courses which are nothing but arrays of facts arranged chronologically or topically; there is no apparent rationale either to the selection or arrangement of factual materials included. Among the worst offenders on this score have been the social studies. However, readers will be able to think of several other culprits, including the natural sciences. Biology, for example, may emphasize taxonomy—classification—to the point-where everything else is omitted or treated only incidentally; albeit, in certain areas of biology, it is difficult to escape if-then generalizations and the building of at least partial structures. Ecology, genetics, and speciation are examples of such areas.

Shortly before this manuscript went to press, a most interesting article appeared in *Saturday Review.* Its author, Professor Richard H. Brown, endeavours to describe what he sees as a revolution in the social studies. He maintains that Professor Bruner articulated the original message. However, in so doing, Professor Brown appears to reveal some unawareness of what had happened in the years B.B. (Before Bruner). In fact, kernels of Bruner's thinking can be traced back to Charles Peirce, William James, John Dewey, Kurt Lewin, E. C. Tolman, Gestalt psychologists, organismic biologists, and other progenitors of contemporary cognitive psychology. Bruner himself acknowledges the hypothesizing and research of numerous persons, going back for decades, which have helped shape his thinking. Accordingly, Bruner's major contribution, perhaps, lies in two directions: First, he has collected a wealth of empirical research and contributed much of his own, so as to provide a fairly impressive empirical underpinning for his conclusions. Second, he has stated his conclusions in a way which is fresh, which has captured the attention of educators everywhere, and which has set in motion innovations for which there was a plausible theoretical base half a century ago but which somehow had not caught hold.

Our purpose here is not to eulogize Bruner and his associates, but to make a point about the blind spots of some persons who work in scholarly disciplines in which generic thinking is not the rule. Professor Brown is a historian. He is not only convinced that Bruner's concept of structure needs fuller definition (which may well be the case) but that in the field of history the meaning of structure is particularly elusive. Professor Brown says that "... if it [structure] exists at all it lies in the methods and purposes of the discipline rather than in the way what is known about it is organized." Is Professor Brown saying that the content of history is not amenable to structuring? Further assertions in the article suggest that this is exactly what he is saying.[27] Yet, it appears to the present writers that this is equivalent to saying that the actual content of history is not susceptible to understanding-level teaching and learning. Perhaps if Professor Brown were to take a second look, he would realize that certain early-entry historians, such as James Harvey Robinson and Charles A. Beard, were coding and structuring history almost fifty years ago. The fact that some of their generalizations did not hold in the light of further inquiry in no way negates the proposition that history can be structured. It seems reasonable that, once we learn how, any subject matter taught in school can be taught at least on an understanding level and that a greater part of it actually can be taught on the reflection-level as described in the next chapter.

The following suggestions may be of value to teachers who wish to implement classroom understanding-level learning. Some of the points are suggested in Bruner's works, others come from several different sources, and some are our own. They centre upon teachers, the teaching process, and appropriate evaluation.

Necessary Characteristics of a Teacher

It appears evident that a teacher must manifest the right kind of attitudes, values, and knowledge to be able to teach effectively on an understanding level. Hopefully, these can be acquired at any age. Let us examine some of the factors which are involved in a teacher's acquisition of these traits. These are as follows: (1) the way in which a teacher has learned the subject, (2) the degree to which the teacher has learned the subject, and (3) the personality characteristics of a teacher.

The way in which a teacher has learned the subject. If prospective teachers have been taught on an understanding level the subjects which they in turn plan to teach, then it is unlikely that they will need much further instruction. It is a truism that the way in which teachers have learned will reflect itself in the way they teach. If a teacher has not himself learned his subjects by moving from instances (facts) to categories (concepts) to codes (generalizations), then it would appear that he needs to relearn his subjects over again, following those steps. The practical problems involved in doing this might in many cases seem insurmountable. One wonders just what this suggests—perhaps that many teachers should think of retiring young. It certainly does suggest the need for changed methods of instruction in many college classes, for more discriminating selection of the "master teachers" with whom student teachers or interns work, and for changed in-service teacher-education programmes.

The degree to which a teacher has learned the subject. Bruner comes very close to a "self-evident truth" (if such exists) when he says, "It takes no elaborate research to know that communicating knowledge depends in enormous measure upon one's mastery of the knowledge to be communicated.... It is also quite plain from recent surveys that many primary and secondary school teachers are not, in the view of various official bodies, sufficiently well trained initially to teach their subject."[28] Our only advice to prospective or in-service teachers is, "If you are not a master of your subject, then take whatever steps are necessary to insure mastery." For the undergraduate, this may mean studying far beyond the minimal graduation requirements. For those already teaching it may mean returning to college for study in depth of the subjects they now teach or it may mean a carefully planned programme of self-study.

The personality characteristics of a teacher. It is fairly simple to deduce what kind of person is most likely to be successful at understanding-level teaching. He must be fairly bright—by which we mean capable to exercising intelligence on a fairly high level. He must have the kind of mind set which finds it easy to see particulars in relation to one another—the kind which leans toward conceptualization, generalization, and abstraction. Another way of putting it is to say an effective teacher is a person with a penchant for theorizing and who understands that "nothing is so practical as a good theory."

Another capacity of crucial importance is patience. Teaching for understanding is not something that can be hurried. The "frantic ground-covering" type of teacher is suited only for memory-level or rote teaching—which is to say good for not very much at all. More is said about this subject under a later head. To discuss other personality characteristics would run us into a series of cliches which potential or practicing teachers already have heard entirely too many times. Of course, a teacher should be dedicated, conscientious, honest, tactful ... etc., etc. Readers can make up their own list of what is required.

The Teaching Process

Most advocates of understanding-level teaching have taken for granted that a teacher begins with truths which he knows but which students do not. Students struggle to find these truths, with the teacher providing what cues are necessary along the way. The student has successfully completed his learning task when he emerges with an understanding of the preordained truths which the teacher already knew. This approach permits inquiry, investigation, and exploration on the part of the student—all of which undoubtedly does not help him greatly in *understanding* the foregone conclusions he eventually will reach. But there is an issue here which is of notable importance and Richard Brown states it brilliantly in the article previously mentioned:

> Are the proponents of the revolution willing to follow through where they argue that they want to make the student a fledgling scholar, a free inquirer after truth? Or do they want him merely to find on his own the truths they already know? In dealing with the original sources ... should the student do any more than play a game with the compiler of the materials, looking for clues so that he may come to a preordained answer? Dare he find things the compiler did not know were there, or ask questions which will carry him outside the materials altogether?[29]

Professor Brown obviously sees the issue between teaching which remains on an understanding level and teaching which moves to the level of reflection. If a student dares find things the compiler did not know and if he dares ask questions which lead outside the previously prepared materials, then clearly reflective teaching and learning are operating. This will be explained in the ensuing chapter. But now let us examine the attributes of an effective understanding-level teaching process.

To teach effectually on an understanding level, a teacher must (1) keep his objectives clear, (2) understand the proper role of practice, (3) practice productive motivational techniques, (4) pace students and lessons advantageously, (5) use lesson plans properly, and (6) recognize the significance of a spiral curriculum.

Keeping objectives clear. Bruner stresses in several of his writings that most students will make an effort to achieve the learning goals which a teacher announces to them. However, this does not mean that prior announcements of conclusions are desirable; such action would destroy the "discovery aspect" of learning. What should be explained to students before the learning act is the *kind* of learning they are expected to achieve. A teacher is either misled or shoddy if, in making assignments, he requests his students to memorize something, to spend so-much-time-at-drill, or just to "learn this by tomorrow" (which students almost always construe to mean "memorize"). Students must be taught, and not through mere memorization, the nature of a concept, a generalization, and a structured subject. This can be done by inductive type of questioning coupled with the study of examples of people in the process of achieving these goals. When students not only can explain in their own words but also can invent their own examples of these processes, then they are ready for effective statements of objectives.

Obviously students should be taught as soon as possible the road to abstract thought. Once this is done, it is possible to proceed with the content of the subject. Assignments will carry instructions such as this: "Here we have some facts which seem unconnected. See to what extent you can categorize them," or "We have reached three generalizations concerning this topic. Try to see if you can combine them into a single, more-inclusive generalization," or "After conceptualizing the known facts, we have invented a generalization. See how many presently unknown but possible facts you can deduce from the generalization." If a student is always reminded that the object of learning is some level of conceptualization, and if no other approach works, then this is the way he will learn.

The role of practice. Practice—sometimes extending over a long period of time—often is necessary to achieve a learning task. This is perhaps more true of gaining voluntary control of motor skills than of cognition of an academic sort, but practice is an important factor in both. In the past, practice has all too often been construed as repetitive drill—the repeating of a static item in identical form. As observed earlier in the book, one of the early proponents of repetition as a means of learning, Thorndike, as a result of further experimentation, later retracted his original assertions in regard to the value of repetition. Only the most naive teacher nowadays knows so little about learning that he thinks he can teach anything of significance by mere repetition.

Practice, on the other hand, has a special connotation. Practice can be construed as the experimental trying of an act over again—and again and again, if necessary. However, a crucial difference between mechanical repetition and experimental practice is that with practice the subject performs the act a little differently each time and observes or experiences the consequences. Bruner maintains that generic learning cannot occur in the absence of a changing situation. Accordingly, he comments on a statement of Kurt Lewin as follows: "Kurt Lewin had a subtle point when he urged that the best way to understand the nature of a social process was to try to change it, for only in the face of changes in events does one begin to have the information necessary to abstract generic properties."[30]

Productive motivation. Educators who operate within an understanding-level frame of reference assume that once a student is acquainted with a subject, told of the expected goals in learning it, and begins to experience some success, motivation generates rather spontaneously. This is not a false theory of motivation, but it may be an inadequate one. It is true that some students become very much interested in a subject merely through exposure to it. But this is the exception rather than the rule.

Like others before him whose chief focus was on teaching for understanding, Bruner does not come to grips with the problem of inducing students to want to involve themselves in study. It appears that teaching which does not go beyond the objectives of helping students see the relatedness of things seeks motivation from wherever it can be found. Bruner stresses the importance of students having a purpose of learning. However, he is not clear—and sometimes is contradictory—with respect to how such purpose can be instilled. Much of his discussion seems to centre on extrinsic purposes—those arising from something other than the fascination of the subject matter itself.[31] But he also refers to a natural tendency toward curiosity and drops it at that. Then, in one book he devotes a chapter to motivation and attributes it to cultural pressures on the learner deriving from the general social milieu.

In any case, student motivation is one area in which Bruner and his like-minded forerunners do not have much to say. The reason is not concealed: Professor Bruner is wary enough to try to steer some middle path between vitalism and the unadulterated environmentalism of most advocates of S-R associationism. What seems to be lacking is an emergent synthesis which will suggest fresh lines of inquiry. Cognitive-field psychologists have worked on this problem.

Pacing advantageously. We come now to one of the major points concerning classroom procedure. By "pace" we refer to speed of movement from one topic to another; it logically follows that the number of topics studied in a year is of great significance. The pace of understanding-level learning is usually slow. It is much more analogous to the steady thrust of a glacier than to the speed of a greyhound chasing a rabbit. As we pointed out earlier in the chapter, categorizing, generalizing, and structuring cannot be rushed. This is the case even in spite of "intuitive leaps"—after all, the leaps produce only hypotheses and not firm knowledge. If a learner is to emerge with something solid, each leap must be followed by a careful series of verifying tests.

Any subject matter *worth* confronting students with is worth careful, penetrating, thorough study. If it is not worth this kind of study, it is not worth inclusion in the curriculum. Typically, we try to teach too many items—and they remain nothing more than items—quickly to be forgotten. To achieve genuine understanding, and consequent retention and transfer, it may be necessary to eliminate half or more of the present curriculum. The problem of the relationship of teaching methodology to curriculum needs a great deal more study than it, to date, has had.

Proper use of lesson plans. Historically, carefully drawn day-by-day lesson plans have been considered essential to understanding-level-teaching and learning. It appears likely that, until a teacher has structured his subject matter in his own thinking, he not only should read and think copiously, but also should take notes which can be translated into lesson plans as necessary. But, Herbartian lesson planning is overly rigid and leads to indoctrination. Morrison's mastery units represent an advance over Herbartian lesson plans. However, they, too, set the stage for a teacher's indoctrinating students in a rather mechanistic fashion. Bruner appears to have nothing to say on the subject of lesson plans. Possibly he assumes that a competent teacher will have his lesson plans in his head.

Our own feeling is that a beginning teacher, striving for understanding level teaching, should have a tentative plan for each class session. For safety, he should probably have an alternate plan in case the first does not work. We do not recommend a rigid plan with 1-2-3 steps. Thought does not take this pattern. Plans should be informal and flexible. They should include reminders of factual material to be presented when needed, key questions to ask, and tentative conclusions. One manner of distinguishing understanding from reflection-level teaching is the tendency of the former to adhere quite closely to lesson plans as drawn and to wrap up each unit in a complete package with no loose ends. This tendency has significant implications for motivation, as we shall see in the next chapter on reflection-level teaching.

The proper use of lesson plans in reflective teaching was summated, and not facetiously, by Boyd H. Bode when he wrote, "... the lesson plan has its merits, provided we do not use it, *i.e.*, provided we do not follow it as a plan of campaign in the classroom... It is as preposterous to concoct a recipe for learning as for invention."[32]

Evaluating Understanding-Level Learning

Traditionally, evaluation of understanding-level learning has been achieved either through tests which give students raw data and have them show how well they can conceptualize and generalize from the data or through application of principles tests which require students to deduce new facts from principles which presumably they understand. A variety of formats are available for each of these two fundamental tests. Essay formats can be used, but it is also possible to test for understanding with short-answer examinations. Such examinations are much harder to construct than the simple and relatively meaningless measuring devices that teachers use to test rote learning. Short-answer tests for the measurement of thinking on any level require a substantial amount of thinking to construct; if their results are to be valid probably more time is required in making them than in grading easier-to-make essay examinations. However, time economies can be effected by constructing more than one version of a short-answer test for each unit and, by switching versions, using the same tests repeatedly.

The pioneering work in devising tests to measure understanding was undertaken by the Evaluation Staff of the Eight Year Study.[33] Ways were devised for constructing short-answer tests under such heads as the following: Interpretation of Data, Logical Reasoning, Nature of Proof, and Application of Principles. The usual format was to describe a situation in one or two paragraphs. These "real life" situations were described concretely and vividly. They were followed by a series of statements about the situation which were to be checked true or false, and in some cases by a second series of statements to reveal possible reasons for the conclusions indicated in the first set of statements. Thus, students had an opportunity to show the reasons which guided their own thinking.

If designed with the specific intent of testing a student's ability to conceptualize, generalize, and apply generalizations to novel situations, a multiple-choice question of the more-or-less standard format of an initial statement followed by four or five choices can be satisfactorily valid. If the test writer is ingenious enough, he might even adapt a simple yes-no format in a way to reveal understanding (*e.g.*, a T-F test, or a dual-choice test of some sort).

Below is an example of a test item which should measure students' ability to apply an understanding *provided* none of the five specific instances which make up the five choices has been used previously by the students in arriving inductively at the principle of flotation.

If, in a liquid or gaseous fluid, an object will float if the fluid it displaces has more mass than the volume displaced, then it follows that (check one):

(a) it would be impossible to construct an object of lead that would float

(b) there is no substance on which a solid iron ball would float

(c) a feather will literally float on air

(d) a model airplane with a frame of balsa should glide farther than one with an oak frame

(e) a man-made orbiting satellite stays in orbit because of its capacity to float.

The foregoing item is not free of bugs; one must assume that students know the vocabulary used in stating the specific instances and that they know certain crucial facts, such as that mercury (a fluid) is almost four times heavier than iron and that oak is a much heavier wood than balsa. There are also assumptions which are not stated, such as that the two model airplanes are of identical design and would perform the same aerodynamically except for the difference in weight.

A simpler and perhaps more valid question would simply ask students to name and discuss one or more instances not previously studied in which the principle of flotation could be put to practical use. But, it could not be machine-scored; the instructor would be faced with the problem of evaluating the quality of a great many ambiguous, half-true, and illegible answers. However, any way one approaches it, teaching and testing for understanding or reflection places a heavier burden on a teacher than mere memory-level teaching.

Most teachers make unnecessarily great the burden imposed by evaluating the results of teaching. There is no evidence we know of which suggests that, with teaching pitched on an understanding level, very many examinations need be given. If a teacher encourages discussion, he learns to sense whether students are categorizing and coding with satisfactory accuracy. He can rate students, one against another, simply by listening or watching. Apparently, understanding-level learning is best promoted and evaluated by widely spaced examinations which are not only announced well in advance but whose format and general content are also announced and explained in advance, preferably by giving students specimen examinations to serve as cues for study. After tests are given, they should be returned to students and the class given time to discuss test results with thoroughness. Unless a teacher uses a short-answer type of test which he expects to use again, he should allow students to keep tests for study purposes. Possession of a file of test answers, with notes indicating how they could have been improved, each successive test demanding higher levels of abstraction, should be a useful tool in helping a student structure a body of subject matter.

Significance of a spiral curriculum. Bruner, with the concurrence of numerous other experimental psychologists, appears to reject the concept of readiness, so popular a few decades back. He asserts that "...the foundations of any subject may be taught to anybody at any age in some form."[34] Even infants learn to use rules long before they can talk about them. First-graders can be taught the rudiments of the idea structure of much of what we now refer to as "higher mathematics." At successive grade levels, or, in an ungraded school, at successive time intervals, it is essential to come back to the rudiments already learned and build upon them by adding more complex and subtle categories and codes. This is the road to successful structuring of a subject matter. It calls for what Bruner refers to as the "spiral curriculum"—*i.e.,* a curriculum in which content keeps "circling back" to build upon previous understandings.

HOW SHOULD WE REGARD PROGRAMMED LEARNING AND MACHINE TEACHING?

In an era when the workload of teachers tends to become constantly heavier, any kind of teaching aid which might relieve a teacher's burden is intriguing to contemplate—especially if the aid potentially is capable of instruction of as high quality as that of the teacher himself. Certain widely used aids have a long history; others are more recent. In the middle 1950s a new (at least in its labeling and the claims made for it) development began attracting wide attention. This was programmed teaching and learning, plus the special kinds of aids for which it seemed to call—primarily "programmed textbooks" and/or teaching machines.

If mechanical aids can be of major assistance in promoting understanding level learning—or reflective learning as it is described in the following chapter—then it seems obvious that we should use them unless their expense is greater than that of hiring more teachers who can do the job equally well or better. On the other hand, if programming and the use of associated devices lead only to memory-level or rote learning, teachers should be wary of their use.

What is Programming?

Except in the thinking of a small group of mavericks, current programming, both in its underlying philosophical and psychological premises and in its implementation, is rooted in S-R associationism and primarily in B.F. Skinner's concept of operant conditioning. Programmed teaching assumes that there is a "correct" subject matter (*i.e.,* body of appropriate responses for each subject taught). This is to say, a programmer *knows* ahead of time rather precisely what should be included in a subject matter, what is true and what is false, and the order in which individual items should be presented. In line with its S-R orientation, subject matter is taught through a process of conditioning but at a pace determined by the student. A "programme" refers simply to a block of subject matter in which stimuli and responses have been arranged to lead a student as expeditiously as possible to the planned outcome—a more-or-less complicated repertoire of over responses.

Sidney L. Pressey—the Pioneer

In 1924, Sidney L. Pressey, of Ohio State University, designed the first system of programming and the first machine to implement it. In 1926, he formally published a report of his work. The original Pressey system involved a series of four-choice multiple-choice questions which could be inserted into a machine which exposed one question at a time to students by revolving them over a rotating drum. By depressing one of four keys which corresponded to what the student thought was the correct answer, he was "told" immediately by the machine whether he was right. A correct answer caused the drum to roll into position to expose the next question; a wrong answer caused the drum to lock.

It appears the Pressey was influenced by two of Thorndike's "laws" of learning—the laws of effect and exercise. He experimented with rewards, one of which was to build into the machine a device which dispensed a "congratulatory" coupon when a student achieved the ability to run through the entire sequence of questions without error. At one time he experimented with a machine which dispensed candy wafers. Mastering the answers was done through sheer repetition—students kept trying over and over again until they had memorized them. We mention this only so readers will note the different theoretical bases of programming, old and new.

Widespread interest in the Pressey system did not develop. One reason often expressed is that it was not truly a scheme for programming. It presented no rationale for the sequential arrangement of subject matter, but rather only seemed to add to the traditional multiple-choice test immediate feedback, reward for success, and an opportunity for students to work at their own speed. Undoubtedly, the Depression and the war also diverted attention from Pressey's work.[35]

Skinner's Linear Programming

By 1954, B.F. Skinner was ready to present a system of programming, and designs for machines to implement it. By 1958, Skinner's system was widely known and under extensive experimentation in industry and schools. More than a dozen types of Skinner teaching machines have been developed.

Skinner's system of programming presents in order of difficulty a series of "frames"—that is to say a stimulus, usually in the form of an incomplete statement, and the response made by the student when he writes in the incomplete part of the statement. One book tells us "...a frame is ... best defined as a behavioural unit designed to add to a complex repertoire that is being learned ... each programme frame must have reason for existence inherent in the behaviour that is being built."[36] It is assumed that making a right response and immediately learning that it is right is in itself a sufficient reinforcer (reward) to cause the student to be more likely to repeat that response in the future and to move on to the next frame.

Often a student cannot respond without a cue of some sort—usually called a "prompt." There are two general types: formal and thematic. A formal prompt includes within the stimulus a part of the response. A thematic prompt includes in the stimulus general properties which suggest the correct response. The following frame contains no prompt:

A warm-blooded animal which suckles its young is called a/an ________________

The following frame contains two formal prompts, one the use of the article "a" which suggests that the correct word begins with a consonant and the other a broken line which shows how many letters the word contains:

A warm blooded animal which suckles its young is called a ____________________

The following frame contains a thematic prompt:

> A warm blooded animal which suckles its young with milk-producing mammary glands is called a/an
>
> _______________ .

In the opinion of many programmers, formal prompts are most useful when one's aim is rote learning, but properly constructed thematic prompts lead to understanding-level learning. Whether the latter is a defensible contention hinges upon factors which we discuss at the end of the chapter.

Skinnerians strongly prefer *constructed* responses to those requiring multiple-choice or true-false answer formats. That is, a student should not identify a right response from a choice presented, but should originate his response. This is in harmony with Skinner's theory of operant conditioning.

As in all programming, linear programming permits students to move at their own rate of speed. Skinner and most of his adherents prefer the use of machines to programmed textbooks. In fact, one of Skinner's more extreme followers, Edward Green, seems to decry the use of books in most or all situations. He says, after commenting that only a machine can *force* overt responses from students, that "Books present material in organized, logical sequences and students do sometimes make overt responses to them. The customary overt response to a book is to sit down, open it, orient the eyes toward the page, and turn the pages. Covertly we read. *There is no direct indication that reading occurs during the time of its occurrence."*[37] After pointing out the dangers of all other forms of teaching, including the use of all traditional teaching aids, he concludes that the machine "...represents the first practical application of laboratory techniques to education." The machine is the only way by which we can bring the behaviours we wish to establish "under the control of particular features of the environment." Since "This is the task of teaching, whether it be directed to the rat, to the high school sophomore, or to the graduate student in philosophy," we presume that the teaching of all types of organisms except by machine is inappropriate.[38]

Linear programmes present new learnings in very small, relatively easy increments. Thus, the jump from one response to the next is sufficiently easy that the error rate is very low. One fairly common idea among linear programmers is that the error rate should not be permitted to exceed 5 per cent. The object of this is to reduce the risk that wrong responses are implanted. The error rate can be controlled without difficulty by providing prompts in sufficient number and degree of helpfulness.

In linear programming it is assumed that students will move by the most direct path possible to mastery of the repertoire of responses which constitutes the subject matter. As we have indicated, all responses are overt—they involve observable and physically measurable action. Unless responses are of this character, learning cannot be said to have occurred. The final repertoire may be very complex, with a great deal of relating of responses in a manner which programmers often refer to as forming concepts, generalizations, or understandings.

Branched or Intrinsic Programming

Approaches to branched programming are associated with such names as Norman Crowder and O. K. Moore—the first famous for his "scrambled textbooks" and the latter for his "talking typewriters." Crowder generally is considered a cognitive rather than a neobehaviourist psychologist. His philosophical and psychological premises seem very different from those of the Skinnerians. Persons of this school of thought are seeking a teaching aid which is as much like an individual live tutor as possible.

Crowder explains the rationale of nonlinear or branched (also called intrinsic programming as follows:

> ....in an automatic tutoring device the programme of instructional material is completely flexible. Each piece of material that the student sees is determined directly by that individual student's immediately precedent behaviour in choosing an answer to a multiple-choice question. Since the student's behaviour in choosing an answer to the multiple-choice question is determined, presumably, by his state of knowledge at the time he makes his choice, the automatic tutoring device adapts the programme of material directly to the present state of knowledge of the individual student.....Evidently any teaching machine which employs a variable programme must incorporate some means of varying the programme on the basis of the student's responses.[19]

The general idea of automatic tutoring, then, is that the teaching device "talks back" to the student and what it says is relevant to the student's attempted answer. Mistake-making is not discouraged—in fact, it even may be encouraged. When a student errs, the teaching device-explains to him why, sometimes quite lengthily, and ask him to try again. When the student answers correctly, he is told why his answer was correct, usually provided with further illustrations of correct solving of similar type problems, and even may be asked to apply his solution in novel situations. Thus, there is no step-by-step progression. Nor does a student necessarily proceed by short, easy steps. Intrinsic programming can urge him to make daring leaps of the imagination, to play hunches—or anything it "chooses" to do. If a student appears especially weak in one area of knowledge, the automatic tutor may stop at that point and take him on a lengthy voyage of exploration in that area. Then, when the tutor is "satisfied" that the student has achieved adequate mastery, it returns him to the main subject.

Obviously, it takes imagination and an immense amount of work to programme a course in this latter manner. In the case of such complicated machines as those formed by combining special typewriters, computers and playback tape recorders, a teacher can programme his own course, taking into consideration the characteristics of his own students. He might even go so far as to make separate tapes for certain individual students. If the programmer knows what teaching for understanding involves and if we are willing to settle for understanding-level teaching, then it appears that, should economy force us to move to more use of programming and automatic teaching devices, we do have a way through intrinsic programming which in some situations might even be more effective than a live teacher. The machine will not supplant teachers, but it may become a very useful aid where classes and workloads are so heavy that even a teacher who knows how to teach for understanding cannot do so effectively.

After succinctly reviewing Skinner's linear programming and its aims (organisms emitting correct responses) Crowder argues that in contrast, his approach is based essentially upon two-way *communication.* Also, the form of communication is left open—the programmer may keep it dully routine, or, if he is capable, he may make it wildly imaginative.

Crowder has devised a format for both a book and a machine which he feels will accomplish what he has in mind. The book begins each new item to be learned with a multiple-choice question, often preceded by considerable explanation. Whichever choice the student selects requests him to turn to a specific page in the book. He is then told whether he was right and why or why not. If wrong, he is asked to return to the page from which he departed and try again. If wrong a second time, he is directed to a page or pages where appear a more comprehensive explanation of the reasons for his error. If right, he is directed to the page which presents the next learning task. Since such a book appears *on the surface* to be disorganized, it has acquired the label mentioned earlier—"scrambled." Crowder's machine (named the Auto Tutor) projects slides similar to the pages of a microfilmed book onto a screen. The slides are numbered and can be projected rapidly by pressing a button with a number corresponding to the desired slide. The machine also contains a device for recording student errors and rates of progress. The machine basically is an automated version of the scrambled textbook. With it a student saves considerable time which would otherwise be wasted in page flipping.[40]

How May We Evaluate Programming and Teaching Machines?

Intrinsic programming, at least in the forms in which we so far have encountered it, can teach for understanding but probably not for reflection. Even with intrinsic programming, the conclusions are decided upon in advance. Students have no opportunity to attempt to refute the arguments of a live teacher or to arrive at an answer which is correct but was not anticipated by the teacher or programmer. Crowder's concept of inquiry does not entail the interplay of teacher and student intellect. Nor does it involve creative, innovative thought and its possible consequences—one of which is the teacher's recognition that he may be wrong.

A common criticism of linear programming is that its advocates fail to make clear what they mean by the so-called "higher thought processes." Their determination to remain "objective" in a physicalistic sense denies them adequate concepts and generalizations to describe what happens when a person thinks (in fact, the word think is very bothersome to them).

Taber, Glaser, and Schaefer concede that it has been widely charged that the only outcome of linear programming is rote learning. They then defend such programming against the charge by saying, "The answer to this question is related to the important fact that the educational technology underlying programmed instruction equates with [overt] behaviour such terms as concept formation, understanding and reasoning."[41] Finally, drawing heavily upon Skinner, they make a valiant attempt to carry their defense even farther. Accordingly, they state, "Programmed instructional sequences can provide a series of well-organized examples leading the student to develop abstractions and complicated concepts," and, quoting Skinner, "An important goal is to 'enrich the student's understanding' by inducing him to permute and recombine the elements of his repertoire." Taber, Glaser, and Schaefer go on to say. "The objective is that the student acquire not a uniform and explicit set of responses about a particular concept, but rather a repertoire which is applicable in a variety of situations."[42]

Consequently, the chief question for students to answer is whether learning on the sophisticated level of generalized insight, or to use Bruner's term, coding and structuring, is achievable through a process of conditioning. Dedicated programmers insist that it is, but S-R associationists define such terms as concept, generalization, and understanding quite differently from the way in which cognitive-field psychologists do. Hence, their case hinges on whether one is willing to accept their definitions. And at the base of the issue are two very different views of the nature of man and his world as we have noted frequently throughout the book.

In conclusion, it would appear that whether Skinnerian linear programming can teach for understanding is in considerable doubt. Crowder appears to summarize his feeling on this matter when he says. "The point is that it has seemed to me preferable to have all of these communication techniques available, and to employ a check on the success of the communication at each step, rather than attempting to reduce the communication process to specific conditioning model *which does not seem well adapted to the teaching of complex meaningful material.*"[43]

REFERENCES

1. Henry C. Morrison, *Basic Principles in Education,* Houghton Mifflin, 1934, Chapter 4.
2. *Ibid.,* p. 39.
3. *Ibid.,* p. 38.
4. Henry C. Morrison, *The Practice of Teaching in the Secondary School,* University of Chicago Press, 1931, pp. 21-22.
5. Morrison, *Basic Principles,* p. 338.
6. *Ibid.,* p. 340.
7. *The Practice of Teaching in the Secondary School,* p. 101. (Italics ours.)
8. Jerome S. Bruner, *A Study of Thinking,* Science Editions, 1962, pp. 245-46.
9. *Ibid.,* p. viii.
10. *Ibid.,* p. 6
11. See Jerome S. Bruner, "Going Beyond the Information Given," *Contemporary Approaches to Cognition,* Harvard University Press, 1957.
12. *Ibid.,* p. 46.
13. *Ibid.,* p. 50.
14. *Ibid.,* p. 46.
15. *Ibid.,* p. 48. (Italics ours.)
16. *Ibid.,* p. 52. (Italics ours.)
17. Jerome S. Bruner, *The Process of Education,* Harvard University Press, 1962, p. 6.
18. *Ibid.,* p. 7.
19. *Ibid.,* pp. 6-7.
20. *Ibid.,* p. 8.
21. Bruner, A *Study of Thinking, op. cit.,* p. 14.
22. *Ibid.,* p. 14.
23. *Ibid.,* pp. 14-15.
24. *Ibid.,* p. 16.
25. *Ibid.,* p. 17.
26. Bruner, *The Process of Education, op. cit.,* p. 72.
27. Richard H. Brown, "History and the New Social Studies," *Saturday Review,* October 15, 1966, pp. 80-81, 92.
28. Bruner, *The Process of Education,* p. 88.
29. Brown, *op. cit.,* pp. 80-81.
30. Bruner, *Contemporary Approaches to Cognition,* p. 61.
31. Bruner, *The Process of Education,* Chapter 5.

32. Boyd H. Bode, *How We Learn*, Heath, 1940, p. 156.
33. See Eugene Smith and Ralph Tyler, *Appraising and Recording Student Progress*, Harper & Row, 1942.
34. *Ibid.*, p. 12.
35. Most of the above was drawn from John Leo Hughes, *Programmed Instruction for Schools and Industry.* Science Research Associates, 1962, pp. 10-20; also Jerome P. Lysaught and Clarence M. Williams, *A Guide to Programmed Instruction*, Wiley, 1963. Lumsdaine's and Glaser's comprehensive source book (see chapter-end bibliography) devotes an entire section to Pressey and includes his own key articles.
36. Julian Taber, Robert Glaser, and Halmutn Schaefer, *Learning and Programmed Instruction*, Addison-Wesley, 1965.
37. Edward J. Green, *The Learning Process and Programmed Instruction*, Holt., 1962, p. 121. (Italics ours.)
38. *Ibid.*, p. 122.
39. Norman A. Crowder, "Automatic Tutoring by Means of Intrinsic Programming," in Eugene Galanter, ed., *Automatic Teaching: The State of the Art.*, Wiley, 1959, pp. 109-10.
40. For a good description of the Auto Tutor, see John Leo Hughes, *Programmed Instruction for Schools and Industry*, Science Research Associates, 1962, p. 27.
41. Taber, Glaser, and Schaefer, *op. cit.*, p. 12.
42. *Ibid.*, p. 13.
43. *Ibid.*, p. 115 (Italics ours).

9
Teaching Reflectively

Since reflective teaching is problem-centred teaching, that which distinguishes reflective from nonreflective teaching and learning is the presence of genuine problems which students feel a need to solve. At the outset of study, a real question develops for which students have no answer, or at least no adequate one. And through the study the students and teacher, working cooperatively, develop a new or more adequate solution.

When reflective teaching is successful, students emerge with an enlarged store of tested insights of a generalized character and an enhanced ability to develop and solve problems on their own. The latter product is as important as the former. If only the first were accomplished, no claims could be made for reflection-level which could not also be made for understanding-level teaching. However, within genuine problem-centred teaching, students learn the very nature and techniques of problem-solving processes. And, if well taught, problem-solving approaches and procedures carry over to be applied to a wide range of problems both in and outside school.

An understanding of how to solve problems according to principles of scientific reflection is perhaps the most useful intellectual tool a person can possess. If the central goal of education is to foster-intelligence, reflective teaching should be the basic approach used by teachers everywhere. Let us visit a college class in introductory psychology being taught *reflectively* and see whether we can discern what is unique to reflection-teaching procedures.

The problem of immediate concern to the class is, "What is

the nature of *mind*?" Most of the students previously have adhered to a dualistic view of mind and body; they have held the idea that man is composed of two distinctly different kinds of substances—mental and physical. As mutual inquiry proceeds, the following discussion between the teacher and various class members ensues. When a student speaks, he probably is verbalizing the thoughts of most of his classmates. The teacher's goal is to help the students sharpen their insights in regard to the meaning of *mind.* The teacher speaks first.

"Mr. J., do you have a mind?"

"Why yes, I think so."

'Then, possibly, you can tell us what is mind?"

"It is the thing with which we think."

"You have said that mind is a thing. But a chair and a table are things. You were not referring to this type of thing?"

"No! I really meant that we think with the mind."

"What about the use of gray matter? Don't we think with our brains?"

"Well, yes."

"Then, If we think with our minds and we also think with our brains, they must be the same thing,"

"No, they are not the same."

"In that case we must arrive at the conclusion that the mind is not a thing and we do not think with the mind?"

The teacher continues. 'Are we able to store ideas and knowledge in the mind or are they stored in the brain? We are able to use our memory and imagination. Aren't these two different phases of thinking?"

"Yes."

'We have just said that we think with our brain. Thus, our ideas seem to be stored in the brain and not in the mind. Besides, there are ideas and knowledge in your textbook. But certainly your textbook does not function in any way like a mind. Is the mind separate from the body?"

"Yes, it seems to be."

"What makes you think so?"

"Well, we always think of mind as one thing and body as another."

"But we agreed that mind is not a thing."

"It just-makes common sense."

"Is common sense a valid method by which to judge truth?"

"No!"

"You know that it was once common sense to believe that the earth is flat and that it is the centre of the universe. You said that the mind is separate from the body or that it seems that way. Have you ever said to yourself that you are going to raise your arm and your arm rises?"

"Yes."

"And you have seen the effect of physical illness upon mental processes. Then, how can the mind and body be considered as separate? Obviously, there must be some connection if we continue to hold this theory."

"Has anyone ever seen electricity?"

"No."

"Will electricity flow through a copper wire?"

"Yes."

"And you know other facts about electricity and what it will do. This description of what electricity can accomplish makes it possible to describe electricity. Let us see if we can apply this same technique to our problem of mind."

"You have said that you have a mind. What did you mean when you said that you have a mind? Did you mean that you act as if you have a mind?"

"Why, yes."

"How would you describe that action?"

"I act normally."

"In other words, the difference between the way you behave and the way someone behaves who we say has lost his mind is that you act in a sensible way. And how do you act if you are sensible?"

"I am reasonable."

"You say you act reasonably. But this does not completely

describe your action. Therefore, let us look at your behaviour from another angle. Imagine that you are looking at a tree. How do you know that the tree is a tree."

"It looks like a tree and everyone agrees that it is a tree."

"Are you suggesting that such a simple object as the tree has a number of specific meanings?"

"Yes."

"For instance, you will know that a tree isn't metal, that it grows, that it has leaves in summer, and much other material of factual nature. In addition, you won't mistake a tree for anything else. Now, what does this tell you about the way you should behave with reference to a tree? What would you do with a tree?"

"I might cut it down for lumber."

"And you might use it for shade. But in any case, you will not try to eat a tree and you will avoid it if it stands in your path? If you understand the meanings which ordinarily are attached to the word tree and you act accordingly, it might be said that you are behaving intelligently. Couldn't this understanding of meaning be the function which we think of as mind?"

"Thus, we have arrived at our definition that mind is a function. We take it to be the function which makes it possible for us to anticipate future consequences of present or proposed lines of action. What is meant by predicting future consequences? Don't we mean that we try to comprehend meaning and use foresight? Then, if we act on the basis of our predictions can we be said to act intelligently?"[1]

Because of space limitation the discussion between students and teacher is to some degree in outline form. In actual practice there would be more digressions, and many statements would be made which were not pertinent to the problem at hand. The latter part of the discussion particularly would be more involved and much longer than is reported.

Now, just what is there about this teacher-student reflective classroom procedure which makes it different from either memory- or understanding-level teaching? *Perhaps it could be summarized by describing the classroom atmosphere as one of teacher-student mutual inquiry within which genuine problems are developed and solved.*

Problem-centred teaching then, involves problem raising and

problem solving. In problem-centred or reflective classes, instruction begins with introduction of an "I don't know" or problematic situation—one in which students are faced with a question they cannot answer. The problem should be so compelling that students really want to study it, but not so overwhelming that they are prone to give up. Accordingly, it should generate an urge to analyze the possible obstacles and dilemmas in the situation, to understand them, and to devise means for resolving the difficulties. After aiding students in raising a problem, the teacher then helps them investigate it until an answer is found. Problem solving consists of the steps of formulating hypotheses and testing them-with all available pertinent evidence. Facts are gathered in profusion, but teachers make no attempt to encourage fact learning or fact recall *as such.* Problems which make for ideal classroom study involve situations which are difficult enough to be challenging, yet simple enough that most students in a class will be able to cast and test hypotheses leading to a solution.

WHEN IS A PROBLEM A PROBLEM?

Too many teachers who have attempted a problems approach to teaching have not adequately understood the psychology of learning as it relates to problem-centred study. Older psychologies— mental discipline, apperception, S-R associationism—had little to say about problem-centred study. Nor have neobehaviourists, with their more sophisticated S-R associationisms, contributed much understanding of reflective teaching. Prior to the twentieth century, Herbart probably came closer than any other psychologist or educator to formulating a problem-centred approach to teaching, but even Herbartian teaching was not problem-centred or reflective in any true sense.

Often "problem-centred teaching" has failed because what teachers have chosen as "problems" have not actually been problems in a psychological sense. Contributions of Gestalt and field psychologists enable us to understand better what happens to a person psychologically when he has a problem. A learning problem is not just an objective issue to be resolved; it must involve *psychological tension in a learner.*

If a learning problem can be defined successfully in psychological terms, this should help resolve a common dilemma which arises in connection with a problems approach to teaching. The dilemma is this: students have a great variety of real problems, but often the "problems" which a teacher thinks students should study arouse no tension in his students; and if students do feel personally some of the problems posed by a teacher, they feel some much less intensely than others. Consequently, the motivation which should accompany problem study often does develop; students remain cold and uninterested and their work proves to be lackadaisical. An analysis of pertinent psychological factors should help readers understand what lies behind this dilemma.

Some problems may be designated as *personal* in that students are personally involved and so experience tension, which is the essence of a true learning problem. While they are experienced, personal problems hold a dominant place in the life spaces of students. Problems of another category may be identified as *social or societal* ; they represent social needs which some adults believe exist in a community, region, or nation. They constitute part of the social matrix and, as such, are atleast in the foreign hulls of the life space of students. But often they constitute no part of their actual life spaces.

These problems are felt personally by someone or they never would have been identified as problems in the first place; but commonly they are received only by some adults, and sometimes only by experts in fields of knowledge relevant to specific questions. To students, societal problems often seem quite remote; the students' function of living does not bring them into play. Posed by a teacher, such problems, unless students feel themselves personally involved, are not real problems at all.

Students Not Motivated by "Other Persons' " Problems

Reactions of students to the two types of problems—personal and societal—are likely to be quite different. A student can see the point of studying problems in which he is personally involved. The necessary emotional steam already exists; often all a teacher needs to do is direct study so that it will be as mature as possible. But when students are asked to study problems which they do not accept as their own, they are likely to remain unresponsive. Furthermore, since no personally felt goals are involved, an inwardly motivated search for solutions is unlikely. Because of this detachment, relevant facts are seen not as data contributing toward a solution but only as lessons to be learned. Consequently, the quality of learning which results when students study someone else's problems is likely to be little different from that produced by conventional textbook-recitation teaching.

Textbook writers often include "problems" at the ends of chapters. Several years ago one of the authors paraphrased the following list of such "problems" from a social studies textbook.

> To learn about the public utility companies of your community.
>
> To see how many articles devoted to farming and rural life appear in the local newspaper.
>
> To find out how many ways there are to send money from one city to another.
>
> To find out what instructions are given to Boy Scouts for the protection of forests.
>
> To learn more facts about life insurance.
>
> To determine the advantages and disadvantages of good roads.[2]

These are tasks, not problems. Thus, there is little reason to suppose that, without skilful preliminary discussion led by a teacher, any of these "problems" as stated will induce any significant kind of psychological tensions in students. All too often textbook writers, authors of syllabi and courses of study, and classroom teachers themselves label as problems exercises which, no matter what their potential in the teaching-learning process, do not function *per se* as true psychological problems for students.

Since study of other people's problems results in learning which qualitatively is little different from traditional fact memorization, some writers have suggested that teachers exclude from study any problem in which students do not already feel involved, and confine instruction to problems which students, because of their life situations, spontaneously feel. Thus, they argue that the role of a teacher is to help students define carefully problems which, for them, already exist, and then to help them conduct whatever research and discussion seem to be appropriate in solving these problems. Although it should not be denied that in any school there is an important place for this kind of problem study, exclusive emphasis on it is highly reminiscent of the

Rousselllian natural unfoldment outlook. There is a strong flavour of "letting students do as they please." Of course, in the hands of a capable teacher, considerable freedom may be permitted students in *selection* of their problems and at the same time considerable rigor demanded in their study.

Certain persons prominent in the Progressive Education movement of the 1920 and 1930s endorsed a highly permissive approach to teaching. It was at this time that the concept of the "child-centred school" developed. One of the authors once visited a class in a Progressive school in which the teacher asked the class, quite literally, "Well, boys and girls, what do you want to study next?" After a period marked by considerable confusion, the students agreed that they wanted to study American Indians—a subject to which they had devoted units on numerous past occasions.

Need for Classroom Study of Serious Societal Problems

Exclusion of the whole range of adult-felt concerns from classroom study, when it occurs, troubles most persons. One might defend confinement of problem-centred study to problems which students already feel on the ground that it teaches them a method of problem solving which will be useful all through life. However, there are a number of significant, persistent societal problems which, for the good of the community, state, and nation, students should come to understand and appreciate. Study of those problems, about which normally only specialists or other adults are concerned, may be of great importance in preparing students for intelligent citizenship. But how can we motivate students to study, in a serious and sustained way, problems which do not seem real to them? *In this question is the crux ofproblem-centred teaching.* Failure to give serious consideration to it is the reason why a problems approach so often bogs down, why students are uninterested, and why, after having tried "Problem-centred teaching" teachers frequently return to "teaching the facts straight."

In recent years, teachers have tried to devise ways of interesting students in problems which intrinsically are not challenging to them. "Solutions" to the engima in which teachers find themselves have included suggestions that they explain to students just how the problems are bound to affect them eventually, that students be confronted face to face with the problems (as when we take a class to visit a slum), and that teachers use more eye-catching teaching materials (such as pictures).

But, as every practicing teacher knows, these "solutions" often fail to produce real intellectual involvement. Students still do not feel the problems as their own. Of course, some students always will do whatever work a teacher assigns, and seemingly do it with enthusiasm. But what seems to be intellectual involvement and a desire to study a genuine problem often is a desire to achieve other goals such as high marks, praise, and social status.

At this point, we should review the distinction between what psychologists often call *extrinsic and intrinsic motivation.*

Instead of striking out blindly and trying everything he can think of, willy-nilly, to motivate students to study seriously what does not seem to them any of their own concern, a teacher could try a drastically different approach; he could view his teaching problems in the light of a clear and adequate understanding of the learning process. Basic to such understanding would be knowledge of what it means for a person to experience a problem as a felt tension, and formulation, based on this knowledge, of an approach to teaching which holds promise in many cases of effectively translating the "problems of others" into thee problems of students.

How is a problem a Felt Tension?

To have a problem, a person must first have a goal or goals which he accepts as his own. A problem arises when he finds it impossible to proceed quickly and directly to the goal. When he cannot achieve his goal readily, it is either because he sees no open path to it or because he sees two or more competing paths, or two or more competing goals, and cannot decide which to pursue. These are the familiar "no-path" or "forked-path" situations described by John Dewey, and diagrammed in Figure 9.1

Problematic Situations Defined in Lewinian or Cognitive-field Terms

Lewinian or cognitive-field concepts and terminology also may be used to express the basic elements of a problematic situation. Either there is a goal region in a person's life space which has a positive valence and a barrier between his person and the region of positive valence, or there are several conflicting goal regions toward which or away from which a person might want to make psychological movement. These two types of situations are barrier or no-path situations and conflicting path situations and shown in Figure 9.2.

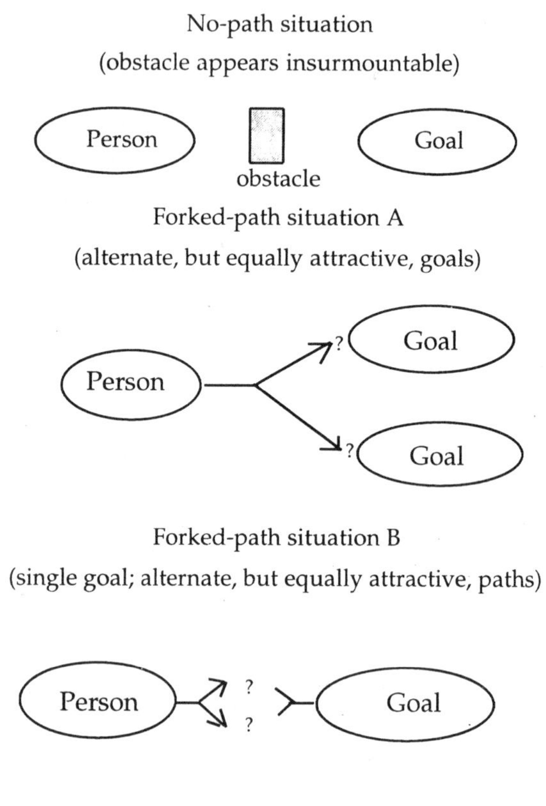

Fig. 9.1 Dewey's problematic situations

Conflicting-path situations lend themselves best to reflective or problem-centred teaching. In a Type I situation, a person has two conflicting goals or two opposite regions of his life space both with positive valences. (Positive goal regions being opposite means that both cannot be achieved at the same time.) In the Type I illustration, vector *vb* represents a psychological force equal to the valence of region *b*, and vector *va* represents a force equal to the valence of region *a*. In a Type II situation, the person is faced with two opposite significant regions of his life space, each having a negative valence; he wants to escape both, and they are of such nature that this is impossible. In a Type III situation, a region of positive valence and a region of negative valence are in the same psychological direction from the person; they are functionally similar or perhaps identical. Movement toward or away from regions is determined by the relative strength of the pertinent forces at the time of movement.

Barrier or no-path situation

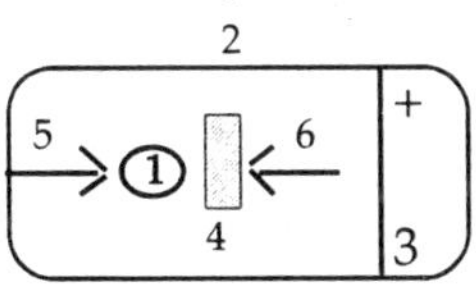

1. Person
2. Boundary of psychological environment
3. Goal; region of positive valence
4. Barrier
5. Vector of driving force toward goal
6. Vector of restraining force of barrier

Conflicting-path situations

Type I Type II Type III

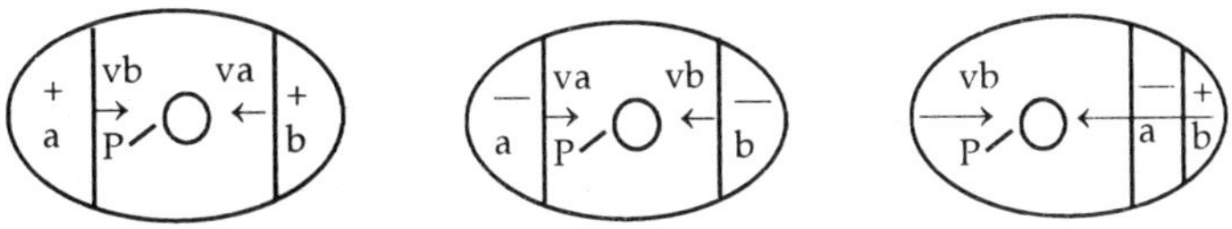

Fig. 9.2 Field-conflict situations

Superficially, Type I and Type II situations appear much alike; however, they are crucially different. A person in a Type II situation is like a ball being pushed from opposite directions by two sticks; once it gives a little, it flies off to the side out of the picture. A person in such a situation is trying to escape two opposite negative driving forces and is likely to become completely frustrated and, like the ball, leave the field—psychologically flee from the scene or become irrationally aggressive; this means that he suddenly moves from a relatively concrete level of his life space to an extremely imaginative level. In contrast, a person in a Type I situation, like a ball being pulled in opposite directions, usually will stay in the field, *i.e.*, remain engaged with the problem and try to resolve his conflict at the level of reality at which he meets it. He is influenced by two goals, both with positive valences. The goal toward which he moves is the one with the higher value or valence. (Should his two opposing goals be exactly equal, would he be like the donkey who starved to death while standing exactly halfway between two stacks of hay?)

Since type II situations (two opposite negative goals) give rise to frustrations, they should be avoided in teaching procedures. Contrastedly, since type I situations (two opposite positive goals) involve and perplex but do not frustrate students, they should be sought.

A type III conflict situation develops when a person contemplates violating one of the basic mores of his society, especially if it is for the first time. He wants to perform the tabooed act and simultaneously he wants not to do it; thus it has both positive and negative valence. The person involved might perceive the taboo not as a negative goal region but as a barrier between him and the positive goal region. In this event, the barrier would have a negative valence which would need to be counteracted by the stronger positive valence of the act, if it is to be performed.

What Level of Tension is Best?

A characteristic of the kind of goal-centred situation which we have described is the presence of a certain amount of felt tension or discomfort. A person confronted with a no-path or forked-path situation feels to some degree doubtful, puzzled, bewildered, uncertain. How strongly he feels this way depends upon at least three factors: (1) desirability of the goal or goals; (2) apparent difficulty of the obstacle; and (3) his own personality make-up. Whether a person finds himself between opposite positive goals which he is trying to achieve or opposite negative aversions which he is trying to escape depends largely upon *how he construes himself and his psychological environment.*

In a sense a teacher must be a tightrope walker. He will get best results if he keeps his students in a state of full enthusiasm. When he has involved them to the point that, during discussions, they sit on the edges of their seats, arms waving and eyes glistening and all wanting to talk at once, he has a potentially fine teaching situation. However, there is a rather fine line between this type of situation and situations in which students either become so excited that their emotions are chaotic, feel despair because the problem posed is too difficult, or are bored because it is too easy.

Necessity for maintaining control of students cannot be over-emphasized. One of the difficulties which commonly arises when a teacher attempts reflective teaching is loss of control. When youngsters are either bored or highly excited, they are difficult to manage. A teacher following the reflective approach usually learns from experience when it is time to sidetrack a discussion that is producing too much heat.

Whenever two more competing alternatives are at stake, there is an *issue.* And since, by definition, all issues are "controversial," *controversy is a fundamental aspect of any truly problem-centred teaching.* Controversy invariably leads to conflict, of which we may distinguish two levels. *Inter-personal* conflict arises when individuals or groups hold beliefs sharply opposed to those of other individuals or groups. We often refer to conflicts on this level as "controversial issues." Persons on each side of an interpersonal conflict, or dispute, may be quite consistent in their own outlooks, even though in sharp disagreement with the opposing position.

Interpersonal conflict tends to become internalized within the personalities of individuals so that they are at war with themselves. Caught in a culture in which interpersonal conflict is always present, they often accept as true and good *both* sides of many issues, thus incorporating cultural conflicts into their own personalities. When they become aware of their incompatibilities of outlook, the resulting internal struggle may be referred to as *intrapersonal* conflict. Although the content of an intrapersonal conflict may be no different from that of an interpersonal conflict, it may exact a greater toll because it can lead to disintegration of personality.

Naturally, we do not desire conflict, on the extreme levels just mentioned, to exist in learning situations which are wholesome. But for a reflective learning situation to exist at all, issues must come to be felt by students so that they find themselves to some degree in *controversy with themselves.* Each individual must be attracted to some extent by two or more competing hypotheses and feel temporarily unable to make a choice between them; otherwise, no problem exists for him.

We now turn to description of the basic procedure for reflective teaching, which includes both problem-raising and problem-solving aspects. *Problem raising* is a process of discovering and identifying inadequacies and disharmonies of outlook or insights; *problem solving,* in turn, is a process of reconstructing outlooks or insights to make them more adequate and harmonious.

HOW DOES PROBLEM RAISING PROCEED?

For a student, a problem arises whenever he can be induced to feel dissatisfied (that is, in doubt) with some one or more of his present attitudes, values, beliefs, or items of knowledge. Introduction of dissatisfaction produces a forked-path or a no-path situation. Is the questioned attitude, value, belief, or knowledge valid, or is it not? Is some alternative more promising than others? In adherence to a certain pattern of thought, is there a basic contradiction which stands in the way? In this sort of situation, it is the element of uncertainty that provides the problematic aspect. The goal of learning now becomes the desire to remove doubt, to restore a degree of certitude.

Very often, doubt can be induced by leading a student to see that he simultaneously holds contradictory attitudes, beliefs, or items of knowledge or that his behaviour does not square with what he says are his convictions. By being made aware of his inconsistency, he is made doubtful. There appears to be something in the make-up of most persons in our culture—not yet well understood—which, once inconsistency is clearly recognized, produces a desire for consistency, a desire for a sense of personal harmony, for integration of self. When, over long periods of time, people display gross inconsistencies without appearing to feel unhappy, it is usually because they simply do not see themselves as being inconsistent.

The foregoing paragraph requires qualification. If we are to judge from experience common to us all, a frequent—in fact, the usual—response to awareness of inconsistency is irritation or anger. This is particularly likely if an emotionally charged issue is involved. However, a person's reaction when he is confronted with his own inconsistencies depends largely on how the confrontation occurs. There are appropriate techniques for helping people see their inconsistencies; an elaboration of them is a major theme of the next section.

How May Contradictions and Loopholes in Students' Thinking Be Exposed?

Before a teacher can do much about helping students see their inconsistencies, he needs a good idea of what to expect—what kinds of contradictions his students are likely to hold. This knowledge will enable a reasonably skilful teacher to pursue a line of discourse and questioning which exposes a student's inconsistencies to himself. Some techniques for raising problems in the thinking of students are use of a *subject matter switch,* introduction of *disturbing data,* and permitting students to *make mistakes.*

A subject-matter switch. A subject-matter switch is performed when we generalize, or reduce to principle, a particular idea, then demonstrate how a further thought is incompatible with the principle and, consequently, with the first idea. For example, a student expresses the opinion that "Government price supports for cotton are ridiculous." The teacher then seeks agreement with the principle that, "The federal government should not interfere with the economy." If the student agrees, the teacher then places the principle in a different context, that is, gives it different subject matter, with a question like, "Do you favour a protective tariff on cotton?" The student, who also adheres firmly to the principle "A high protective tariff brings prosperity to a nation," is thus placed in a position which forces some kind of revision (if he attempts to extricate himself) of one or both of the contradictory opinions.

The foregoing example is hypothetical and, of course, very much simplified. To make the contradiction explicit to most students in a class, much more discussion would be necessary. Furthermore, this example, and any other which we might substitute, can be misleading. A teacher may ask questions which appear to reveal a contradiction that actually does not exist. If a student is permitted to qualify his opinions by introducing exceptions, he may extricate himself readily without having to do any serious thinking. On the other hand, the general technique of the subject matter switch is useful, and every teacher should experiment with it. Often, when it does not provoke the particular student who is trapped by it to constructive thought, it will motivate other students in the class.

In the preceding sentence we use the word *trapped* advisedly. Yet some explanation is needed. A teacher who wishes to teach reflectively probably is justified in using any device which works to get reflection going. Some devices may seem so teacher-centred—that is, the teacher is so fully in charge—that the whole procedure appears to be rigged in favour of the teacher's biases. But remember that this is only the beginning. When it comes time to cast and scrutinize hypotheses and draw conclusions there can be no rigging. Although the teacher performs key functions throughout the process, the relationship between students and teacher is interactive. Students remain free to reach whatever conclusions they choose, when the teacher sees to it that they give reasoned consideration to alternatives and the data which support them.

Introduction of disturbing data. Another means of inducing students to feel problems is to introduce them to data from outside their life spaces which have the effect of making them doubt some attitude, value, belief, or supposed item of knowledge. In other words, the teacher asks students to read a book, to watch a television programme or motion picture, to go on a field trip, or to engage in some other activity which confronts them with facts contrary to what they have taken for granted. Of course, this approach, like any other, may not work; students may refuse to admit the new facts into their life spaces. Unless they recognize the significance of the facts and truly come to doubt, no problem is created. Use of negative evidence to shake the confidence of students in their own knowledge and beliefs is often more effective if evidence comes from some source other than the teacher; for example, other students or reading references.

Permitting students to make mistakes. Making a mistake often encourages us to re-examine something which we have regarded as provides motivation and direction for the problem-solving aspect of reflective inquiry. Once doubt has been induced, reflective teaching and learning enters its second important step. Students are encouraged to formulate as many hypotheses—considered guesses or hunches—as possible which might resolve the discrepancies in thought that have been exposed. Or, in many instances, students formulate questions, that is, "negative" hypotheses, the answering of which will solve the problem. In the third aspect of reflective teaching, *students are encouraged to examine the hypotheses, or answer the questions, in the light of all obtainable, pertinent evidence.* Formulation and testing of hypotheses should be conducted in an atmosphere which, as far as possible, resembles that of a scientific laboratory; the same open-minded and objective attitudes which characterize any scientific investigation should prevail.

We should note carefully that, in the process of testing hypotheses, a teacher does not play the role of a softhearted baby-sitter. At times he must be quite tough-minded in his insistence that students examine and think about all pertinent available evidence. He also must guard against snap conclusions and any other liberties which students might want to take with the reflective method.

Ideally, problem-centred study should culminate in at least a tentative conclusion about how a problem might be alleviated or solved; however, in many instances a definite conclusion will not be achieved. A teacher should emphasize the tentativeness of conclusions. An irrevocable conclusion is like a locked door, whose key someone has thrown in the ocean. Students should be taught that the door to knowledge must always be left unlocked or even ajar. Nevertheless, at the termination of an inquiry, a conclusion should be considered a warranted assertion; it should provide greater predictive accuracy than any alternative hypotheses which have been entertained and examined.

A conclusion may involve reacceptance of the idea originally brought under question, modification of the idea, or formulation of a substitute one. The important concern is that students push their thinking further than it had gone before. Reaffirmation of an idea which a teacher has induced students to doubt is equally acceptable, provided that in the course of their study the students come to understand the idea better and to have a better grasp of pertinent evidence.

We should stress two points regarding the over-all process of reflective, problem-centred study. One relates to thoroughness and the other to orderliness.

Thoroughness and Reflective Teaching

When a teacher and a class of ninth-graders purport to "solve" some highly difficult problem during the course of a unit of study which covers a period of, say, three days, we can only feel that the procedure has been a travesty on education. It is conceivable that students might inform themselves a little better, might push their thinking forward a little more, in this length of time. But to talk about their achieving solutions so quickly is nonsense. True problem-centred teaching, like any teaching which leads to understanding, is necessarily an unhurried procedure. Consequently it is very difficulty, and usually impossible, to pursue problem-centred teaching in situations characterized by rigid scheduling of time or units to be covered.

To make problem-centred teaching a success, a teacher may need to make several false starts; when one plan for bringing students to feel a problem fails, he tries another until he hits on one that works. The period during which a given problem is studied is necessarily rather unstructured and it frequently is impossible to predict how soon a class will devise anything resembling an answer. Even though a problem has been under study a week or more and nothing educational seems to have happened, so long as the teacher feels there is still a chance that some useful insights will emerge, study should be continued.

The length of time students will struggle with a problem depends upon their age and maturity. First-graders need to come to a conclusion soon after they develop a problem, perhaps the same day. However, college seniors may accomplish their best learning when they have struggled with a problem for a semester of longer.

As a practical matter, of course, there must be limits to thoroughness. Something like a "law of diminishing returns" operates in education; in connection with each problem, a time is reached when further pursuit of the problem obviously will not be worth the time and effort involved. Other equally important problems may be pressing for attention.

Most textbooks and courses of study contain entirely too many topics for each to be treated in problem-centred fashion. Thus, teachers who wish to experiment with problem-centred teaching must free themselves somewhat from the dictates of standard printed guides (textbooks, courses of study, state curriculum frameworks). This does not necessarily mean ignoring such guides, which seldom is possible anyway, but rather using them judiciously with clear recognition that they need not be followed literally.

Orderliness and Reflective Teaching

Problem-centred study is rarely, if ever, as orderly as written descriptions of it imply. To realize this, one needs only to listen carefully to a group discussion of some matter about which most members of the group have a sizable personal concern. Hypotheses are advanced, evidence is stated, and conclusions are suggested in what appears on the surface to be random order. Thought even for the best organized person, is seldom completely ordered in a one-two-three fashion. Although we may list a series of aspects involved in reflective thinking (corresponding to aspects of scientific procedure), they are rarely steps taken in their "logical" order. A thinker moves continuously; back and forth from problem to hypotheses to evidence to conclusions in varying order, and at any given moment an idea may strike him which sets off an entirely different train of thought (sometimes about a quite different problem).

In good group inquiry there are always two types of discussion in progress—one the public discussion which an observer can hear, the other a series of private discussions in which each interested student debates the issue with himself. Most of the questions and assertions which are uttered aloud emerge from, or are influenced by, the private, silent debates. An aim of vocal discussion is to help each individual in the classroom, including the teacher, push forward the thinking he is doing privately. Hence, during the course of a single discussion, Mary may reach a conclusion which seems satisfactory to her, John may have his faith badly shaken in conclusion he once had, and Fred may merely formulate a hypothesis. In each case, the student may have thought the problem through to a point farther advanced than any previously reached by him. Hence, in a discussion which appears chaotic to an observer, individuals may achieve a considerable amount of pointed thinking.

Althought we stress the inevitable disorderly appearance which characterizes most highly motivated discussions, we must not forget that a teacher is obligated to preside in such a way as to see that appropriate questions do get asked, that obvious hypotheses are not ignored, that pertinent evidence is not glossed over, and that conclusions are presented and debated (when conclusions seem warranted). In short, he is obligated to see that all aspects of reflective study are evidenced at some time during the public part of a discussion. Only then will individual students have available for their private reflection all that a group study situation can contribute.

Although in the forgoing paragraphs we have concentrated upon the discussion aspect of reflective teaching, we wish to emphasize that, provided the teacher promotes an atmosphere of mutual inquiry, problem-centred study in school may encompass a variety of activities. It is likely to include periods set aside for individual or group research, home study, trips and guest speakers. It may even include considerable talking, explaining, and illustrating on the part of a teacher; an informal lecture can be a highly useful tool for providing data for students' consideration and for instigating and promoting their reflection.

HOW CAN CLASSROOM ATMOSPHERE PROMOTE REFLECTIVE LEARNING?

A Teacher's success in inducing reflective learning hinges upon his ability to bring students to involve themselves in issues to the point of perplexity and yet to remain curious and open-minded in regard to their solution. The aim of this section is to consider means of keeping students so involved without frustrating them, and to explore ways in which they can be made more receptive to points of view based on empirical—scientific—evidence.

The type of atmosphere in which a person feels so secure that he dares entertain evidence contrary to his present knowledge and values seems best achieved in a small, face-to-face group in which warmth and considerable permissiveness have been deliberately cultivated. Some techniques which a teacher may use in creating such an atmosphere, and in leading a class to change its views and thereby its behaviour, are (1) encouraging group membership, (2) reducing threat and promoting open-mindedness, (3) practicing democratic group leadership, and (4) fostering group decisions.

Encouraging Group Membership

A student is more likely to drop prejudices, revise his moral values, or make almost any other type of significant ideological change if he is a member of a group of individuals *who are making the same change together.* Although significant learning may occur in discussion groups formed of strangers, learning in areas of strong prejudice (such as in the closed areas) seems more likely to occur in groups charactorized by friendships and some degree of mutual intimacy. Thus, there may be sound pedagogical advantages in helping students become well acquainted with each other, whether simply through classroom informality or by deliberately fostering out-of-school contacts.

Cliques, self-contained groupings based on religious or social-class affiliations, racial groupings, or associations based on academic achievement may develop within any school and be reflected in subgroups within a single classroom. Such groupings may entirely omit certain students, who in turn become social isolates. With development of subgroups of this sort, especially if chauvinistic attitudes are involved, a class may become badly split and team spirit difficult to achieve. Hence, if observation or use of sociometric devices suggests to a teacher that an unhealthy social situation exists in his classroom, he should take steps to alleviate it.[3]

In establishing group feeling, there are possible advantages to be gained from group study and group projects. However, when this sort of thing is attempted, it is best to divide a class into small groups and to see that the same students do not always work together. A committee system can ordinarily be made to work fairly well for gathering information. Whether it can be made to function in reflective evaluation of data and the productive solution of problems depends on the maturity of students and their familiarity with the rules of reflection. Generally, a teacher must be central to reflective deliberation if it is to be productive.

Encouragement of full and free communication among its members will heighten the cohesiveness of a group. If students understand each other, they will almost inevitably work together better as a group. A teacher should urge and help students to state opinions and propositions meaningfully. Also, he should discourage use of emotive language, particularly when students are inclined to direct personal jibes at each other. Furthermore, he should make certain that every member has a chance to be heard and is correctly interpreted.

A deep-seated desire of human beings is for security, and a common means of achieving security is through membership in a group. When a person feels that he has a place in a group, that he "fits in," that he is wanted, he feels secure. As Lewin points out, "The social climate in which a child lives is for the child as important as the air it breathes. The group to which a child belongs is the ground on which he stands. His relation to the group and his status in it are the most important factors for his feeling of security or insecurity."[4] One achieves membership in a group by conforming, at least to a degree, to the mores of the group. To be accepted in a group of thieves, one must act like a thief; to be accepted in a group of saints, one must act like a saint.

This is not to say that an individual is completely subject to group control. He may develop beliefs and values which are novel to a group and may get them accepted by others in the group. With widening acceptance, the new beliefs and values become effective in controlling group behaviour. However, there is little chance that large changes will occur in individuals outside their relationship to their primary group associations. For example, a psychotherapist is constantly aware of the fact that there is little he can do to help a patient reorganize his personality *as an individual.* Such reorganization as may occur must fit exigencies posed by a patient's associations—the various needs and pressures, often highly subtle and complex, which grow out of the fact of group membership itself. This is particularly the case where values are concerned, and even more particularly, values in "closed areas."

Reducing Threat and Promoting Open-Mindedness

When a student regards his convictions to be under fire, he feels threat to his ego. The intensity of the threat depends on its source, its power, and the valuation placed on the ideas which are in jeopardy. Unless threat can be largely eliminated, a student is not likely to entertain evidence contrary to present convictions or, when facts warrant, to change his mind. Several techniques are available for keeping a sense of threat to a minimum.

A teacher should always treat student opinions with respect. This does not necessarily mean that a teacher expresses approval; but he avoids ridicule, sarcasm, or any expressions which might be so interpreted by students. Furthermore, he does not cast aspersions on the intelligence or motives of students who render serious opinions. Opinions offered in good faith are taken for what they are —the best insights which students have been able to achieve up to then. A student needs to feel complete freedom to express his opinions without danger of censure, no matter how ill-formed or unorthodox they may be.

On occasion, as during relatively indirected discussion preceding serious study of an issue, it may be advisable for a teacher to give students plenty of opportunity to express the very views which he hopes later to bring under question. It may even help for him to express considerable sympathy with these ideas for the time being. Lewin recommended that a group leader may get farther by letting members of a group freely express the very values which he hopes to change because "a feeling of complete freedom and a heightened group identification are frequently more important at a particular stage of re-education than learning not to break specific rules."[5]

When a teacher wishes to challenge an opinion expressed by a student, he should do it in such a way that conflict is internalized. That is, the student is made to feel the conflict within his own personality. If he sees the conflict merely as a contest between him and someone else, he may not feel a problem, or at least the problem which the learning situation demands. Accordingly, when a teacher wishes to contest the opinion of a student, he may best handle it something like this: "You have an opinion, and I think I understand and appreciate your reasons. But there are contrary opinions which are widely held in this country. I wonder if there is any merit in a point of view such as .....?" Thus, the student is asked to entertain, not an opinion of the teacher or a classmate, but simply an opinion which "some persons" hold. Experiments cited by Lewin[6] suggest that, when a group is presented with a problem to discuss, beliefs and behaviours contrary to those accepted by group members are more likely seriously to be entertained and later adopted if the problem is discussed with reference to persons other than themselves, at least in early phases of discussion.

It is well to arrange the learning situation so that facts "speak for themselves." Other things being equal, facts—especially if impersonal, sharply relevant, and simple enough to be easily grasped—are more likely than expressions of opinion to break through an emotional barrier, particularly if the facts come to students in life situations. It may then only be necessary to remind a student of their relevance and their bearing on a problem. For example, a trip to a slum may speak eloquently against the notion that everyone is adequately housed, or the witnessing of a congressional investigation over television may show quite convincingly that traditional American principles of fair play are not always employed. Lewin has suggested that "An individual will believe facts he himself has discovered in the same way he believes in himself or in his group."[7]

In most instances it probably pays to minimize, or at least not encourage, emphasis on personal opinion in discussion. Issues may be handled as issues and propositions discussed on their merits. The learning enterprise should focus on raising questions about what will come of acting in accordance with a given proposition or hypothesis. An opinion may be converted to a proposition by saying, "Here is an opinion which is before the class. Let us take it as a proposition to be tested. If it is true, what consequences may we deduce from it?" If propositions are relevant to beliefs of students, then students often make their own connections. Even though beliefs are not studied directly, significant revisions may come. It is necessary, of course, that students *see* connections; if emotional blocking prevents this, steps must be taken to expand perception. Perhaps only mentioning the connections will be enough; perhaps patient effort will be needed further to reduce emotional barriers.

Practicing Democratic Group Leadership

The aim of democratic group leadership is to translate a democratic philosophy into group action. Thus, democratic group leadership combines traditional democratic philosophy with a relatively recent personal-social psychology such as cognitive-field psychology.

Democratic philosophy—We define democracy as a social arrangement in which all members of a group share equally in determining which freedoms and restraints shall apply. It is presumed that, in general, freedoms and restraints shall apply with the same force to all. But democracy must allow for the granting of special powers for special purposes (as in the case of its executive officers). If we think of democracy as a system of *equally limited* freedom, characterized by shared decisions regarding which specific rules are to prevail, then we have a simple criterion for distinguishing democracy from other social arrangements. A social system may provide *unlimited freedoms,* in which case it is called anarchy. Or it may provide *unequally limited freedoms,* in which case it is called autocracy. Or it may provide for *equally limited freedoms,* in which case it is called democracy.

The nature of a democratic group—A democratic group is self-governing. But it must provide for situations where disagreement occurs. Ideally, democratic decisions are by consensus, *i.e.*, mutually agreeable decisions reached through discussion and compromise. Then, by common consent, action is taken. However, if it is time for action and consensus is not yet possible, a democratic group votes. Each person has an equal vote, and a majority vote wins. So, votes are taken to facilitate action, not to enforce views or opinions.

Successful and permanent operation of democracy seems to require that a group maintain certain conditions which, although not a part of the central idea of democracy, contribute to its functioning. For example, if participation is to be full and free, a group must establish an accepting atmosphere—an atmosphere in which every member is considered important and has his opinions guaranteed a hearing. Participation implies reasonable freedom of communication, and freedom of speech and thought. It any single individual or minority group gains disproportionate control over agencies of communication and opinion, the society has lost equality of participation in decision making.

It also would seem that, if a democratic society is to survive over time, a majority of its members must learn to make reflective decisions where socially important questions are involved. A democratic society assumes competence on the part of its members; any different assumption would lead to distrust and rejection of the principle of equal participation. Without wise leadership no society can solve its problems and endure. However, in a democracy wise leadership is a function of a wise citizenship. If democracy is to survive, its members must take steps to insure that the principle of reflection is employed as widely as possible in making choices of group concern.

The role of democratic leadership—Behaviour of a group is influenced significantly by its leaders. Particularly if a group is immature, its over-all emotional and intellectual climate as well as its direction and extent of growth depend largely on the conduct of its leadership. However, as a group matures, it become less dependent on particular leaders, it develops capacity to produce leaders from its own ranks, and reject and select leaders according to need.

The role of democratic leadership is to *help a group realize its own potentialities for growth*. Such a statement becomes meaningful only when growth is defined in operational terms. One attempt at an operational definition specifies a number of "dimensions" of group growth, including the following.[8]

1. Progress toward closer intercommunication among members. This includes increasing understanding and acceptance by members of standards of language usage, with especial reference to problems of semantics.
2. Progress toward seeing the functioning of the group objectively. This includes both capacity of all participants to make, and agree with, interpretations about the proper functioning of the group and its individual members, and ability to accumulate, and make use of, relevant information about itself.
3. Progress toward achieving shared responsibilities. This includes personal movement toward sharing functions of leadership, as well as participation in the determination of goals and cooperation in their achievement.
4. Progress toward achieving group cohesion. Cohesion should be sufficient to make possible absorption of new ideas without group disintegration, assimilation of new participants in a way which will strengthen rather than weaken group feeling, maintenance of long-range goals when a situation so demands, and putting to constructive ends whatever internal conflict may arise.
5. Progress toward acquiring the capacity to inform itself, to think clearly, and to make creative choices when problems must be resolved. This embraces learning to make maximum use of whatever contributions members are potentially capable of supplying and uncovering and rectifying falacious conclusions.

If a group is to move in these directions, what functions does a democratic leader perform? He may execute or administer, serve as judge or arbiter, be an advocate (or shaper of opinion), or render expert advice. He also serves as discussion leader. Although a discussion leader may on occasion assume any of the above roles, his function as discussion leader is distinctively different from and more inclusive than that of any of the others; he helps the group members, including himself, achieve self-growth. Or, as one writer puts it, he tries to "release the creative talents of the members of a group, help them solve their own problems, and reach their own decisions."[9]

Fostering Group Decisions

No matter how great their internal rapport, groups do not change beliefs automatically, As we have observed, the most effectual situation for producing group change appears to be a democratically led discussion. For purposes of this analysis, probably the most important requirement of discussion (or other modes of study) designed to change basic attitudes is that it have the quality of freely permitting self-learning. (This should not be taken to mean absence of directedness.) We have already noted that students resist outside pressure to change opinions. As Lewin has indicated, the object in achieving change is not to apply pressure from outside but to remove counterforces within the individual.[10]

Although a teacher can and usually must help in eliminating these counterforces, students must perform the actual removal. If they can explore a problem independently, feeling no authoritarian pressure from above to explore it in a particular way or emerge with particular conclusions, they are much more likely than otherwise to undergo real and permanent changes in conceptual patterns. They need to be encouraged to use investigatory techniques of their won, to explore by themselves provocative readings, trips, interviews, and radio and television programmes. A teacher's role here is to suggest possible directions of exploration and to help students evaluate facts which are exposed.

For maximum change, reflective discussion of problems should culminate in group decisions. That is, in addition to discussing and studying a problem, students as a group should consider what conclusions are warranted, what the conclusions mean to them, and what if anything they intend to do about them. Students need to communicate their views to each other, so that intentions of each are known to all. If it is evident to individuals that most members of a group have revised their outlooks and expect to change their behaviour in stated ways, then members who are reluctant to change because of long-standing attachment to certain views may find change easier. This should not be interpreted to mean that a group or its leader should pressure individual members to accept conformity. We are referring to changes which individuals see the logic of making but find difficult because of opposing forces. The opposing forces are often social pressures exerted by peer culture, community mores, or parental dictates. These may be combated more successfully if a student feels that others intend to combat them with him.

IN WHAT SUBJECT FIELDS IS PROBLEM-CENTRED TEACHING APPLICABLE?

Many teachers see problem-centred teaching as a possible approach to instruction in a very limited number of courses, such as social studies, and problems as if they were all the same. We should make a clear distinction between these terms.

A project is an individualized work assignment. Although all members of a class may be given the same general kind of task, each student is free to arrange variations. Furthermore, although there may be a deadline for completion of a project, students work on an individualized time schedule. Projects involve physical activity and almost always result in some kind of physical product. Examples of projects are making a table, as in a shop class; raising a calf, as in an agriculture class; making an insect collection, as in a biology class; making a clippings scrapbook, as in a social studies class.

A unit, in its most general sense, is a collection of subject matter which is unified by a single theme. The unit concept has been applied extensively in courses of an academic or semiacademic nature, such as English and social studies. In a given course, units constitute the organizational foci. A succession of units arranged sequentially in some presumably logical fashion, gives a course its form. Obviously, unit organization is designed, among other things, to make a course independent, or relatively independent, of a textbook. Since teachers themselves usually are responsible for developing each unit and collecting teaching materials to go with it, a unit organization offers considerable flexibility. Units may be selected and designed to fit a particular situation. Educators have devised a great variety of unit plans, the nature of which depends largely on how the educator defines the learning process and what he sees as the goals of education.

Morrison's mastery units are but one conception of what unit teaching means. So far as contemporary practice is concerned, most teachers view a unit as very much like a textbook chapter except that, to a large degree, it is their own creation. They see a unit of work as simply a bloc of subject matter dealing with a common subject. For example, a geography course may contain a unit on France. This simply includes all the factual data on France which the course provides, pulled together in a bundle so that they can be studied together.

Project and unit teaching is not necessarily *problem centred or reflective*. Both project and unit approaches to teaching may fail to confront students with issues and to challenge independent thought. Furthermore, as popularly conceived, projects and units may not even lead to learning on an understanding level. The outcome of project and unit teaching depends almost entirely on the wisdom of the particular teacher involved.

Popularization of project teaching and unit teaching may have done more harm than good in the sense that, to many teachers, these approaches have been seized upon as the heart of the educational process. A teacher may develop a collection of projects and units which look good to him and consider his major teaching problem solved. Consequently, project and unit teaching may misdirect a teacher's effort. Instead of regarding as all-important the development of the kind of unique interaction among teacher and students which leads to reflection and understanding, he is likely to focus on the more or less mechanical arrangement of predetermined subject matter so it will look neat on paper. Teachers so occupied lose sight of what is central in all learning: the intelligent interplay of a person's ideas with those of others.

Because there is so much confusion over the meaning of a unit and particularly because units often are handled in a kind of pseudo problem solving manner, it is well to sharpen the distinction between the "problemlike" unit and true reflective problem solving. Fortunately, Dr. Elizabeth Berry has provided us with a very apt illustration which could fit any of the subjects of English, social studies, or journalism—and, by implication, probably almost any other. Dr. Berry uses the term *process unit* as equivalent to what we mean by a true problem-centred, or reflective, unit. In her own words, the story is as follows:

> A few years ago I visited and observed in the classroom of an English teacher who was conducting a unit on "The Role of the

Newspaper in the World Today." This teacher began the unit by announcing that the students were going to undertake a unit on the aforementioned title. The teacher spent considerable time telling the students why it was important for them to make a study of the newspaper, then she told them that the next day the class would set up objectives for the unit study.

In the meantime, class members were to give some attention to the objectives. The next day in class, the students agreed upon a list of objectives for the unit, questions they wished to answer. It was interesting to note that their questions were primarily material that the teacher had given them in the lecture the day before. The teacher then announced a series of activities that the class would undertake in the study of the unit. These activities proceeded in a systematic way. As each activity was undertaken, the teacher brought to the class any materials needed, gave specific instructions on how each piece of work was to be done and saw that these activities were carried out. Some of the activities undertaken included the daily reading of the local newspaper and a discussion of local news items. No attention was given to the accuracy of reporting. There seemed to be a feeling that if an article appears in the press it is valid. A local newsman spoke to the class and built up a strong argument for his paper and the press in general. He was a delightful speaker and won the support of the group. The students then wrote letters to the editor on a rather non-controversial subject. The letters were graded, returned to the students, and presumably mailed. Students were encouraged to write articles of school interest for the school newspaper. Several did. Some vocabulary words relating to the press were studied. During the month that the unit was in progress, the daily work laboriously dragged on. By the end of the unit, the students were restless and ready for a change. The teacher, realizing that the students had lost interest, decided to bring the unit to an end with a class evaluation. In the evaluation, the students agreed that they had learned how to read the newspaper, recognized the importance of reading, and expected to confirm their interest by making a daily reading of the newspaper a part of their lives. The teacher then announced that it was time to move on to another unit, which would be a study of *Macbeth*.

After I had observed the teaching of the newspaper unit, I determined to try this unit using a different approach, method, and plan. I decided to use the unit process. My own personal goals were not only to help students improve their use of specific language skills, but also to make them critical readers of newspapers. From past experiences, I knew that many of the students believed that anything in print was truth. They had probably developed such a belief because most of their educational experience had been rooted in a firm belief in the word of the press. Many had gone through school proving their points with such remarks as this, "I can prove it because I read it in . . . . . " Also I had observed that many of my students equated being arrested with being guilty, considered all advertising as an honest presentation of fact, thought almost any sale a good buy, and generally felt that the highest honour that a girl could achieve would be a photograph in the society section.

Now I could have told the students the strengths and weaknesses of a newspaper, of its worth and limitations. But I knew that learning comes from within, not from without, and that students are more apt to use fruitfully knowledge gained through self-discovery. For this reason, I presented the unit in a problem solving context. I did this by making reprints of articles on the same subject but from different newspapers. I used three different newspapers for this and selected an article from each on the same topic but with varying interpretations. I passed out reprints of the first article for the class to read. Class discussion followed but there were few comments. In general, the class members agreed with the reporter. I then gave them a second article to read. There were some comments that this article was not in complete agreement with the first, but not much excitement about it. Then I gave them the third article . But this time students were puzzled at discrepancies and differences in class discussion before I took action. In other words, I allowed them to come face to face with a felt difficulty and problem. Finally I halted the discussion and said, "What is the issue in this discussion? What is it that you want to know? Let's define the problem."

Now the students entered the second phase of the unit process, when they defined the problem as they say it in view of their recent experiences. I did not define the problem for the students. Through the use of the chalkboard to examine carefully selected answers, I patiently took time for the students to agree upon a statement of the problem and a series of questions that they should answer if they were to become intelligent readers of the news. Now I asked how the class could proceed to make a study of this problem so as to gain the needed insight. The students suggested numerous ways: (1) Daily reading of different papers to see differences or similarities in reporting, (2) Reading news magazines for a similar purpose, (3) Searching for books in the library that discuss the magazine and newspaper field, (4) Calling in local reporters for class interviews, (5) Getting personal accounts of news reporting from biographies of famous newsmen, (6) Interviewing people in the community who had complained about being misrepresented in the news, (7) Practicing news reporting themselves to see what difficulties arise. I shared in the suggestions for this cooperative research, but I did not dictate them. For I did not wish to kill initiative and creativity.

Next the class co-operatively agreed upon a plan of action. They then proceeded to carry to their plans, and I acted as a catalyst and guide. As the students began the study and exploration, they found a need to go to the library for resource materials pertaining to the problem at hand. The librarian helped the students find books and materials relating to their study. Perhaps it was necessary for both librarian and students to consult the card catalogue, the *Reader's Guide*, encylopaedias, and bibliograhies. In addition, students used the library to investigate current magazines and newspapers. It was through the resources of the library, for example, that they were able to compare original articles with *Reader's Digest* condensations of them. It was from the *Reader's Guide* that students discovered articles on "How to Read the Chicago Tribune" and "All the News that Fits the Pattern." (April and May issues of Harpers, 1949.) The students found especially helpful William H. Burton's *Education for Effective Thinking* and S. I. Hayakawa's *Language in Thought and Action*. Copies of Liebling's *The Press* and Edgar Dale's *How to Read a Newspaper* were also found on the library shelves. In addition there were the autobiographies of newsmen and journalists telling their own personal experiences in the newspaper field. The unit took the students to the school library, to the public library, and into the community. It made them active researchers and problem solvers . . . . . [11]

HOW EFFECTIVE IS REFLECTIVE TEACHING?

A person who experiences reflective learning should thereby gain an increased store of generalized insights related to the subject studied; and these should be incorporated at the personality level so that a permanent change in him occurs. Furthermore, he should show a greater disposition and ability than before to apply the method of scientific reflection to problems outside the school subject in which reflective learning occurs.

It is difficult to measure insightful changes which occur in people as a result of school experiences. The most significant changes may not be evident in a person's outward behaviour while he is still in school. Perhaps the best sources of evidence as to the effectiveness of reflective learning are the subjective reactions of students themselves, the reactions of teachers and administrators, and the results of objective objective studies of the accomplishments of reflective teaching as compared with those of the other two levels.

Subjective Student Reaction to Reflection-Level Teaching

How does a student feel toward a course taught reflectively compared to one taught on a memory or understanding level? Students react to reflective teaching in various ways, but usually with intensity. Some of them despise their first experience in a reflectively taught course—but not because of boredom. Students who actively dislike reflective situations usually do so because such situations encourage them to think about ideas which they would prefer not to expose to rigorous examination. Other students react positively and express gratitude for having been "made to think." In fact, some conclude that they "will never again be quite the same". A third group, the lesson learners, prefers to have the answers given to them completely predigested. Members of this group probably are victims of habit; through experiences of the wrong kind they have learned to work for grades rather than insights.

Reactions of Teachers and Administrators to Reflective Teaching

Adherents of reflective teaching agree that students need facts to think with, ideas from which to feed, and understandings from which to develop new insights, and they think that reflective teaching is the best instrument for achievement of necessary facts, ideas and understandings. They are convinced that even facts are learned best when they are pertinent to meaningful, problem-centred study. Furthermore, they think that, in addition to the unique nature of its teaching-learning process, there are other advantages of reflective teaching. If conducted in the right manner, it produces a high level of motivation in most students. This leads them to work with a great deal of perseverance and tends to eliminate discipline problems. Students often become so enthusiastic in problem-centred classes that they do twice as much work as would normally be expected, sometimes to the point of neglecting other classes. Work in a reflectively taught class also is likely to be more self-directed and self-sustained than in nonreflective classes. That is, students voluntarily dig for information in libraries and elsewhere. Furthermore, they hold frequent out-of class discussions concerning their work in class, with cross fertilization of ideas contributing to their learning.

Of course, not all attempts at reflective teaching work out so well. In fact, the "problems approach," as it has been called, is in bad repute among some teachers and administrators. The most common charges levelled against it is that students fail to acquire the basic background—principles and facts—essential to a subject. Now what do studies of the results of reflective teaching show in this regard?

Studies of the Results of Reflective Teaching

It might seem logical to assume that, on a test designed to measure recall of facts, students taught on a memory or an understanding level would fare better than those taught reflectively. However, if we are to take at face value a group of studies extending from 1940 into the 1950s, this apparently is not the case. These studies, all designed to test the results of reflective teaching, have been reported by Bayles.[12]

The studies were conducted by public school teachers in

Kansas and Missouri and culminated in the form of master's theses. Four of the six studies reported were conducted in high school social studies and the other two in fifth-and sixth-grade classes.

The general procedure was as follows: students were given IQ tests to determine the average IQ of a class. Only those classes were used which were approximately "average." Then, insofar as the teachers were able to do so, the classes were taught reflectively. The teachers measured the effects of reflective instruction by giving various standardized achievement tests and by observing such changes of students' overt behaviour as made it possible to infer the quality of their learning.

The control group used in evaluation of test results was in each case the group upon which the test had been standardized. All tests used had been standardized on groups of students of average or better IQ. The control against which teachers judged student behaviour was much more subjective—the behaviour of students of other classes which the teachers had taught in conventional fashion. However, since each of the teachers was experienced and able, subjective impressions reported by them were considered worthy of respect.

The results of each study were very clear cut. Irrespective of whether the achievement tests emphasized fact recall or the application of principles, students who had been taught reflectively scored conspicuously higher in almost all cases than the national or regional norms. Those who did not actually score higher than the norms made exceptionally large gains during the school term. With respect to informally gathered data, teachers reported the following results: (1) apparent heightened interest among students; (2) more work done; (3) more voluntary reporting of data which had been encountered out of school—data gathered from radio, newspapers, magazines, etc.; (4) increased tendency to be critical—to demand evidence; (5) increased participation in discussions, particularly among students formerly reticent; and (6) much more reading. Some of the teachers obtained librarians' records of magazines and books checked out by students; they found that those in their reflectively taught classes were reading more than any other students in school.

To measure the amount of gain during a term, one of the investigators continued for a period of six years to give achievement tests to respective classes at the beginning and end of each school term. She found that the net gain in learning increased from year to year. This indicated that with continued experience with reflective teaching a teacher becomes more effective. If the six teachers participating in these studies had had several years of reflective teaching experience behind them (most were trying it for the first time), it seems likely that the studies would have revealed even more spectacular results.

Many teachers, when discussing the merits of reflective teaching, argue that it works only with the best students. One of the studies reported by Bayles suggests that this is not true; in the instance reported, reflective teaching was used in a class containing a wide range of ability. *Students of low ability made greater percentage gains than did those of high ability.* However, the investigator concluded that her teaching had not been pitched on a challenging enough level for the high group. Probably a safe conclusion is that reflective teaching, when effective, tends to bring students of all levels of ability up to maximum or near maximum performance.

We shall mention only one more conclusion, but it is a significant one. The teachers who participated in the studies which Bayles reports adapted reflective teaching to school situations which were quite conventional. The fact that they achieved good results suggests that effectiveness of teaching in our public schools could be greatly increased without drastically upsetting the conventional framework of subject matter and school organization. It is reasonable to assume that, in a school administratively committed to reflective teaching, results would be even more impressive.

REFERENCES

1. Unit originally written by Leslie A. McKinnis quoted from Ernest E. Bayles, *The Theory and Practice of Teaching*, Harper & Row, 1950, pp. 272-274. Reprinted by permission of Harper & Row, New York.
2. Maurice P. Hunt and Lawrence E. Metcalf, *Teaching High School Social Studies*, Harper & Row, 1955, p. 44.
3. One of the most useful references on means of analyzing the social structure of groups and techniques to use in establishing greater cohesiveness is Helen Hall Jennings, *Sociometry in Group Relations: A Work Guide for Teachers*, American Council on Education, 1949.
4. Kurt Lewin, *Resolving Social Conflicts*, Harper & Row, 1948, p. 82.
5. Lewin, *Resolving Social Conflicts*, p. 68.

6. See Kurt Lewin, "Group Decision and Social Change," in Theodore Newcomb and Eugene Hartley, eds., *Readings in Social Psychology*, Holt, 1947, pp. 330-344.
7. Lewin, *Resolving Social Conflicts*, p. 68.
8. National Training Laboratory in Group Development, *Report of the Second Summer Laboratory*, Washington, D. C., Department of Adult Education, 1948, pp. 113-114.
9. Franklin S. Haiman, *Group Leadership and Democratic Action*, Houghton Mifflin, 1951, p. 71.
10. Lewin, "Group Decision and Social Change," in *Readings in Social Psychology*, p. 342.
11. Elizabeth Berry, "The Unit Process," The *Educational Forum*, March, 1963, pp. 364-366. Recommended is her textbook, *Guiding Students in the English Class*, Appleton, 1957. This material is used by permission of Kappa Delta Pi, an honorary society in education, owners of the copyright.
12. "Experiments with Reflective Teaching," *Kansas Studies in Education*, April, 1956. This monograph is reproduced in essentially its original form in Chapter 1 of Bayles' book *Democratic Educational Theory*, Harper & Row, 1960.

Index